The Anatomy of the Confederate Congress

A Study of the Influences of Member Characteristics on Legislative Voting Behavior, 1861-1865

THOMAS B. ALEXANDER
RICHARD E. BERINGER

What manner of men were the members of the Confederate Congress? What personal, economic, and political conditions motivated them to vote as they did? And how did the performance of these men affect the outcome of the Civil War?

These and other penetrating questions are answered in this first computer-aided analysis of the voting patterns of the members of the Confederate Congress. Using such data as former party affiliation, attitude toward secession, wealth and slaveholding status of each member and his constituents, and the proximity of the members' home districts to actual military operations, the authors have analyzed 1,490 of 1,900 roll-call votes to determine the relationship between a congressman's legislative performance and the factors which might have influenced him. The research has revealed clear patterns of personal attributes, political behavior, and external forces that affected congressmen's votes and thus the fate of the South.

A milestone in Civil War historiography, this work reveals, and substantiates through tables, more about the Confederate Congress than has been shown heretofore. An extensive biographical directory of the congressmen is appended.

The Anatomy of the Confederate Congress

A Study of the Influences of Member
Characteristics on Legislative
Voting Behavior, 1861–1865

Thomas B. Alexander
and
Richard E. Beringer

Vanderbilt University Press
Nashville, 1972

Library of Congress Cataloguing in Publication Data

Alexander, Thomas Benjamin, 1918-
  The Anatomy of the Confederate Congress.
  Bibliography: p. 420-423
  1. Confederate States of America. Congress.
2. Confederate States of America—Politics and
government. 3. Legislators—Confederate States
of America. I. Beringer, Richard E., 1933-
joint author. II. Title.
JK9937.A65   328.73'09   76-138985
ISBN 0-8265-1175-9

Composed by Gulbenk Typesetting Co., Nashville, Tennessee
Printed in the United States of America by
Reed Printing Company, Nashville, Tennessee

For Luise
and
For Elaine

Contents

Tables

Tables

Maps

Preface

T HIS study is principally an investigation of the associations that may have existed between congressional voting behavior and personal or constituent characteristics of the individual members of the Confederate Congress. We are keenly aware that causal relationships may not be assumed to exist simply because numerical association has been discovered. We are equally convinced that numerical associations constitute one kind of evidence bearing on causation, and we are satisfied that this kind of evidence is neither better nor worse, as a general rule, than other types of evidence long used by historians to determine causation. Although we reach conclusions in this study about the likelihood of causal relationships, we do not attempt at every pertinent point to enter a caveat about limitations that scholars should habitually assume to exist for any kind of evidence, whether statistical or not. In deference to reservations that may be more keenly felt about statistical inference than about some other familiar forms of inference, we have erred on the side of excessive qualification in the larger portion of the presentation. Only in the latter chapters, after evidence has been reiterated, do we intentionally abandon the safeguarding modifiers. We ask our readers to be generous enough to have in mind that we are not thoughtlessly overlooking the ultimate doubt that lies beneath any generalization. We are trying to state our findings, difficult at best to phrase felicitously, as simply as we dare, while acknowledging our own willingness to accept the thrust of the evidence at those points where we· do not harbor reasonable doubt.

We have been at extensive pains to provide the basis for replication of what we consider the most important parts of our work, but only by incorporating more data than could be accepted by the publisher would it have been possible to provide for total replication. Our research design has been fully stated, and the data we employed have been largely reproduced in the appendices. Judgments have naturally and repeatedly entered into the classification of our information, but we have tried to employ justifiable principles of classification and to describe them fully.

Professor Alexander wishes to express appreciation for support of his general investigation of nineteenth-century two-party politics, of which this study is an important element, to the John Simon Guggenheim

Memorial Foundation, which provided a year's research leave; the Institute of Southern History of the Johns Hopkins University, which provided a semester's research leave; and to the Social Science Research Council, the University Research Committee of the University of Alabama, and the University Research Council of the University of Missouri—Columbia, which together have furnished support for research assistants, data assembling and processing, and computing services.

Professor Beringer adds his thanks to Northwestern University for a fellowship in 1962–1963 which enabled him to continue research on the Confederate Congress for his doctoral dissertation, and for a grant to aid in meeting some of the early costs of data processing. He is also indebted to the Research Committee of California State College, Hayward, and to the trustees of the California State Colleges for a research leave for the winter quarter of 1968. His personal obligations include those to his father, who passed to his son his interest in history; Professor Grady McWhiney, who originally encouraged him to undertake a study of the Confederate Congress; and Professor Duncan MacRae, Jr., who has provided stimulation not only through his publications but also through personal contacts.

We acknowledge, with keen awareness of our dependence on staffs and facilities, the services of the computer centers of the University of Alabama, the University of Missouri—Columbia, and, through the aid and interest of Professor MacRae, the National Opinion Research Center at the University of Chicago.

Friends and colleagues who have assisted us with counsel and criticism include Duncan MacRae, Jr., David Donald, Charles B. Dew, Richard Jensen, Charles M. Dollar, Joel H. Silbey, and Dewey W. Grantham. Ralph A. Wooster graciously provided apportionment information and verification of census listings for those congressmen who also served in secession conventions. The late Daniel M. Robison generously provided biographical information from his research files. We have profited from the advice of the readers designated by Vanderbilt University Press, and we are greatly indebted to Martha I. Strayhorn and Gary G. Gore of the Press staff.

We also owe debts of gratitude to the several typists who undertook to bring this intractable material into acceptable form. Luise T. Beringer accomplished an initial draft of text, tables, and appendices for us; Segail I. Friedman produced the camera-ready copy for all tables; Mary L. Watkins and Mary Ellen Case typed the appendices. Many assistants labored with us in the analyses and checking stages, and our special thanks go to Warner O. Moore, Jr., Richard Lindsey, and Margaret Lindsey Smith for assistance with computer programs, to Harry D.

Preface

Holmes for both research and supervisory aid, and to Karli Brasch, Karen Ann Stoner, Paul E. McAllister, C. Murray Joekel II, Charles Baker, Robert Cowherd, and Richard N. Stover. Harry R. Weitkemper provided the needed draftsman's skills.

For permission to quote manuscripts or other items from their collections, we are indebted to the Huntington Library, San Marino, California; the Massachusetts Historical Society, Boston; the University of Texas Library, Austin; and the Southern Historical Collection of the University of North Carolina, Chapel Hill.

Perhaps it should go without saying, but we want to express our appreciation for the generous help we have so often received from our wives, Elise P. Alexander and Luise T. Beringer.

The nature of this study almost dictates that we would be indebted to many people for many kinds of assistance. It is all the more necessary, therefore, to acknowledge that no one except the authors is responsible for the errors that remain.

Columbia, Missouri   T.B.A.
Grand Forks, North Dakota   R.E.B.
March 1971

The Anatomy of the Confederate Congress

Research Design

THIS study of the Confederate Congress is limited primarily to an exploration of the patterns to be found in the roll-call behavior of the members and a search for explanations of political attitudes in the background characteristics of the congressmen. Among the kinds of surviving information for individuals of the 1860s, those used to clarify voting behavior in the Confederate Congress include former party affiliation, attitude toward secession in the crisis of 1860–1861, wealth and slaveholding status of each member and his constituents, and the relation of each member's home district to the location of military operations.

Personal attitudes or temperamental considerations, together with a considerable range of unknown influences not readily discoverable nor measurable in units of quantity, surely accounted for a large part of the reaction of many legislators on any particular roll call. No student of the Confederate Congress, or of any but a most unusual legislative body, could seriously proffer an explanation of voting patterns for which he claimed even approximate completeness, but the authors are convinced that a significant portion of these roll-call reactions can be understood in terms of member characteristics or circumstances that do yield to measurement. The intent of this study is to describe the relationship between a congressman's legislative performance and some of the known considerations that could have influenced him.

The principal approach for this study has been to divide the membership of the Congress into groups reflecting background differences and to compare the voting record of one group with that of another in a search for distinctions that might point to influences on roll-call decisions. Specifically, former Whigs have been compared with former Democrats to gauge the possible significance of previous party affiliation. Secessionists have been compared with Unionists in search of lingering influences of attitudes that had undergirded the individual's stand in the secession crisis. Several levels of wealth have been used to separate members and districts into groups for comparative study, to provide evidence for judgments about the role of personal or constituent economic status in dictating decisions on roll calls. A further search for influences flowing from economic status has been made by dividing the membership according to the relative standing of each within the wealth structure

3

of his own county. Levels of slaveholding for members and for their home counties have in a similar manner been employed to subdivide the congressmen for comparison of voting records of one group with another, and an additional division has been based on the slaveholding of each member relative to the pattern of ownership in his own county.

Whether the district represented by a member was behind Federal lines, threatened by Federal occupation, or for the time being safely Confederate, was another individual variable that injected a troublesome consideration into the decisions of each representative. Energetic military effort and extraordinary sacrifice might have been just the thing envisioned by a legislator as the appropriate way either to liberate his district or to protect it against imminent invasion. In the same context, remoteness of Federal military operations could have engendered indifference and reluctance to make sacrifices. And few representatives could have been unaware of the obvious point that personal and property commitments called for by congressional action would be exacted only from those within Confederate reach, especially since their colleagues and the newspapers were not loath to remind them of it. As the war approached the desperation stage for the Confederacy, each member must also have begun to balance cost against possibility of victory. Since the sacrifices demanded in the twilight of the Confederacy had to be borne primarily by those within an ever diminishing core of the South's territory, the question whether there were distinctions between representatives from within and without that core justified the closest investigation. For each of the six sessions of the First and Second Congresses, therefore, the membership was divided into those representing occupied or imminently threatened areas and those representing the remainder of the Confederacy. Comparison of the roll-call responses of these groups (changing somewhat from session to session) provides one of the avenues of search for explanation of the decisions recorded on the roll calls.

The divisions selected for use in the analysis are intended to represent essentially full coverage of that legislative business brought to the roll-call stage. Of approximately 1,900 recorded votes in the Confederate Congress journals, 1,490 have been incorporated in this study. All except a few unanimous or duplicated votes have been taken from the Senate journals, totaling 492; the same is true for the two sessions of the Second House, totaling 415. From the four sessions of the First House, 437 of the almost 700 votes appeared to incorporate everything except essentially repetitive or insignificant items. Approximately half of the roll calls from the five Provisional Congress sessions (a total of 146) provided as much coverage as could usefully be exploited; for reasons indicated in the chapter on the Provisional Congress, the number of votes cast and the subject matter

were useful selection guides for these early divisions. Injection of judg-
mental selection has been accepted in preference to a substantial increase
in data-preparation effort. There is no reason to think that addition
of the one fifth of the roll calls omitted could have affected the findings
significantly; on the contrary, the indications are that far more were
included than would have been necessary. An excess of caution is not
misplaced, however, when grappling in such murky water as the Confederate Congress proved to be.

Several methods have been used to compare the votes of one group
with another. Some involve group voting records; others require attention
to individual performances on the roll calls. Whatever the form of
investigation, it was designed to throw light on the same question: how
much and what part of a member's decision making in the Confederate
Congresses was associated with and, perhaps, may be attributed to the
measurable personal characteristics and circumstances employed in the
analysis?

Agreement Scores

One way of comparing group performances on roll calls is an agreement score that provides a measure of the amount of concurrence or
antagonism between any two sets of the voting members. The score
employed for this study is obtained by determining the number of roll
calls on which the two groups under comparison concurred, were antagonistic, or were simply dissimilar. The distinction used is between a
two-thirds vote within a group of congressmen and one more closely
dividing the group. Thus, if two thirds of both groups in a comparison
stood on the same side, the groups are classified as concurring. If neither
segment of congressmen recorded two thirds of its followers on either
side of a question, the relationship is also classified as concurrence, in
the sense that the two were taking a similar posture—largely uncommitted
to either position. Antagonism is defined as an instance in which one
group voted two-thirds "Yea" and the other voted two-thirds "Nay."
On the other hand, if one set of congressmen recorded a two-thirds
majority on either side while the other was more closely divided, the
classification assigned is one of dissimilarity. The agreement score is
obtained by subtracting the percentage of antagonisms from the percentage of concurrences in the total number of roll calls.

For example, if 150 roll calls were analyzed, 80 instances of concurrence between two groups (53 percent), reduced by 30 instances of
antagonism (20 percent), would be scored as 53 minus 20, or 33 percent,
for a score of +33. Since it is possible for more instances of antagonism
than of concurrence to appear, the agreement score may be negative.

In the above case of 150 roll calls, if only 30 had produced concurrence patterns and 80 had been instances of antagonism, the result would have been 20 percent minus 53 percent, or a score of −33. The range of agreement scores, therefore, may be from +100 to −100. This score, appropriately compared with the score produced by a random division of the same membership, can be useful in estimating whether the descriptive characteristics dividing the groups (former party affiliation, secession stand, or slaveholding, for instance) had an appreciable relation to the roll-call responses. Agreement scores have been computed for the various groups of congressmen from all of the roll calls examined in a particular session; additional agreement scores were calculated using subsets of votes, each set relating to one of the more important subjects of congressional business.[1]

Cohesion Level

Some members of Congress who share a particular personal or political characteristic may be compared with members of a differing characteristic on the basis of the extent to which each group drew together and voted as a bloc, e.g., former Whigs can be compared with former Democrats. The level of cohesion displayed by each of the various membership segments under comparison in this study has been determined in the form of the proportion of roll calls which brought each segment to a degree of unity of 90 percent or more, 80 to 89 percent unity, 70 to 79 percent, 60 to 69 percent, and that proportion producing a division so close as to allow only 50 to 59 percent on the prevailing side. Comparison of cohesion levels for an identified group with the levels of cohesion displayed by the entire voting membership of the body is another method, generally parallel to the agreement-score measure, for estimating whether significant influence on voting behavior may be attributed to the characteristics employed in dividing the membership. If, for example, Unionists and Secessionists are found to have, as separate categories, notably greater cohesion than that displayed by the entire membership, it is

1. The familiar Rice Index of Likeness has been calculated for many of the pairwise comparisons for which agreement scores are used to investigate whether significant inferences might be drawn from differences between these two index numbers. The purposes for which we used pairwise group comparisons, however, were better served by the agreement score we employed. This results principally from the fact that we were not so much interested in the average difference in performance over many roll calls as in the relationship between the proportion of roll calls producing something like partisan antagonism to the proportion suggesting very different relationships between the groups. The Rice Index of Likeness is discussed in relation to many forms of comparison in Duncan MacRae, Jr., *Issues and Parties in Legislative Voting: Methods of Statistical Analysis* (New York: Harper and Row, 1970), p. 183.

reasonable to conclude that the member's stand at the time of the secession crisis did have some relation to his decisions as a member of Congress.[2] Again, if members in each of five separate levels of wealth display significantly greater unity than is the case for the entire membership, this is evidence that some influence on the representatives may be stemming from their personal economic status.

Minority Status Analysis

Whether there was a persisting minority element in any house or session of the Confederate Congress has been investigated by determining what proportion of each member's roll-call responses placed him in a minority of one third or less of those voting. This proportion has been determined for each member for each session in which he served. Resulting distinctions in the frequency with which members were in a minority of one third or less have, in turn, been compared with the characteristics and circumstances of the individual members for evidence of incipient clusters or blocs along lines of some common interest not otherwise anticipated. This serves as a rather crude but nonetheless useful type of cluster bloc analysis.

Performance Score

Each member of the Confederate Congress who voted more than a few times provided a record of his contributions to the objective of establishing an independent Confederacy with a central government adequate to the tasks imposed upon it in war or in peace. A pro-Confederate (or "strong") side for a large majority of the roll calls has been assigned by content analyses, value judgments, and inspection of relationships between pairs of such votes. These roll calls have been clustered according to the nature of the issues. Members with adequate voting participation have been assigned a score for each of the several subject-content areas that represented important congressional business during each of the sessions in which they served.[3] (Including all sessions, sixty-six

2. The probability of random cohesion is affected by the number of members involved, so that "notably greater cohesion" must be judged in relation to whether the whole Congress, the House, the Senate, or a portion of one house is involved. The Rice Index of Cohesion, which reduces the measurement conveniently to a single statistic, sacrifices more information than we thought disposable, so that the more cumbersome but revealing cohesion pattern is employed herein. For discussion of the Rice Index of Cohesion, see MacRae, *Issues and Parties in Legislative Voting*, p. 179.

3. A Performance Score was calculated for each member for each content-area set of roll calls as follows:

(*a*). The member was not assigned a score unless he voted on at least one third of

content areas of congressional business have been used for assignment of scores—six from the Provisional Congress, twenty-five from the Senate, and thirty-five from the House). These individual scores are the basis for comparison of member performance with individual characteristics, again in pursuit of clues as to the factors affecting the extent of each member's willingness to take "strong" positions on each of several topics of legislation.

The performance score may not provide as precise inferences about member attitudes as does the cumulative scaling procedure discussed below, but such a score has other advantages, including coverage of some issues for which cumulative scales were not found. In this type of score, which is simply a measure of the proportion of a content group of roll calls on which a member voted the "strong" side, there is no weighting of divisions according to their importance. Accordingly, some of the specific subjects within a topical set used to assign a score speak more loudly than other portions of that topic simply because they produced more roll calls. Some consideration has been given to this difficulty, and some roll calls were intentionally omitted when it was apparent that they would only enlarge a limited subject beyond its proper significance.[4] Notwithstanding its limitations, a performance score has the

---

the roll calls in a normal set. The exceptions were very large sets, containing many essentially repetitive roll calls, which required less than one-third participation if votes were adequately scattered over the topics included, and sets that included very few roll calls, on which greater than one-third participation was required for score assignment.

(b). The number of the member's responses on the "strong" side was expressed as a percentage of the total number of responses he made to roll calls in the set.

(c). A score was assigned by dividing the possible range of percentages into ten spans, as follows:

$$
\begin{aligned}
90\text{–}100 &= 9, \text{ the "strongest" score} \\
80\text{–}89 &= 8 \\
70\text{–}79 &= 7 \\
60\text{–}69 &= 6 \\
50\text{–}59 &= 5 \\
41\text{–}49 &= 4 \\
31\text{–}40 &= 3 \\
21\text{–}30 &= 2 \\
11\text{–}20 &= 1 \\
0\text{–}10 &= 0, \text{ the "weakest" score}
\end{aligned}
$$

The 101 possible percentile values, 0 through 100, were thereby allocated equally to the extremes (eleven each) and ten to each of the other scores except that one of the middle scores, 4, includes only nine. This resulted not from an undue emphasis on precise equality for the most significant scores, 0 and 9, but from converting these scores from an earlier design that spread them over a range from $+100$ to -100.

4. This has not, however, been necessary very often because in the Confederate Congress the number of roll calls is usually found to be a rough index of the degree to which

advantage of incorporating a vast amount of the legislative business that could not be brought into a Guttman scale arrangement of roll-call sets. Performance scores measure the extent to which a member's voting record leans toward full sacrifice of short-term rights, privileges, and enjoyments for the sake of increasing the chances of securing the long-term goal of independence. The sets of votes measured by this score may be multidimensional, rather than limited to one dimension or attitude, as is implied in scale analysis.

Scale Analysis

The most refined form of analysis used in this study is cumulative scaling, a procedure developed for purposes unrelated to the study of legislative roll-call responses but adapted by political scientists and historians to the investigation of roll-call patterns. The desired objective is to wrest from large quantities of divisions two types of useful information. One is identification of groups of specific choices which the voting members evidently treated as though they were closely related and which are subject to ordinal ranking from easiest-to-accept to hardest-to-accept. The second is a position on the resulting scale set of roll calls for almost every member of the body—a position that measures how far the member would go in support of the policy defined by the scale set. One of the procedures employed in this study to search for scalable groups of roll calls provides a wide scanning over large numbers of subjects for inter-relations between topics that might not have been anticipated by an investigator. Another of the methods employed makes possible scrutiny of a predetermined content area among the roll calls to identify all that may be incorporated within a satisfactory scale set on the specific subject involved. Scale positions have been assigned to the appropriate Confederate congressmen for each of forty-two scalograms identified in the various sessions (four in the Provisional Congress, sixteen in the Senate, and twenty-two in the House). These positions, in turn, have been compared with individual member characteristics for evidence of the relation between wealth, former party affiliation, or some other personal or constituent consideration, and the extent to which a congressman would support the various programs involved in the scale sets.

Performance scores and scale positions for congressmen are similar in that both devices provide ordinal measurement, meaning that although we are unable to state precisely how much of a legislative-behavior

---

a particular subject pressed upon the business of the session. This is not to say that mere numbers of roll calls are an index of importance, for on some critical topics few roll calls were taken for the very reason that congressmen successfully postponed or evaded issues they feared to face.

attribute characterizes individuals, we can be certain of being able to place them in ordered categories in accordance with the degree (however great) of the attribute being examined. The extent to which one congressman took the "strong" or pro-Confederate view of the conscription issue, for example, is an uncertainty, but the performance scores and scale positions can indicate that Congressman A (score 7) did take a stronger stand than Congressman B (score 5), and that both took a stronger stand than Congressman C (score 3). The rank values assigned to each lawmaker do not stand for absolute values, but merely indicate which persons are equal to, somewhat greater than, or somewhat less than another person in the characteristic under discussion. Nevertheless, the two methods are far from identical ways to measure voting behavior. The performance score is based on a very large number of roll calls and approximates a member's total impact on the major business of a session. The scale score for each scale set is a more precise way to determine each member's relative standing on a single dimension—but necessarily on a much smaller number of roll calls and in some cases on an extremely narrow segment of legislative activity. If broad scales had been discovered on all important subjects, performance scores would have been unnecessary. Since this was not possible, the two scores for an individual complement each other in assessing his role in the Congress.[5]

Cross-Tabulation

To study and display the possible effect of individual characteristics on voting behavior, both performance scores and scale positions have been cross-tabulated with each of the nine above-mentioned forms of personal and constituent information gathered for the congressmen. In those instances in which a very similar performance-score topic was established for both Senate and House for the same session of Congress, the members of the two houses were first cross-tabulated as one group. Scale sets from House roll calls are not sufficiently similar to those from Senate roll calls to justify tabulation together, even on almost identical subjects, so that separate tabulations for each house are provided. The resulting cross-tabulations involve forty-nine sets of scores with each of the nine individual considerations and forty-two sets of scale positions with each of the same nine characteristics.

In those cases for which it became evident that senators behaved in

---

5. For a helpful discussion of the uses of and differences between simple indexes such as the performance score, which may be multidimensional, and unidimensional scales such as the Guttman scale, see Lee F. Anderson, Meredith W. Watts, Jr., and Allen R. Wilcox, *Legislative Roll-Call Analysis* (Evanston, Illinois: Northwestern University Press, 1966).

roll-call responses differently from the bulk of the House members, separate cross-tabulations for senators and representatives have been made for performance scores. In some instances the two houses may be merged for analysis; in other instances they must be treated separately. Furthermore, after the significance of a district's being outside the area of Confederate control became apparent, cross-tabulations were added incorporating only members whose districts remained within Confederate military lines. Some summary cross-tabulations, designed to approximate average or central-tendency over-all behavior, were based on appropriate combinations of an individual's performance scores or scale positions.

More than three thousand of these cross-tabulations have been searched for justifiable inferences about influences on congressmen.[6] Many of those which reveal significant relationships between individual member considerations and voting records have been selected for presentation. Although only a small portion can suitably be provided for readers of this study, generalizations about the nature and import of all such comparisons appear at appropriate places in the discussion of findings.

6. The contingency coefficient C has been calculated for each of the cross-tabulations that included enough members to make possible a trustworthy measure. This was done to sift out efficiently the tabulations with enough evidence of association to justify close attention. The strength of association indicated by C is provided in Appendix V for each cross-tabulation offered in this study when the test was feasible. For a discussion of the contingency coefficient C, see Sidney Siegel, *Nonparametric Statistics for the Behavioral Sciences* (New York: McGraw-Hill, 1956), pp. 196–202.

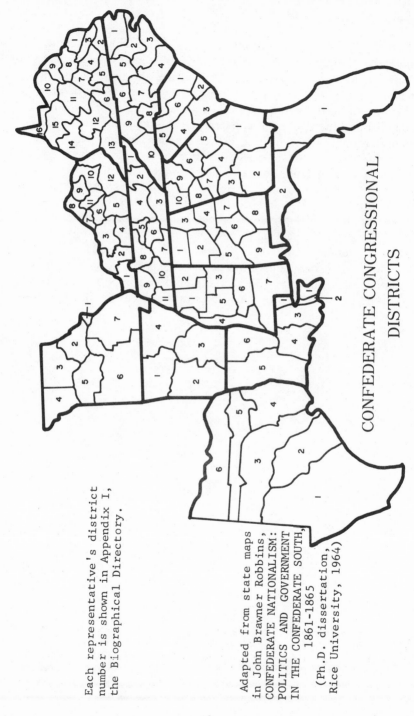

CONFEDERATE CONGRESSIONAL
DISTRICTS

Each representative's district
number is shown in Appendix I,
the Biographical Directory.

Adapted from state maps
in John Brawner Robbins,
CONFEDERATE NATIONALISM:
POLITICS AND GOVERNMENT
IN THE CONFEDERATE SOUTH,
1861-1865
(Ph.D. dissertation,
Rice University, 1964)

1 Profile and Personalities

WHEN the Confederate congressmen arrived in Montgomery or Richmond, part of the contents of their intellectual baggage was their widely differing backgrounds. Each man had a somewhat different reservoir of experience, which made him act apart from his fellows. It is difficult at best to create a composite picture of such a group, but the attempt will nevertheless be made, acknowledging that the sketch which emerges will fit no one exactly. The actual workings of the Congress will become apparent in later pages. Here, it is the biographical profile of 267 men which is offered.

These delegates represented the eleven states of the Confederacy, but they claimed to represent Missouri and Kentucky as well. These two states in effect remained within the Union, for they had representatives in the United States Congress throughout the war and made handsome contributions of blood and treasure to the Union cause. But in both cases, groups within the state organized a rump state government pledged to follow the fortunes of the South. This was significant for the later history of the Confederate Congress. In addition, the Arizona Territory and the Indians of the Cherokee, Choctaw, Creek, Seminole, and Chickasaw nations had the right of representation. These territorial and Indian delegates could not vote, however, and are therefore of no importance in the roll-call studies further on. But where information on their biographical backgrounds is known, it is included in this chapter.

The largest delegation was from Virginia, which sent thirty-five men

1. Much of the material in this chapter was originally published with some variations in Richard E. Beringer, "A Profile of the Members of the Confederate Congress," *Journal of Southern History*, XXXIII (November 1967), 518–541. Copyright 1967 by the Southern Historical Association. Reprinted by permission of the Managing Editor. Figures here may differ from those in the article because somewhat different criteria are used to determine secession view and nominal party affiliation and because additional information has been uncovered by further research. A few of these differences are significant. Percentages have usually been figured from a base which includes only those members for whom information is available. Exceptions have been made when there are so few unknowns that the results would be much the same, or when the percentage of unknowns is itself significant. Although economic characteristics of members' constituencies are among the important variables examined in this study for possible relation to and influence on voting behavior, they will be omitted here since this chapter concerns the individual congressmen and not their constituents.

to Congress during the life of the Confederacy. By contrast, Arkansas, Florida, and Louisiana together sent fewer than Virginia, for each of the former states selected altogether only eleven congressmen. Virginia was also the leading birthplace, for one fourth of the membership was born there, while only four each were born in Louisiana and Mississippi, and none was born in Arkansas, Florida, Missouri, or Texas. This is a predictable pattern in a region which still had large areas of frontier, or districts only one step beyond the pioneering stage. Indeed, many of the congressmen from the western states of the Confederacy are good illustrations of the settlement process and of restless American mobility.

One of the best examples of this mobility is Williamson S. Oldham of Texas. Born in Tennessee in 1813, Oldham seems to have had to work from an early age. If one of his contemporaries can be believed, Oldham's education was a Lincolnesque experience, for "necessity compelled him to work in the field during the day, [so] he usually sat up late in the night, and mastered the common textbooks by the light of a brush fire." [2] With this meager background, he opened his own school and briefly tried teaching. He then studied law, was admitted to the bar, and became district clerk in Franklin County, Tennessee. He moved to Arkansas, where he became speaker of the state house of representatives by the age of twenty-nine, and later sat on the state supreme court. Moving again in 1849, Oldham went to Texas, prepared a digest of Texas law, edited a newspaper, joined in the call for a secession convention in 1860, sat in that convention, and attended the Confederate Congress throughout its existence.[3] Few congressmen illustrate this frontier process as well as Oldham, but there were other interesting examples. Of the fifty-seven trans-Mississippi congressmen, for example, only four Louisianans were born west of the river; Kentucky, Tennessee, or Virginia was the birthplace of thirty-one of them. On the other hand, congressmen from the eastern coastal states were overwhelmingly native to the state they represented—and Virginia sent all native-born legislators to the Confederate Congress. A mere handful were born in the North and only four were born in Europe.

Their terms of office, however, were more varied. Since only seven states had left the Union by the time the Provisional Congress opened at Montgomery, and Texas did not have a delegation on hand until

---

2. E. Fontaine, "Hon. Williamson S. Oldham," *DeBow's Review*, ser. 2, vol. VII (October 1869), p. 873.

3. James D. Lynch, *The Bench and Bar of Texas* (St. Louis: Nixon-Jones Printing Co., 1885), p. 254; Fontaine, "Oldham," pp. 873–880; Ernest William Winkler, editor, *Journal of the Secession Convention of Texas, 1861* (Austin: Austin Printing Co., 1912), p. 406; Allan Johnson and Dumas Malone, editors, *Dictionary of American Biography* (New York: C. Scribner's Sons, 1928–1958), XIV, 12 (hereinafter cited as *DAB*).

February 15 and did not formally secede until March 2, 1861, there was a limited charter membership; only eight lawmakers served in Congress from start to finish, February 4, 1861, to March 18, 1865. There were three separate Congresses, Provisional (February 4, 1861, to February 17, 1862), First (February 18, 1862, to February 17, 1864), and Second (May 2, 1864, to March 18, 1865), and twenty-eight men (about 10 percent of the membership) sat in all three. Some, like Senator Oldham, had the way eased by not having to face elections in 1863. Others were from districts where the normal electoral process was interrupted by Federal occupation. But a number of these representatives, while appointed to the Provisional Congress, had to meet the voters in the fall of 1861 and again in 1863.

More important from the viewpoint of membership continuity were the nineteen "short termers," men who served less than three months. The leading example was John P. Sanderson, of Florida, who served only the last thirteen days of the Provisional Congress. An obscure Baptist minister from Louisville, Kentucky, came close to equaling that record. After attending during only the last month and a half of the Provisional Congress, S. H. Ford abandoned his political duties and once again took up his spiritual labors; he became the Chaplain of the House of Representatives for a short time. The reasons for such brief terms were many. Senator Edwin G. Reade, for example, was appointed by Governor Zebulon B. Vance of North Carolina to attend part of the "lame duck" session of the First Congress. The incumbent, George Davis, had moved up to the attorney-generalship of the Confederacy, and the senator already elected to the Second Congress was unable to go to Richmond until his regular term began. So Whig Unionist Reade got the nod from Vance, and he got it because Vance thought that Reade would follow the antiadministration line in Congress that Vance was following in the statehouse.[4] Vance's expectation appears to have been justified, if one can trust what can be gleaned from the twenty-seven days of Reade's participation. David P. Lewis of Alabama (a future Republican governor), resigned after less than three months, apparently because he had had his fill of the Confederacy, which he had not liked very much to begin with.[5] John W. Lewis of Georgia, like Reade, owed his appointment to a special relationship with the governor of his state, Joseph E. Brown.

4. Robert D. W. Connor, *North Carolina: Rebuilding an Ancient Commonwealth* (Chicago: American Historical Society, 1928-1929), II, 228; Pardon petition of Edwin G. Reade, Amnesty Papers, North Carolina, National Archives, Record Group 94 (hereinafter cited as Amnesty Papers).
5. David P. Lewis petition, Amnesty Papers, Alabama.

In earlier years, Lewis had been Brown's patron, as Brown had taught Lewis's children and borrowed Lewis's money.[6] ˙

Men like Sanderson and Reade are indicative of one of the problems that plagued the Confederate Congress. Not only did the membership change at elections; it changed between them as well. Of course, the former problem was the greater of the two. A mid-twentieth-century United States Congress may have a turnover at election time of as much as 15 or 20 percent; in the Confederacy, the 1861 elections caused a two-thirds turnover in membership and those in 1863 caused a one-third replacement.[7] In the first case, new congressmen tended to be Democrats and Secessionists, but in 1863 about two thirds of the newly elected congressmen were Whigs and Unionists. Some states furnished more than their share of replacements in 1863, as nine of the twelve Georgians and eight of the twelve North Carolinians were new. Such shifts played an important role in changing the directions of the legislative process.

Former political affiliation apparently was one of the most important determinants of congressional behavior.[8] It is a moot question whether men with similar political views created a party or whether members of a party adopted views most likely to achieve success. In either case, there is a marked similarity, for example, between party affiliation and views on secession (Table 1-1). At least 92 former Whigs served in the Confederate Congress at one time or another. Of those whose views are known, 81 percent were Unionists, while the same proportion of the 138 Democrats were Secessionists. Four fifths of the 206 members for whom both party and secession stand are known fit into one of these two categories. Although only 39 legislators are known to have crossed what was virtually a party line on this vital issue, Whig-Secessionists and Democrat-Unionists were by no means inconspicuous. Louisiana congressmen, for example, were heavily Whig, but they were

6. Isaac W. Avery, *The History of the State of Georgia from 1850 to 1881* . . . (New York: Brown and Derby, 1881), pp. 12-13.

7. The United States Congress in the period also had extensive turnover. In the Thirty-fifth Congress (1857-1859), 46 percent of the membership was new, and the corresponding figure for the Thirty-sixth Congress (1859-1861) was 43 percent. Replacements declined to about one third after the 1864 elections.

8. It should be remembered that although parties changed names in the South in the 1850s, much of the membership avoided actual realignment. While some Whigs moved directly into the Democratic party, at least 53 of the Whig Confederate congressmen simply changed their labels, calling themselves Americans or Constitutional Unionists before their eventual assimilation by the Democrats. There were a few who still called themselves Whigs in 1860, and the most persistent Whigs kept the title into the postwar period. Those who eventually became Constitutional Unionists were the most Union-oriented of the Whigs, as may be expected. Criteria for determining party affiliation in this study are discussed in Appendix I.

TABLE 1-1

FORMER PARTY AFFILIATIONS OF CONFEDERATE CONGRESSMEN
ARRANGED BY POSITION ON SECESSION

Former Party Affiliation	Secessionists		Unionists		Sub-total		Unknown	Total
	No.	%	No.	%	No.	%	No.	No.
Democrats	99	81	23	19	122	100	16	138
Whigs	16	19	68	81	84	100	8	92
Unknown	9	60	6	40	15	100	22	37
Total	124	56	97	44	221	100	46	267

heavily Secessionist too, just as the Democratic Arkansas delegation tended to be Unionist. Geographically, the Florida, Louisiana, Mississippi, South Carolina, and Texas delegations were most Secessionist, while Arkansans, North Carolinians, and Tennesseans were most likely to be Unionist. The Louisianans and North Carolinians were most Whiggish, while the Democrats were strongest in the Arkansas, Florida, Mississippi, Missouri, South Carolina, and Texas delegations. In line with expectation, Upper South delegates were more conservative than those from the Lower South; the difference along party lines is small, but on the secession issue, 57 percent of Upper South congressmen were Unionists, while 67 percent from the Lower South were Secessionists.

One of the most important parts of this profile is the size of the individual's estate and slaveholding. Most of the information on these points is from the 1860 census, a convenient if sometimes inaccurate source—and usually the only source. Some people thought the census taker was a tax man and so gave little account of their fortunes. Others seemed to see the census interview as an opportunity to brag; the reality of their estates was stretched or rounded off for effect. And sometimes the census taker seems never to have visited at all. The census may therefore be unreliable on occasional individuals, but the impression it gives of the entire group should be essentially valid.

One immediate impression is that the congressmen could not have divided along lines of rich and poor—there simply were not enough of the latter to allow this. Some were poor, but the mere handful who could be so considered by 1860 standards was not enough to create a significant bloc, even if the desire had existed. In fact, of those whose estates are known, only 5 percent were worth less than $5,000—a comfortable amount in 1860. On the other hand, a large number of the congressmen could be considered wealthy even by standards of later generations. The median estate was quite substantial: $47,335. Secessionists and Unionists did not differ on this point of comparison, both having a median estate of $50,000. The median estate for Democrats was $47,335 (the same as for the entire membership), but the Whig median was somewhat higher, at $53,100.

Wealth levels may be illustrated more vividly by comparing each congressman's estate with the average estate in his home county (see Table 1-2). More than half (130, or 54 percent) of the congressmen for whom this information has been located held estates that were at least 600 percent of the average ownership in their home counties. Only twelve held estates that were less than 51 percent of average. In every state (except Missouri but including Kentucky and Arkansas, from which a disproportionate number of the less wealthy congressmen came) the majority of congressmen had estates at least twice as valuable as the county average. As this would seem to hint, there were significant differences in estate between congressmen from the Upper South and those from the Lower South. Among the former, the median estate was $35,000 (the twelfth estate below the over-all congressional median of $47,335). The estates in the Deep South, predictably, were much larger, for the median there was $60,000 (the thirteenth estate above the over-all median); but about the same percentage of Lower South and Upper South congressmen had estates 600 percent or more of their county average. Only one legislator from an Upper South state, Robert W. Johnson of Pine Bluff, Arkansas (actually in Delta country), had an estate worth more than $400,000: his was $800,000; but six lawmakers from the deep South passed that mark, including one each from Alabama, Georgia, and Texas, and three from Louisiana. Despite the lower general wealth of the border-state members, however, it is obvious that most of the congressmen were rich, not only by the standards of their own neighborhoods but by those of the entire South as well.

As Table 1-2 indicates, however, these relative estate evaluations had only a small relation to a congressman's views on secession. Unionists tended to be somewhat richer than Secessionists on this relative basis, but the difference is too small to be considered very significant and might even be pared if the unknown estate group could be assigned. Nor is any pattern observable when party affiliations are taken into account (see Table 1-3), for again the distinction is very slight. Relatively speaking, Whigs were perhaps richer than Democrats, but again the difference is small; in fact, Tables 1-2 and 1-3 show almost the same relative wealth distribution on secession stand as on party.

Slaveholding was also an important index of wealth, at least in a group almost 60 percent agricultural and resident primarily in rural areas or very small towns. Here the contrasts of affluence are not as great as with estate value, for only 17 percent of the lawmakers owned more than 600 percent of the average holding in their respective counties. Some nonslaveholders, one should be aware, were actually quite prosperous. Wiley P. Harris of Mississippi, for example, owned no slaves but was worth about $36,000 in 1860. Small holders, as expected, tended to come from the Upper South, both as compared relatively in their own counties and as compared with the entire region. The median slaveholding among the Upper South congressmen was 12 slaves, with only 13 percent owning over 600 percent of the local average. The larger slaveholdings, just like the larger estates, generally were in the Lower South, where the median holding was 23 slaves, with 22 percent of the lawmakers possessing at least 600 percent of the average in their home

TABLE 1-2

RELATIVE VALUES OF ESTATE OF CONFEDERATE CONGRESSMEN ARRANGED BY POSITION ON SECESSION

Relative Value of Estate	Secessionists		Unionists		Unknown	Total
	No.	%[a]	No.	%	No.	No.
No Estate (0%)	0	0	1	1	0	1
Below Average (1-50%)	9	7	0	0	2	11
Average (51-200%)	11	9	16	16	8	35
Above Average (201-600%)	32	26	21	22	11	64
Much Above Average (601%+)	62	50	53	55	15	130
Unknown Estate Category	10	8	6	6	10	26
Total	124	100	97	100	46	267

a. Percentages are based on the number whose secession views are known. Relative estate categories are based upon computed average values for each congressman's county of residence. See Appendix I for explanation of categories.

20

TABLE 1-3

RELATIVE VALUES OF ESTATE OF CONFEDERATE CONGRESSMEN
ARRANGED BY FORMER PARTY AFFILIATION

Relative Value of Estate	Democrats		Whigs		Unknown	Total
	No.	%[a]	No.	%	No.	No.
No Estate (0%)	0	0	1	1	0	1
Below Average (1-50%)	9	7	0	0	2	11
Average (51-200%)	13	9	13	14	9	35
Above Average (201-600%)	36	26	22	24	6	64
Much Above Average (601%+)	68	49	50	54	12	130
Unknown Estate Category	12	9	6	7	8	26
Total	138	100	92	100	37	267

a. Percentages are based on the number whose party affiliations are known. Relative estate categories are based upon computed average values for each congressman's county of residence. See Appendix I for explanation of categories.

counties. Only one congressman in the Upper South—Robert W. Johnson, again—owned more than 140 slaves; but fifteen Lower South legislators exceeded that mark, with the top four men coming from the Mississippi River country of Louisiana. While the median slaveholding for the entire Congress was 16 slaves and that for Whigs and Unionists was 15 and 14 slaves respectively, the median for Democrats was 19 and for Secessionists it was a noteworthy 25 slaves.

Wealth, especially in slaves, was so greatly concentrated in the Lower South, however, that Democrats and Secessionists as a group necessarily held significantly more slaves than Whigs and Unionists. But this merely reflects the customarily smaller slaveholdings of the Upper South, where Whigs and Unionists had some of their most important concentrations of strength. It is safe to say that almost all congressmen were affluent and that estates and slaveholdings had no significant or direct relationship to party or secession stand except perhaps for occasional individuals. Such findings may warn that the roll-call behavior of these lawmakers could be only slightly differentiated according to economic status, since most were wealthy until hope of victory died, after which almost all faced the future with uncertain prospects.

Extremes of wealth in Congress may be illustrated more graphically by the poorest and richest members. Thomas C. Fuller of North Carolina was the poorest of the legislators, a fact which is explained in part, but only in part, by his relative youth. Born in North Carolina in 1832, Fuller had studied law, but his practice must have been rather meager for the support of his wife and two young children, for the 1860 census lists him as possessing no estate whatever. He was a Whig who had supported John Bell the previous fall; and, until Abraham Lincoln called for troops in April 1861, he was a Unionist. He entered the army, apparently under some compulsion, and attained the modest rank of first lieutenant. (It is notable that almost no congressmen were lieutenants. If they went into the army at all, they were usually colonels, at least.) In 1863, despite his lack of previous political experience, Fuller was elected to the House of Representatives by what he termed the "Conservative party" and voted with the Leaches "of N.C., with Boyce of S.C. and Wickham of Va." If the "conservative party" was an anticentralization faction, Fuller did indeed vote with it. The various methods of analysis used in later chapters show him to have been no friend of the measures necessary for Confederate independence. If everyone in the Confederate Congress had voted with Fuller, the war would certainly not have lasted as long as it did. While in Congress, he took a minor role, serving on committees dealing with commerce (which was not very important by then), patents (which was never important), and enrolled bills (which was a clerk-like position). Unlike many of his colleagues, he attended sessions with reasonable regularity and was very seldom heard in debate.[9]

Edward Sparrow of Louisiana is a startling contrast. Born in Ireland in 1810, he was one of the few immigrants in Congress. He apparently studied law and continued to practice, but it is clear that he never worried about the size of his practice as Fuller must have done. His estate, as reported for the 1860 census, was $1,248,050, and included the ownership, according to his postwar statement, of about 460 slaves. Sparrow was thus one of the richest men of the South, both in wealth and slaves, and he was by far the richest man in Congress. Even among other planters from the Mississippi River country, Sparrow was rich; he produced the seventh largest cotton crop in Louisiana in 1859. Like Fuller, Sparrow was a Whig, but unlike him, Sparrow was a Secessionist and voted as such in the Louisiana secession convention. He did not enter the army (he was over fifty years of age by 1860), but he had served as a brigadier general in the Mexican War. Sparrow was a man of some officeholding experience, having served in the state legislature as well as in the secession convention, which sent him to the Provisional Congress. Later, the legislature chose him to be senator at Richmond, so that he was one of the eight men to be members of the Congress from first day to last. Here he took a generally nationalist position, which his speeches reflected, while playing a major role in congressional affairs. He was chairman of the Senate Committee on Military Affairs, the importance of which more than made up for his membership on the relatively minor committees on Indian Affairs and the Flag and Seal. He did not give speeches on the merest excuse, as some congressmen did, but he did participate in debate often.[10]

Sparrow's role in the Confederate Congress was significant; Fuller's was minor, as far as his contemporaries could tell, and it is only by

9. Thomas C. Fuller petition, Amnesty Papers, North Carolina; *DAB*, VII, 66; *Journal of the Congress of the Confederate States of America, 1861-1865* (Washington: Government Printing Office, 1904-1905), VII (hereinafter cited as *Journal of the Confederate Congress)*; Bell I. Wiley and Hirst D. Milhollen, *Embattled Confederates: An Illustrated History of Southerners at War* (New York: Harper and Row, 1964), p. 264; Eighth Census of the United States, 1860, Manuscript, North Carolina, Schedule I, vol. V, p. 472, National Archives, Record Group 29 (hereinafter cited as Manuscript Census).

10. Manuscript Census, Louisiana, Schedule I, vol. II, p. 367; Edward Sparrow petition, Amnesty Papers, Louisiana; Joseph Karl Menn, *The Large Slaveholders of Louisiana—1860* (New Orleans: Pelican Publishing Company, 1964), p. 108; Charles Robert Lee, Jr., *The Confederate Constitutions* (Chapel Hill: University of North Carolina Press, 1963), p. 44; Wilfred Buck Yearns, *The Confederate Congress* (Athens: University of Georgia Press, 1960), p. 244; Wiley and Milhollen, *Embattled Confederates*, p. 271.

TABLE 1-4

PRIOR POLITICAL EXPERIENCE OF CONFEDERATE CONGRESSMEN

Type of Experience	Number	Percentage[a]
State Legislature	172	64
Federal Congress	85	32
State Secession Convention or Equivalent	86	32
State Supreme Court	13	5
State Circuit, Superior, and Other Courts	25	9
Governor or Lieutenant Governor	14	5
Other State Office	25	9
City Office	10	4
Federal Cabinet or Diplomatic Post	8	3
Other Political Experience	140	52
No Political Experience	27	10

a. Percentages are based on total membership and do not equal 100 since most legislators had several types of experience.

considerable effort that he is brought out of the shadows at all. It does not follow, however, that all rich men were outstanding congressmen. Some, like Alexander M. Clayton, who resigned in the middle of the second session of the Provisional Congress, got off the train when it had barely left the station.

Of importance to an understanding of the Confederate Congress is the political experience these legislators had before 1861 (see Table 1–4). As a group, they cannot be considered mere newcomers thrown into the political arena by the force of revolutionary events. Rather, most congressmen were well-informed public men. Only 10 percent of them had no discoverable political experience. Even this figure is undoubtedly too large, since we can assume that pertinent information on some individuals was not located. Furthermore, it is to be expected that any legislative body would find itself with some members of limited first-hand political background.

Only seven of the inexperienced lawmakers sat in the Provisional Congress, ten more came to the First Congress, and eleven more attended the Second Congress, which is remarkably few in view of the fact that many Southern leaders preferred military to civil service. No less than two thirds of the members had sat in state legislatures, and one third had served in the United States Congress (sixty-two men served in both). Eighty-six congressmen had been delegates to their state secession conventions (or the equivalent legislature in Kentucky).[11]

The experience level was high in the Congress as a whole, yet it did vary over the years and between houses. About 70 percent of the Provisional congressmen had sat in state legislatures; the corresponding proportion for the First and Second House are eight and eleven percentage points lower, respectively. The First Senate had 92 percent former state legislators and the Second Senate had 81 percent. A similar trend occurred regarding former United States congressmen. The Provisional Congress had more (39 percent) than the First House (32 percent), which in turn had more than the Second House (21 percent). In the Senate, there was a larger proportion of antebellum congressmen, although the figure dropped again between the First and Second Congresses, from 55 percent to 48 percent. Despite this, there were more experienced politicians in the Second Congress than one might expect. The largest proportion of inexperienced legislators sat in the Second House, but they made up only 15 percent of that body, and some of them had

11. Tennessee did not hold a secession convention either, disunion being accomplished by action of the governor and state legislature; but no member of Tennessee's 1861 legislature ever sat in the Confederate Congress.

become familiar with politics and legislative procedures in the Provisional and First Congresses. The experience level was, as a rule, very high, with the senators not unexpectedly more acquainted with political life than the representatives.

In a more general context, the assembling of information about the members, including their prior political experience, provides evidence that there was no jolting change of leadership because of secession. The state conventions or legislatures sent to the Provisional Congress men similar in accomplishments to those formerly chosen by legislators to be United States senators or statewide officials. The legislators subsequently followed customary practice in choosing Confederate senators. A majority of the First Senate had formerly been in the United States Congress, and nearly every state sent at least one senator with such experience. The voters in the first general elections were offered a familiar array of congressional candidates and selected a House that fairly closely reflected both the party and the secession divisions within the Confederacy, and that was in many ways a replication of antebellum Southern congressional delegations. Thirty-seven men with prior experience in the United States Congress were elected to the First House and constituted one third of its membership. Moreover, the other members differed little from these thirty-seven in slaveholding or value of estate when the somewhat greater age of the former congressmen is taken into consideration. Mid-war elections sent to Richmond more men who had been outspoken against secession from within the ranks of acknowledged political leaders of 1860. This, in itself, was largely a turning toward a pre-existing option rather than a fundamental revolt against the leadership patterns of Southern political society.

Some of the newcomers to the Second House, however, were men of such former political obscurity and modesty of estate as to reflect some voter reaction against the whole familiar corps of politicos. In this connection, it is instructive that, while about half of the representatives with antebellum congressional background were able to cash in on their experience and return to their seats, few such men were among the freshman members of the Second House. Of the half a hundred new members, only six had served in the federal Congress—and four of these represented constituencies in Kentucky, Missouri, or occupied portions of Virginia where no valid election among civilians could be held. Even better than lack of political experience to illustrate the possibility of significant changes in attitude on the part of numerous voters is the economic status of many new figures in the Second House. Men with estates valued no higher than $25,000 constituted only 25 percent of the First House, but amounted to 40 percent of those elected to the Second House by civilian constituencies free to vote, and 50 percent of the freshman representatives so elected. Slaveholding tells the same story: men below the small planter level (holding fewer than twenty slaves) made up less than 50 percent of the House elected in 1861, but totaled 60 percent of the representatives elected by voters inside Confederate-held territory in 1863, and 67 percent of the new members of the Second House sent from such protected districts.

We may illustrate some of the involvements of experience and wealth by again using extremes. Thomas J. Foster of Courtland, Alabama, was born in Tennessee in 1809 and moved to Alabama in 1830. By 1860, he owned 128 slaves and had an estate of $178,000, which was about twenty times the local average. He must have been a very visible figure, for he had not only planting but manufacturing interests as well. Although he was not engaged in politics, he was elected representative to the First and Second Congresses. A former Whig and a supporter of Stephen A. Douglas in 1860, he was predictably a Unionist, who went along with his state in 1861. His congressional record shows a half-hearted dedication to the Confederate cause.[12]

If the politically inexperienced Foster was not unknown, there were other neophyte congressmen who were. Of Nimrod L. Norton, for example, we know relatively little and can only assume his contemporaries knew little more. He was born in Kentucky in 1830 and moved to Missouri as a young man. By 1860, he was a comfortable, reasonably prosperous farmer near Fulton, Missouri, with an estate of $6,000 and no slaves. He opposed Lincoln's policy after Fort Sumter, became a lieutenant colonel in the Missouri State Guard, and later was a staff officer in the Confederate Army. He was elected to the Second Congress, apparently from the army, but because of illness did not sit until the Second Session was two weeks old. He cast his last vote a month before the end of the Congress, when he received leave of absence for the remainder of the session. After the war, he moved to Texas and returned to farming. His chief claim to fame seems to have been his work in finding the stone used for the construction of the Texas statehouse.[13]

Although politically inexperienced delegates might be either obscure or well known, the experienced legislators would naturally be well ac-

12. Manuscript Census, Alabama, Schedule I, vol. VI, p. 1013, Schedule II, vol. III, p. 164; Thomas J. Foster petition, Amnesty Papers, Alabama; Thomas M. Owen, *History of Alabama and Dictionary of Alabama Biography* (Chicago: S. J. Clark Co., 1921), III, 606; Yearns, *Confederate Congress,* p. 239.

13. Manuscript Census, Missouri, Schedule I, vol. III, p. 1057; *Journal of the Confederate Congress,* VII; Nimrod L. Norton petition, Amnesty Papers, Missouri; John Henry Brown, *Indian Wars and Pioneers of Texas* (Austin, Texas: L. E. Daniell, n.d.), pp. 697–700.

quainted with political leaders, at least in their own states. Several
Confederate congressmen, moreover, had extremely broad experience,
and they illustrate that aggregate information on such officeholders as
state legislators, governors, and United States congressmen, may be
misleading since one individual frequently held several such positions.
Howell Cobb, who considered his role as President of the Provisional
Congress the greatest achievement of his long political career, had been
state solicitor general, United States congressman (and speaker of the
U.S. House of Representatives in the Thirty-first Congress), governor
of Georgia, and Secretary of the Treasury under Buchanan.[14] Herschel
V. Johnson had been a federal judge, governor of Georgia, United States
congressman, and Douglas's vice-presidential running mate in 1860.[15]
Others had experience without lasting fame, such as Edmund S. Dargan
of Alabama, who had been chief justice of the Alabama supreme court,
mayor of Mobile, state senator, congressman, and a member of the
secession convention.[16]

By contrast, some had fame with little formal office. William L. Yancey
of Alabama was in the state legislature in the 1840s and served in
Congress from 1844 to 1846. Between then and the secession crisis, he
served only in party conventions and as presidential elector. Yet he
remained in the forefront of his party in Alabama, stirring up enough
sectional trouble to merit his selection as Confederate senator in 1862.[17]
George Davis of North Carolina held no formal office until the secession
crisis, although he had come close to securing the Whig nomination
for governor in 1848. Yet he was well enough known to be sent to
the Washington Peace Conference, he was chosen to attend the Provisional Congress and the Senate of the First Congress, and he was selected
by Jefferson Davis for the post of attorney general.[18] Indeed, Confederate
senators, being chosen by the state legislatures, had to have reputations
known to the legislators though not necessarily to the voting public.
Party wheel horses who had seldom held formal office might therefore
have a good chance of election. Landon C. Haynes was in the Tennessee
legislature in the late 1840s, lost a race for Congress in 1859, and was

---

14. *Biographical Directory of the American Congress 1774–1961* . . . , revised edition
(Washington: Government Printing Office, 1961), p. 711 (hereinafter cited as *BDAC*);
DAB, IV, 241–244.

15. *DAB*, X, 102–103.

16. Owen, *History of Alabama*, III, 454; *DAB*, V, 74.

17. *BDAC*, p. 1855; *DAB*, XX, 592–595.

18. *DAB*, V, 114–115; Samuel A'Court Ashe, editor, *Biographical History of North
Carolina from Colonial Times to the Present* (Greensboro, N.C.: Charles L. Van Noppen,
1905–1917), II, 71.

a Breckinridge elector in 1860.[19] Despite this slim record, he was in the top echelon of the Democratic leadership in East Tennessee; his political experience fully entitled him to be picked for the senatorship. But other Confederate congressmen had such wide officeholding experience that their names became political bywords among historians of the antebellum period: Robert M. T. Hunter, Alexander H. Stephens, Robert A. Toombs, Albert G. Brown, Robert Barnwell Rhett, Sr., William C. Rives, and John Tyler.

The vocations of the Confederate congressmen were as varied as their political experience and, in some cases, a good deal more colorful. But much of the variety included lines of work no longer followed by 1860. While the membership did include a former slave-trader, a part-time horse breeder, a one-time stage coach driver, several former soldiers, and a once-aspiring poet, the vast majority were either engaged in the practice of law (77 percent) or in agriculture (58 percent), with 107 congressmen (40 percent) engaged in both. Eleven congressmen were journalists and ten were in finance. Another ten were merchants, and there was a sprinkling of clergymen, physicians, manufacturers, and educators. Occupations show little or no relation to previous political affiliation or secession view, except for the twenty-four men who had mercantile, financial, or manufacturing interests, and who were more likely than their fellow congressmen to have been Whigs or Unionists. This is most notable in regard to secession view, as thirteen of the entrepreneurs were Unionists and only four were Secessionists (though nine were of unknown stand). As to party, with only three unknowns, this group included thirteen Whigs and ten Democrats.

Most of the Confederate legislators were in the prime of political life, though they were younger than congressmen of the twentieth century. Slightly less than three quarters were in their thirties or forties in 1860. Nine of the youngest were born in 1830, and another seven were even younger. Robert J. Breckinridge, Jr., of Kentucky, and Elias C. Boudinot, Cherokee Nation, were the youngest: each was only twenty-five years old in 1860. Twenty-two percent of the members were fifty years of age or older. Ten were born in the eighteenth century, and the oldest, Thomas Fearn of Alabama, was born in 1789. The younger the congressmen, the more likely they were to have been Democrats, even though all but a bare handful came to maturity while the Whig party was still active. Men in their fifties and sixties were evenly divided between parties,

19. Philip M. Hamer, editor, *Tennessee: A History, 1673–1932* (New York: American Historical Society, 1933), I, 518; Joshua William Caldwell, *Sketches of the Bench and Bar of Tennessee* (Knoxville: Ogden Brothers and Co., 1898), pp. 330–331.

while twice as many men in their thirties or younger were Democrats
as were Whigs. Younger men were also more likely to be Secessionists.
Those aged fifty or more were somewhat more inclined toward Unionism;
those less than forty were in favor of disruption by a 1.6-to-1 ratio.
As to both party and secession, the younger group included about five
times as many unknowns as the older.

It is also interesting to examine the rather tangled and extensive social,
political, and familial relations among these representatives and senators.
Congress was not a gathering of strangers, for many of these men had
known each other for years. Except for a few on the outside circles,
it sometimes seems that everybody knew almost everybody else and
would soon be introduced to the few they had missed. This is an exagger-
ation to be sure, but family trees spread their branches far. Each of
about thirty members, for example, had a relative among the congressmen or other high-ranking Confederates. There were at least three pairs
of brothers and two pairs of cousins, and ten or more others were related
by marriage.[20] At least seven more were related to high civil or military
officers. The story does not stop with family ties. There were eight sets
of law partners, and several legislators discovered their law teachers
among their congressional colleagues. A few senators and representatives
had other business dealings with one another. Some congressmen were
neighbors back home (Reuben Davis, for example, lived next door to
James Phelan), as more than one third of the membership lived in a
small town that was home to at least one other lawmaker. Little Ocala,
Florida, for example, had four of its citizens in the Congress at one
time or other; and Greensboro, North Carolina, Little Rock, Arkansas,
Holly Springs, Mississippi, and Huntsville, Alabama, had three members
each. Brief reference to the membership rolls of the state legislatures
would widen the horizon of acquaintanceship, while forty of the men
in the last antebellum United States Congress eventually sat in the
Confederate Congress.[21] Still others got to know each other during their
sojourn in Richmond. Alexander H. Stephens, Augustus H. Garland,
and Edward Sparrow, for example, regularly frequented the home of
fellow-congressman Thomas J. Semmes; while Richard W. Walker, Herschel V. Johnson, James L. Pugh, and W. W. Boyce lived in the same
rooming house. In 1864, more than sixty congressmen were living in
the same hotel, rooming house, or home as at least one other congress-

20. We may be sure that there were more relationships than these, but precise information
is lacking in several cases.
    21. *BDAC*, pp. 169–172.

man, as legislators maintained joint accommodations in order to cut costs in the wartime capital.[22]

These interrelationships were even more widespread because some of these men had political experience, and therefore contacts, outside the states they later represented in Montgomery or Richmond. The volatile Henry S. Foote is one of the best examples. A Tennessee congressman, he was born and educated in Virginia, practiced law in Alabama, and served Mississippi as a state legislator and United States senator. While in Washington in 1847, he quarrelled with and on Christmas Day came to blows with the other Mississippi senator, Jefferson Davis. The two men developed a lifelong enmity which was only heightened when Foote defeated Davis for the Mississippi governorship in 1851. In 1854, Foote sought re-election to the U.S. Senate and upon losing moved to California, where he again sought a senate seat, losing this time by a single vote. In 1858, he returned to Mississippi and was a member of the Knoxville Southern Commercial Convention in 1859. Soon after, he moved to Nashville, Tennessee, and represented that district for three years at Richmond.[23]

J. Patton Anderson had similar nomadic experiences. Born in Tennessee and educated in Pennsylvania, he studied law in Kentucky, practiced in Mississippi, and was a lieutenant colonel in the Mexican War. He was a member of the Mississippi legislature before accepting appointment to the post of federal marshal in the Washington Territory. He later served as delegate to Congress from Washington. He turned down an appointment to be territorial governor before moving to Florida, where he established himself as a planter and lawyer, sat in the secession convention, and was elected to the Confederate Congress.[24] Other individuals such as Oldham, mentioned above, had experiences which were almost as diverse, enabling them to be acquainted with many fellow congressmen.

It is interesting to note that these men were in many ways like those who had sat in the secession conventions. Ralph A. Wooster has pointed out that those conventions were quite similar to one another.[25] They

22. *Directory of the House of Representatives* (Richmond: R. M. Smith, 1864); *Directory of the Confederate States Senate for the Second Session of the Second Congress . . .* (Richmond: R. M. Smith, 1864).

23. *BDAC*, p. 902; *DAB*, VI, 500–501; John E. Gonzales, "Henry Stuart Foote: Confederate Congressman and Exile," *Civil War History*, XI (December 1965), 385.

24. *DAB*, I, 266–267; *BDAC*, p. 479.

25. See Ralph A. Wooster, *The Secession Conventions of the South* (Princeton: Princeton University Press, 1962), pp. 256–266, and Wooster, "An Analysis of the Membership of Secession Conventions in the Lower South," *Journal of Southern History*, XXIV (August 1958), 360–368.

were composed of middle-aged men, most of whom made their living in either law or agriculture and a majority of whom were rich slave-holders. This is also true of the congressmen. In addition, the percentage of natives of the state within the congressional delegations varied substantially the same way as in the conventions. The older, established states furnished the most natives, Virginia and the Carolinas heading the list, with Arkansas, Florida, Missouri, and Texas at the bottom in both instances. In both convention and Congress, Secessionists had more slaves than Unionists; and in both, members from the Upper South owned fewer slaves than those from the Lower South. Nevertheless, it cannot be said that the Confederate Congress was merely a projection of the conventions, for there were some important differences. Congressmen, for example, were richer than the convention delegates; only the South Carolina, Louisiana, and Mississippi conventions had a higher median estate than that of Congress, and in the case of Mississippi the margin of difference was slight. Although Secessionists in the conventions had larger estates than their Unionist opponents, among congressmen, estates were distributed almost evenly between the antagonists of 1861— and the median estate sizes were identical. As expected, congressmen were better known than the average member of the secession conventions, although it is certainly not the case that each one was necessarily a leading statesman.

Confederate congressmen were also much like other members of the Southern ruling élite as described in Professor Wooster's study of office-holders in the Lower South between 1850 and 1860.[26] State legislators from the Deep South, like congressmen from the same region, were "middle-aged planters, farmers, or lawyers, holders of property, including slaves, who were born in the slaveholding states and usually in the lower South." To be more specific, the age distribution was much the same except that a slightly smaller proportion of the congressmen were men below thirty years of age. On a proportional basis, fewer Lower South congressmen than Lower South legislators were born in the states of

26. Ralph A. Wooster, *The People in Power: Courthouse and Statehouse in the Lower South, 1850–1860* (Knoxville: University of Tennessee Press, 1969); especially pp. 27–42, 95–105, 110–111, 121–163. Some of the figures used to compare Wooster's findings with ours are aggregates derived from Appendix I of *People in Power*. In view of the large turnover among Confederate congressmen, it is important to note that rotation in office was even greater among state legislators and county officers. In the Mississippi legislature of the 1850s, for example, 61 percent of the members served only one term and another 31 percent served only two (Wooster, *People in Power*, pp. 41–42). Compared with these figures, the continuity of congressional membership appears greater than one might have expected.

the Atlantic Seaboard or the Deep South, but these differences are not particularly striking. Other characteristics display more notable variations. Although the same proportion of both groups engaged in agriculture, congressmen were far more likely to be lawyers.[27] And while slaveholders were a majority among both, more than 20 percent more congressmen than legislators owned the twenty or more slaves considered to be the lower limit of the planter class; the distribution of estate was similar. Wooster also found that members of county governing boards were like state legislators, except that there were far fewer lawyers and fewer men of great wealth. Such differences as these are certainly not unexpected, and may be attributed in part to the natural tendency of voters to support men of greater prominence for the national capital than for the statehouse, and for the statehouse than for the county seat. Moreover, only the more affluent could readily afford the cost of campaigning over larger districts and of abandoning professional or other responsibilities while serving at a considerable distance from home for little if anything more than expenses.

The average Confederate congressman may be described as a man of some political experience, having served in his state legislature and perhaps as a congressman or member of his state secession convention. He came to Congress knowing, and knowing of, many of his colleagues, and was in turn known by many of them. As to his other characteristics, he was likely to be a Breckinridge Democrat and a Secessionist. He lived in a rural area, and he practiced law but also had some agricultural interests. He was born in one of the established eastern states, or perhaps Kentucky, and the chances are a little better than even that he was sent to Congress by the state of his nativity. He had a substantial estate, which was valued well above the average for his county, and if he owned slaves he owned at least as many as his neighbors. He was between the ages of thirty and sixty, a Protestant, and had some college education. He probably was never in the Confederate army.

27. It is difficult to say how great the distinction is, for Wooster used a different procedure for the assignment of occupational labels. He finds 20 percent of the state legislators in the Lower South in 1860 to have been engaged in law (aggregate figure derived from tables in Appendix I of *People in Power*). The corresponding figure for Lower South congressmen is 77 percent if all be included who may have been engaged in both law and agriculture. A count of occupations as given only in the manuscript census lowers the figure to a 60 percent minimum, and if all those engaged (by our criteria) in both law and agriculture be counted only as agriculturalists, which really would be quite misleading, 37 percent of the Lower South congressmen could be classed as lawyers. It is the opinion of the authors that the proper comparable figure for Congress would be in the 70 percent range, but in any case there is no doubt that, proportionally, far more Deep South congressmen than state legislators were practicing law.

This composite picture of the ever-elusive average man as Confederate congressman fits no one exactly. Nevertheless, these are the characteristics which tended to be most prevalent, and which may be presumed to have affected, in some degree at least, the behavior of the legislators on the multitude of issues they faced. In the following chapters, several of these attributes will be examined closely, in an effort to judge the extent of their influence on voting behavior.

2 Political Parties

THE Confederate Congress under the Permanent Constitution was constituted exactly like the United States Congress, and Confederate congressmen were naturally well acquainted with a two-party system operating in such a national legislative body. Politics, in both Confederate congressional elections and legislative work, ought to have continued along lines similar to national partisan activity of the late antebellum years, and parallel to Northern patterns of the war years, or so one might reasonably expect. Exhortations to bury the political hatchet for the duration of the war, heard on both sides of the battle lines, obviously cannot be taken seriously for the United States Congress. The Confederate Congress, however, had no overt party organization, so that to discover whether partisan divisions were quietly present requires extensive study of popular votes and of the roll-call responses of the members.

Either a Democrat-Whig axis or a Secessionist-Unionist axis might have yielded a two-party alignment in the Confederate Congress. As indicated in the previous chapter, these two classifications of rivalry were almost the same, for among the congressmen for whom both party and secession stand have been determined, 81 percent were either Democrat-Secessionists or Whig-Unionists. A sufficiently close balance between Democrats and Whigs, or between Secessionists and Unionists, prevailed in both House and Senate at all times to furnish an adequate basis for a two-party structure (see Table 2–1).

The presence of intense antagonism between Democrats and Whigs, or between Secessionists and Unionists, is well attested to in private and public communications of the war years. In North Carolina, Unionists were bitterly frustrated by having the state's decision almost preempted by the secession of Virginia, so that deeper animosities may be found here than in any other Confederate state. Jonathan Worth, postwar governor, wrote in May of 1861: "I leave the Union and the flag of Washington because I am subjected and forced to submit to my master—democracy, detesting it with more and more intensity, as I become better acquainted with its leaders and its objects." At the end of the summer, he complained that Democrats and Secessionists would

TABLE 2-1

FORMER PARTY AFFILIATION AND POSITION ON SECESSION OF CONFEDERATE CONGRESSMEN, BY STATES

State	Provisional Congress						First House						Second House		
	Former Party			Secession Position			Former Party			Secession Position			Former Party		
	D	W	Not Known	S	U	Not Known	D	W	Not Known	S	U	Not Known	D	W	Not Known
Ala.	5	6	1	3	9	0	6	3	0	6	3	0	4	4	0
Ark.	3	1	1	1	4	0	2	1	1	2	2	0	1	2	2
Fla.	3	2	0	3	2	0	2	0	1	3	0	0	1	0	1
Ga.	4	7	1	6	5	1	4	5	2	5	5	1	3	3	4
Ky.	3	3	4	0	3	7	6	5	1	2	3	7	5	5	2
La.	1	4	1	4	1	1	1	3	2	3	1	2	1	5	1
Miss.	6	3	0	6	3	0	6	1	1	6	1	1	4	2	1
Mo.	6	1	1	3	3	2	4	1	1	3	2	1	5	0	2
N.C.	5	5	0	5	5	0	6	4	0	5	5	0	1	9	0
S.C.	9	0	0	9	0	0	6	0	1	7	0	0	5	0	1
Tenn.	4	3	0	2	4	1	6	5	0	3	5	3	6	5	0
Texas	6	1	0	7	0	0	5	1	0	6	0	0	3	0	3
Va.	7	8	1	9	6	1	10	6	3	9	7	3	6	5	5
Total	62	44	10	58	45	13	64	35	13	60	34	18	45	40	22

TABLE 2-1--Continued

State	Second House Secession Position			First Senate Former Party			Secession Position			Second Senate Former Party			Secession Position		
	S	U	Not Known	D	W	Not Known	S	U	Not Known	D	W	Not Known	S	U	Not Known
Ala.	4	4	0	2	1	0	2	1	0	0	2	0	0	2	0
Ark.	2	2	1	2	0	0	1	1	0	2	1	0	1	2	0
Fla.	2	0	0	1	1	0	0	1	1	1	1	0	0	1	1
Ga.	2	5	3	2	1	0	0	2	1	1	1	0	0	2	0
Ky.	2	2	8	2	0	0	1	1	0	2	0	0	1	1	0
La.	3	1	3	1	1	0	2	0	0	1	1	0	2	0	0
Miss.	4	2	1	2	0	0	2	0	0	1	1	0	1	1	0
Mo.	4	1	2	3	0	0	0	2	1	2	0	0	1	1	0
N.C.	1	9	0	1	2	0	2	1	0	1	1	0	1	1	0
S.C.	5	0	1	2	0	0	2	0	0	2	0	0	2	0	0
Tenn.	4	5	2	1	1	0	1	1	0	1	1	0	1	1	0
Texas	3	2	1	2	0	0	2	0	0	2	0	0	2	0	0
Va.	5	6	5	1	2	0	1	2	0	1	1	0	1	1	0
Total	41	39	27	22	9	0	16	12	3	17	10	0	13	13	1

treat Whigs as subjugated vassals when soldiers were no longer needed.[1] Confederate Senator William A. Graham testified after the war that Southern Whigs in general had been zealous adherents to the Union until forced by events to choose simply which side to fight with, "when a favorable result to either, was to be little short of ruin to us."[2] James G. Ramsay, representative to the Second Congress, claimed to have been elected in 1863 by "old Union friends" and commented that he could not have been elected to the First Congress because of the secession fever.[3] Union Whig Zebulon Vance, soon to be elected governor, wrote to his wife in May of 1861 that his spirits were low because of the way things were being managed at Raleigh: "None but Locos and Secessionists will be appointed to the Offices: the old Union Men will be made to take back Seats and do most of the hard work and make bricks without straw." Two years later, Vance, by then governor, received a letter concerning the congressional elections which summarized somewhat inelegantly the attitudes of many Union Whigs: "*I fear very much, the stinking democracy,* will beat Davidson [Allen T., Confederate congressman] . . . Christ—how I hate democracy."[4]

Fears that a Democrat would replace Representative Davidson were ill-founded, in fact, for another Union Whig took his seat in the Second Congress. The sweep of North Carolina by Union Whigs in 1863 was one of the spectacular electoral phenomena of the Confederacy and was accompanied by public as well as private intemperate denunciations of Democrats and Secessionists. Congressman Burgess S. Gaither wrote from Richmond that the truest and boldest men in Congress were

old line Whigs, who wish to preserve in tact [sic], the constitutional rights of both state and the Confederate Governments. The extremist . . . friends of state rights, appear to have lost their reconing [sic] and are upon the wild seas of revolution, without compass and are drifting into the vortex. . . . They showed high capacity for the destruction of the old government and now exhibit none for the construction of the new one.[5]

1. Jonathan Worth to D. G. Worth, May 15, 1861; Worth to E. J. Hale and Sons, August 1, 1861, in J. G. de Roulhac Hamilton, editor, *The Correspondence of Jonathan Worth* (Raleigh: Edwards and Broughton Printing Co., 1909), I, 144–145, 157.

2. Graham to Robert C. Winthrop, February 1, 1867, in Robert Charles Winthrop Papers, Massachusetts Historical Society, Boston, Mass.

3. James G. Ramsay petition, Amnesty Papers, North Carolina.

4. Vance to wife, May 18, 1861, in Frontis W. Johnston, editor, *The Papers of Zebulon Baird Vance* (Raleigh, N.C.: State Department of Archives and History, 1963), I, 100; William L. Lowe to Vance, April 3, 1863, in Zebulon B. Vance Papers, North Carolina State Department of Archives and History, Raleigh, N.C.

5. Gaither to Zebulon B. Vance, April 24, 1863, in Vance Papers.

At home, during the congressional contests, Democrats and Secessionists were scorched in election broadsides by victorious candidates James T. Leach and James M. Leach.[6] Party politics were kept alive in North Carolina throughout the war, and were acerbated through reinforcement of the Democratic-Whig rivalry by a closely paralleling Secessionist-Unionist antagonism. In fact, only two North Carolina congressmen crossed party lines on the secession issue. One of them was Whig George Davis, who became the Confederacy's attorney general in January 1864.

North Carolina was unique in the depth and decisiveness of persisting party consciousness, but it was by no means the only place where party recriminations were heard. By May of 1861, the Richmond *Examiner* was making reference to a tendency in Virginia to elect only old Democrats.[7] John Janney wrote from the Virginia convention exulting that leading Secessionists had been defeated in the contests for seats in the Provisional Confederate Congress. "Mr. Rives [William C., a Union Whig] beat James A. Seddon, a red hot disunionist . . . Judge Brockenbrough [John W.] beat James M. Mason (which does the very inside of my heart good)."[8] Rives was distressed at having been elected and wrote to his brother that he had positively refused to be a candidate, that all knew his opposition to secession, and that he reluctantly quit his retirement because he could not decline a "call thus made upon me by my fellow-citizens, & in the spirit & intention, as I had reason to believe, that my influence should be used, as it was, to promote a termination of the war, as soon as practicable, by mutual agreement & negotiation."[9] Rives evidently had believed that he was selected by Unionists to continue his work against secession at the new stage of escalation of the sectional conflict; and in 1863, he successfully sought a seat in the Second House.

A few days after the 1863 elections in Virginia, a newspaper correspondent wrote that an effort had been made in both state and congressional elections to ostracize those who had not been original Secessionists, "and this in a state where the conservatives or cooperationists had a four to one majority on the date of Lincoln's inauguration." He added

6. James T. Leach, broadside entitled "Fellow-Citizens of the Third Congressional District," dated September 17, 1863, in James T. Leach Papers, Southern Historical Collection, University of North Carolina Library, Chapel Hill, N.C.; James M. Leach, broadside entitled "To the Soldiers of the 7th Congressional District," dated April 5, 1864 (special election to fill seat vacated by death of member-elect), in Vance Papers.

7. Quoted in Washington *National Intelligencer,* May 10, 1861.

8. Janney to wife, April 29, 1861, in John Janney Papers, Southern Historical Collection, University of North Carolina Library, Chapel Hill, N.C.

9. Rives to brother, June 7, 1865 (subsequently forwarded to Andrew Johnson), in Amnesty Papers, Virginia.

that he did not see how anyone could be so blind as to try to proscribe old Unionist Whigs and commented that the folly of that course was seen "in the defeat of Lyons [James, a Secession Whig], present member of Cong from Richmond district by Col Wickham [Williams C., also a Whig], originally a cooperationist who took sword upon secession." [10]

In Alabama, the Secession Convention sent several opponents of secession to the Provisional Congress, allegedly with Secessionists standing aside for the sake of harmony. Not much harmony was restored, however, as William R. Smith, Union Whig delegate to the First and Second Congresses from the Tuscaloosa district, wrote to his wife: "The people will be overwhelmed with troubles—but there will be a day of reckoning for the wicked.... There is a calm and deliberate determination here to hold our enemies accountable in the future before the people whose will has been violated—and whose peace, if not Liberty, has been destroyed." [11] At the war's end, he wrote to President Andrew Johnson that he had refused to sign the secession ordinance, had opposed the Permanent Constitution of the Confederacy, and would have left the South had he been financially able to move his large family. His choices, he claimed, were few: "I found that I should either have to leave the country, be mobbed, or take part." He went on to allege that he had been elected both times by the Union party of his district against the united forces of the Secessionists. [12]

Another Alabama Whig wrote in 1863 to Union Whig Lewis E. Parsons, who became the provisional governor in 1865, that a Confederate senator was needed from among honest men "that love the country more than party." Of the Secessionists he commented: "I find many men who were highly gifted in tearing down the old government are worth but little in building up the new one." [13] The Alabama Senate seat vacated by the death of a prominent Secessionist, Yancey, was filled shortly thereafter by legislative selection of one of the outstanding Unionist leaders in the Alabama secession convention, Robert Jemison, Jr., who was also a former Whig. Thomas H. Watts, elected governor of Alabama in 1863, felt called upon to arrange a post-election speaking tour "to correct the impression that his election represented a Union vote." "The only ground for such an opinion," announced a pro-Confederate editor, was "the

10. [Greensboro] *Alabama Beacon*, June 19, 1863.

11. Smith to wife, January 10, 1861, in William Russell Smith Papers, Division of Manuscripts, Library of Congress, Washington, D.C.

12. William R. Smith petition, Amnesty Papers, Alabama. (Smith's pardon was dated July 29, 1865.)

13. R. A. Baker to Lewis E. Parsons, August 24, 1863, in Lewis E. Parsons Papers, Alabama Department of Archives and History, Montgomery, Ala.

fact of his having been a member of the Whig organization in party times, and a Union man previous to the election of . . . Lincoln." [14]

Hiram P. Bell, Georgia Union Whig representative to the Second Congress, wrote in 1865 that he had opposed disunion with "voice and vote" but found it impossible to do other than go along, although he deeply "deplored the madness and folly of secession." While incapacitated during recovery from a battle wound, he was elected to Congress, according to his account, by those opposed to secession—defeating an avowed Secessionist. [15] Another of the Georgia Union Whig congressmen, Hines Holt, afterward wrote that he accepted election to the Congress only to pour oil on troubled waters and resigned when he saw the hopelessness of that course. [16] Georgia Senator Benjamin H. Hill, prominent Union Whig, spoke of Whig attitudes in 1865 in these terms:

Well, you see all the evils of secession that we prophesied have become true; now we suppose the people will believe us, and not believe the old secession democrats, who wanted to drink all the blood that would be shed by the war; we suppose now that the old whig party will arise from its ashes in some form, at least what we call the anti-democratic element. [17]

A Mississippi Union Whig, Walker Brooke, claimed that his selection as a delegate to the Provisional Congress was by aid of the "more conservative parties" of the convention. [18] A year after the war's end, a Mississippi Whig editor was urging supporters of President Andrew Johnson's reconstruction policies not to adopt a distinctive party name because it would be quite as hard for the old Democrats to become latter-day Whigs as it would for "us old Whigs to become Democrats." [19] Neill S. Brown, formerly Whig governor of Tennessee, wrote sadly in the fall of 1861 that distinctions between Secessionists and Unionists ought to be forgotten but that the administration at Richmond was, in a partisan spirit, awarding all of the high offices, both civil and military, to original Secessionists. [20] But when the war had ended, the shoe was on the other foot, and Democrats, even Unionist Democrats, felt that they were being proscribed by Tennessee Whigs. One disgruntled East Tennessean wrote to President Johnson, a lifelong Democrat, that the

14. Grove Hill (Alabama) *Clarke County Journal,* October 29, 1863.

15. Hiram P. Bell petition, Amnesty Papers, Georgia.

16. Hines Holt petition, Amnesty Papers, Georgia.

17. Walter L. Fleming, editor, *Documentary History of Reconstruction* (Cleveland: A. H. Clark Co., 1906–1907), II, 92.

18. Walker Brooke petition, Amnesty Papers, Mississippi.

19. Raymond (Mississippi) *Hinds County Gazette,* June 15, 1866.

20. Brown to [?], October 25, 1861, Miscellaneous Manuscripts Collection, New York Historical Society, New York, N.Y.

"*old line* Whigs, or the leaders, are your bitter enemies. . . . There is hatred of everything that is Democracy." [21] It was reported from Florida at the end of the war that Whigs there had an understanding that they would vote for no Democrats, whom they accused of having brought on the disaster in the first place.[22]

Continued party antagonism after 1861 is illustrated also by the revealing attempts of congressmen and other civil officers to deny that such discord existed, or that they were at all responsible if it did. Senator Herschel V. Johnson, a pro-Union Democrat who had been Douglas's running mate in the 1860 election, accused Confederate Vice President Alexander H. Stephens of attempting to build up an opposition party. A month before the start of the Second Congress, Union Whig Stephens replied that he did not really desire an opposition party, nor did he dislike Secession Democrat Jefferson Davis, but that he did suspect Davis of creating a despotism. Stephens denied that Georgia's opposition to Davis in 1864, especially on the habeas corpus issue, was a party movement; but he did admit that his half-brother, Linton Stephens, took a leading role, and that he knew about it.[23] Nevertheless, organized opposition could easily lead to the development of parties, as James Madison and Alexander Hamilton had discovered three generations before.

Denials of perpetuating party strife were constantly heard in congressional halls; that they were heard at all indicates lingering (or perhaps developing) party influence. In August 1862, William N. H. Smith felt it necessary to defend newly elected Governor Vance of North Carolina on the floor of Congress against charges of political partisanship. The allegation that Vance was acting in the spirit of party (which in the American tradition would have been the logical way to act) was treated as an insult to both Vance and North Carolina.[24] The idea that opposition was desirable, and that party was the practical vehicle for this opposition, seemed extrinsic. In February 1865, when the denouement of the Confederate drama was speeded by severe internal divisions and constant carping criticism, Representative Thomas S. Gholson of Virginia re-

21. H. B. Williams to Johnson, August 7, 1865, in Andrew Johnson Papers, Division of Manuscripts, Library of Congress, Washington, D.C.

22. William W. Davis, *Civil War and Reconstruction in Florida,* Columbia University Studies in History, Economics and Public Law, vol. LIII (New York: Columbia University, 1913), p. 366n.

23. *The War of the Rebellion: A Compilation of the Official Records of the Union and Confederate Armies* (Washington: Government Printing Office, 1880–1901), ser. IV, vol. III, pp. 278–281 (April 8, 1864) (hereinafter cited as *O.R.*).

24. "Proceedings of the Confederate Congress," *Southern Historical Society Papers* (1925–1959), XLV, 211 (hereinafter cited as "Proceedings").

marked that he was astounded to "hear gentlemen indulge in denunciation and invective. . . . It seems to me they act as if they thought we were engaged in ordinary party conflicts, and that in order to ensure the success of their party, they should render their adversary as odious as possible." [25]

Congressional election results offer some further evidence of rivalry or even bitterness between Democrats and Whigs, or Secessionists and Unionists. The first congressional election, that of 1861, sent to the House about three Democrats to two Whigs—roughly the proportion of the party presidential vote in the Confederate region in 1860.[26] The ratio between Secessionists and Unionists was almost the same. The legislatures in six states apparently agreed to select one Democrat and one Whig for the Senate seats. In the North Carolina legislature, only Democrats were nominated for one of the seats and only Whigs for the other.[27] In South Carolina and Texas, where the Whig party had not been an organized force, and in Alabama and Arkansas, only Democrats were selected for Senate seats. Kentucky and Missouri were also represented exclusively by Democrats, but in each case one of the two senators had been a Unionist as long as possible for a man who cast his lot with the Confederacy. In satisfying rivals, however, less emphasis seems to have been placed on secession position than on party in most of the legislatures. North Carolina's senators represented both political parties but neither was a Unionist. The same was true in Virginia and Louisiana.

Party continuity does not appear very clearly, on the other hand, when the prior voting record of each district is compared with the party affiliation or secession stand of the successful candidate for the House in 1861. Thirty-four Democrats represented Democratic districts, but twenty-five others were returned from Whig districts. Sixteen Whigs came from Whig districts but eleven from Democratic districts. Some of the

25. Thomas S. Gholson, *Speech of Hon. Thos. S. Gholson, of Virginia, on the Policy of Employing Negro Troops, and the Duty of All Classes to Aid in the Prosecution of the War* (Richmond: G. P. Evans and Co., 1865), p. 18. (Pamphlet edition of speech delivered in Congress, February 1, 1865.)

26. John Bell received almost exactly 40 percent of the popular vote in 1860 in either the ten states of the actual Confederacy or the twelve states claimed by the Confederacy (this excludes South Carolina, which had no popular vote for presidential electors until after the Civil War), although the percentage varied widely from state to state. (United States Bureau of the Census, *Historical Statistics of the United States, Colonial Times to 1957* [Washington, D.C.: U.S. Government Printing Office, 1960], p. 688.)

27. Daniel M. Robison, "The Whigs in the Politics of the Confederacy," East Tennessee Historical Society's *Publications,* No. 11 (1939), pp. 3–10; Yearns, *Confederate Congress,* pp. 46–48.

districts were so closely divided between parties, however, that they contribute little to this comparison.[28]

The voters' attitudes toward secession evidently had greater force than party alignments in determining representation in the First House. Among twenty-eight districts that had voted decisively for John C. Breckinridge, the southern Democratic presidential candidate, and thereby had revealed their secessionist bent, twenty-two elected Secessionists.[29] Ten congressional districts that had indicated pro-Union majorities by clearly opposing Breckinridge in favor of Bell or Douglas sent seven Unionists and three Secessionists to Congress.

The next occasion for general voter response in congressional and state elections came in mid-war, in 1863, after critical Confederate reverses and the onset of severe personal sacrifices. There is evidence that discontent among the people was reflected in many areas by a preference for new faces or even by the retirement of Democrat-Secessionists in favor of former Whigs who had been Unionists. This was spectacularly the case in North Carolina, where a House of Representatives delegation three-fifths Democratic was supplanted by one consisting of nine Union Whigs and only one Secession Democrat. And the same result may be observed in scattered districts in other portions of the Confederacy. Approximately one half of the Union Whigs in the First House were elected to the Second, and the same proportion of the Secession Democrats returned to Congress. The replacements, however, were preponderantly Whigs and Unionists. Among the freshman representatives in the Second House, more than two thirds were Unionists and three fifths were Whigs. One consequence was to alter the party balance from almost two-thirds Democratic or Secessionist in the First House to very nearly equal in the Second House. Exclusive of the areas under Federal occupation, fifteen districts replaced Secessionists with Unionists, and sixteen

28. Yearns, *Confederate Congress*, pp. 48–49, discusses the correlation between a district's party or secession position and the kind of congressman who was victorious. Since a large number of Confederate congressmen had not been identified as to party or secession stand by Yearns, his estimates are somewhat different from the ones made here.

29. For a large proportion of the counties of the Confederacy, Secessionist strength is surprisingly difficult to determine with a significant degree of accuracy. Presidential vote for 1860 is known for almost all counties. Hence, the employment of Breckinridge *versus* Bell and Douglas strength provides a far wider base for these estimates of congressmen's attitudes than could the incomplete and often nonexistent Secessionist percentage among the county's voters. Appreciation is expressed to Wilfred B. Yearns for a sketch map of the Confederacy by congressional district. A map of each state by district is in John Brawner Robbins, "Confederate Nationalism: Politics and Government in the Confederate South, 1861-1865" (Ph.D. dissertation, Rice University, 1964), Appendix II.

continued to be represented by Unionists. The bulk of these thirty-one districts formed a nearly contiguous stretch encompassing the Appalachian and Piedmont regions of the South. Few were in the Coastal Plain of the Deep South. There can be little doubt that the approximate area of strongest Unionism in 1861 overwhelmingly elected Unionists to the Second House.[30]

Election of governors and legislators occurred at the same time as the mid-war congressional elections in most of the Confederacy. In nearly every state, Whigs, most of whom had been Unionists, were remarkably successful. Alabama and Mississippi elected Whigs to the governorships for the first time in their histories. Several of the other governors elected at this time were Whigs. What Jonathan Worth said of North Carolina was evidently true for many other portions of the Confederacy: those who had been the most determined opponents of secession and of the Democratic party had become by 1863 the most popular.[31]

These Whig-Unionist victories were not necessarily evidence of a peace movement, except perhaps in a few local areas, nor even of conscious judgments on the voting records of congressmen seeking re-election.[32] Almost all of the newly elected Union Whigs had, during the election, at least posed as warm advocates of sustaining Southern independence; and the dedication of congressmen to sacrificial measures during the First Congress usually appears to have had little if any weight in determining which ones were re-elected and which ones were not. Nonetheless, there is reason to believe that the general aura of discontent and discouragement led to greater popularity at the polls for men who had been more cautious in the secession crisis and had accepted secession reluctantly after warning their constituents of the dangers and hardships ahead. The voting records of the newly elected congressmen bear out

30. Appendix I provides party and secession position for each member of Congress, as well as terms served and other biographical information. Table 2-1 provides for each state the number of men of each party and secession position who served in each Congress. The association of a representative with a specific district was done by establishing county of residence and then consulting either the district map provided by Yearns, or the maps in Robbins, "Confederate Nationalism," or the apportionment laws of the states. When necessary, district numbers could be established by resort to *The Confederate States Almanac* . . . [title varies] (Vicksburg and Mobile: H. C. Clarke, 1861-1864) or miscellaneous biographical sources.

31. Thomas B. Alexander, "Persistent Whiggery in the Confederate South, 1860-1877," *Journal of Southern History*, XXVII (August 1961), 309.

32. *Ibid.;* Yearns, *Confederate Congress*, pp. 49-59, discusses the 1863 congressional elections, but generally in terms of whether the victors were pro-President Davis or anti-Davis. The authors doubt the validity of such a simple dichotomy; and, in any case, Yearns apparently established a position for each congressman on the basis of only a relatively small number of selected votes.

the assumption that they were not decisively committed to Southern independence at any cost. On the sensitive subjects of conscription, impressment, and suspension of the writ of habeas corpus, the new members of the Second House registered significantly less belligerent stands than did the two-term congressmen.[33]

James M. Leach, one of the North Carolina Union Whigs swept into the House in 1863, recalled, a decade later, when he was in Washington as a United States congressman, that he had been the leader of what had been known as the peace party in the Confederate House and that it had consisted of about thirty-five men, who were actually reconstructionists, believing that the Union should be restored.[34] One would not have to trust implicitly in Congressman Leach's memory to suspect the presence of some form of party alignments in the Confederate Congress. Comments of members, during and after the war, together with election returns from both general elections, suggest that, however quiet, rivalry between Secessionists and Unionists, if not between Democrats and Whigs, was a conscious consideration for many Confederate congressmen.

The roll-call responses in Congress should reveal whether a two-faction alignment existed on any large portion of the legislative business. One of the most obvious measures of partisan antagonism is the proportion of roll calls on which two rival contingents are on opposite sides of the issue and display a high degree of unity within each party group. It is rare for all members of one party in a legislative body to vote together on a roll call. Complete unity would not, therefore, be expected. On the other hand, unity to the extent of two thirds of the group voting together is not unusual in a party-oriented congress and may serve as a convenient level of unity, or cohesion level, by which to distinguish divisions that may be described as party-antagonism issues. The United States House of Representatives during the late antebellum and Civil War years provides a bench mark from which to survey the extent of party alignment that existed in the Confederate Congress. For each session of the United States Congress in these years, instances in which at least two thirds of the Democratic representatives voted in opposition to at least two thirds of the opposition party usually accounted for between half and three fourths of the significant roll calls recorded during a session.[35]

The almost total absence of such party-antagonism roll calls in the

33. Appendices II and III provide sets of performance scores and scale positions for each member of Congress, which provide the basis upon which this conclusion was reached.

34. William H. Barnes, *A History of the Congress of the United States, 1875–1877* (New York: W. H. Barnes and Co., 1878), II, biographical entry for Representative James M. Leach.

35. Thomas B. Alexander, *Sectional Stress and Party Strength: A Study of Roll-Call*

Confederate Congress, regardless of whether a Democrat-Whig or a Secessionist-Unionist axis is used, is in startling contrast to this customary pattern as well as to the warnings and complaints voiced by many Confederates. The table of comparison of roll-call voting by pairs of groups (Table 2–2) shows how very small a percentage of the roll calls produced antagonism patterns. Often there were none and the index for the Provisional Congress or House reached even as high as 10 percent only once (except for the constitutional convention). There is only one session found in the Confederate Senate in which even 11 percent of the roll calls could be classed as antagonisms (when using a party axis).[36]

Another meaningful differential in the voting behavior of groups such as rival party contingents is that between unity and division. Dissimilarity between Democrats and Whigs or between Secessionists and Unionists may be noted on the table of comparisons (Table 2–2) to have varied from session to session, and tended to increase in some of the later sessions of the House. Issues which united one group more than another may have had two-party implications. One form of summarizing the relations between two voting groups so as to incorporate in a single figure the weight of concurrence, dissimilarity, and antagonism is an agreement score (obtained, for this study, by subtracting the percentage of antagonisms from the percentage of concurrences among the number of roll calls selected for study from a given session). Such an agreement score may fall anywhere between + 100 and −100. In a typical mid-nineteenth-century United States House in which party lines were so firm that perhaps three fourths of the roll calls produced antagonism patterns, the agreement score between rival party segments were well into the minus range, at least in the −20s and more frequently in the −30s or even more deeply negative. The last two United States Houses of Representatives prior to the Civil War (Thirty-fifth and Thirty-sixth), for

---

Voting Patterns in the United States House of Representatives, 1836–1860 (Nashville: Vanderbilt University Press, 1967), p. 107.

36. Among the very few roll-call votes taken in the Constitutional Convention, 16 percent were antagonism instances between both Democrats and Whigs and Secessionists and Unionists. Even this highest antagonism level (only three roll calls, in fact) is far below the customary 50 to 75 percent found to be antagonism instances in the typical contemporary United States House session. The proportion of antagonism instances in the United States House during the Civil War years is drawn from roll-call analysis yet unpublished but comparable to that in Alexander, *Sectional Stress and Party Strength*. It may seem that analysis by secession view is a repetition of that by party, since 81 percent of those for whom both types of information are known were either Union Whigs or Secession Democrats. Thirty-nine men, however, were either Union Democrats or Secession Whigs; and for another thirty-nine only one of these attributes is known. These seventy-eight members prevent analysis by secession stand from duplicating the party analysis and often cause these two measurements to be based on significantly differing groups.

TABLE 2-2

COMPARISON OF ROLL-CALL VOTING BY INDICATED PAIRS OF GROUPS
IN THE CONFEDERATE CONGRESS

Pairs of Groups and Voting Pattern	Prov. Cong.[a]	Prov. Cong. as Const. Conv.	First House			
			Session			
			1st	2d	3d	4th
Democrats-Whigs						
Percentage of Concurrence Instances[b]	59	16	76	74	68	65
Percentage of Dissimilarity Instances[c]	40	68	24	26	33	32
Percentage of Antagonism Instances[d]	1	16	0	0	0	2
Agreement Score (% Concurrence minus % Antagonism)	58	0	76	74	68	63
Secessionists-Unionists						
Percentage of Concurrence Instances[b]	61	16	74	63	68	60
Percentage of Dissimilarity Instances[c]	39	68	25	36	33	38
Percentage of Antagonism Instances[d]	1	16	1	1	0	2
Agreement Score	60	0	73	62	68	58

a. Due to rounding off, percentages for each session may not always total 100.

b. Concurrence = at least 2/3 of each group on the same side of the issue, or neither group recording a 2/3 majority.

c. Dissimilarity = at least 2/3 of one group voting together while the other group was more closely divided.

d. Antagonism = at least 2/3 of one group opposing at least 2/3 of the other.

TABLE 2-2--Continued

Pairs of Groups and Voting Pattern	Second House		First Senate				Second Senate	
	Session		Session				Session	
	1st	2d	1st	2d	3d	4th	1st	2d
Democrats-Whigs								
Percentage Concurrence	69	57	49	51	49	44	51	61
Percentage Dissimilarity	31	40	47	38	44	52	41	36
Percentage Antagonism	1	3	4	11	7	4	8	3
Agreement Score (% Concurrence minum % Antagonism)	68	54	45	40	42	40	43	58
Secessionists-Unionists								
Percentage Concurrence	58	47	63	52	54	57	57	60
Percentage Dissimilarity	38	42	35	45	43	40	39	37
Percentage Antagonism	4	10	2	2	3	2	4	3
Agreement Score	54	37	61	50	51	55	53	57

example, had this type of agreement score between Democrats and Republicans on wide selections of roll calls at −48 and −73 respectively.

The agreement scores shown on Table 2-2 make it obvious that very significant rivalry in the over-all roll-call voting of the Confederate Congress is highly improbable (using either a party or secession axis), for none of the scores is in the minus range and the large majority are high into the plus range. There is much variation among the several agreement scores, suggesting that at times there may have been some influence flowing from the former party affiliation or the secession stand of a member. Such influence as may have been present from these sources, however, cannot be said to have divided Confederate congressmen into anything even faintly resembling a two-party system, insofar as this may be seen in the over-all agreement scores.

Certain specific areas of legislation may have produced divisions in the Confederate Congress along the lines of a two-party rivalry even though such division failed to be evident in the total mass of recorded roll calls. Agreement scores have therefore been determined for several specific content areas of congressional business, especially for economic issues and the more sensational problems associated with wartime sacrifices. The most impressive aspect of these content-area agreement scores between Democrats and Whigs, and between Secessionists and Unionists, is that they generally are found in the high positive ranges instead of in the minus ranges, where scores for antagonistic party groups would be found. A few of these are lower than the ones for the total roll-call analysis, but only one is minus—the one measuring relations between House Secessionists and Unionists on the explosive issue of suspending the writ of habeas corpus during the dying days of the Confederacy. The implications of some subtle persistence of attitudes associated with having been a Democrat rather than a Whig or of having favored rather than opposed secession will be explored further in chapters concerned with specific subjects of legislation. These agreement scores buttress the conclusion that no significant partisan awareness existed in terms of former party or of position on the secession question.

Another yardstick for measuring the impact of party on roll-call responses is the level of unity, or cohesion, registered by each party contingent. In a typical session of the United States House of Representatives between 1836 and 1865, each major party was able to hold at least 80 percent of its voting members together on three fifths of the roll calls. Since the parties were normally antagonistic to each other on the majority of roll calls, the cohesion levels for the entire House membership were low. Customarily, the prevailing side in the entire House vote reached not even 70 percent on three fifths of the roll calls and not

TABLE 2-3

COHESION IN ROLL-CALL VOTING IN THE CONFEDERATE CONGRESS

Percentage of Selected Roll Calls in Each Session on Which
Indicated Groups Voted Together to the Extent of at Least
90%, 80-89%, 70-79%, 60-69%, or 50-59%

Confederate Congress[a]	Level of Cohesion	Entire House[b]	Former Democrats	Former Whigs	Secessionists	Former Unionists
Provisional Congress (all sessions)	90-100%	4	6	9	4	7
	80-89%	13	9	15	13	14
	70-79%	16	17	18	18	17
	60-69%	31	35	30	33	25
	50-59%	35	33	28	31	37
Provisional Congress as a Constitutional Convention	90-100%	0	11	0	5	26
	80-89%	5	16	21	5	16
	70-79%	16	11	26	16	37
	60-69%	42	42	21	42	11
	50-59%	37	21	32	32	11

a. Comparative Cohesion Levels from a Typical U.S. House of the Period 1836-1865

Level of Cohesion	Entire House Vote	One Party Vote
90-100%	2	40
80-89%	3	20
70-79%	10	15
60-69%	25	13
50-59%	60	12

These approximations are drawn from Alexander, Sectional
Stress and Party Strength, and from unpublished analyses
of 1861-1865 roll calls.

b. Due to rounding off, percentages for each session and
group may not always total 100.

TABLE 2-3--<u>Continued</u>

Confederate Congress	Level of Cohesion	Entire House	Former Demo-crats	Former Whigs	Seces-sionists	Former Union-ists
First House First Session	90-100%	8	8	13	8	10
	80-89%	11	15	11	16	15
	70-79%	14	14	14	8	11
	60-69%	21	28	28	26	31
	50-59%	46	36	34	41	32
First House Second Session	90-100%	5	4	3	6	5
	80-89%	9	14	10	12	6
	70-79%	18	21	15	23	20
	60-69%	30	28	35	30	31
	50-59%	39	33	37	30	38
First House Third Session	90-100%	3	4	6	5	3
	80-89%	10	9	9	7	13
	70-79%	12	10	20	13	19
	60-69%	31	33	32	35	25
	50-59%	44	43	33	41	39
First House Fourth Session	90-100%	2	5	4	2	4
	80-89%	10	10	10	12	12
	70-79%	24	21	20	24	21
	60-69%	24	33	37	29	33
	50-59%	40	31	30	33	30
Second House First Session	90-100%	6	13	10	11	9
	80-89%	11	14	6	17	7
	70-79%	9	11	11	15	21
	60-69%	28	22	29	24	25
	50-59%	45	40	43	33	38
Second House Second Session	90-100%	7	8	10	10	11
	80-89%	8	10	7	14	16
	70-79%	11	17	19	19	20
	60-69%	26	31	26	28	26
	50-59%	48	34	38	30	28

TABLE 2-3--<u>Continued</u>

Confederate Congress	Level of Cohesion	Entire House	Former Demo-crats	Former Whigs	Seces-sionist	Former Union-ists
First Senate	90-100%	8	8	18	14	8
First Session	80-89%	8	10	14	6	20
	70-79%	27	27	14	18	31
	60-69%	20	24	37	31	14
	50-59%	37	31	16	31	27
First Senate	90-100%	9	9	28	12	18
Second Session	80-89%	15	21	26	13	15
	70-79%	24	16	7	16	17
	60-69%	26	27	26	34	28
	50-59%	27	28	13	24	22
First Senate	90-100%	6	7	32	8	12
Third Session	80-89%	15	15	27	19	19
	70-79%	17	15	1	15	14
	60-69%	21	28	31	21	29
	50-59%	41	35	9	38	26
First Senate	90-100%	9	11	22	15	12
Fourth Session	80-89%	11	11	14	17	13
	70-79%	20	24	24	13	12
	60-69%	24	36	24	33	23
	50-59%	36	18	15	22	40
Second Senate	90-100%	8	12	18	8	14
First Session	80-89%	10	6	12	12	10
	70-79%	14	14	22	8	20
	60-69%	18	27	29	41	43
	50-59%	49	41	18	31	12
Second Senate	90-100%	14	18	15	14	17
Second Session	80-89%	9	11	16	19	8
	70-79%	16	15	18	24	13
	60-69%	30	28	32	23	33
	50-59%	32	29	20	21	30

as high as 80 percent on four fifths of the divisions. Typical cohesion patterns for United States House roll calls are shown as a note on the table of cohesion in roll-call voting in the Confederate Congresses (Table 2–3) [37]

The entire vote in either house of the Confederate Congress gives the appearance of a two-party system at work, for on the great majority of roll calls a fairly close division occurred. On the other hand, none of the four groups under analysis (Democrats, Whigs, Secessionists, or Unionists) achieved cohesion levels resembling a party. Instead of achieving unity at the normal party-contingent level of 80 percent or more on three fifths of the roll calls, each of these four groups was lower than 70 percent in degree of unity on three fifths of the House roll calls, with very few exceptions. On the nineteen roll calls employed from the Constitutional Convention, Democrats and Whigs faintly resembled a party in level of unity and Unionists almost delivered a party-type performance (to be discussed in more detail in a later chapter). Furthermore, after the mid-point of the war, Whigs and Unionists began to show somewhat more unity than was found in the total-vote pattern. The probability of higher cohesion levels is far greater for the small numbers in the Confederate Senate, and such levels are expectedly higher. Whigs in the Third Session of the First Senate were remarkably cohesive but, since there were never more than seven sitting at one time, the significance of this fact is probably not great. The over-all impact of cohesion levels, therefore, is to reinforce agreement-score indications that neither former party nor secession position had conditioned the majority of Confederate congressmen to fall into rival factions that could be described as a two-party arrangement. Accusations of acting in the spirit of party usually were, in the term of the day, just so much buncombe; and such partisanship made no apparent impression on the total roll-call pattern.

That no effective two-party structure appeared in the Confederate Congress was doubtlessly the result of many considerations. Limited by the permanent constitution to a single six-year presidential term, Jefferson Davis was relieved from the normal pressure to keep some kind of party lines intact for a re-election effort. The very nearly complete identification of former Whigs with reluctance to secede would have placed the members of that party in the unenviable position of appearing to persist in or revive a treasonable sort of Unionism, had they continued to band together. The Democrats had been the majority party within almost

---

37. Alexander, *Sectional Stress and Party Strength*, pp. 20–22, and comparable analyses for the 1860–1865 period in possession of the authors.

all of the legislatures of the Deep South long enough to have considerable confidence in their ability to exercise political control in the Confederate Congress without firm party discipline. In the elections in those states, Whigs had for several years before 1860 been too weak to hope for success in a state-wide election or even for a victory in more than a small proportion of the congressional districts. Only in the presidential elections had Whigs of the South managed to keep high morale and produce a respectable showing at the polls. In addition, the small Southern Whig delegation to the United States Congress in the last few years before the war had not been voting in antagonism to Southern Democrats in Congress. On the contrary, levels of agreement between Whigs and Democrats from the South had been so high as to resemble agreement between two groups of congressmen from the same party. Sectionalism had so triumphed over party before 1858 that the customary partisan antagonism posture no longer functioned between Whigs and Democrats from the area soon to be the Confederacy. Perhaps the failure of partisan antagonism to appear promptly in the Confederate Congress can be attributed partly to the continuation of this late antebellum trend.[38]

In stark contrast to the Confederate party circumstances, conditions in the North fostered the continuity of partisan antagonism. The Democrats had not opposed saving the Union, and their minority status in Congress was a very recently suffered affliction, which they had no intentions of bearing any longer than necessary. Lincoln's party activity and his policies regarding slavery disrupted the Union party fusion arrangements before the end of 1862 and offered convenient issues for northern Democrats planning party recovery. Within the Confederacy, sentiment against Jefferson Davis did arise and even included a certain amount of former party antagonism. But the primary basis of open political opposition to the Davis policies was couched in the idiom of state rights and was chiefly the indignant reaction of localism and individualism to the centralizing policies forced on the Confederate government by war pressures. This localistic state-rights theme, in turn, was more compatible with former Democratic party attitudes than with Whig views. Hence, anti-Davis manifestations never took as distinct a party orientation as did anti-Lincoln sentiment.

There is also the matter of practical options for members of the Confederate Congress. Once seated and confronted with the major issues of policy making, almost all of which were related to survival of the Confederacy, what choices did they have? Support of the war effort seemed impossible to avoid unless outright submissionism could be

38. *Ibid.*, p. 126.

acknowledged. Much talk about maintaining constitutional government and civil rights against tyrannical central government was heard, and a rising tide of pleas for substituting conference table for battlefield accompanied the ebbing fortunes of Confederate arms. But unless independence and slavery could be surrendered, no practical compromise peace was possible, although some congressmen evidently did not realize this—or perhaps could not risk admitting it openly. And pending such negotiations as might wishfully be dreamed up by desperate Confederates, who could deny that the best terms would be obtained by maintaining maximum military resistance. Short of admitting that reconstruction without slavery should be attempted, a congressman had to face day-to-day roll calls with considerably less latitude in his reactions than he could exercise in the realm of rhetoric.

Many evidently did become totally defeatist, but as long as Jefferson Davis commanded the armies to fight, a defeatist may have felt in danger of prosecution for treason. Congressman William R. Smith of Alabama phrased a defeatist rationale when he said: "In all modern wars the statesman as well as the warrior has his part to act . . . it has been the pride, as well as the policy of great leaders, to carry the sword in one hand and the olive branch in the other. The soldier in the trenches, knee-deep in blood and mire, has a right *to look to the statesman* and require him to act his part." [39] This he said, however, in the safety of the fall of 1865, long after the fighting had died away. He had acknowledged earlier that he had retired from Congress because his policies about peace were considered treasonable. Alexander H. H. Stuart, Virginia Union Whig, was invited by Davis and Judah P. Benjamin to come to Richmond in March of 1864 and hastened there, his mind teeming with peace plans on terms of gradual emancipation with compensation. He was stunned to learn that what they wanted him to do was to go to Canada to stir up the peace movement in the Old Northwest. He said that Benjamin and especially Davis were carried away by wild notions of the strength of that peace movement. He tried to mention his peace plans but found it unsafe to continue.[40] Davis never accepted defeat as inevitable until he was a prisoner of the Federals, and as long as military resistance was feasible it was not safe for a congressman to do so. If a congressman felt he had to act directly to bring peace, the only thing he could do was go to the North, as Foote of Tennessee did shortly before the end of the war.

Whatever the reasons, the spirit of party did not dominate the Confed-

39. Selma (Alabama) *Times,* October 19, 1865.

40. Stuart to Robert C. Winthrop, December 25, 1889, in Robert Charles Winthrop Papers.

erate Congress as a major determinant in congressional decision making. If one knew the party and section of a member of the United States Congress during the generation before 1861, one could come very close to predicting that congressman's position on a wide array of antebellum issues—so powerful were party and section in molding the roll-call patterns of that period. No such ready direction finders are available to explain Confederate congressional voting behavior. Sectionalism had in a sense been muted by its own fulfillment. So, without either sectional or party directives, the Confederate congressman was left almost entirely to individual decision making; and ephemeral groupings formed separately on each issue and dissolved when a decision had been made. Congressmen made impromptu judgments from day to day, almost as if Congress were a lodge meeting.[41]

Without party caucus, formal lines of communication, party newspapers, or substantial concepts to act as guides, party lines and policies were only a remnant of a more innocent political past. The legislator was in a situation in which his personal characteristics and circumstances, as well as the subject under immediate consideration, were more likely to be highly significant than in normal legislative situations. Party consciousness certainly remained from prewar experience, but organized party behavior did not. Party labels were important as epithets, not as guides for action. Moreover, because opposition to administration proposals lacked the cover of reputable party policy, it was all too likely to be treated as carping, petty, selfish, and unpatriotic. A congressman could bear such opprobrium only so long, perhaps, without actually becoming unpatriotic insofar as the Confederacy was the country to which he was supposed to be devoted. As Senator Oldham of Texas put it, "The principle was inculcated, and almost universally accepted, that our political and military leaders knew best, what should be done for the

41. In later chapters, another probable reason for the lack of party paraphernalia will be suggested. The powerful influence on a congressman's votes that may be attributed to his district's being in Federal hands introduced a crosscurrent effect that actually masked some of the Secessionist-Unionist rivalry in the Confederate Congress. Among representatives from within the perimeter of Confederate military control, appreciably more evidence of antagonism between Secessionists and Unionists does appear in the over-all voting record. For this condition to have generated party structures, however, would have required the conscious separation of Interior members from Exterior-district members so as to achieve a caucus and some consensus within each of these factions. Interior-Exterior tensions did develop, as will be discussed later; but rarely so openly and persistently as to lay the basis for a separate political pattern emerging among the Interior members only. The probable effects on one man of such mutually antagonistic influences as Unionism and Exterior status can better be analyzed after the presentation of subsequent chapters of this study.

safety of the country and therefore, patriotism demanded the support of all their acts, and opposition to any, could but result from treasonable sentiment." [42] For many reasons, therefore, one who seeks an explanation of the demeanor of the Confederate Congress must delve deeply into the effects of individual member considerations and the varied subjects to which they were applied. What other influences might have borne on each congressman's decisions and what, if any, consequences may be traced to the nature of those influences will be pursued in subsequent chapters.

Confederate Senator Yancey is supposed to have said in 1847 that "if this foul spell of party which binds and divides and distracts the South can be broken, hail to him who shall break it." [43] This same antiparty hope prevailed fourteen years later, at the end of the Provisional Congress. "The spirit of party has never shown itself for an instant in your deliberations," said Howell Cobb in his valedictory as presiding officer of that body, "and I would that it should be the good fortune of each successive presiding officer in the closing scene of every Congress to be able to bear the testimony I now publicly give to the honor of this body." [44] President Cobb's wish was substantially realized, but whether it was good fortune for either presiding officer or Confederacy may be questioned.

42. "Memoirs of W. S. Oldham, Confederate Senator, 1861–1865," typescript, University of Texas Library, Austin, Tex., p. 190.

43. John W. DuBose, *The Life and Times of William Lowndes Yancey* . . . (Birmingham, Ala.: Roberts and Son, 1892), p. 206, quoted in *DAB*, XX, 593.

44. *Journal of the Confederate Congress*, I, 846.

3 Nonpartisan Bases of Factionalism

A LARGE portion of the many roll calls in the Confederate Congress produced fairly close divisions. The extraordinary number of votes, along with their closeness, is an indicator that much of the legislative work was carried on without even approximate consensus. If former party association or attitude about secession are unable to go very far toward explaining these numerous close votes, the question remains whether some other discoverable grouping of congressmen is able to account for such substantial rivalry.

Economic distinctions could have provided one pervasive basis of dichotomy. Many students of bipartisan politics in the nineteenth century have stressed one or more economic explanations for antebellum parties. The nation's separation in 1861, it is true, eliminated traditional United States' economic issues from the politics of the Confederacy, for by 1860 most Southerners, whether Democrats or Whigs, had come close to consensus in opposing tariff protection and other forms of central government encouragement or direction of economic development. The Confederacy was not, however, an economic monolith; and many possibilities existed for new contests along lines of economic interest groups. One of the most obvious possibilities would have pitted small farmers or even holders of one or two families of slaves against planters, factors, merchants, and others more directly concerned with large-scale commercial agriculture and its marketing, credit, and transportation involvements.

The roll-call records of different economic groups among the congressmen have been compared in an effort to find evidence of existing or emerging class antagonisms. Slaveholding, reported for the 1860 census, was the basis for one of these searches, employing separate groupings of farmers with few if any slaves, large farmers with three or four slave families, small planters with up to fifty slaves, and large planters holding more than fifty slaves. Since a man may have thought of himself in terms of his standing within his own community rather than in the whole Confederacy (and this is surely how his constituents thought of him), an additional distinction has been made on the basis of a delegate's status in relation to other slaveholders in his home county. Value of estate, as of 1860, also provided information upon which the legislators have been divided into five groups ranging from the few poor, through the moderately prosperous and intermediate levels, to the extremely wealthy, who had estates of two hundred thousand dollars or more. And finally, like slaveholding, the status of each member was classified relatively, comparing his wealth with the average estate in his own county.[1]

Two measurements have been used to test the influence of the economic characteristics of the members on their over-all roll-call records. These have been applied to the Provisional Congress and to the House of Representatives of the Permanent Congress. One is the study of levels of agreement between each pair of economic groups; the other is a scrutiny of the amount of unity, or cohesion, each separate group was able to achieve in a session. The significance of levels of agreement between economic groups can be assessed realistically only if compared with levels of agreement on the same roll calls achieved by random groupings within the Congress. As for the implications of cohesion, the degree of unity that one group may demonstrate is meaningful roughly to the extent that it differs from the cohesion pattern of the entire house on the same votes.

In the several sessions of the Provisional Congress, the agreement level between random groups of congressmen is measured at $+70$ on a scale that ranges from -100 to $+100$. The levels of agreement between the most significant pairings of economic categories are far enough below $+70$ to suggest a very slight but probably meaningful tendency for each of these groups to differ with other economic groups on some of the issues. That these scores may have some significance is also suggested by the fact that they are always lower than the random score. Were these chance scores, if these results carried no meaning at all, some of them would probably have been higher than the random score. (Caution is in order, however, because the sizes of groups vary somewhat and agreement scores can be affected by the number of members involved.) Table 3±1 presents for each of the four types of economic characteristics of congressmen the *differences* between the approximate average of the pairwise agreement scores and the appropriate random score. The amount of the differences between the subsets by random and those by slaveholding or personal wealth for the Provisional Congress, for example, may be read from the first column of the table (-25, -15, -30, -21), and it is these lower levels that suggest the possibility of the above-mentioned slight significance of economic status. Except

1. More specific descriptions of these groupings will be found in Appendix I.

TABLE 3-1

RELATION BETWEEN ECONOMIC STATUS OF CONFEDERATE CONGRESSMEN
AND THEIR OVER-ALL VOTING PERFORMANCE ON ROLL CALLS

Differences Between Random-Division Agreement Scores and
Average Agreement Scores for Significant Groups of Congressmen
Divided According to Indicated Economic Characteristic[a]

Basis of Division into Groups	Provisional Congress	First House				Second House	
		Session				Session	
		1st	2d	3d	4th	1st	2d
Random Division	70	82	74	67	73	73	75
Absolute Slaveholding	-25	-17	-12	-5	-15	-21	-25
Relative Slaveholding	-15	-25	-12	-7	-20	-20	-25
Absolute Wealth	-30	-32	-14	-10	-25	-18	-47
Relative Wealth	-21	-40	-8	-4	-8	-13	-15

a. Agreement score is the percentage of Concurrence instances
reduced by the percentage of Antagonism instances. Concurrence
= at least two thirds of each group on the same side of the issue,
or neither group recording a two-thirds majority. Antagonism
= at least two thirds of one group opposing at least two thirds
of the other.

for one of the economic indicators, divergence from the random score is greater in the First Session of the First Congress than in the Provisional Congress. All of them dip in the next session and reach their low points in the Third Session of the First Congress. The four economic indicators then rise until, with one exception, they equal or exceed their earlier divergence in the last session of Congress. To translate: the Second and Third sessions of the First Congress were the periods of greatest harmony among the economic groups represented here, but this harmony tended to disintegrate until political stratification along lines of personal economic characteristics was most marked, although still not very striking, in the winter of 1864–1865. Matched against the possible range of scores, however, these indicators measure only slight political vibrations.

The cohesion pattern for each type of economic division of the membership is the other basis for gauging whether personal economic consideration significantly influenced member response to issues. Table 3–2 offers selected, instructive examples of cohesion patterns. For the Provisional Congress, as may be seen, the entire house achieved a 90-percent-or-more level of unity on only 4 percent of the roll calls—and an 80–89 percent level on only 13 percent more. The division of membership according to absolute slave ownership resulted in patterns of cohesion for several groups that are summarized in the table, which shows, for the Provisional Congress, that substantially the same proportion of the roll calls (6 and 13 percent) produced the two highest levels of cohesion. These differ little from the entire house performances, but the 23 percent figure for a degree of unity within the 70–79 percent bracket is somewhat higher than the comparable figure for the entire house (16 percent). Correspondingly, very close votes on which less than 60 percent were on the prevailing side were slightly more common for the entire house. The other three bases for economic grouping of congressmen provided a slightly greater evidence of unity: 10, 13, and 11 percent respectively of the roll calls falling into the 90-percent-or-better bracket. The few votes in the Constitutional Convention provide too narrow a base for inferences without more decisive evidence of cohesion than is found. Greater cohesion might be expected with the smaller subsets than within the entire house, however, and this dilutes any suggestion of influences flowing from economic attributes. These faint clues—and they are extremely faint in both cohesion and agreement levels—will be pursued by further search into the major topics of business in the Provisional Congress for instances of economic influences. This more intensive examination is discussed in the next chapter.

Roll calls from the First Session of the First House, which was deeply concerned with the initial establishment of a manpower conscription

TABLE 3-2

RELATION BETWEEN ECONOMIC STATUS OF CONFEDERATE CONGRESSMEN
AND THEIR OVER-ALL VOTING PERFORMANCE ON ROLL CALLS
AS MEASURED BY COHESION LEVEL

Percentage of Selected Roll Calls in Each Congress on Which
Indicated Groups Voted Together to the Extent of at Least 90%,
80-89%, 70-79%, 60-69%, or 50-59%

Congress	Level of Cohesion	Entire House Vote[a]	Approximate Average Cohesion Level for Groups of Congressmen Divided According to			
			Absolute Slave-holding	Relative Slave-holding	Absolute Wealth	Relative Wealth
Provisional Congress (all sessions)	90-100%	4	6	10	13	11
	80-89%	13	13	13	13	14
	70-79%	16	23	18	19	19
	60-69%	31	30	30	25	30
	50-59%	35	28	29	29	25
Provisional Congress as a Constitutional Convention	90-100%	0	8	8	5	b
	80-89%	5	34	13	16	
	70-79%	16	18	8	11	
	60-69%	42	29	50	42	
	50-59%	37	11	21	26	

a. Due to rounding off, percentages for each session and characteristic may not always total 100.

b. Blanks indicate that no satisfactory average level could be calculated because of erratic variations in the cohesion of each category within a group, or that no pattern justifying attention appeared in cohesion measurement.

63

TABLE 3-2--Continued

Congress	Level of Cohesion	Entire House	Absolute Slaveholding	Relative Slaveholding	Absolute Wealth	Relative Wealth
			Approximate Average Cohesion Level for Groups of Congressmen Divided According to			
First House First Session	90-100%	8	15		14	
	80-89%	11	12		11	
	70-79%	14	16		17	
	60-69%	21	24		25	
	50-59%	46	33		33	
First House Fourth Session	90-100%	2	7		10	
	80-89%	10	15		15	
	70-79%	24	21		20	
	60-69%	24	27		27	
	50-59%	40	31		28	
Second House First Session	90-100%	6	14	15[c]		
	80-89%	11	9	23		
	70-79%	9	18	26		
	60-69%	28	29	18		
	50-59%	45	31	19		
Second House Second Session Nov.-Feb.	90-100%	7	11	10	27[d]	
	80-89%	7	8	8	18	
	70-79%	12	17	18	23	
	60-69%	28	34	26	18	
	50-59%	46	31	35	14	
Second House Second Session Feb.-Mar.	90-100%	7	15	10	11	10
	80-89%	9	15	9	8	6
	70-79%	10	20	20	17	19
	60-69%	24	23	24	27	22
	50-59%	50	27	37	37	44

c. Largest Slaveholding category only.

d. Largest Estate category only.

64

system and appropriate exemptions, reveal a persistent although slight trace of these economic influences. Each of the groupings produced, for this session, agreement scores between congressmen farthest apart on the economic scales lower than those between more similar groups. Furthermore, the average levels of agreement between pairs of economic groups were lower than for the random grouping. Cohesion levels, however, do not suggest as much economic influence as do the agreement scores. Further analysis of the roll calls by subject groups appears to be indicated and is therefore described in appropriate topical chapters.

By contrast, the Second and Third Sessions of the First House, which were faced with problems of conscription extension, habeas corpus suspension, inflation, taxes, and Lincoln's Emancipation Proclamation, apparently were hardly affected in over-all voting behavior by personal economic considerations. Neither the agreement nor the cohesion levels indicate the presence of significant numbers of votes swayed by such influences. The "lame duck" session (fourth) of the First House, may have witnessed some resurgence of economic influences in a small portion of its business, as the increasing pressure of the Union army forced Congress to deal with the serious need to extend conscription further, deal with inflation, regulate impressment, and again consider the issue of suspending the writ of habeas corpus. In some instances, pairs composed of the groups most different with regard to wealth or slaveholding developed levels of agreement significantly lower than that for random grouping. And cohesion levels for slaveholding groupings appear distinctly, though only moderately, higher than for the entire house vote.

As in the preceding session, the First Session of the Second House— which did almost nothing of significance despite the enormous problems facing the Confederacy—yields both agreement levels and cohesion patterns only slightly indicative of economic influences. The next session, however, saw the Confederacy standing on the brink of total dissolution. Problems of inflation, taxes, and the use of slaves as soldiers had to be met squarely. Now Congress was apparently more involved in issues arousing conflict along lines of individual economic circumstances. Average agreement scores differ from the random more than in any other session, while categories of congressmen farthest apart in wealth or slaveholdings are found to be distinctly below those for other pairings. In addition, some of the specific groups of congressmen within both the slaveholding and the estate-value categories reached an 80 percent or 90 percent level of cohesion on a significantly larger proportion of the roll calls than did the entire house. This is especially true for absolute slaveholding, which may be due to congressional consideration of the bill to conscript slaves.

Despite these few significant scores, the general implications of analysis of over-all roll-call performance in terms of member economic status are severely limited, and should be considered as little more than straws in the wind. Although a slight amount of economic influence may be indicated in some of the sessions, especially in early 1862 and early 1865, never did antagonistic economic groups actually dominate alignment on substantial proportions of the roll calls, or even come close to doing so. Had a two-party pattern been emerging with personal economic aspects as its dimension, agreement scores presumably would have been in the minus range for pairs of widely divergent economic groups, and cohesion patterns for some groups would have resembled a pyramid standing on its point, with the larger proportion of roll calls producing the higher levels of unity. It follows, then, that only a few clues worth pursuing into specific content areas are contained in this analysis of member performance according to personal economic status—certainly not a general explanation for the large number of close divisions on roll calls.

Another divisive consideration to be investigated—one outside the arenas of party, secession stand, or economic factionalism—is the distinction between representatives from the core of the Confederacy and those from Kentucky and Missouri or other areas beyond the control of the Confederate authorities. Each succeeding session of Congress contained an ever larger proportion of members from constituencies no longer under effective Confederate political or military administration or, as in the cases of Missouri, Kentucky, Arizona, and the Indian nations, never under effective Southern control. Emphasis upon a distinction between districts inside and outside the perimeter of Davis's domain, voiced often and with asperity, provoked George W. Ewing of Kentucky to introduce on January 31, 1865, a set of resolutions in hot retort (quoted here in full so that the reader can get the full flavor of their vitriol):

Whereas a resolution has been introduced in the legislature of the State of North Carolina, bearing date nineteenth January, eighteen hundred and sixty-five, calling for a convention to amend the Constitution of the Confederate States so as to prohibit members from some of the States which have been overrun by the enemy from voting or having a representation in the Confederate Congress only in a territorial capacity, for the passage of which said resolution there were cast thirty-nine votes out of ninety-seven; and

Whereas all the oppressive and unconstitutional measures which are charged to have been passed by said Congress are attributed to the States thus overrun and in the possession of the enemy, and who, it is charged, are exercising this high privilege without constituents and in violation of the Constitution and laws of the said Confederate States; and

Whereas this opinion has often been intimated in this House, and also by various persons and newspaper publications from several of the States, thus showing that the services of those brave men who have left their property, their homes and families, and all that is dear to them on this earth, to defend that of these neighboring States, are not appreciated and not entitled to that consideration which is extended to other troops who have not been so unfortunate as to have their States overrun and their property despoiled: Therefore,

Resolved, That the Committee on the Judiciary be, and is hereby, instructed to inquire whether or not any member or members of the States or parts of States thus in the hands of the enemy are occupying their seats in violation of the laws and Constitution of the said Confederate States, or without constituents.

Resolved, That if any such State or states, or parts of a State, should be thus represented, that said committee report the same to this House, and that they also report a bill repealing so much of all acts or laws passed by said Congress as give the Confederate authorities the right to conscript or force into the Army any person whose residence shall be in any one of the States or parts of States thus in the enemy's possession.

Resolved further, That it is the duty of the President, and he is hereby directed upon the report of said committee showing that any States or parts of States have such members, immediately to discharge all the soldiers now in the Confederate service from such States or parts of States, unless they shall voluntarily reenlist and agree to serve without the privilege of having their interests represented in the said Congress.

Resolved further, That upon the repeal of the said laws and the discharge of the troops as aforesaid that the members of Congress elected from said States or parts of States should and will resign their seats, and will further organize under our own banner and with our brave soldiers march upon the soil of our own States and there live or die freemen.[2]

The surprising thing is not that these sardonic resolutions were tabled, but that a voice vote could not dispose of them; "Yeas" and "Nays" had to be called and twenty-four congressmen were in opposition. Perhaps this minority desired more serious consideration, and it is worth noting that while these twenty-four men included some of the most determined congressmen, from Missouri, Kentucky, Tennessee, and other occupied areas, it also included several of the most reluctant, preponderantly North Carolinians. Evidently some of the latter thought the proposed North Carolina resolutions had real merit.

A difference in attitudes on an important array of subjects had undoubtedly become characteristic of the "Outsiders" and "Insiders" by the time this resolution was introduced. The relation between a congressman's place of residence and his roll-call performance will, therefore, be placed under scrutiny in later chapters concerned with several sensitive issues. As for the over-all legislative activity of the Congress, members from

2. *Journal of the Confederate Congress,* VII, 524. See also the debate which followed, in "Proceedings," LII, 266–269.

beyond the battle lines were actually not very different from the other congressmen until the last session of Congress. At this point, it is sufficient merely to note that neither the levels of agreement between representatives from occupied and those from unoccupied districts nor the cohesion patterns of the two groups indicate significant differences until 1864, except on certain issues, such as conscription. Even at the end of 1864 agreement scores between insiders and outsiders ran far into the positive range at +52 (for the earlier part of the last congressional session), and at +39 for the desperate last few weeks in early 1865 (these scores are 23 and 36 points respectively below the random score).

None of the individual member characteristics or circumstances so far discussed, therefore, can explain more than a small part of the total roll-call responses. That small part is undoubtedly a very significant portion and will be appropriately analyzed below in association with several of the most important subjects of legislation. The great mass of member responses simply does not sustain any interpretation premised upon a persistent rivalry along partisan, economic, or occupied-status lines. What then did produce the close division in the vote on so many of the roll calls? Was it the result of some reasonably coherent two-group antagonism on some basis not investigated thus far? It seems likely, from these aggregate data findings, that congressmen were split, not by a single attribute, but by a number of them working sometimes at cross-purposes and other times in concert. This could well be both a cause and an effect of an ever-changing division of the congressmen in which a member had no continuing group of colleagues with whom he customarily voted.

And yet, if there had been an unidentified bloc of individual congressmen who habitually voted together, these measurements could have failed to expose them and so masked the presence of a substantial collaborating minority. One way to test for the existence of such a minority is to determine the proportion of each congressman's roll-call responses on which he was among a minority of one third or less of those voting. Almost six hundred, or approximately one third of the selected roll calls from the Confederate Congress, produced at least a two-to-one majority in the total vote. The recorded vote of every congressman has been measured against the majority position on those two-to-one divisions in which he participated. A cohesive minority of anything close to one third of the membership would have produced for each of its members a record of disagreement with the majority position on a substantial proportion of these roll calls. A portion of the membership of either house behaving in a manner typical of a minority party or faction would, in fact, be in the minority much more frequently than in the majority on those roll calls for which the prevailing side included at least two thirds of those voting.

Not a single Confederate congressman, not even the most discontented, has been found to occupy the position of consistent loser on roll calls of this nature. All except a bare handful of the congressmen were aligned with the majority in more than half of these instances (see Table 3-3). In the Provisional Congress, only three members were even slightly more often on the losing side. These voted on so few roll calls that their minority status may be accidental, except perhaps for George G. Vest of Missouri, who voted on one fourth of the roll calls and was in a minority of one third or less in fourteen instances out of twenty-six votes. The Constitutional Convention recorded only six two-to-one roll-call instances among the nineteen employed in the analysis. Ben Hill of Georgia and Duncan F. Kenner of Louisiana were in the minority four times. No other instances of such minority position appear, except for one delegate who voted only once.

During all four sessions of the First Congress, only one representative and one senator were for a single session in the minority more often than not. The representative, Lewis M. Ayer of South Carolina, did not vote frequently enough to justify considering his position a significant one, and he is not represented on Table 3-3. Senator Oldham of Texas remains the sole significant instance of a member's being in the minority most of the time for a single session—yet, in every other session, even the intractable Oldham was usually on the winning side of the two-to-one divisions.

In neither session of the Second Congress was a senator preponderantly in the minority status. Three representatives were in the minority barely more than half of the time during the First Session of the Second Congress—James T. Leach and George W. Logan, both of North Carolina, and John T. Shewmake of Georgia. Leach and Logan were elected to Congress because they opposed the course of the administration and were suspected of being reconstructionists, yet Shewmake was there because it had been thought he would support Jefferson Davis. It seems obvious that no small minority bloc served as a persistent faction in any session of Congress.

One possible influence on the minority status of any congressman is the fraction of the roll calls involving nearly unanimous consent. The Confederate Congress recorded an extraordinary number of votes, far more than the United States Congress in a comparable period, and it is doubtful that any great significance can be attached to a vast number of them. If near unanimity had been characteristic of these insignificant items, obviously each member must have been aligned with at least

TABLE 3-3

TENDENCY OF CONFEDERATE CONGRESSMEN TO VOTE
WITH A MAJORITY OF TWO THIRDS OR MORE

Percentage of Congressmen at Each Indicated Level
of Agreement with the Prevailing Side
on Roll Calls Producing Two-to-One Majorities[a]

Percentage of Member's Responses in Agreement with a Two-thirds Majority	Prov. Cong.	Prov. Cong. as Const. Conv.	First House			
			1st	2d	3d	4th
90-100%	12	28	21	13	15	6
80-89%	28	17	39	32	26	34
70-79%	36	0	22	33	33	30
60-69%	18	35	11	19	23	25
50-59%	2	13	6	3	1	5
40-49%	2					
30-39%	1	4				

a. In the Senate one individual equals 4 percent of
the membership, while in the House one individual equals
about 1 percent. In the constitutional convention each
member equals close to 2 percent.

70

TABLE 3-3--<u>Continued</u>

Percentage of Member's Responses in Agreement with a Two-thirds Majority	Second House		First Senate				Second Senate	
	Session			Session			Session	
	1st	2d	1st	2d	3d	4th	1st	2d
90-100%	19	11	23	8	0	8	25	29
80-89%	34	43	27	24	36	44	34	29
70-79%	20	29	38	44	39	40	17	25
60-69%	14	15	8	12	14	0	17	12
50-59%	10	3	4	8	11	8	8	4
40-49%	3		4					
30-39%								

a two-thirds majority much of the time. This, in effect, would have reduced the chances of his falling among a minority of less than one third and would have weakened considerably the thrust of the preceding analysis. Such, however, was not the case: near unanimity (90 percent at least on the prevailing side) was reached on only about 5 percent of the House votes and less than 10 percent of those in the Senate. The prevailing side of a division recorded more than 80 percent of those present and voting on only about 15 percent of the roll calls in either house. As a consequence, the issues that produced the two-thirds majorities also generally left at least one fifth in the minority. This substantial minority could have been an important obstructionist bloc if it had had a steadfast membership. It would then have been exposed as a hard core of dissidents on the great majority of the divisions of a two-to-one character. But, as has been shown, there was never a significant number of such losers.

There were, indeed, differences among members of the Congress with regard to how often they were among a two-thirds majority. A few were almost always in line with such a majority, although not many had consistent records from one session to another. Some were almost continually, from session to session, lower than average in percentage of agreement with a two-thirds majority, though even this did not mean that they were in the minority very often. Among the one fourth of the Confederate congressmen who did have this type of record, very little distinction existed as to former party affiliation or secession stand. The North Carolina Whig-Unionists in the Second Congress, who comprised a notoriously disaffected and obstructionist delegation, were in this category, as would be expected. But even among these North Carolinians all except two voted with the two-thirds majority more than half of the time; J. T. Leach and Logan, mentioned above, were in the one-third minority on barely more than half of the votes during the First Session of the Second Congress, but not in the vastly more critical Second Session.

The absence of any persistent minority bloc in any of the sessions of the Confederate Congress is, therefore, apparent from the members' proportion of agreement with the two-thirds majority position, and it is one of the most interesting and significant findings of this study. Minority opposition to a procession of *pro tem.* majorities appears to have involved a kaleidoscopic shifting of membership alignments, without noticeable clustering of more than a few members at a time. The limited differences which have been noted among the members' records in this respect were not associated with the normally expected bases of a partisan type of division. It is evident that such understanding of influences on

Confederate congressional voting behavior as may be reached will have to emerge from close analysis of specific issues and from attention to individual member performances on definite problems, rather than from across-the-board examination of political background, economic status, geographic location, or minority voting. Accordingly, congressional business must be divided into subject-content areas for further study.

4 The Provisional Congress

Exceptional Character

IN many ways, the Provisional Congress was anomalous. It was unicameral in the face of American bicameral tradition, and it was the forerunner of the bicameral Permanent Congress. For a time, it was the executive as well as the legislative branch of government. Its early membership was quite abbreviated, consisting of a mere handful of delegates from six states of the Deep South (Texans arrived late), whereas it ended with more than a hundred members from thirteen states and a territory. Voting was by states, rather than by individuals as under the Permanent Constitution. It was a constitutional convention that was not intended to be a legislature, but it turned out to be both, with much more of the latter than of the former. Most important, it was the only season in the life of the Confederate Congress when a significant part of its effort could be devoted to peacetime legislation, yet ironically the nation it sought to create was never to have a peaceful existence.

The fleeting nature of this foundation-laying effort is indicative of a basic theme of the Confederate Congress. One of the major differences between the governments in Washington and in Richmond lay in the tasks each faced. Both sides had to prepare for war; and, although few people North or South in 1861 realized the magnitude of what was to come, before the end of the Provisional Congress in February 1862 it was apparent that a long conflict loomed. The protracted war itself was an enormous challenge, and the exertions made by both Union and Confederacy demonstrate this. But the Confederate Congress had not only to meet the problems of almost total war with insufficient resources, it had the additional task of building a nation with what proved to be insufficient commitment.

Nation-building dominated the first half of 1861. But as Confederates saw that Northern Unionists would not give up their dreams any more quickly than Southern sectionalists would give up theirs, the Provisional Congress was forced to turn more and more to the problem of achieving victory. This was a chronic malady of the Confederate Congress: nation-building had continually to be subordinated to the ever more pressing necessities of the struggle for national survival. The Provisional Congress

was able to do more toward creating a real country than either the
First or Second Congresses. But even its attention was turned by the
pressure of events; and by the time of its termination on February 17,
1862, it was a war legislature, with the normal peacetime problems of
any country quite definitely in a subordinate place. If there were those
who thought that the Confederacy would have a "business as usual"
legislature, it was not long before they were disabused of the idea. The
heady overconfidence of July 1861 was, by February 1862, succeeded
by a less impassioned and more realistic outlook.

For a variety of reasons, then, the Provisional Congress was unique,
and it may well stand alone in a consideration of the problems of the
Confederacy. Many issues threshed out in the first year, such as seques-
tration and railroad construction, got much less attention in later sessions.
The best example is the work of constitution making—a phase of the
Provisional Congress important enough for separate discussion below.

The first year of the Confederate Congress is also quite distinctive
because it was too early to see the shape of the future. By 1863, one
could foretell the important issues of 1864 and 1865, but in 1861 such
prediction would have been impossible. Although some issues in the
Provisional Congress remained to plague the Confederacy throughout
its existence, they usually took on a different aspect. The financial issue
was never absent, but in 1861 the problem was simply how to get the
monetary wheels to turn. Since these wheels were, for the most part,
geared to the printing press, future Congresses had inflation to face.
The army was also a continuing concern, but again one with a difference.
All Congresses had to recruit men, but while the Provisional Congress
established a volunteer army, the First Session of the First Congress
was forced into a conscription system with its ever-attendant exemption
laws. The suspension of the writ of habeas corpus was also an important
issue, with several incidents during the Provisional Congress heralding
its future importance. But the writ was not actually suspended, and the
real controversy did not arise until the First Congress. Similar illustrations
could be offered for other issues.

If the Provisional Congress is worthy of separate attention, it is no
easier to understand on that account. Indeed, it is perhaps more difficult
to approach this provisional legislature through quantitative methods
than it is thus to approach any other period or topic of Confederate
legislation. There are several reasons for this, only some of which were
suggested above. Voting was by states, and this had several important
consequences, sometimes making the roll-call record quite difficult to
assess. There were occasions when the majority of the delegates favored
a measure, but because those supporters were concentrated in two or

three states, the opponents dominated enough delegations to carry the point. In this way, the totals of "Yeas" and "Nays" sometimes had an inverse relation to the outcome of a vote. State voting also meant that legislators were absent even more frequently than in later years, since one man could register a state's single vote. Often a five- or six-man delegation would be represented by a solitary individual on the floor. If the lawmakers from a single state were in substantial agreement on the basic issues of the day, there was no reason for all of them to attend the sessions. Often it seems as if one man stayed to cast a state's vote, while the rest of the delegation went to the War Department to get appointments for constituents or engaged in other business. There is also evidence of bloc voting. All members of a state's delegation are recorded as voting alike on an unusual number of occasions. While this created no problems for the Confederacy, it does create more than a few for the historian who relies on roll-call analysis.

There are other difficulties. One is that of shifting membership, which, as indicated in a previous chapter, was serious throughout the life of the Confederate Congress, but which seems to have been most prevalent in 1861. Some members served only briefly and then resigned. Thomas Fearn and David P. Lewis of Alabama, and William S. Wilson of Mississippi, resigned after the First Session, and Alexander M. Clayton of Mississippi followed suit during the Second Session. A much greater problem is the steady growth of the Congress as new states were admitted. Texas sent five delegates in March, and five Arkansans came in May. The sixteen Virginians trickled in during the last days of the Second Session and the early days of the Third (convening on July 20), but one came as late as August and another did not appear until November. North Carolina added ten in July and Tennessee seven in August 1861. Most Kentuckians and Missourians arrived in December 1861 or January 1862. Two men are surpassing examples of this expansion problem. George W. Ewing of Kentucky served only the last three days of the Provisional Congress, and James L. Orr of South Carolina served only the last day, casting but a single vote. Thus, when the Provisional Congress adjourned, on February 17, 1862, it had 107 members, less than one third of whom (thirty-four) had been present at the first rap of the gavel February 4, 1861. It is hard to analyze such a legislative body, as factions and coalitions might well have changed every time a new state was seated. Performance scores will have less meaning when many of the legislators were not present long enough to make their real feelings known, and cumulative scales are difficult to detect when two roll calls frequently have an insignificant number of recorded names in common. Cohesion scores and agreement scores should be almost as useful as for other sessions. But with some of our tools unsuited to the raw material available, roll-call analysis is very difficult, and it must be acknowledged that findings will be tentative.

Roll-Call Issues

The issues confronted by the Provisional Congress were extremely varied, but they fell into several primary content areas: military, economic (mostly taxation), and sequestration were very important. Also noteworthy and involving several different areas is a state-rights cluster; and a final area can only be designated as miscellaneous. The issues underlying some of these topics are obvious. Sequestration involved confiscating debts owed to Northerners, at least temporarily, and using the proceeds to indemnify Confederates who were owed by Northerners or whose property might be damaged by the war. The financial area dealt with the use of Treasury notes, issuance of bonds, establishment of import and export duties, and, most frequently, the War Tax passed in August of 1861. The military subject area was a seemingly endless conglomeration of items dealing with surgeons, furloughs, appointments and confirmations, recruitment, subsistence, reports of the First Battle of Manassas, elections of officers, and pay—to mention only a few topics. The issues which conjured up the state-rights bogy included railroad construction, supreme court jurisdiction, slave importation, precedence of Confederate general officers over those of the states, expansion of the Quartermaster Department, and a variety of others. The miscellaneous issues were just what the name implies. They were few, but covered such diverse items as the postwar status of Maryland, supplies for volunteers from border states not in the Confederacy, a regiment for the Texas frontier, and the slave trade.

Only a few of these roll calls were ordinally related to each other, however, judged by the response patterns necessary for scale analysis. In spite of the several significant content areas and the importance of the subjects of the individual divisions, only two significant scales were found. Limited results from a search for cumulative scales are not uncommon for any session of the Confederate Congress but are especially notable here because of such above-mentioned influences as bloc voting, increasing membership, and absenteeism.

One of the two scales relates to the raising of revenue. All except two of the divisions found to be scalable here were details of the War Tax bill of 1861, which was a major effort to raise revenue by taxing slaves, real estate, and other specified property. The second scale is much the clearer of the two. All roll calls included were found in the state-rights content area (they were the only issues in this content area that would scale), and they concern the specific subject of government-sponsored railway construction, recognized as a military necessity. The proposed rail links were vitally needed to fill strategic gaps in the thin Southern transportation network, so the votes were quite important. Yet the strict state-rights viewpoint did not encompass central government financing of railroad construction, let alone interference with state-owned railroad properties, as will be demonstrated below.

Association of Member Characteristics with Roll-Call Voting Behavior

The major question of this study, which will recur again and again, then poses itself: how much, if any, might each member characteristic have helped to determine voting behavior? In the years immediately preceding secession, much had been made in the North and even among Southern Unionists of the machinations of a supposed slave power, and there were Northerners on the eve of war who thought that slavery was so self-evidently the source of conflict that the mass of nonslave-holders would have nothing to do with secession. Taking a different tack, some historians have seen a motivation for secession in plantation owners' desire to end a colonial relationship reminiscent of that obtaining between England and the Thirteen Colonies in 1775. If such consid-erations were influential, they should be discernible in the votes of congressmen—distinguishing large slaveholders in Congress from those who owned few if any slaves. Acknowledging the limitations on roll-call analysis imposed by the special nature of the Provisional Congress, we offer the following results of comparing member characteristics with voting performance.

Slaveholding

So few members of the Provisional Congress were nonslaveholders that their voting records provide very little basis for comparison with the several levels of slaveholding, but each of the four categories of absolute ownership was represented by enough voting members to make possible some comparison of one group with another. Relative ownership, determined by a member's relative standing in his home county, provides sufficient numbers in only the highest three levels for intergroup compar-ison. Between ten and twenty-five members were usually recorded for each of the sufficiently populated slaveowning subdivisions of the house.

Agreement Scores. These several groups of congressmen display very slightly but yet perceptibly lower agreement levels with one another than would have been expected from chance relationships. Random division of the voting membership provides the basis for comparison, with agreement scores averaging about +70. The scores for the various pairings of slaveholding levels are usually fifteen to twenty-five points below the random one, which seems rather insignificant when the number of persons in each level of slaveholding is taken into account. This is true for divisions on the basis of relative as well as absolute slaveholding status, when all selected roll calls are used in the calculations (see Table 3-1). The twenty roll calls relating to sequestration of enemy property and the eighteen roll calls on taxation show no significant distinctions based on size of slaveholdings. Almost forty votes on military matters, however, do expose some correlation with slaveholding because agreement scores are substantially below the random-division scores for this particular content area (about +40). And the thirty votes associated with state-rights considerations yield further evidence of this same influence. None of these agreement-score distinctions is signal, however, and nothing more than a hint of influence from this member characteristic is present.

Cohesion Levels. No significance may be attached to the degree of cohesion achieved by each of the slaveholding classifications of congressmen. Some are found to be slightly more cohesive than the entire house, but the approximate average cohesion pattern for each of these subdivisions differs very little from that of the entire house vote (see Table 3-2). If cohesion configurations were usable for specific subject-content groups of roll calls, probably some distinctions could be located; but the small number of roll calls in each such set renders cohesion measurement too sensitive to one or two specific instances to be employed with much confidence.

Performance Scores. The four topical areas mentioned above and a group of miscellaneous subjects have been used as bases for five different scores. No very significant distinctions based on numbers of slaves held or relative slaveholding status in home community have been found. Although some variations appear in the cross-tabulation of these scores with member slaveholding characteristics (for example, see Table 4-1A), only one variation is sufficiently large to merit an inference that the characteristic may actually have contributed to roll-call stance; on the state-rights group of roll calls, the weaker, or less nationalistic, standings are disproportionately among the large slaveowners (Table 4-1B). This apparently lesser devotion to the cause among the large slaveholders is frequently found, though it is usually not marked enough to merit comment.

Scale Positions. Two cumulative scales, one on economic issues and the other on central government underwriting of railroad extensions, provide some further evidence that on economic matters no decisive

TABLE 4-1

PROVISIONAL CONGRESS ISSUES AND SLAVEHOLDING

(A)
Diverse Issues

Diverse Issues Score	Number of Individuals Assigned Each Score	
	Owners of Less than 20 Slaves	Owners of 20 or More Slaves
0		
1		1
2	2	2
3	1	4
4		
5	4	5*
6	5*	1
7	7	4
8	1	4
9		3
Median Score	5.60	5.00
Difference	0.60	
% 0-4	15%	29%
% 5-9	85%	71%

*
Median score.

80

TABLE 4-1--Continued

Format Description

Part A of Table 4-1 is in a format that is to appear very frequently in the remainder of this volume. The numbers in the body of the table represent the members of Congress who are assigned the indicated scores. As an example, for this table no member was assigned a score of 0, no small slaveholder but one large slaveholder was assigned a score of 1, and two of each slaveholding level were assigned the score of 2. The very highest score, 9, was assigned to no small slaveholder but to three large slaveholders.

The asterisk in each column marks the score assigned for the median individual in the column. In this table, scores are included for twenty small slaveholders, and the median actually falls between the tenth and eleventh man. Because both of these men are found at score 6, that is where the median is marked. In the other column, twenty-four large slaveholders are shown, and again the median falls between two men, the twelfth and thirteenth. In this case, counting twelve men from either the high or the low end of this column incorporates all of the men in the last score incorporated (score 5 counting from the top, score 6 counting at the opposite end of the column). The asterisk is therefore placed between these two scores to mark the median.

In the space below the tabulation of members assigned to each score category, a calculated median score is shown as a basis of comparison between the two columns. The members assigned a score of 6 in the small slaveholding column did not actually have identical performances on the roll calls included in the set. The collapsing of all possible scores into only ten categories is a convenience that simplifies a commentary on the pattern observed. On the assumption, for convenience only, that the five small slaveholders assigned a score of 6 are distributed evenly within this range, the median is calculated so as to place half of the men in the column higher and half lower. The calculated median score in this case is 5.60, indicating that 60 percent (three) of these men belong in the lower half of the range encompassed within score 6, while the other two belong in the higher.

The use of zero to designate the lowest category produces some undesirable aspects of calculated medians, but common usage of zero for the lowest scale position in cumulative scale analysis has seemed to us to justify a comparable use for performance scores in the interest of ready comparisons to scale positions on the same subjects. A straightforward description of the calculated median in the instance above is that it lies 60 percent of the way through the range of values encompassed within category 6 when proceeding in the low-toward-high-score direction. This might be expressed a different way: all the way through score 5 and .60 into a higher category (6), or 5.60. Perhaps unfortunately, when a median falls within the zero score, a negative calculated median results, as, for example, -0.50 to mean mid-point of the zero category.

In some usages, a calculated median proceeds from assumptions that boundaries between categories lie mid-way in a theoretical range between the values assigned to each score or other category designation. In other words, a score of 6 would be thought of as the center of a range from 5.50 to 6.49. We have chosen to employ our score designations just as though they were nominal category labels, and to assume that the range spanned by score 6 terminates at a full 6.00 (in the same manner used in referring precisely to a five-year-old as being in his sixth year until his sixth birthday). Hence, category 6 incorporates all values greater than 5 and not greater than 6. Score 1, therefore, covers a range from greater than 0 to and including 1; and score 0 covers an equal span below 0 (from greater than -1 to and including 0).

The difference between the calculated medians for the two columns is shown in the center below these median scores, and furnishes one clue to the configurations in the table and one basis for inference. This difference, however, is unrelated to the way in which the scores are distributed above and below the medians. For example, in this table, the median would not be altered if the seven small slave-holders with the lowest scores (scores 2, 3, and 5) were all located at score 0, although the significance of the distribution would obviously be changed. There are standard ways to summarize various characteristics of distribution, but for as few men as are dealt with in the Confederate Congress, inspection of the pattern is both the simplest and the best way to perceive the distinctions.

At the bottom of the table is a four-cell tabulation that gives for each column the percentage of scores in the lower half and the percentage in the higher half of the set range. This percentage display, like the difference between calculated medians, offers one form of summary image of the distributions. No summary statistic, however, can fully replace the close visual inspection that is required for an appreciation of the implications of each distribution of members' scores.

TABLE 4-1--Continued

(B)
State Rights

State Rights Score	Number of Individuals Assigned Each Score				
	Relative Slaveholding[a]				
	0	1	2	3	4
0	1		1	3	1
1		1	1	4	1
2		1		3	1
3		2	2	2	4
4			1		1
5	1	1		3*	2*
6	1	1	5*	2	
7		1*	2	5	1
8	3*	2	2	1	7
9	2	4	4	3	1

*
Median score.

a. Relative Slaveholding:
   0 = No slaves
   1 = 1-50% of average
       slave ownership in
       county of residence
   2 = 51-200%
   3 = 201-600%
   4 = 600%+

TABLE 4-1--<u>Continued</u>

(C)
State Rights Railroad Issues

State Rights Railroad Issues Scale Position	Number of Individuals Assigned Each Position	
	Relative Slaveholding	
	600% or Less	More than 600%
0	4	7
1	3	7
2	3	
3	11*	13*
4	14	11
Median Position	2.68	2.38
Difference	0.30	
% 0-2[a]	24%	37%
% 2-4	76%	63%

*Median position.

a. In scale sets with an odd number of positions, the number of members assigned to the center position is divided into halves for percentage calculation.

differences can be traced to slaveholding. Accepting the general assumption that the war would be short, both large and small holders opposed vital tax measures. But on the railroad scale, with its state-rights connotations, a moderately disproportionate number of the larger slaveholders are found in weak scale positions (Table 4-1C). The strength of association is not very high in this scale set but, taken together with corroborating evidence from the agreement and performance scores, justifies very cautious inferences.

Value of Estate

Value of individual estate is a measure of affluence somewhat different from slaveholding because some very valuable possessions other than slaves or the land they worked were held by many members of the Confederate Congress. Almost none of the Confederate congressmen was really poor, but wide gaps did exist between the economic status of the less affluent and those who were most wealthy. Probably not enough Provisional congressmen with estates of less than $20,000 voted to justify much confidence in the analysis of the two groups below that level. However, each of the other three ($20,000 but less than $50,000, $50,000 but less than $200,000, $200,000 or above), was represented by adequate numbers. When these men are classified by relative wealth standing in their county, only the two highest categories (200 percent to 600 percent, and above 600 percent of the county average) include enough voting members to be employed. Nevertheless, if major economic differentials in voting behavior existed on any basis apart from size of slaveholdings, these categories should serve to uncover them.

Agreement Scores. Scores for pairings of congressional groups subdivided by value of estate, either absolute estate or relative estate, are too close to random expectation to justify inferences of influence from values of personal estate; except that the small number of men valuing their estates at less than $10,000 are found at appreciably lower agreement levels with the more wealthy than could be attributed to chance. The small number of men involved, however, suggests caution in drawing conclusions. The poorer legislators appear, to a greater extent than their wealthy colleagues, to have desired expanded compensation benefits from sequestration receipts, lower assessments of land and slaves for the War Tax (by back-dating assessments to January 1, 1861, before the start of inflationary pressures), election of army officers, and payment of bounties to soldiers.

Agreement scores based on the content areas display no significant differences between wealth levels except on diverse state-rights-oriented issues. Here a decidedly lower level of agreement appears between men who had estates of less than $50,000 and those in the two higher brackets. Agreement scores of +17 and +13 contrast with random expectation of about +50. Apparently there were differing ideas about railroads, court jurisdiction, slave importation, and relative rank of Confederate and State general officers, and these differences were associated at least in part with economic background.

Cohesion Levels. Evidence similar to that furnished by agreement scores appears in the cohesion levels for the several wealth categories. On the average there is no great difference between these group cohesion patterns and that for the entire house (see Table 3-2), and the modestly larger proportion of roll calls producing cohesion above the 80 percent level for the individual groupings may reflect only the fact that each such group was smaller than the entire house.

Performance Scores. These scores for the five groups of roll calls (including the miscellaneous one) yield no real evidence of the influence of individual economic status except in two instances. On the miscellaneous content area, the only substantial bloc of men occupying a weak or antinationalistic stance are men of middling wealth (not shown). And on state-rights-related issues, the wealthiest are seen to be somewhat weaker or less nationalistic (Table 4-2A).

Scale Positions. Positions on two cumulative scale sets offer a little further insight. On an economic scale, the wealthier members are the more polarized (clustering at both positive and weak ends of the scale). One effect of this polarization is that the strongest positions are occupied by men of great wealth (Table 4-2B), although by far the majority of congressmen placed in this table occupied positions at the weak, presumably antinationalist, end of the scale. The scale consisting of railroad issues (not shown) also shows wealth more polarized, with the weakest positions usually occupied by richer members.

It is apparent that the roll-call divisions in the Provisional Congress were not significantly associated with personal economic status of the members. In any event, in the earliest stages of the war, dissatisfactions were minimal and sacrifices limited. Nevertheless, some slight distinctions do appear in the voting records of differentiated economic groups; the results of searches in subsequent legislative activity for possible influences arising from personal economic distinctions will appear in appropriate later chapters.

Former Party Affiliation

Confederate Provisional congressmen had only very recently been either Democrats, Whigs, or Whig-oriented Americans and Constitutional Unionists. And whether or not personal economic status had been a conscious basis of distinction among political leaders, party affiliation surely had been. The absence of party antagonism in the patterns appearing in the total business of each session of the Confederate Congress has already been discussed in Chapter 2. The specific content areas emerging from the Provisional Congress votes, however, deserve further examination for possible influences deriving from former party affiliation.

The absence of partisan antagonism on the roll calls of the Provisional Congress is actually a continuation of Southern sectional voting behavior of the late antebellum years. Political parties in the South had come to a remarkable degree of accord in the years just preceding the Civil War. There was a two-party system at work in the United States Congress, with normal partisan antagonism between Democrats and their northern, Republican opponents; but Southern Democrats and their Southern Whig opponents, as pointed out earlier, generally had agreement scores high in the plus range after 1856, and going higher. The level of partisan agreement in the Confederate Congress in 1861 was merely a projection of a trend which had been well developed in the United States Congress by 1860.[1] Only the arena, not the voting behavior, was changed.

Agreement Scores. The over-all agreement score between former Whigs and former Democrats is insignificantly lower than the random score, and the only individual subject-content area revealing an agreement score between Democrats and Whigs below random expectation is the one associated with state rights. But this one is distinctive only because of votes taken during the meetings when the Provisional Congress was acting as the Constitutional Convention—votes that will be discussed below. As a matter of fact, the content areas generally had agreement scores at least slightly above the random score, rather than below it. This method of analysis therefore reveals no voting distinction on the basis of party during the Provisional Congress.

Cohesion Levels. As was noted earlier in the discussion of Table 2–3, in Chapter 2, cohesion levels for party contingents do not differ greatly from each other or from the entire house pattern. Cohesion measures on small sets of content-area roll calls are equally small and not of much value since no striking differentials appeared. About all that can be observed in over-all cohesion data is a slight tendency for Whigs to draw together more than did the entire house. Roll calls bringing as much as 80 percent of the entire house together on the prevailing side made up but 17 percent of the total number of roll calls used; the less numerous Whig contingent achieved this level of cohesion on 24 percent of the roll calls, perhaps only because it was a smaller group.

1. See Alexander, *Sectional Stress and Party Strength,* p. 126.

TABLE 4-2

PROVISIONAL CONGRESS ISSUES AND WEALTH

(A)
State Rights

State Rights Score	Number of Individuals Assigned Each Score				
	Absolute Estate[a]				
	0	1	2	3	4
0	1		1	4	
1			2	3	1
2	1		1	1	2
3	1	1		4	4*
4			1	1	
5	1	1		5*	
6	1	2*	4*	2	
7	1		3	4	1
8	3*		1	6	4
9	5	2	3	3	1

(B)
Economic

Economic Scale Position	Number of Individuals Assigned Each Position				
	Absolute Estate[a]				
	0	1	2	3	4
0		1	4	1	3
1		2*	2	6	1
2			*	6*	2*
3	1	1	4	5	2
4	1*		1	1	1
5	1	1	1		1
6				4	2
7				2	

*Median score or position.

a. Absolute Estate: 2 = $20,000 - $49,999
   0 = Below $10,000   3 = $50,000 - $199,999
   1 = $10,000 - $19,999   4 = $200,000+

TABLE 4-3

PROVISIONAL CONGRESS ISSUES AND FORMER PARTY

Score on Issue Area	(A) Economic		(B) Diverse Issues	
	Number of Individuals Assigned Each Score			
	Democrat	Whig	Democrat	Whig
0	3	3	1	
1	5	6	1	
2	1	2	4	
3	2	8*	4	1
4	3	1		
5	5*	5	6*	4
6	4	4	2	4
7	5	3	5	5*
8	5	2	1	4
9	3		2	1
Median Score	4.80	2.75	4.50	6.10
Difference	2.05		1.60	
% 0-4	39%	59%	38%	5%
% 5-9	61%	41%	62%	95%

*
Median score.

Performance Scores. On issues associated with military matters or sequestration, no distinction on the basis of party is found in the performance scores. Economic issues, chiefly tax matters, exposed former Whigs as inclined to be more hesitant about steps that would strengthen the hand of Confederate authorities (Table 4–3A). On some miscellaneous subjects and, to a lesser extent, on the state-rights group of divisions, it is the former Democrats who are found to fall significantly more frequently into the less nationalist positions (Table 4–3B and C).

Scale Positions. The two scale sets, relating principally to revenue questions and railroad considerations (the latter not shown), add only slight weight to the conjecture that Whigs were less enthusiastic on taxation but a bit more consolidationist on railroad appropriations than were Democrats (Table 4–3D). Both parties were polarized on the railroad question and therefore furnished a significant number of the men in both the weak and strong positions, but the percentage quadrants on the economic scale show party distinctions to have been more important than the narrow median difference would indicate.

Position on Secession

Divisions about the propriety or timing of secession represented the most recent basis for political distinctions among the Provisional Congress members. It has already been noted in Chapter 2 that no party structure along these lines developed in this early Confederate legislature, although a strong correlation existed between secession views and prewar party affiliations. Over-all voting patterns generally exposed little to distinguish Secessionists from Unionists. It remains only to test the content areas in this Congress for evidence of such distinction.

Agreement Scores. This score, as noted, is almost exactly the same for Secessionists and Unionists as for random groupings of the entire house when all roll calls are included. On the subjects of sequestration and taxation, the scores are signally higher than for random groups, very strongly implying that this basis of division was most decidedly not the one exerting divisive influence on these subjects. On military matters, the Secessionist-Unionist score is about the same as for random groups. Only on state-rights issues does the score uncover a significant differential.

Cohesion Levels. Patterns of cohesion for Secessionists and for Unionists are almost identical to that for the entire house (see Table 2–3).

Performance Scores. These scores for the military and sequestration areas show no distinction on the basis of secession stand. The state-rights topic exposed even less distinction between Secessionists and Unionists than it did between Democrats and Whigs. But both taxation and diverse issues revealed a significant split. On the former subject, the Secessionists are seen to be much more polarized than the Unionists and to average higher scores (Table 4–4A). The odd, miscellaneous group of roll calls places the Unionists overwhelmingly in the more determined posture as illustrated by both medians and percentages in Table 4–4B. Unionists, perhaps because so many of them had the border-state attitudes of the Upper South, took much stronger pro-Confederate positions on the status of Maryland, volunteers from the Union border states, a regiment for the Texas frontier, and the slave trade. Men from both camps are, of course, found on almost all levels of performance on most topics; and this one distinction may not go very far toward explaining the positions taken by individuals. It does appear, nevertheless, that one of the measurable associations here relates to the stand on secession. The precise nature of this can better be observed in later chapters concerned with specific subjects of legislation, when the lawmakers were under far more pressure than they were during the Provisional Congress.

Scale Positions. The two cumulative scales discovered in the Provisional Congress roll calls (exclusive of the Constitutional Convention activity) furnish only minor and probably insignificant evidence of persistent influence of secession position on the Provisional congressmen.

Interior or Exterior Constituency

During most of the life of the Provisional Congress, a distinction between members whose constituencies were occupied or threatened by Federal forces and those from unoccupied areas is meaningless. Missouri and Kentucky were admitted in December 1861, but even in early 1862 there were still hopes of quick Confederate liberation of occupied territory. That there would be ever increasing areas lost to the Confederacy more or less permanently was certainly not yet foreseen. For all practical purposes, a comparison of Interior with Exterior representatives in the Provisional Congress can be applied only to the Fifth Session. It distinguishes the voting records only of delegates from Missouri, Kentucky, western Virginia, and a very few others, though we may question the extent to which an occupied-territory mentality was created this early.

Agreement Scores. The score between Interior and Exterior members is significantly low (33). Actual antagonism instances are few. But there are almost twice as many dissimilar relationships as the random calculations produced (56 percent contrasted with 31 percent), and the subjects of these instances of dissimilarity involve much of the business of the Fifth Session of the Provisional Congress.

Cohesion Levels. Delegates with Exterior constituencies proved to be much more cohesive, with a significantly larger proportion of roll calls

TABLE 4-3--Continued

	(C) State Rights			(D) Economic		

State Rights Score	Number of Individuals Assigned Each Score		Economic Issues Scale Position	Number of Individuals Assigned Each Position	
	Democrat	Whig		Democrat	Whig
0	5		0	3	7
1	5	2	1	4	6
2	4	1	2	5	3*
3	5	4	3	5*	9
4		2	4	3	2
5	4	3	5	4	
6	7*	2	6	3	4
7	6	4*	7	2	
8	7	10			
9	6	4			

Median Score	5.21	6.50	Median Position	2.50	1.83
Difference	1.29		Difference	0.67	

% 0-4	39%	28%	% 0-3	59%	81%
% 5-9	61%	72%	% 4-7	41%	19%

*Median score or position.

TABLE 4-4

PROVISIONAL CONGRESS ISSUES AND STAND ON SECESSION

	(A) Economic		(B) Diverse Issues	
Score on Issue Area	Number of Individuals Assigned Each Score			
	Secessionist	Unionist	Secessionist	Unionist
0	5	1	1	
1	7	4	1	
2	1	3	4	
3	3	7*	4	1
4	2	2		
5	7*	3	7*	2
6	4	4	1	5
7	6	2	5	6*
8	5	2	3	2
9	3		2	1
Median Score	4.50	2.86	4.57	6.08
Difference	1.64		1.51	
% 0-4	42%	61%	36%	6%
% 5-9	58%	39%	64%	94%

*
 Median score.

in the high range of cohesion than the entire house had. These men were chiefly from Kentucky or Missouri and may have been displaying a typical state-delegation unity, although the low agreement score suggests further bases for difference from the bulk of the membership, who represented Interior constituencies.

Performance Scores. Three content areas—military subjects, state-rights issues, and sequestration of enemy property—incorporated the votes of enough Exterior delegates to make possible a comparison with Interior membership. On the first, there was very little difference, but while both groups took the strong (or nationalist) position on the other two, the Exterior (occupied) group is found to have taken a far stronger position than the Interior (unoccupied).

Scale Positions. The only cumulative scale set involving enough Exterior members to allow reliable scoring was that relating to railroad extensions by the Confederate authorities. It further demonstrates the very strong relative stand taken by those legislators with Exterior constituencies (Table 4–5). Seventeen of the eighteen Exterior members assigned scale positions are in one of the two most positive levels, and the only weak one of the group is Barnwell of South Carolina, who is classed as occupied because of Federal seizure of sea islands in his district and the destruction of his home. The conclusion reached by the use of the other tools of analysis on this problem seems to be confirmed. This early in the life of the Confederate Congress, a meaningful distinction is found between those whose voting constituencies were outside the perimeter of effective Confederate control and those who spoke for citizens actually subject to Confederate authority.

Intra-Confederate Sectionalism

The search for bases of division within the Confederate Provisional Congress revealed a reasonable, if ironic, possibility—sectionalism. It is not an unexpected possibility, given the cleavages revealed in the secession movement, and although it was a much milder case than had afflicted the United States, sectionalism within the Confederacy often was a more significant factor than some of the others considered above. Southerners did not refer to this. Instead, they ranted about delegates from "imaginary constituencies," as the occupied areas came to be known, or about a "rich man's war but a poor man's fight," or about party or secession alignments. But an Upper South *versus* Lower South lineup may be discerned in the patterns of voting in the Provisional Congress. The differences are more than marginal and are sometimes quite marked. On taxation and military questions, Lower South members are usually found in the stronger, or more nationalistic, position, while on other

TABLE 4-5

PROVISIONAL CONGRESS ISSUES AND FEDERAL OCCUPATION

State Rights Railroad Issues

State Rights Railroad Issues Scale Position	Number of Individuals Assigned Each Position	
	Exterior Members	Interior Members
0		11
1	1	9
2		4
3	4	21*
4	13*	16
Median Position	3.31	2.31
Differ- ence	1.00	
% 0-2 [a]	6%	36%
% 2-4	94%	64%

*Median position.

a. In scale sets with an odd number of positions, the number of members assigned to the
center position is divided into halves for percentage calculation.

questions, dealing with sequestration, a few state-rights-oriented issues, and some miscellaneous items. Upper South members were willing to support sterner measures. To be sure, it cannot be said that sectionalism was the basis of factionalism in the first year of the Confederate Congress, but it does seem to have been an important consideration. On the taxation scale, it was the Upper South (not yet including Kentucky or Missouri) that preferred a weak system of levies. On the other hand, the railroad scale, which developed only in the Fifth Session, shows very strong Upper South pressure for having the Confederacy build these strategic lines, while the Lower South appears to have been too well satisfied with its navigable river system to support such a policy.

It is significant that the railway problem is one of the best illustrations of an Upper South-Lower South cleavage, and that it is related to the state-rights content area. Indeed, when that area of roll-call response was searched for scalable sets, only the railroad votes fell into a cumulative scale pattern. Consequently, it is not surprising that many of the extreme state righters opposed, with a special fervor, central government assistance in constructing railroads, and that the localistic point of view was the minority cry of the Lower South. Ten members from that region spread a protest on the pages of the *Journal* that is peppered with phrases like "invade public, corporate, and individual rights," "dictatorial powers," and "sovereign State," and included what was surely one of the worst prophecies of the war, asserting that "armies and munitions and military supplies have been, are now, and probably always will be mainly transported by other means [than railway]." With warnings against sapping "the foundation of the Constitution," the protesters reminded their countrymen that "the old Government never exercised this power." All ten of the signers were from the Lower South.[2]

It is perhaps worth noting that all of the Georgia delegates except Ben Hill were opposed to any Confederate railroad construction, and that four of them signed the protest. Georgia had a major state-owned railroad, and Georgians might have feared for the independence or prosperity of their line if Confederate underwriting had been provided for its potential competitors. Jackson Morton of Florida signed the protest but did not vote this sentiment consistently. Apparently he did not think that every instance of government railroad building would destroy the liberty of the people.

Although limited, this Upper South-Lower South antagonism was very real, as even Jefferson Davis noted; in February 1862 the Confederate President, while the Provisional Congress was still in session, had ex-

2. *Journal of the Confederate Congress*, I, 781–782.

pressed a fear that the South might disintegrate into a middle Confederacy and a southern Confederacy. "No doubt," wrote Attorney General Thomas Bragg, "there is such a party line . . . which will be headed by disappointed men."[3] Whatever the roots of the discontent, had the Confederacy either existed in peace or prevented Union domination of the Upper South it might well have been plagued by the sectional problems Southerners were trying to escape. This schism can only be observed during the Provisional Congress because, during the First Session of the First Congress, Federal forces occupied important new areas in Missouri, Kentucky, Tennessee, Louisiana, and along the Confederate coasts. In later years, the Upper South was itself politically split by the forces of war, so that, in the 1863 elections, Kentucky and Tennessee sent to Congress delegates who were distinctly different in character and goals from congressmen from other parts of the Upper South, such as North Carolina. Sectionalism in the Provisional Congress furnishes an intriguing glimpse into what might have been, but no more than that. Soon thereafter, occupied status so critically affected portions of the Upper South as to obscure almost all else.

Provisional Congress as Constitutional Convention

Because the character of the Constitutional Convention was much different from that of the rest of the Provisional Congress, its consideration has intentionally been avoided thus far in this chapter. It was a small body without turnover or excessive absentee problems, and, even more notable, its mission was of a unique nature. Here was the most consequential task in the nation-building process, the establishment of organic law which, it was hoped, would shield the Confederate States of America from the mistakes made under the constitution of the United States. This was a vital job, not to build a new machine but to tune the old one carefully, and delicately, until it hummed in the proper state-rights rhythm. The delegates possessed a sense of the magnitude of their task, for had the Confederacy survived, the convention would have been the most noteworthy part of the Congress. The score of roll calls recorded by the Provisional Congress for constitution-making was on substantial issues, and from February 28 to March 11, 1861, a portion of each legislative day was spent in convention while the permanent constitution was being hammered out.

The nineteen votes employed in this analysis of the Constitutional Convention represent almost all of the recorded divisions and every one

3. Thomas Bragg Diary, 1861–1862, microfilm copy of original, Southern Historical Collection, University of North Carolina Library, Chapel Hill, N.C.

with individual significance. Their subjects are an index of more than thirty years' accumulation of Southern grievances. Seven of the votes were on attempts to decide whether nonslaveholding states should be allowed to be members of the Confederacy. Four dealt with the sensitive question of supreme court jurisdiction, with state-rights implications heavily involved in the relations between highest state courts and the national judiciary. Two more concerned the long-standing problem of central government appropriations for internal improvements. Other proposals reaching roll-call stage would have restricted the right of petitioning the government to those problems which Congress was constitutionally authorized to consider (a reminder of the perennial gag-rule controversy), limited the power of Congress to make appropriations not specifically requested by the president (reminiscent of floor fights about rivers and harbors bills), and restricted slave trade with slaveholding states of the United States. The nationalist position on such issues, in the sense of supporting a strong central government and contemplating a viable and developing nation, would have been to make it possible for free states to be in the Confederacy, to press for adequately broad supreme court powers, to grant considerable latitude to Congress in selecting the objects of appropriations regardless of executive attitudes, and to authorize central government participation in providing the new nation with a transportation network suited to its future development.

It is immediately evident that the convention was distinct from the rest of the Provisional Congress in voting behavior. Not only was the content of the divisions different, but more important, the roll calls are more scalable than are divisions of the other sessions of this Congress. Two scales were identified in the nineteen roll calls, whereas the remaining 125 votes employed from the Provisional Congress produced only two more scales. The subjects of these convention scales intersect, but they are nonetheless distinct, with one concentrating on slavery-related questions and the other involving a somewhat broader range of concerns at least tangential to state-rights issues.

Slaveholding

Personal economic status may first be examined in terms of slaveholding, as we turn again to the basic question of this study, how much influence on voting may have been exerted by individual member characteristics. *Agreement scores* based on as few roll calls as were recorded in the convention cannot be employed with much confidence unless more glaring differentials appear than are found here. *Cohesion levels* are rendered equally untrustworthy by the small number of roll calls. Therefore, although some variations from random expectations for the entire house are observable, other methods of measurement are preferred as bases for inference. *Performance scores* are available for the entire set of selected roll calls but provide little if any basis for concluding that size of slaveholdings was influential. The *scale sets,* involving state rights and slavery, yield equally little evidence that any such distinctions existed.

Value of Estate

Much the same may be said for value of estate as a differentiating consideration as was observed for slaveholding classification. Due to the small number of divisions being considered, neither *agreement scores* nor *cohesion levels* may be trusted, and the *performance scores* and *scale sets* show no significant distinctions between the more and the less wealthy members.

Former Party Affiliation

When comparisons are made on the basis of former party affiliation, however, significant distinctions appear immediately. The *agreement score* is zero for Democrats and Whigs; while it is not in the negative range, as would have been normal for traditional party antagonism, it is nonetheless below the lowest level of agreement so far noted (see Table 2-2), and is about 60 points below the level of agreement these two parties displayed in the Lower South in 1860. In short, by this measurement, members of the Lower South's old parties acted more in accordance with usual behavior in the Constitutional Convention than they had since 1848.[4] On only three convention votes were these delegates in agreement, and they score 47 points below the random score on these same issues. *Cohesion levels* for both Democrats and Whigs are so much higher than for the entire house as to suggest significance despite the small number of roll calls involved (Table 2-3). *Performance scores* definitely place Whigs in a stronger or more nationalistic posture than Democrats; and the two *scale sets* decisively identify the Whigs as having a more positive attitude toward the establishment of central authority (Table 4-6A, C, and E).

Position on Secession

Secessionists and Unionists in the convention were, with few exceptions, the same individuals as Democrats and Whigs respectively, for only 10 of the 50 convention members were neither Secession Democrats nor Union Whigs. It is therefore not surprising that this *agreement score,*

---

4. Alexander, *Sectional Stress and Party Strength,* p. 126. States of the Upper South were not represented in the Constitutional Convention since they had not yet seceded.

TABLE 4-6

CONSTITUTIONAL CONVENTION ISSUES AND FORMER PARTY
OR STAND ON SECESSION

	(A) All Issues		(B) All Issues	
Const. Conv. Score	Number of Individuals Assigned Each Score			
	Democrat	Whig	Secessionist	Unionist
0				
1	1		1	
2	5	1	6	
3	3		4	
4	5*	4	6*	2
5	2	2	3	1
6	3	6*	4	5*
7	4	3	4	3
8	1	2	2	2
9		1		1
Median Score	3.60	5.42	3.67	5.80
Difference	1.82		2.13	
% 0-4	58%	26%	57%	14%
% 5-9	42%	74%	43%	86%

*
Median score.

TABLE 4-6--<u>Continued</u>

Issue Area Scale Position	(C) Slavery and State Rights		(D) Slavery and State Rights	
	Number of Individuals Assigned Each Position			
	Democrat	Whig	Secessionist	Unionist
0		2		2
1	11	1	12	
2	3*	1	4*	
3		1	1	1
4	7	5*	8	3
5	1	4	3	2*
6	1	5	1	6
Median Position	1.17	3.90	1.63	4.50
Difference	2.73		2.87	
% 0-3[a]	61%	24%	57%	18%
% 3-6	39%	76%	43%	82%

*Median position.

a. In scale sets with an odd number of positions, the number of members assigned to the center position is divided into halves for percentage calculation.

TABLE 4-6--Continued

State Rights Scale Position	(E) State Rights		(F) State Rights	
	Number of Individuals Assigned Each Position			
	Democrat	Whig	Secessionist	Unionist
0	6	2	9	
1	7*		7*	
2	6	4	7	2
3	6	7*	5	8*
4		6	3	4
Median Position	0.93	2.50	0.93	2.63
Difference	1.57		1.70	
% 0-2 [a]	64%	21%	63%	7%
% 2-4	36%	79%	37%	93%

*
Median position.

a. In scale sets with an odd number of positions, the number of members assigned to the center position is divided into halves for percentage calculation.

like the score for Democrats and Whigs, is zero, 47 points below random (see Table 2-2), with only three instances of agreement. *Cohesion levels* for Secessionists are not significantly different from the pattern for the entire house, but Unionist cohesion is so impressive as to resemble more nearly the pattern of a normal political party (see Table 2-3). It appears evident that Unionism in the just concluded secession contests was associated with a greater degree of uniformity than was pro-secession feeling or party alignment of members. This cohesion pattern for Unionists is particularly impressive when the closeness of the roll-call divisions is examined. With only one exception the divisions were close, certainly not heavily lopsided votes that could skew the results of this analysis. The relative cohesiveness of the Unionists is illustrated in Table 4-7, where it is contrasted with the cohesiveness of party and two sample economic segments. Both the *performance scores* and the two *scale sets* repeat the thrust of the comparison by party alignment: Unionists were decisively more nationalistic than were Secessionists in that they were willing to entrust far more authority and power to the central government (Table 4-6B, D, and F). It may be noted that both median scores and percentage quadrants show secession stand to be a more devisive variable than party.

Considering earlier party views, there is nothing especially surprising about the nationalistic position of Unionists and Whigs if one assumes that those present had turned their backs on the old Union and, however regretfully, had looked forward to a Confederate new day. Whigs had long been on the nationalistic side of allocation of governmental powers as a matter of ideology. Some Southern Whigs who resented this had been forced to identify themselves by the label "State Rights Whigs." What was more natural than that Whigs in the Confederate convention would seek to create a new edifice as nearly in the image of Henry Clay's dream as possible, or that Unionists who had only reluctantly accepted citizenship in the Confederacy, would seek to make the new structure as much like the old as possible. Democrats had led in secession, on the other hand, precisely because they were perturbed by the prospective consequences of alleged abuse of central government power and by what they thought they had recognized as a compelling current toward "centralism." Again, what was more natural than that Democrats would seek to emasculate the new national government at its birth.

In the proceedings of the convention, Confederate delegates encountered something different from the rest of the Provisional Congress business. Here was something fundamental—no votes on adjournment or pay and mileage, nor succession of minor details of legislation. Logrolling had little place. The difference was between organic law and

TABLE 4-7

COHESION IN ROLL-CALL VOTING IN THE CONFEDERATE
CONSTITUTIONAL CONVENTION

Percentage of Roll Calls on Which Indicated Groups
Voted Together to the Extent of at Least 80%,
70-79%, or 50-69%

Cohesion Level	Entire Convention	Secession Stand		Former Party		Relative Wealth	
		Seces-sionist	Union-ist	Demo-crat	Whig	Cate-gory 3 (201-600%)	Cate-gory 4 (600%+)
80-100%	5	10	42	27	21	16	11
70-79%	16	16	37	11	26	21	11
50-69%	79	74	22	63	53	66	79

statutory provisions, principles as opposed to everyday expediency. Here was something basic enough for everyone to grasp and address in terms of political ideologies. It is no coincidence that disciples of Henry Clay and John J. Crittenden took more nationalistic ground than those from the party of Franklin Pierce and James Buchanan.

Summary

The roll calls of the Provisional Congress are a challenging proving ground in a search for influences on member responses that can be traced, at least by inference, to the individual legislator's background characteristics. That in most respects these characteristics proved to furnish little explanation is perfectly apparent. On the other hand, some flashes of relationship give promise of better yields as we turn to the significant content areas confronted by the Permanent Congress. Although little effect has been traced to personal economic status of the members, some signal consequences of former party affiliation and stand on secession have apparently been turned up. And the very limited employment of a distinction between Exterior and Interior representatives has been very promising in the few content areas to which it is at all applicable. In any event, the most revealing evidence of persisting influences on the congressmen would not normally be expected in the halcyon days of dreaming of a bright new future. The Confederacy's subsequent struggle to realize that future despite ever-darkening prospects should reasonably be expected to expose more of the character of individual motivation.[5]

---

5. Constituency characteristics are of minimal significance for the Provisional Congress because the delegates were not elected by their constituents. Discussion of these variables is therefore omitted from this chapter.

It is evident beyond reasonable doubt from internal evidence that the *Journal* erroneously records the votes of the South Carolina delegation on one of the nineteen Convention votes, as indicated in Appendix VI. The effect of correcting this roll call would not be extensive. Democratic and Secessionist cohesion in the Constitutional Convention would become somewhat more parallel to that of the Whigs, but the performance set would show only minor alteration, produced by a one-position change for some of the South Carolinians. It was decided, therefore, to follow the roll-call record as found in the *Journal,* as must necessarily have been done for undiscovered errors in the record.

5　Conscription

CONSCRIPTION was more than an attempt to raise an adequate army; it also involved many of the other problems faced by the Confederate Congress. It was, for example, a constitutional issue that helped to define the nature of Confederate-state relations. Some of the congressmen, occasionally with logic but often without, saw conscription as a key state-rights issue. Senator Oldham of Texas accordingly denied that Congress had the power to conscript unless the states gave their consent: "This was not circumlocution; it was the theory of our government." The other senator from Texas, fire-breathing Louis T. Wigfall, who divided his emotions by fervently committing himself to Confederate victory and intensely hating Jefferson Davis, disagreed. Raising armies was part of the war power, he thought, which was exclusively possessed by the Confederate government. But many were not convinced by Wigfall's rejoinder. In August of 1862, Congressman Caleb C. Herbert, also of Texas, took the ultimate state-rights position, which the entire Confederacy had taken only a few months before, by asserting that it "would not do to press the conscription law too far upon the people. If it became necessary to violate the Constitution, as some gentleman had admitted, he would be for raising in his State the 'lone star' flag that had twice been raised before."

The relationship of conscription to state rights became more direct and more obvious when Congress tried to establish an exemption system, for there were those who wished to exempt all state officers from required military service, even justices of the peace. At the heart of the issue was the fear expressed by Senator Henry C. Burnett of Kentucky, "that Congress had no power to take the humblest State officers, for if it could take the Justices of the Peace, it could take the Governor, and thus overthrow government." [2] Illustrative of inequalities created by such localism, Georgia declared in 1865 that it had 8,229 state officers eligible for exemptions, and North Carolina declared 5,589 state officers exempt; but Alabama, with approximately the same population as Georgia or North Carolina, exempted only 1,333 state officers, and South

1. "Proceedings," XLV, 26–27, 213.
2. *Ibid.*, XLVI, 154.

Carolina, with about three fourths as many people, reported only 307.[3] The right of men in the ranks, even men who were conscripted, to elect their own officers was also a cherished privilege which state-rights-oriented congressmen guarded jealously.

Conscription was linked with other issues as well. When a system of exemption by substitute was established and then repealed, there was extensive debate over whether a contract was being violated by drafting the principal who had furnished the substitute—especially since the latter was kept in the army. The habeas corpus issue was also involved, as we shall see in Chapter 7, for state judges frequently used the writ to order the army to release a man who was allegedly forced to serve in violation of his constitutional rights. Equally as important is the relationship of conscription to slavery. One of the hottest issues every time exemptions were discussed was an exemption for overseers of twenty or more slaves; and when manpower was short, the army used blacks to serve in various menial positions, including that of laborer on vital fortifications. Most important was the ever-growing agitation in a few quarters for the conscription of slaves and free blacks as soldiers, but this issue will be examined in a later chapter.

Conscription was basic. Without it, there could have been no army and without an army there could have been no Confederacy, so the close link to other issues is not unexpected. One might go so far as to say that a man's position on conscription was one of the best indices of his support of the Confederate cause.

Roll-Call Issues

Despite its ultimate importance, conscription was not passed into law until the Confederacy was more than a year old. Until then, fighting men were volunteers, usually enlisted for twelve months and organized by states under officers selected according to state laws. Originally, a state might volunteer militia units or permit these organizations to sign up as units on their own initiative; but after actual fighting began, individual citizens were allowed to contribute their services by volunteering and assembling into units. Later, the requirement of state consent for volunteer organizations was removed; yet, President Davis was still uncomfortable about twelve-month enlistments and tried without much success to obtain three-year volunteers. When the spring of 1862 brought extensive and sometimes disastrous military operations, Davis justifiably

3. *O.R.,* ser. IV, vol. III, p. 1102. The Georgia figures included 1,350 justices of the peace, 1,350 tax collectors, and 2,751 militia officers (*ibid.,* p. 1112), for an 1860 population of 1,057,000. North Carolina's population was 993,000; Alabama's, 964,000; and South Carolina's 704,000. (United States Bureau of the Census, *Historical Statistics of the United States,* p. 13.)

complained to Congress that the short enlistment period "contributed in no immaterial degree to the recent reverses which we have suffered, and even now renders it difficult to furnish you an accurate statement of the Army."[4] Furthermore, about half of the Confederacy's trained soldiers were nearing the end of their one-year terms, and thereby future success was threatened. Congress initially reacted by authorizing lures to re-enlist for three years or for the duration of the war, principally in the form of a fifty-dollar bounty, a sixty-day furlough, and extension of the privileges of reorganizing units and electing officers.

Compulsory conscription was the next logical step, and Davis called for it in March 1862, lecturing Congress upon the need to simplify the complicated manpower laws, avoid conflicts of state and Confederate authority, and mitigate the excessive enlistment zeal of young boys and older men. In a masterpiece of periphrasis, he went on to request for these purposes the conscription of men aged eighteen to thirty-five who would "pay their debt of military service to the country, that the burdens should not fall exclusively on the most ardent and patriotic."[5] No mention was made of the fact that enlistment, far from being too popular, was no longer popular enough, and the impending dissolution of much of the army was ignored with an official evasiveness that must have fooled no one, least of all the men in the field.

Obedient to Davis's request, Congress passed the first conscription law in April 1862, making able-bodied white men between eighteen and thirty-five liable for a maximum of three years of military duty. Its most immediate value was obviously its application to men already in the army, for it extended their twelve-month enlistments to a maximum of three years, saving the veteran forces for the major campaigns of 1862 and in effect preventing military disintegration. States were no longer to be principal instrumentalities in raising military forces, although the coveted privilege of serving with friends and neighbors and being commanded by officers from one's own state was retained. The objections of anticonscription congressmen to such far-reaching legislation were never stilled, and insofar as they objected to the subversion of state

---

4. James D. Richardson, editor, *The Messages and Papers of Jefferson Davis and the Confederacy, Including Diplomatic Correspondence, 1861–1865* (New York: Chelsea House-R. Hector, 1966), I, 190-191 (hereinafter cited as *Messages*). President Davis tried to be encouraging by adding: "The people, incredulous of a long war, were naturally averse to long enlistments, and the early legislation of Congress rendered it impracticable to obtain volunteers for a greater period than twelve months. Now that it has become probable that the war will be continued through a series of years, our high-spirited and gallant soldiers, while generally reënlisting, are from the fact of having entered the service for a short term, compelled in many instances to go home to make the necessary arrangements for their families during their prolonged absence." *Ibid.*

5. *Ibid.*, 205–206.

rights, they were probably correct. Writing in 1880, Emory Upton pointed to the serious Confederate setbacks of early 1862 and praised the Confederate Congress for explaining "for all time, the meaning and extent of the power to raise and support armies. Appalled, but not unmanned, it rose to the occasion . . . treating the principle [of state sovereignty] as a dead letter." "The temerity of this legislation," Upton had previously asserted, "finds no parallel in the history of the world." [6]

Exemptions under the conscription system were instituted from the first. The primary justifications were physical or mental unsuitability for service or employment in an essential civil occupation. A proposal to permit states to define additional exemptions for their citizens was rejected by Congress. The burden of patriotism rested more lightly upon rich than upon poor, however, for exemptions would be granted those who could hire an able-bodied white substitute who was not liable to conscription.

The First Session of the First Congress adjourned on April 21, 1862, not to meet in Second Session until the following August. In the interim, major battles were fought, and while General George B. McClellan's Union Army of the Potomac was defeated and recalled from the peninsula before Richmond, General Henry W. Halleck's Federals in the West advanced into northern Mississippi, and Fort Pillow and Memphis fell to Union forces. Under the pressures of these military events, it became obvious that even the laws of April were not adequate to produce the needed men. It is apparent that the full impact of conscription was only understood now, several months after its passage. Manpower was still a pressing concern when Congress reassembled on August 18, for military campaigning continued in full swing; and two of the most critical issues considered at this session were extension of the draft age to forty-five and overhaul of the generous exemption arrangement. The former was accomplished, but the latter proved to be a thorny problem throughout the life of the Confederacy.

Almost every congressman seemed to have a pet type of exemption, providing an excellent logrolling opportunity that, with true political instinct, they could not overlook. In addition to Confederate and state governmental officials, exemptions were allowed for "pilots and persons engaged in the merchant marine service; the president, superintendents, conductors, treasurer, chief clerk, engineers, managers, station agents, section masters, two expert track hands to each section of eight miles, and mechanics in the active service and employment of railroad companies, not to embrace laborers, porters and messengers. . . ." The multitude of other included classes numbered Dunkards and Friends, "shoemakers,

6. Emory Upton, *The Military Policy of the United States* (Washington: Government Printing Office, 1912), pp. 468–469.

tanners, blacksmiths, wagon-makers, millers and their engineers," public printers, "superintendents of public hospitals," "teachers employed in the institutions for the deaf, dumb and blind," and "miners employed in the production and manufacture of salt to the extent of twenty bushels per day." The list seemed endless and even included "one male citizen for every five hundred head of cattle." [7]

It was all very finely, even painfully, drawn out, especially for someone like Senator Albert G. Brown of Mississippi, who looked at such legislation and thought things were going the wrong way. Daily, bills were "introduced, not to increase the army, but to weaken it, and now this bill is brought in, which, if passed, would virtually disband it. We should legislate men into the army, and not . . . [be] attempting to legislate them out of it." If the bill should pass, he suggested, the Confederacy might just as well give up. [8] Brown exaggerated, of course; but by February 1865, the superintendent of the Bureau of Conscription reported 67,000 men exempt from conscription under act of Congress. [9]

It was in this Second Session of the First Congress that the twenty-Negro law exempted either the owner or an overseer for every plantation containing twenty or more slaves or for any plantation which by state law was required to have a white man in residence. This, together with the substitute system, is what provoked so many to use the sarcastic cliché, a "rich man's war and a poor man's fight." Since some boys under eighteen years of age had managed to get into the army, Congress also considered legislation to discharge such youthful volunteers and to regulate the acceptance of those under eighteen.

Before adjournment on October 13, 1862, additional legislation was enacted that was intended to obtain soldiers from areas occupied by Federal forces. Special volunteering arrangements were extended as privileges to obtain border-state soldiers for Confederate service; and for those border-state refugees who ungratefully refused to take advantage of this law by enlisting, another law applied conscription even when a man was not in his home county by tapping him for enrollment wherever he might be found.

Exemptions were the main manpower concerns of Congress during the Third Session, January 12 to May 1, 1863. President Davis wanted the power to make the decisions about essential civilian activity through a system of executive detailing of individuals to nonmilitary activity.

7. James M. Matthews, editor, *The Statutes at Large of the Confederate States of America, Passed at the Second Session of the First Congress: 1862* . . . (Richmond: R. M. Smith, 1862), pp. 77–79.

8. "Proceedings," XLVI, 20–21.

9. *O.R.,* ser. IV, vol. III, p. 1103.

He would have preferred to have all men of draft age subject to service and detailed to fight or work according to the Confederacy's need for specific skills. Congress was unsympathetic with this concentration of power in the hands of the executive and failed to respond satisfactorily. The President could and did detail men for nonmilitary service beyond the exemptions offered by the laws. This session also confronted a rising discontent about the exemption for slave overseers, leading Davis to recommend revision to eliminate class distinctions. Congress proved to be willing to correct only the worst abuses of the system.

Maintenance of state militia organizations represented a severe withholding of manpower from active Confederate service. When the draft age was extended from thirty-five to forty-five, men in this age group were exempt if in active service under state authority. Governors, especially Joseph E. Brown of Georgia, were latitudinarian in interpreting what constituted "active service" and prevented conscription of many men who were not receiving effective military training or experience or contributing adequately to Confederate defense. Constrained by its localism and state-rights ideology, Congress refused to take any steps to alleviate this weakness in the conscription system.

Congress adjourned on May 1, 1863, not to meet again until the following December, by which time the Confederacy had suffered disastrous defeats in the field. Lee's army had reeled back from Gettysburg, Vicksburg had fallen, and Braxton Bragg's Army of Tennessee, betrayed by the incompetence of its commander, had suffered stunning defeat at Chattanooga. That the campaigns had opened more auspiciously for the Confederacy only deepened the gloom at the baneful termination of the season's operations. A congressional election had been held, furthermore, and this Fourth Session of the First Congress operated with a generous proportion of "lame ducks."

It was to this body that Davis displayed the demoralization of the Confederacy for all to see when, four days before the end of the session, he sent a special message asking Congress (as he had before) for greater executive control of local defense forces. Here again conscription impinged upon state rights, for this was simply an effort to replace the state militia with a Confederate reserve. As Davis himself pointed out, "if the spirit which rendered the volunteering so general among all classes of citizens at the beginning of the war were still prevalent, there would be no necessity for the proposed legislation." Since this was not so, it was "necessary that conscription for local defense should replace volunteering." [10]

10. *Messages,* I, 405.

The most pressing manpower problem faced by this session arose because the army suffered grievously from desertions, which even Davis's amnesty proclamation of August 1863 could not stem, and many of the Confederacy's most seasoned campaigners were to be eligible for discharge in 1864 at the expiration of their three-year obligation. In February, therefore, Congress redefined the term of military obligation; thereafter it was for the duration of the war. At the same time, age limits for conscription were expanded to include seventeen-year-olds and men from forty-six through fifty. Exemptions were curtailed, and substitution was ended because of desertions by many substitutes—the principals being made liable for conscription on the grounds that substitution was a privilege and not a contract, as some had contended. The generally satisfactory effectiveness of this legislation, together with the influx of new congressmen not likely to be as willing as their predecessors to tighten conscription, persuaded the administration to leave this problem alone during most of the First Session of the new Congress, which met during May and June of 1864.

The last session of the Congress assembled in November of 1864, amid signs of hopelessness on all sides. Lee's army was pinned down at Petersburg. Atlanta had fallen and William T. Sherman's army was deep in the heart of the Confederacy—soon to be deeper. Manpower problems had reached the level of desperation for the Confederacy and Davis, hopefully seeking new sources of troops, lectured Congress on occupational exemptions, saying that they were not only unwise but also were not even "defensible in theory." He went on to assert that "in a form of government like ours, where each citizen enjoys an equality of rights and privileges, nothing can be more invidious than an unequal distribution of duties and obligations." [11] His solution to the problem was to make the president a manpower czar by concentrating all exemption power in a system of details by the executive and by passing his oft-suggested general militia law, under which militia would be called to duty by Confederate authority, not by that of the states. Despite a frantic appeal on March 13, 1865, five days before the last adjournment of the Confederate Congress, Davis never got as full control of manpower as he desired, either by a satisfactory exemption law (which would have been helpful) or by central control of the militia (which was absolutely essential). Congress debated at length and often with hostility, producing last-minute legislation that was of little use. The most important conscription measure in this session involved an entirely different dimension:

---

11. *Ibid.*, p. 491.

the use of blacks as soldiers. This proposal and the continued examination of the twenty-Negro exemption will be considered in a later chapter.

Association of Member Characteristics with Roll-Call Voting Behavior

Every session of Congress under the Permanent Constitution except the First Session of the Second Congress was extensively concerned with the conscription-exemption issue, and with several related topics which had a bearing on the status and condition of the Confederate fighting man—even including the exchange of prisoners with the Federals. Scores of roll calls were taken on one or another aspect of this complicated and persisting problem. The dimensions of the subject were too numerous to expect congressmen to divide into permanent factions, and analysis reveals that they did not. Exemptions alone were exceedingly varied because of their occupational nature, and every trade seems to have had its champions. A single member of Congress was very likely to favor some exemptions fervently while denouncing others as vicious.

Large groups of roll calls on the subject of conscription have been included in performance-score calculations for each congressman. Some of the roll calls from each session involved have also proved to fit in scalable sets, i.e., subject to consistent ordering from easiest-to-support to hardest-to-support, with concomitant scale-position assignment for almost every member who voted on enough of the issues to be included. Comparison of several member characteristics with these scores and scale positions brings to light some of the possible influences affecting the attitudes and votes of members on conscription.[12] To turn to A. B. Moore's apt characterization, if on conscription the Confederacy was a house divided, on what basis did it divide?[13]

Former Party Affiliation

Former party affiliation evidently had no significant relation to attitudes toward conscription during the First Congress, with the possible exception of the initial establishment of conscription in the First Session. When the measure was first adopted, Democrats were quite commonly in the highly favorable positions (scores 7, 8, and 9), as may be seen in Table 5-1A. There is also a difference of some significance between

12. Agreement scores between selected groups of the members on this issue add some further insight but are limited in value because the number of roll calls on conscription in any one session is not large enough to provide stability in this scoring system.

13. Albert Burton Moore, *Conscription and Conflict in the Confederacy* (New York: Macmillan, 1924), p. 353.

the median score of Democrats and Whigs. This difference is not extraordinary, however, and both Democrats and Whigs are found at all levels. Interior members in this session were evidently somewhat less conscript-prone than the Exterior representatives, but no greater distinction is found on the basis of party among the Interior members only. During the other three sessions of the First Congress, Democrats and Whigs were not significantly different on the conscription issue, judging by the comparison of scores.

Cumulative scale sets of roll calls on conscription, often fragmentary, were identified for three House sessions and for all four Senate sessions of the First Congress. They bear out the conclusion that former party affiliation was not a significant basis of distinction on this topic during this Congress. The median scale position for Democrats is very nearly identical with that of the Whigs for each of these scales. Only in the First Session does it appear from the scale set that the Democrats were somewhat more likely to fall into the positive extremity of the scale positions. This buttresses the equally limited evidence in Table 5–1A about the voting pattern during the parliamentary maneuvers leading to the initial enactment of conscription.

In the Second Congress, conscription questions clearly evoked differing responses from Democrats and Whigs. Table 5–1B and C provides evidence of this differentiation.[14] The conscription scores for the entire Congress during the disheartening winter months of 1864–1865 suggest substantially greater zeal among former Democrats than among former Whigs. When the Interior members alone are measured, the distinction increases dramatically because the bulk of the Whigs taking a strong posture on conscription were those from occupied territory. Note on Table 5–1B that of the fourteen Whigs in the high levels, 6, 7, 8, and 9, only two were Interior members.

During the dying weeks of the Confederacy, February and March of 1865, Congress continued to wrestle with conscription. Table 5–1C illustrates the difference between those Democrats and Whigs who still remained to vote in the House. Just about the only Whigs left to represent Internal constituencies are seen to be at the lowest level. These men were predominantly the North Carolinians, but within the limited scope

14. Table 5–1B combines the scores of both representatives and senators. While this is a theoretically risky procedure, since the roll calls in one house may not be very comparable to those in the other, in practice it has created little difficulty. The subject-content area is the same for both houses, and the number of roll calls and their distribution by percent voting positive has proved to be remarkably similar. Where these two criteria are not met, a combined score has not been used. This combination table has not, of course, been used for scale sets, which rarely measure up to a desired level of comparability.

of this final comparison, former party affiliation is found strikingly related to conscription roll-call behavior.

Position on Secession

A Confederate congressman's attitudes toward conscription issues were more decidedly related to his stand on secession than to his former party affiliation. Table 5–2A indicates the greater firmness of the Secessionists during the initial legislative work on the general conscription measures passed in the First Session of the First Congress, and eliminating the impact of the Exterior members makes the distinction greater. Almost half of the Unionists in the entire Congress falling into the highest three levels were Exterior members, but only one of the nine Unionists in the lowest three levels was from an occupied district. As a result, the Unionist median score is notably lower when only the Interior members are tabulated, while the Secessionist median score for the larger Secessionist segment is not as greatly affected. A scale set of roll calls from this same session (not shown) reinforced the inference that Unionism influenced a member toward a lower scale position than that of his Secessionist counterpart.

Conscription issues during the Second and Third Sessions did not produce such great distinctions between Unionists and Secessionists. Whatever variance appeared always showed Secessionists more pro-conscription than Unionists, even though the Second Session Secessionists populated both very high and very low levels; this is in contrast with the Unionists, who were more inclined to bunch around their own median. Very probably the state-rights zeal that had made some of the members Secessionists in the first place was inhibiting their acceptance of such centralism as was involved in compulsory military service. Willingness to support exemptions for slaveowners or overseers, adopted in this Second Session, may also have drawn some Deep South planters into the lower level of scores. On the other hand, both the highest performance scores and the most positive scale positions on conscription in this session are occupied disproportionately by Secessionists. In the scale set from the Second Session, fourteen of the sixteen congressmen found in the most positive scale position were Secessionists.

During the struggles over exemptions that occupied much time in the Third Session, only very modest differences appear. A limited number of the conscription votes were found to be scalable in the Senate, but the scale positions of Secessionists were found to be only slightly higher than those of Unionists. A renewal of distinctions that occurred in the Fourth Session may be observed in Table 5–2B, which reveals signal differences at both the lowest two and the highest three levels.

TABLE 5-1

CONSCRIPTION AND FORMER PARTY

(A)
1 Cong. , 1 Sess.

Conscrip-tion Score	Number of Individuals Assigned Each Score			
	House		Interior Members	
	Democrat	Whig	Democrat	Whig
0	3	3	2	2
1	4	1	4	3
2	5	2	5	2
3	3	5	4	5
4	3	3	3	2
5	4	3*	8	3*
6	4	2	4*	1
7	7*	2	9	2
8	8	6	8	4
9	12	3	7	5
Median Score	6.07	4.33	5.25	4.17
Differ-ence	1.74		1.08	
% 0-4	34%	47%	33%	48%
% 5-9	66%	53%	67%	52%

*
 Median score.

116

TABLE 5-1--Continued

(B)
2 Cong., 2 Sess., Nov.-Feb.

| Conscrip-tion Score | Number of Individuals Assigned Each Score | | | |
| | Congress | | Interior Members[a] | |
	Democrat	Whig	Democrat	Whig
0	1	7 (6)[b]	1	6 (6)[b]
1	3	4 (3)	2	3 (3)*
2	2	2	1	1*
3	2	4		2
4	5		4	
5	3	7*(1)	1	4 (1)
6	8	4	5*	
7	7*	3	3	
8	11	3	3	2
9	8	4		
Median Score	6.14	4.29 (5.00)[c]	5.20	1.00 (4.33)[c]
Difference	1.85 (1.14)[c]		4.20 (0.87)[c]	
% 0-4	26%	45%	40%	67%
% 5-9	74%	55%	60%	33%

* Median score.

a. Interior at least until the beginning of Second Session.

b. N.C. Union Whigs.

c. Without the N.C. Union Whigs.

117

TABLE 5-1--Continued

(C)
2 Cong., 2 Sess., Feb.-Mar.

Conscription Score	Number of Individuals Assigned Each Score			
	House		Interior Representatives[a]	
	Democrat	Whig	Democrat	Whig
0	1	8 (5)[b]	1	6*(5)[b]
1	8	1	5	
2	1	3*(1)		1 (1)
3	5	2 (1)	4*	2 (1)
4	5*	2	3	
5	2	2		1
6	4	1	1	
7	1	2		
8	3	2		
9	3			
Median Score	3.30	1.83 (3.50)[c]	2.25	-0.17 (2.50)[c]
Difference	1.47 (0.20)[c]		2.42 (0.25)[c]	
% 0-4	61%	70%	93%	90%
% 5-9	39%	30%	7%	10%

*Median score.

a. Interior at least until the beginning of Second Session.

b. N.C. Union Whigs.

c. Without the N.C. Union Whigs.

TABLE 5-2

CONSCRIPTION AND STAND ON SECESSION

(A)
1 Cong., 1 Sess.

Conscrip-tion Score	Number of Individuals Assigned Each Score			
	Congress		Interior Members	
	Secessionist	Unionist	Secessionist	Unionist
0	3	3	2	2
1	4	3	4	3
2	4	3	3	3
3	9	5	7	5*
4	3	3*	3	2
5	8	2	8	1
6	5*		5*	
7	11	4	9	2
8	10	4	8	3
9	12	6	9	3
Median Score	5.70	3.83	5.40	2.80
Difference	1.87		2.60	
% 0-4	33%	52%	33%	63%
% 5-9	67%	48%	67%	38%

*
Median score.

119

TABLE 5-2--Continued

(B)
1 Cong., 4 Sess.

Conscrip-tion Score	Number of Individuals Assigned Each Score			
	Congress		Interior Members	
	Secessionist	Unionist	Secessionist	Unionist
0	1		1	
1		5		5
2	5	7	4	5*
3	11	4 *	9	2
4	10	2	7 *	
5	13*	5	9	3
6	6	3	4	2
7	12	3	8	2
8	2	2		
9	1	1		
Median Score	4.27	3.00	4.00	1.90
Difference	1.27		2.10	
% 0-4	44%	56%	50%	63%
% 5-9	56%	44%	50%	37%

*
Median score.

TABLE 5-2--<u>Continued</u>

(C)
2 Cong., 2 Sess., Nov.-Feb.

Conscription Score	Number of Individuals Assigned Each Score			
	Congress		Interior Members[a]	
	Secessionist	Unionist	Secessionist	Unionist
0	1	7 (6)[b]	1	6 (6)[b]
1	1	5 (3)	1	4 (3)
2	1	2		1*
3	1	6		3
4	3	1*	2	1
5	5	6 (1)	3	4 (1)
6	7	5	4*	2
7	8*	2	3	
8	8	2	3	
9	5	5	1	
Median Score	6.13	3.50 (4.70)[c]	5.50	1.50 (3.50)[c]
Difference		2.63 (1.43)[c]		4.00 (2.00)[c]
% 0-4	18%	51%	22%	71%
% 5-9	83%	49%	78%	29%

*
Median score.

a. Interior at least until the beginning of the Second Session.

b. N.C. Union Whigs.

c. Without N.C. Union Whigs.

The First Session of the Second Congress was not asked by the administration to wrestle with further conscription adjustments, but the Second Session meeting in November 1864 could not avoid the issue any longer. Table 5-2C shows the widening gap between Secessionists and Unionists on the issue. Almost all of the congressmen located in the lowest levels were Unionists, and of the twenty Unionists in the strong half of the conscription levels, all but six were Exterior. Furthermore, median score differences are more substantial than in earlier sessions of Congress. (For Interior members only, differentiation on the basis of secession view is most vivid.) The scalable roll calls from this period of the session yield a similar variation in scale positions. The North Carolina delegation accounts for many of the Unionists at low score levels or in the weakest scale position, and some Unionists are found at almost every level and scale position. Yet, it is perfectly clear that, by the dismal winter of 1864–1865, secession stand was proving to be an excellent predictor of votes on conscription matters for all members, not just those from North Carolina.

Conscription continued at issue even during the last weeks of Congress, in February and March 1865. Attendance was declining steadily during this period, and the more dispirited were evidently inclined to depart early if they had any hope at all of getting home before the end. Table 5-2D offers a last glimpse of the relative defeatism of Unionists in the House. Interior members alone included no Unionists except in the lowest levels, yet it is evident that in the last weeks Secessionists also tended to take weaker positions than they had previously taken. While the general will to persist was collapsing (compare Parts C and D of Table 5-2), even in the debacle the Unionists outstripped the Secessionists in their willingness to abandon the effort.

Slaveholding

The number of slaves held by a congressman exerted considerably less influence on his conscription votes than did his party or secession position. For the large majority of both performance-score and scale-position patterns, little if any significance may be attached to slaveholding, either in terms of absolute numbers held or relative status of the member of Congress in his home county. Two points at which one might expect slaveholding to emerge as a consideration are the adoption of the twenty-Negro law, exempting a white man for each twenty slaves on a plantation, and the debates concerning use of slaves as soldiers. The exemption provision was adopted in the Second Session of the First Congress; the debate about possible military service for slaves came in the Second Session of the Second Congress, although it had been debated outside of Congress long before then. Table 5–3A gives the scale positions on the exemption issue. Only a modest difference is noted between owners of less than twenty slaves and owners of twenty or more. There is some difference, however, and it is in the pattern to be expected: larger slaveowners tended to give less support to a strong conscription-exemption system, scoring lower and scaling less positively than did nonslaveowners and small slaveowners. Although the differences between median scores are not large, the distinguishing tendency is clear. Although large and small slaveowners are found in every scale position, the dominance of the small owners among those in the two most positive scale positions, 4 and 5, is especially significant. Furthermore, such contrasts as may be seen in Table 5–3A on slaveholding are not equaled in conscription voting performances in the other sessions of the First Congress. But in the Senate, during the Third Session, a bitter battle over repeal of the exemption of overseers sharply divided large from small slaveowners in a cumulative scale set.

The slave-soldier debate is more carefully analyzed in a later chapter. It should be noted here, however, that in the last weeks of the Congress, in 1865, a very sharp distinction between large and small slaveowners appeared among the Interior members only. The Interior group had been reduced to such a small number by that date that it is risky to draw any inferences about the importance of slaveownership. Nonetheless, in the final days of the Confederacy small slaveowners from unoccupied territory did appear to be much less willing to see drastic steps taken on conscription than were the large planters. Perhaps this was only a reflection of high stakes and desperation play by men who stood to lose the most in slave property in the impending debacle. It may also include some of the aversions of the plain people and even the smaller slaveowners to encouragement of black aspirations through military service and probable consequent emancipation.

The reverse is the case for the First Congress, where one may observe a recurring tendency for large slaveowners to be slightly less sacrificing on conscription votes than their nonslaveowning or small slaveowning colleagues. The significance of this repeated pattern is clearer when it is noted that the difference is narrowed or eliminated, especially in scale positions, if only the Interior members are tabulated. Since the Exterior members in the First Congress were generally from a land of smaller slaveholdings and were, at the same time, more willing to support Confederate defense at whatever sacrifice, the result is simply that the Exterior members moved the median position for the smaller slaveowners toward a more positive stance. Whatever the actual causative element may have been, therefore, it is more likely to have been Exterior status

TABLE 5-2--Continued

(D)
2 Cong., 2 Sess., Feb.-Mar.

Conscription Score	Number of Individuals Assigned Each Score			
	House		Interior Representatives[a]	
	Secessionist	Unionist	Secessionist	Unionist
0	2	8 (5)[b]	2	6*(5)[b]
1	5	3*	4	1
2	1	3 (1)		1 (1)
3	5	2 (1)	4*	2 (1)
4	6*	1	3	
5	3			
6	4	1	2	
7	1			
8	1	2		
9	2	1		
Median Score	3.33	0.83 (1.50)[c]	2.38	-0.17 (0.50)[c]
Difference	2.50 (1.83)[c]		2.55 (1.88)[c]	
% 0-4	63%	81%	87%	100%
% 5-9	37%	19%	13%	0%

*Median score.

a. Interior at least until the beginning of the Second Session.

b. N.C. Union Whigs.

c. Without N.C. Union Whigs.

TABLE 5-3

CONSCRIPTION AND SLAVEHOLDING

(A)
1 Cong., 2 Sess.

Conscription Scale Position	Number of Individuals Assigned Each Position			
	House		Interior Representatives	
	Absolute Slaveholding		Absolute Slaveholding	
	0-19 Slaves	20 or More Slaves	0-19 Slaves	20 or More Slaves
0	9	11	7	10
1	3	1	2	1
2	7	8*	4	6*
3	11*	10	10*	9
4	9	2	3	1
5	11	5	7	3
Median Position	2.55	1.81	2.35	1.67
Difference	0.74		0.68	
% 0-2	38%	54%	39%	57%
% 3-5	62%	46%	61%	43%

*Median position.

125

(which is to be discussed in a separate section below), than slaveholding level.

This same point is reiterated by reference to the character of slaveholding in each representative's district. The average-sized slaveholding in the home county of each representative has been used to divide the districts into three categories. The small slaveowning areas are those in which the average number of slaves held by each owner was less than eight; the middle rankings are assigned where the average holding was eight but not as many as fourteen; the large slaveowning category consists of instances in which the average holding was fourteen or more (see Appendix I for further explanation). With few exceptions, by this standard the land of small slaveowners is, as mentioned above, the border states—especially those regions where Federal control existed from the beginning of the war or was very soon established.

The strong relationship that is found between a constituency's slaveholding characteristics and a representative's initial stand on conscription in the First Session of the First Congress is easily accounted for by straightforward considerations (Table 5-3B). The section of the Confederacy characterized by large slaveholdings was at that early date still generally safe and its delegates to the House were reluctant about conscription. Their colleagues from small-slaveholding counties were, at the same time, representing constituencies either under Federal occupation or clearly slated for battle. Even among Interior representatives exclusively, the strong conscription scores and scale positions are disproportionately among these small-slaveholding spokesmen, most of whom came from zones seriously exposed to invasion. The fifteen Interior representatives from small slaveholding districts who scaled in one of the highest three positions, for example, were preponderantly from districts barely within the perimeter of Confederate defense. They included all four Tennessee districts not yet invaded, an Alabama district just up the Tennessee River from an invading Federal army, and districts around the target ports of New Orleans and Mobile. Two North Carolina mountain districts plagued by Unionism are also represented among the five with the strongest stand.

No significant association between size of slaveholdings and the district's vote in the House is noted for later sessions of Congress among Interior representatives only. The area of small slaveholding was occupied by Federal troops very rapidly, so that almost twenty such districts originally classified as Interior were cut to half that number before the end of the First Congress and to one fourth that number for the sessions of the Second Congress. Thereafter, although small slaveholders' representatives continued to merit strong conscription scores or scale positions,

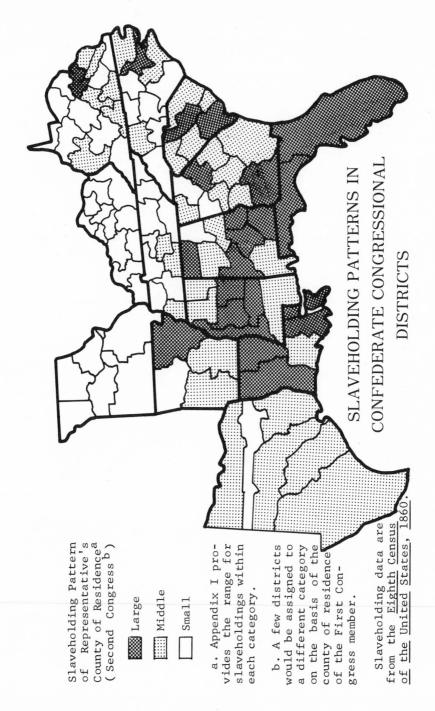

SLAVEHOLDING PATTERNS IN
CONFEDERATE CONGRESSIONAL
DISTRICTS

Slaveholding Pattern
of Representative's
County of Residence[a]
(Second Congress[b])

▨ Large

▦ Middle

☐ Small

a. Appendix I pro-
vides the range for
slaveholdings within
each category.

b. A few districts
would be assigned to
a different category
on the basis of the
county of residence
of the First Con-
gress member.

Slaveholding data are
from the Eighth Census
of the United States, 1860.

TABLE 5-3--Continued

(B)

1 Cong., 1 Sess.

Conscrip-tion Scale Position	Number of Individuals Assigned Each Position					
	Slaveholding Pattern of Congressman's County					
	House			Interior Representatives		
	Size of Slaveholdings			Size of Slaveholdings		
	Small	Middle	Large	Small	Middle	Large
0	3	3	5	2	2	4
1	2	7	8*	1	7	8*
2	5	2	3	3	2	3
3	5	5*	1	4	5*	1
4	8*	5	1	6*	4	1
5	12	3	7	5	3	7
Median Position	3.31	2.10	0.94	3.08	2.10	1.00
Difference	1.21	1.16		0.98	1.10	
	2.37			2.08		
% 0-2	29%	48%	64%	29%	48%	63%
% 3-5	71%	52%	36%	71%	52%	38%

*Median position.

128

TABLE 5-4

CONSCRIPTION AND WEALTH

(A)
1 Cong., 1 Sess.

Conscrip-tion Score	Number of Individuals Assigned Each Score				
	Entire Congress				
	Absolute Estate Category[a]				
	0	1	2	3	4
0			1	5	
1		2		7	
2	1		3	2	2
3	1	3	5	5	1
4	2	3	1	*	
5	1	2	6*	4	1
6		3*		3	1
7	2*	3	4	4	3*
8	2	5	3	4	
9	4		5	4	3

(B)
2 Cong., 2 Sess.

Conscrip-tion Scale Position	Number of Individuals Assigned Each Position				
	Interior Representatives[b]				
	Absolute Estate Category[a]				
	0	1	2	3	4
0	3*	1	2	4	1
1	1			*	
2	1	1	2*	2	*
3		1	1		
4	1	2*	1	2	1
5		3	1		
6					
7					

*Median score or position.

a. Absolute Estate: 2 = $20,000 - $49,999
  0 = Below $10,000   3 = $50,000 - $199,999
  1 = $10,000 - $19,999 4 = $200,000+

b. Interior at least until the beginning of the Second Session.

these men were almost all Exterior spokesmen at the time. Few remained Interior, probably too few to justify an inference about the pattern observed (not shown). The significance appears to be chiefly in the fact that almost all of the strong-position men from small slaveholding districts were Exterior representatives; twenty-five of the twenty-seven such representatives in the strong part of the scale were Exterior. When the consideration of military jeopardy has been controlled, therefore, slave ownership patterns in a member's home county are no longer significantly associated with his conscription votes.

Value of Estate

A Confederate congressman's estate value was in most instances related to the number of slaves he held. It is not surprising, therefore, to find that the same sessions of Congress that yielded distinctions between large and small slaveowners also show distinctions among wealth groupings. This is true for the Second Session of the First Congress and for the Second Session of the Second Congress. In addition, during the First Session of the First Congress, when conscription was initially adopted, a clear pattern based on wealth may be seen (Table 5-4A). For the entire Congress the level of support is highest for the smallest wealth category and progressively weaker for each greater level of wealth except for the most wealthy (who have a very high median). There appears to have been more reluctance about the draft and exemption legislation among the prosperous congressmen than among those of modest estate, with the exception of the great planters. Whether this was actually a result of wealth is a question that may be difficult to answer; but the fact that the Interior members (separate table not shown) do not display such marked pattern as the Congress or House alone casts much doubt on the hypothesis that wealth was the source of the influence. Rather, as with slaveholding, the delegates from occupied districts were generally both more zealous and less wealthy. Furthermore, when it is noted how widely each wealth category is spread over the range of levels, even less confidence in wealth as an influence seems justified. Despite the fact that the scale set for the Second Congress shows a distinction according to wealth for the Interior members (Table 5-4B), one should be deterred from drawing inference by widely varying medians and the very small number of men involved at that date. Since the Federal forces had overrun such a large portion of the Confederacy, there were simply too few Interior members remaining. The clues that do exist are insufficient justification for any attempt to include personal wealth considerations among the formative forces acting on congressmen as they made their decisions about manpower mobilization.

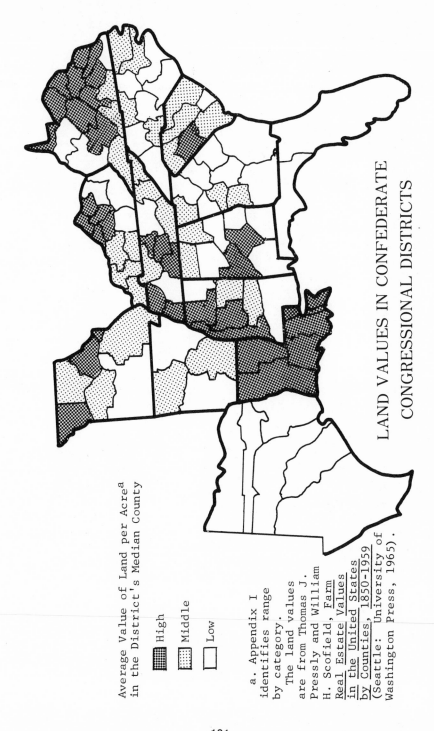

Average Value of Land per Acre[a]
in the District's Median County

■ High

▨ Middle

☐ Low

a. Appendix I
identifies range
by category.
    The land values
are from Thomas J.
Pressly and William
H. Scofield, Farm
Real Estate Values
in the United States
by Counties, 1850-1959
(Seattle: University of
Washington Press, 1965).

LAND VALUES IN CONFEDERATE
CONGRESSIONAL DISTRICTS

TABLE 5-5

CONSCRIPTION AND FEDERAL OCCUPATION

Conscription Score	(A) 1 Cong., 1 Sess.		(B) 1 Cong., 4 Sess.	
	Number of Individuals Assigned Each Score			
	Exterior Members	Interior Members	Exterior Members	Interior Members
0	2	4		1
1	1	8		5
2	1	7	3	9
3	2	13	4	12
4	1	5	8	7*
5	3	11*	8*	13
6	2	6	7	6
7	5*	11	6	10
8	3	13	4	
9	5	13	2	
Median Score	6.10	4.77	4.75	3.64
Difference	1.33		1.11	
% 0-4	28%	41%	36%	54%
% 5-9	72%	59%	64%	46%

*
Median score.

The general level of prosperity among a representative's constituents is no more helpful than his own wealth in predicting his conscription stand. The information used to make rough divisions of the congressional districts into high, middle, and low categories is the average per-acre value of land and improvements in 1860 (see Appendix I for further explanation). Since this information is available by county, the median county in each district has been used to establish the district's economic level. The most prosperous districts, with few exceptions, are those either outside the area of effective Confederate control from the beginning or threatened if not invaded early in the war. In effect, then, a distinction between representatives from the high-level districts and those from middle and low levels is necessarily at the same time an Exterior-Interior differential. Almost all levels of the conscription scores and of the scale positions on this subject are found to be peopled by representatives from each land-value category. This is about equally true, until the last session of Congress, for all districts together or for the Interior districts exclusively. In the final session, conscription scores for representatives from the high-land-value districts are notably bunched at the higher levels of support for conscription. Yet, it turns out that almost all of these high-scoring men were by that date representing Exterior districts and very probably responding to this latter consideration.

Interior or Exterior Constituency

The fact that some members of Congress represented areas occupied by or threatened by Federal forces and had, therefore, an Exterior constituency, has repeatedly shouldered its way into notice during analyses of other individual member circumstances. This, among the considerations we are studying, seems to have exerted the most ever-present influence on conscription votes of Confederate congressmen.

Table 5-5 (parts A, B, and C) includes conscription-score tabulations for the First and Fourth Sessions of the First Congress and one for each part of the Second Session, Second Congress. In every one of the comparisons, the Exterior members display a higher median level, the lowest levels being occupied very disproportionately by Interior members. In the Second Congress, the Exterior members are found overwhelmingly in the highest levels—exclusively so during the last few weeks. The percentage quadrants reveal only weak associations for the First Congress but much stronger ones for the Second Session of the Second Congress.

Table 5-5 (parts D, E, and F) is the comparable set of cumulative scale analyses. These deal with more limited aspects of the conscription topic than do the performance scores. The differences between Interior and Exterior representatives are not as great but are nonetheless along

TABLE 5-5--Continued

(C)
2 Cong., 2 Sess.

Conscrip-tion Score	Nov.-Feb.		Feb.-Mar.	
	Number of Individuals Assigned Each Score			
	Exterior Members	Interior Members	Exterior Representatives	Interior
0	1	7 (6)[a]	3	7 (5)[a]
1	3	4 (3)	7	2
2	3	1	4	2 (1)
3	6	1	2	6*(1)
4	3	3	5	3
5	9	4*(1)	5*	1
6	8	5	5	3
7	8*	4	4	
8	18	3	7	
9	14	1	4	
Median Score	6.44	4.13 (5.30)[b]	4.40	2.17 (2.70)[b]
Differ-ence	2.31 (1.14)[b]		2.23 (1.70)[b]	
% 0-4	22%	48%	46%	83%
% 5-9	78%	52%	54%	17%

*
 Median score.

a. N.C. Union Whigs.

b. Without N.C. Union Whigs.

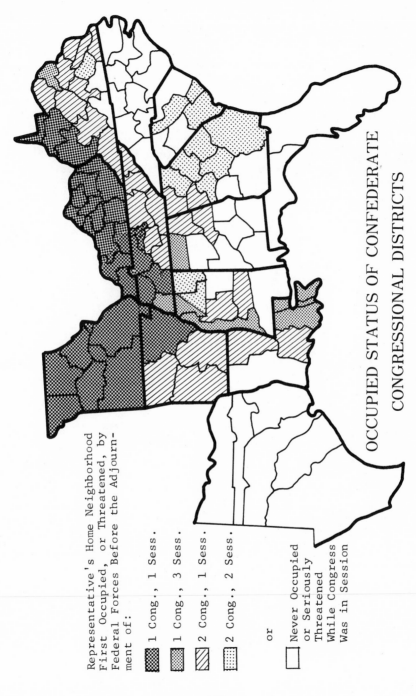

Representative's Home Neighborhood
First Occupied, or Threatened, by
Federal Forces Before the Adjourn-
ment of:

1 Cong., 1 Sess.

1 Cong., 3 Sess.

2 Cong., 1 Sess.

2 Cong., 2 Sess.

or

Never Occupied
or Seriously
Threatened
While Congress
Was in Session

OCCUPIED STATUS OF CONFEDERATE
CONGRESSIONAL DISTRICTS

135

TABLE 5-5--Continued

	(D) 1 Cong., 1 Sess.		(E) 1 Cong., 4 Sess.		(F) 2 Cong., 2 Sess.	
Conscription Scale Position	Number of Individuals Assigned Each Position					
	Exterior Representatives	Interior	Exterior Representatives	Interior	Exterior Representatives	Interior
0	3	8	1	8	6	8 (7)[a]
1	1	16	1	3	3	3
2	2	8	8	11	5	4* (1)
3	1	10*	7	13*	5	1
4	5*	10	11*	7	19*	6 (1)
5	8	16	2	3	17	5
6			7	3		
Median Position	3.60	2.20	3.14	2.15	3.45	1.63 (3.20)[b]
Difference	1.40		0.99		1.82 (0.25)[b]	
	% 0-2	30% | 47%	% 0-3[c] 36% | 59%		% 0-2 25% | 56%	
	% 3-5	70% | 53%	% 3-6 64% | 41%		% 3-5 75% | 44%	

*
Median position.

a. N.C. Union Whigs.

b. Without N.C. Union Whigs.

c. In scale sets with an odd number of positions, the number of members assigned to the center position is divided into halves for percentage calculation.

the same lines. Moreover, the differences between median scores are, in scale sets, affected by the number of positions (usually less than ten). The first scale, for example, is constructed with only six positions (0 through 5), so that the size of the contrast between median scores would not be expected to be as great as the difference in a ten-level performance-score tabulation. Dominance of the weak positions by Interior members is observable in all of the tabulations, and, after mid-war, the thinning of Interior members in the strong or high-scale positions is almost as evident as for the high performance-score levels.

The first session of Congress to get tough on exemptions and produce a conscription law that almost satisfied the Davis administration was the Fourth Session of the First Congress. That greater differentiation between Exterior and Interior members did not occur at that time probably requires some explanation. One plausible idea is that defeated congressmen and those who had not sought re-election might have felt less constrained by prospective reactions among their constituents and hence have taken a stronger position. A check, however, reveals that the scores for the "lame ducks" fall into a pattern almost identical to that for the re-elected members. It is possible that a re-elected congressman felt released from restraint anyway. Furthermore, many of the defeated congressmen knew the strength of the peace movement at first hand. A product of the counsels of despair, it was sweeping large areas of the South and had contributed to the defeat of a significant number of Interior representatives in the 1863 elections. The Second Congress was therefore likely to be of a different character, and "lame ducks" knew well that their terminal session was probably the last chance to enact a strong conscription law. But the primary reason for the strength of the measure, and for the support it received from even Interior members, seems to have been simply the obvious necessity arising from military disasters.

Summary

What influenced a member to decide as he did on conscription issues? Many of his personal views were undoubtedly involved; perhaps the liability for service of relatives or friends could not be ignored; his personal estimate of the chances of gaining anything by further fighting must eventually have entered into the equation. Knowing the number of slaves he held or the value of his estate would not help in predicting his voting behavior, with the possible exception of divisions on the twenty-Negro exemption. The same may, in general, be said of knowing the slaveholding pattern in his home county or the land values in his district, insofar as Exterior status is set aside. To know his party affiliation in the antebellum period would be a valuable clue; to know his position on secession would help even more; and to know whether his home district was occupied at the time of his decision might be the most revealing of all. Put these three characteristics together, and very favorable odds would exist that his stand could be at least approximately predicted.[15]

15. Confederate senators differed from their House colleagues in roll-call behavior on many content-area sets. The House and the Senate record of both performance scores and scale positions have been cross-tabulated separately in the tables when it is apparent that the inclusion of the senators dilutes or cancels out the associations between voting position and member characteristic of representatives. In general, much less influence from earlier party or secession alignments is found for senators than is the case for representatives. Where chapter-end generalizations are distinctly less applicable to the Senate than to the House, this consideration is noted, at least in a footnote.

For the subject of conscription, former party affiliation is not associated with senators' voting positions until the last session of Congress; and even then the greater dedication of former Democrats in the Senate appears to be traceable chiefly to the fact that Democrats still present to vote at that date were preponderantly Exterior senators, whose attitude may more properly be attributed to the latter consideration. Secession stand is no better as a predictor of a senator's votes on conscription. Exterior status was for senators, as for representatives, almost certainly a significant source of influence, although not uniformly so from session to session. Personal economic status is not clearly associated with conscription positions in either house. The substantial difference between senators and representatives, then, lies in the strength of the evidence for associating voting behavior with party or secession stand, which is not as convincing for senators as for representatives.

6 Impressment

MEN were expected to defend their country with life and property when necessary. So deeply ingrained was this common-sense corollary to the absolute political sovereignty of the nation-state that militia obligations were rarely questioned in principle, even among such individualistic citizens as the preponderantly rural Confederates. Compulsory conscription of manpower by special laws produced more complaint about specific terms or enforcement procedures than about the general idea—except among those who had never accepted the postulated sovereignty of the Confederacy. As with life, so with property; one surrendered it for military use or suffered its destruction to handicap the enemy. Sometimes the property taken was slaves or manufactured goods, or even railroad iron and equipment. Such impressment did not arouse great controversy or debate, although there were always those who would complain. More important was the commandeering of food or forage to supply the army; and for reasons to be noted below, it was this that created the most widespread antagonism toward the government on the part of the individual citizen. In any case, compensation was anticipated for property taken for the common good, but acceptable compensation was not a prerequisite to its seizure. In a nutshell, that was the reality Confederate citizens had to reckon with.

Impressment of private property by armies in the field came so naturally and was sanctioned by so long a history that the Confederate Congress did not pass laws on the subject until the war was half over, in March 1863. Federal invasions and the vulnerability of stored cotton had precipitated a hasty 1862 law permitting authorities to destroy property subject to capture and of value to the enemy, with compensation indicated but without an appropriation of funds. The 1863 general impressment legislation emerged from growing complaints about arbitrary and inequitable procedures, on the one hand, and, on the other, from rising indignation at speculative prices and withholding of critically needed supplies in anticipation of greater profits.

The difficulties in agreeing on prices were many, to start with. Farmers almost always considered their compensation too low; impressment agents were struggling against the inflationary pressure of soaring prices. The presence of a major army in any vicinity was certain to create an immediate shortage of fresh food and a rapid depletion of staple commodities. Each of the principal Confederate armies, for example, had about as many men as there were people in an entire congressional district. Everywhere one of these armies went, food and forage needs doubled over a ten-county area. Furthermore, long-haul transportation facilities were wholly inadequate for funneling army supplies into a few critical areas from the wide reaches of the Confederacy. Stripping of battle theatres like northern Virginia or Middle Tennessee became inevitable; and impressment of everything in sight near the rail lines leading away from these zones was the next obvious consequence. This localized, excessive demand was alone enough to force sharply increased market prices, which impressing officers were likely to view as unpatriotic profiteering on the part of the seller. In addition, speculation did enter into transactions from an early date. Officers rarely paid asking prices, therefore, and often not even local market prices.

Depreciation in the value of Confederate paper money increased the need to resort to seizure; as prices increased, so did reluctance to accept Confederate Treasury notes. If the army could not buy, it had to take. Hence the practice of impressment increased as the currency declined in value. The disastrous campaigns of the summer of 1863 set off a giddy, spiraling inflation; and the exactions of the impressment officer became more burdensome, for it was his goal to obtain goods as cheaply as possible.[1] Even so, men were often outraged at the prices the government had to pay. In the summer of 1864, the army was paying as much as thirty and forty dollars for a bushel of wheat, and among the producers who received such prices was none other than Secretary of War James A. Seddon.[2] Completing the vicious circle, both producers and speculators struggled to hold out for higher prices in the rapidly cycling inflation. Eventually even this profit hope collapsed before rising fear of repudiation of the paper money, so that many producers or merchants actually preferred not to sell staple commodities at all—presumably hoping for payment in gold, or for the war's end. When payments for impressed goods came to be made in certificates of indebtedness, suppliers generally

1. See Richard C. Todd, *Confederate Finance* (Athens: University of Georgia Press, 1954), Appendix C, which illustrates the depreciation of Treasury notes.

2. A list of individuals receiving these prices was reported to Congress on February 14, 1865. ("Proceedings," LII, 343–345.) According to Edward A. Pollard, wartime editor of the Richmond *Examiner*, this incident "gave great dissatisfaction," for when a cabinet member got such high prices public confidence in the value of Confederate currency was lost. The important thing is not the economic effect of Seddon's wheat but that the price paid became public knowledge and apparently affected confidence in the government itself. (Pollard, *The Lost Cause: A New Southern History of the Confederates . . .* [New York: E. B. Treat and Co., 1866], p. 652.)

were dismayed by the prospect of never being paid or of receiving nearly worthless paper.

It is understandable, then, that impressment was both a necessity for the Confederate authorities and a source of rising resentment among agricultural and other affected interests. Congress in this unavoidable yet probably insoluble problem impinged on the private property rights of a dangerously large proportion of Confederate citizens. The impingement was all the more serious because at least some politicians contended that the strike for nationhood had been made in defense of certain forms of private property rights. Here again was the cruel dilemma which Confederate leaders so frequently faced: should independence be pursued by measures that smacked of the very thing Southerners hoped to escape?

Roll-Call Issues

Debates on the original impressment legislation, that of March 1863, exposed a persisting argument not finally settled until the Confederacy was a month away from oblivion. Condemning arbitrary impressments, many congressmen maintained that the only fair compensation for impressed goods was the market price in the vicinity, agreeing with Senator Allen T. Caperton of Virginia that "anyone had sense enough to see the gross injustice of taking his property at less than its real value while the property of his fellow citizens was left untouched." Senator Hill of Georgia replied that this would only create opportunities for speculators, while Gustavus A. Henry of Tennessee attacked the market-price argument with a succinct *reductio ad absurdum* by reminding the Senate that "Richard III when down in the dust and blood of Bosworth field, offered his 'kingdom for a horse.'" Representative John B. Baldwin of Virginia agreed with the market-price concept, however, pointing out that his constituents were unable to ship cattle to Richmond without "the risk of seizure at a little over half the market value," and that the result of such government policy was a shortage of food in some cities. One man had supposedly lost as much as $80,000 by impressment, and Baldwin ominously inquired whether "any one suppose[d] that the people of the country would submit to this sort of thing?"[3]

Such complaints, made before the regularizing of impressment, spoke to very real problems. While some of the complainers were merely malcontents, many others were simple people who opposed the idea of confiscation (for this is what below-market-price impressment amounted to) as a means of financing the war.

The impressment law of March 1863 was intended to keep prices

3. "Proceedings," XLVIII, 253, 255, 281.

at reasonably low levels, while giving full legal sanction to the practice of required surrender of goods by producers or merchants. Property necessary to the owner's own subsistence or even to the operation of his farm or business was not supposed to be taken, though abuses were inevitably created by the zealousness of some impressing officers. The price of any other property grown or purchased by the owner for his own use was to be negotiated between owner and impressing officer if possible. In case of an impasse, each party was to name a disinterested man from the vicinity to settle the price. If these agents could not agree, they were to appoint an umpire, whose decision was to be final.

Property held for sale or resale was to be paid for according to a current schedule of prices for an entire state, set by two commissioners for each state, one appointed by the governor and the other by the president of the Confederate States. These two commissioners were to use an umpire if they disagreed. Impressment officers and owners of this class of property, however, were still to negotiate points of difference or use local men as agents to settle disagreements. The officer had the right of appeal to the state commissioners if he was convinced that a local appraiser had been somewhat less than disinterested. An amendment to the same law soon relieved the officer of having to await a decision on such an appeal. He could leave a receipt and let the owner wait for payment until the decision was known. The temporary labor of slaves could also be impressed under the 1863 law, according to the applicable state code regulating an already existing practice. The secretary of war was to establish regulations if no state laws on the subject had been enacted.

The last session of the First Congress, assembling in December 1863, faced a rash of complaints about illegal or unjust impressment practices. Governor Joseph E. Brown of Georgia wrote Secretary of War Seddon that there were "so many outrages committed in this State under the guise of making impressments for the Army . . . that I have felt it to be my duty to interpose in behalf of common justice and right," and he recommended that his legislature pass enactments to punish such deprivations. He desired market-price impressment, and told Seddon that low prices only made people "withhold the supplies from the market and cause them to be secreted and concealed from the Government agents." [4] Governor John Milton of Florida told his legislature a few days later that seizure was "incompatible with the rights of the citizens and insulting to freemen who know their rights and have proven their loyalty." Like Brown, Milton talked of interposition (a truly significant

4. *O.R.*, ser. IV, vol. II, pp. 943–944 (November 9, 1863).

word in a land of state rights) and requested the legislature to act to protect citizens and their property.[5] Early the next month, the General Assembly of North Carolina begged for an end to illegal impressment,[6] and in January Milton wrote Seddon that "the effect of the impressment made in West Florida was the desertion of a large number of the troops of that part of the State, a portion of whom have joined the enemy."[7]

In his message at the start of the session, President Davis took note of these complaints. He admitted that many of the allegations leveled against the impressment system were true and asserted that only the "disordered condition of the currency" made it necessary to adopt a method of supply which was "unequal in its operation, vexatious to the producer, injurious to the industrial interest, and productive of ...discontent among the people." Contrary to Governor Brown, however, Davis contended that fear of the impressment officers had discouraged hoarding and speculation. He doubted that the problem could be alleviated by tampering with the impressment law and urged instead the "restoration of the currency to such a basis as will enable the [War] Department to purchase necessary supplies in the open market."[8] In other words, impressment evils would end when inflation ended; and since there was little prospect that inflation could be ended while the war continued, Davis was really dismissing the problem as irremediable.

Some congressmen, however, were of a different mind. The House Judiciary Committee, for example, in effect approved payment of local market prices before impressment of any commodities. The entire House would not go this far, but did agree to retention of state-level commissioners only for hearing appeals, not for fixing prices in the first place. In a gracious bow to the planting interests, the House exempted slaves engaged in producing food from impressment except on order of a commanding general. Thus price restraints would have been essentially abandoned by the House in the next session after their establishment. The Senate balked only at emasculating the state commissioners' functions, and on this the House backed down. The new law was, nevertheless, a major concession to speculators as well as to producers, and it weakened the government's legal position while at the same time increasing greatly its financial obligations.

In spite of the fact that complaints about impressment continued to be plentiful, Jefferson Davis did not even mention the subject in his message to the First Session of the Second Congress. Taking their cue

5. *Ibid.*, pp. 974–976 (November 23, 1863).
6. *Ibid.*, p. 1066 (December 12, 1863).
7. *Ibid.*, vol. III, p. 46 (January 26, 1864).
8. *Messages*, I, 373–374.

from the President, congressmen grumbled about the system but did almost nothing to reform it. The Senate, little affected by the 1863 elections, was willing to make the situation worse (from the agriculturalists' point of view) and passed a bill that would have eliminated part of the problem by the simple expedient of legalizing almost any impressment. This would have satisfied the army by allowing nearly unrestricted seizure of anything alleged to be needed, but would have abandoned the purpose of impressment laws, which had been to protect citizens from the abuses that already existed rather than to authorize those practices.

The House, however, was very much affected by the elections and desired to make the situation more bearable for planters and farmers. It therefore rejected the sorely needed yet impolitic measure, even though the cost of army supplies was mounting rapidly and the big Federal drives of 1864 in northern Virginia and Georgia were placing Confederate armies under ever-increasing pressure. In June 1864 Congress did create a claims system, with decision-making at the congressional district level, to furnish some relief for owners of property unjustly seized or appraised. No other substantial legal remedy was offered to owners of impressed property.

The collapsing of the Confederacy's defenses soon wiped out not only co-operation but acquiescence on the part of sellers. To obtain needed supplies for the army, the government was forced to capitulate to the faultfinders; and, by the closing months of the war, Confederate agents had to offer cash in coin for supplies. In his desperation message to Congress on March 13, 1865, Jefferson Davis admitted that Confederate Treasury notes were not being accepted; and he obtained the passage of two acts designed to obtain coin from states, banks, or other sources to meet the emergency. Davis also complained of prices in this frantic, last-minute appeal, pointing out that "none believe that the Government can ever redeem in coin the obligation to pay $50 a bushel for corn, or $700 a barrel for flour." Congress ignored the logic of the appeal, and, on the last day the Confederate Congress was in session, Davis signed a bill that watered down the impressment system drastically by ordering that goods seized be paid for at "the usual market price of such property at the time and place of impressment."[9]

---

9. *Ibid.*, pp. 545–546; Charles W. Ramsdell, editor, *Laws and Joint Resolutions of the Last Session of the Confederate Congress (November 7, 1864-March 18, 1865) Together with the Secret Acts of Previous Congresses* (Durham, N.C.: Duke University Press, 1941, pp. 147-150, 152.

Association of Member Characteristics
with Roll-Call Voting Behavior

Congressmen debated and voted on many aspects of impressment during the Third and Fourth Sessions of the First Congress and in both sessions of the Second Congress. In addition, the closely related matter of destruction of property to prevent cápture by the enemy was confronted as early as 1862. Thus, the confluence of two powerful streams—basic property rights and Confederate self-preservation—provided a turbulent passage which Confederate congressmen could hardly negotiate without exposing some of the influences bearing on their voting behavior.

Former Party Affiliation

The authorization for destruction of private property to prevent its capture by Federal forces was adopted in the First Session of the First House without significant evidence that a congressman's former party affiliation was a factor in his judgment. Neither performance scores nor scale positions sustain any inference of distinction between Democrats and Whigs. When the Third Session tackled the first general impressment legislation, however, the roll-call record provided a basis for some differentiation according to former party (Table 6-1A). It is true that no profoundly differing stance was taken by these two elements in Congress, and that median scores are very close to the same among all members. Every Exterior Whig, however, is scored in the higher half of the range of scores; and although the Interior Whigs are equally split between the two halves of this range, there is a distinct and important cluster of them at the lowest levels. Democrats, by contrast, are divided more evenly, and almost exactly the same whether considered by entire Congress or Interior members only. Without doubt, some clue at least to subsequent Whig behavior is not far below the surface of the apparent similarity between Democrats and Whigs.

The Second Congress contained a substantially different membership and also operated under rapidly deteriorating defense capabilities. Under the impact of these changes, a clearer relationship emerged between attitude on impressment and former party affiliation. Table 6-1B indicates the greater impressment zeal displayed by the Democrats in Congress, and the reverse role played by the Whigs. This is more vividly displayed when even greater party differences among Interior members alone are examined. Except for one man, all Whigs at a higher level than 3 were Exterior members, but no such startling antagonism between Interior and Exterior members can be noted among the Democrats. A scale set on impressment from the House roll calls reveals a pattern similar but less extreme than that found in the performance scores; only

TABLE 6-1

IMPRESSMENT AND FORMER PARTY

(A)

1 Cong., 3 Sess.

Impress-ment Score	Number of Individuals Assigned Each Score			
	Congress		Interior Members	
	Democrat	Whig	Democrat	Whig
0	7	5	7	5
1	6	6	5	6
2	9	1	8	1
3	8		1	
4				*
5	10*	5*	9*	3
6	8	7	5	5
7	6	1	5	1
8	4	2	2	
9	8	6	4	3
Median Score	4.30	4.90	4.22	3.00
Differ-ence	0.60		1.22	
% 0-4	45%	36%	46%	50%
% 5-9	55%	64%	54%	50%

*
 Median score.

146

TABLE 6-1--<u>Continued</u>

(B)
2 Cong., 1 Sess.

Impress-ment Score	Number of Individuals Assigned Each Score			
	Congress		Interior Members	
	Democrat	Whig	Democrat	Whig
0	3	7 (4)[a]	1	6 (4)[a]
1	4	6 (2)		3*(2)
2	2	4	1	2
3	3	3*(2)	2	3 (2)
4	2	2	2	
5	5	1	1	
6	6*	3	3*	
7		1		
8	6	5	1	
9	10	4	6	1
Median Score	5.25	2.33 (4.00)[b]	5.50	0.50 (1.25)[b]
Differ-ence	2.92 (1.25)[b]		5.00 (4.25)[b]	
% 0-4	34%	61%	35%	93%
% 5-9	66%	39%	65%	07%

*Median score.

a. N.C. Union Whigs.

b. Without N.C. Union Whigs.

TABLE 6-1--Continued

(C)
2 Cong., 2 Sess.

Impressment Score	Number of Individuals Assigned Each Score					
	Congress		House		Interior Members[a]	
	Democrat	Whig	Democrat	Whig	Democrat	Whig
0	2	8 (7)[b]	2	7 (6)[b]	1	7 (7)[b]
1	2	3 (1)	1	2 (1)	2	1*(1)
2	3	5	3	4*	3	1
3	6	3*(2)	4	3*(2)	4	2 (2)
4	3		1		*	
5	7	2	3	0	4	
6	5*	2	3*	2	1	1
7	6	3	5*	2	1	1
8	6	3	5	2	3	
9	9	5	7	4	1	2
Median Score	5.30	2.33 (5.50)[c]	6.00	2.00 (5.75)[c]	3.50	0.50 (6.50)[c]
Difference	2.97 (0.20)[c]		4.00 (0.25)[c]		3.00 (3.00)[c]	
% 0-4	33%	56%	32%	62%	50%	73%
% 5-9	67%	44%	68%	38%	50%	27%

* Median score.

a. Interior at least until the beginning of the Second Session.

b. N.C. Union Whigs.

c. Without N.C. Union Whigs.

one Whig among the Interior representatives is assigned a scale position
above the lowest two of a seven-position set.

In the last session of Congress, the impressment issue produced a
repetition of this party contrast in scale positions (not shown) and in
performance scores (Table 6–1C). Again, Whigs press heavily on the
lowest scores, while Democrats tended to gravitate toward the higher,
stronger pro-impressment scores. It is true, of course, that when the last
of the impressment business was conducted, the Interior Whig membership still present and voting was preponderantly the North Carolina
element.

Position on Secession

A member's stand on secession, being so commonly parallel to his
former party affiliation, would be expected to relate to his votes on
impressment in a manner similar to that just described for party. This
is usually found to be the case, even for property destruction, where
neither characteristic was at all important. There are some significant
variations from the party pattern, however, the most consequential being
a generally wider gap between Secessionists and Unionists than between
Democrats and Whigs.

Part A of Table 6–2, for example, shows the difference between median
scores of Secessionists and Unionists among Interior members to be 3.25,
as compared with a difference of only 1.22 between Democrats and
Whigs as shown on Table 6–1A. Such differentials are not unusual, and
their repetition throughout this subject area clearly indicates that stand
on secession was a better predictor of impressment votes than was former
party. A scale set from the Senate of the Third Session of the First
Congress indicates that this party characteristic was equally operative
in the Upper House, as the Unionist senators are found at decidedly
less positive scale positions than Secessionist senators.

During both sessions of the Second Congress, Unionists are scored
at profoundly lower levels and in weaker scale positions than are Secessionists, as Unionists persistently displayed a decided edge in unwillingness to sacrifice property rights for the cause of nationhood. In the Third
Session of the First Congress (Table 6–2A), the antagonists of 1861 had
almost the same percent of their total membership scored in the upper
half of the range. This was not true for the First Session of the Second
Congress (Table 6–2B), and it was less true for the Second Session (Table
6–2D), where the Unionists, though somewhat polarized, are found
chiefly at scores 0 to 3. The scale set illustrated by Table 6–2C supports
the contention that acceptance or rejection of impressment legislation
was associated with Secessionism or Unionism, but also shows that
Interior status softened the impressment attitude of both of these groups.

TABLE 6-2

IMPRESSMENT AND STAND ON SECESSION

(A)

1 Cong., 3 Sess.

Impress-ment Score	Number of Individuals Assigned Each Score			
	Congress		Interior Members	
	Secessionist	Unionist	Secessionist	Unionist
0	6	6	6	6
1	7	5	6	5
2	9	1	8	1*
3	6	1	1	
4				
5	6*	9*	6*	6
6	10	4	9	3
7	6	1	6	1
8	5	1	3	
9	9	3	6	1
Median Score	4.67	4.28	4.75	1.50
Differ-ence	0.39		3.25	
% 0-4	44%	42%	41%	52%
% 5-9	56%	58%	59%	48%

*
Median score.

150

TABLE 6-2--Continued

(B)
2 Cong., 1 Sess.

| Impress-ment Score | Number of Individuals Assigned Each Score | | | |
| | Congress | | Interior Members | |
	Secessionist	Unionist	Secessionist	Unionist
0	3	7 (4)[a]	1	6 (4)[a]
1	2	8 (2)		3* (2)
2	1	6*	1	3
3	5	3 (2)	4	3 (2)
4	3	1	3	
5	5*		2*	
6	3	4	2	
7		1		1
8	5	2	1	
9	7	5	4	1
Median Score	4.60	1.58 (1.92)[b]	4.00	0.83 (1.50)[b]
Differ-ence	3.02 (2.68)[b]		3.17 (2.50)[b]	
% 0-4	41%	68%	50%	88%
% 5-9	59%	32%	50%	12%

*
Median score.

a. N.C. Union Whigs.

b. Without N.C. Union Whigs.

TABLE 6-2--Continued

(C)
2 Cong., 1 Sess.

Impressment Scale Position	Number of Individuals Assigned Each Position			
	House		Interior Representatives	
	Secessionist	Unionist	Secessionist	Unionist
0	4	10 (4)[a]	3	8*(4)[a]
1	2	2* (1)	2	2 (1)
2	7	2	5*	
3		3		
4	6*	3	4	
5	10	4	4	1
Median Position	3.25	1.00 (2.17)[b]	1.80	-0.31 (-0.25)[b]
Difference		2.25 (1.08)[b]		2.11 (2.05)[b]
% 0-2	45%	58%	56%	91%
% 3-5	55%	42%	44%	9%

* Median position.

a. N.C. Union Whigs.

b. Without N.C. Union Whigs.

TABLE 6-2--Continued

(D)
2 Cong., 2 Sess.

Impressment Score	Number of Individuals Assigned Each Score					
	Congress		House		Interior Members[a]	
	Secessionist	Unionist	Secessionist	Unionist	Secessionist	Unionist
0		10 (7)[b]		9 (6)[b]		8* (7)[b]
1	1	4 (1)		3* (1)	1	2* (1)
2	4	4*	4	3*	4	
3	3	4 (2)	2	4 (2)	2	2 (2)
4	3		1			
5	8	3	5	0	4*	1
6	5*		3		2	
7	5	4	5*	2	1	2
8	6	2	5	1	3	1
9	7	4	6	2	2	1
Median Score	5.40	1.88 (4.17)[c]	6.10	1.00 (1.83)[c]	4.63	0.00 (5.50)[c]
Difference	3.52 (1.23)[c]		5.10 (4.27)[c]		4.63 (0.87)[c]	
% 0-4	26%	63%	23%	79%	37%	75%
% 5-9	74%	37%	77%	21%	63%	25%

* Median score.

a. Interior at least until the beginning of the Second Session.

b. N.C. Union Whigs.

c. Without N.C. Union Whigs.

A caveat is in order, however. These distinctions which seem so evident between Secessionists and Unionists were not so great as to indicate party behavior on this issue, for as a previous chapter has indicated, such behavior apparently did not exist. The contrasts uncovered here, while real, are not even close to partisan antagonism, nor are agreement and cohesion scores helpful in detecting party behavior in this limited content area. Furthermore, we must not obscure the fact that almost every impressment-score level or scale position in the Congress as a whole is occupied by men from both sides of these divisions. Secession stand is only one among several influences that were involved in these roll-call decisions.

Slaveholding

In dealing with property destruction to prevent enemy advantage, the First Session of the First House exposed some difference between large and small slaveowners among Interior representatives (Table 6-3A). The distinctions are only slightly greater than those for the entire House (not shown). Since the occupied area was mostly confined to the Upper South at this time, and people did not yet know how long enemy occupation would last, this distinction could actually have had a sectional basis. Although median scores are not especially far apart, percentage tables show a significant 16 percent difference between the proportion of each group located on either half of the range of property destruction scores, with large holders heavily weighted in favor of the proposal. More significantly, the highest scores (7, 8, and 9) could be assigned to disproportionately few of the smaller slaveowners: 15 percent, as compared with 44 percent of those in the planter class. Even so, it should be noted that a majority of both groups is located in the stronger half of the distribution. The scale set on property destruction from this session reinforces the inference that smaller slaveholders were less willing to allow property to be destroyed on the grounds of strategic necessity (Table 6-3B). Once more, this may actually reflect only a sectional difference, because small holders were disproportionately located in the Upper South, where most of the fighting and destruction was taking place, and they were therefore more likely to suffer loss than were their richer colleagues.

Evidence of slaveholding association with impressment scores did not appear in the Third Session of the First Congress, when the first impressment legislation was introduced, but it did emerge in the First Session of the Second Congress, when Interior members' votes indicated less toleration for impressment among the smaller slaveowners (not shown). A scale set on impressment from this same session strongly supports this impression that smaller owners were less willing to sacrifice (Table 6-3C). This difference appears in the total House vote as well as in the vote of Interior representatives only, even though median scale positions for both large and small slaveowners are much lower for the Interior group than for the entire House. The median for the smaller holders of the Interior, furthermore, is at the lowest possible position. If the scale could have been extended to a lower limit, very probably a sizeable number would have placed lower than they did and median differentials would have been significantly greater. On the other hand, medians eroded by almost exactly the same amount as analysis moved from the entire House to Interior representatives only. This might indicate that, as Union armies advanced into areas of heavy slave population, Federal occupation of the home area had much the same effect upon large and small slaveholders in Congress.

During the last session of Congress, impressment brought out voting patterns based on slaveholding classifications that are of a curvilinear nature. Performance scores and scale positions (not shown) are quite high for the lowest category of slaveowning, slightly lower for the next category, much lower for the next, but higher again for the larger of the slaveholders. The small population in each classification provides a very weak basis for inferences, but it would appear that impressment may have alarmed the middle ranges of slaveholders more than either the smallest or largest owners. One might suspect Exterior-member influence in the ranks of the small slaveholders, except that the same performance-score pattern appears for Interior members alone. The scale set provides the same pattern when analyzed for the entire House vote, but the Interior-member analysis offers only weak bases to distinguish one set of slaveholders from another. This tabulation is based on absolute slaveholding; one using relative slaveholdings shows the same general pattern, insofar as differences between large and small owners may be observed.

Ownership of slaves was decidedly not a major influence on the impressment votes of Confederate congressmen. That it was an influence at all in most sessions is in doubt on the basis of the slender variations found. Yet the differences between median scores, together with the general strength of association for the C part of Table 6-3, justify a conclusion that large and small slaveholders in the Second House acted differently, whatever the causative factor may have been.

The size of slaveholdings in a representative's home area shows some strong associations with his voting record on impressment; it is evident in every instance that something other than this consideration is the more probable cause. The destruction of property to avoid capture by

TABLE 6-3

IMPRESSMENT AND SLAVEHOLDING

	(A) 1 Cong., 1 Sess. Property Destruction			(B) 1 Cong., 1 Sess. Property Destruction		
	Number of Individuals Assigned Each Score				Number of Individuals Assigned Each Position	
Property Destruc- tion Score	Interior Representatives		Property Destruc- tion Scale Position		House	
	Absolute Slaveholding				Absolute Slaveholding	
	0-19 Slaves	20 or More Slaves			0-19 Slaves	20 or More Slaves
0	1	2	0		4	4
1	4	2	1		20*	7
2	9	3	2		13	12*
3		2	3		8	8
4	2	2	4		1	3
5	7*	7*				
6	5	1				
7	2	7				
8	2	5				
9	1	3				
Median Score	4.07	4.86	Median Position		0.95	1.50
Differ- ence	0.79		Differ- ence		0.55	
% 0-4	48%	32%	% 0-2 [a]		66%	50%
% 5-9	52%	68%	% 2-4		34%	50%

*Median score or position.

a. In scale sets with an odd number of positions, the number
of members assigned to the center position is divided into halves
for percentage calculation.

156

TABLE 6-3--<u>Continued</u>

(C)
2 Cong., 1 Sess.

Impress-ment Scale Position	Number of Individuals Assigned Each Position			
	House		Interior Representatives	
	Absolute Slaveholding		Absolute Slaveholding	
	0-19 Slaves	20 or More Slaves	0-19 Slaves	20 or More Slaves
0	14	1	11*	1
1	3	3	2	3
2	4*	6	2	3*
3	3	2		
4	5	6*	2	2
5	9	7	3	3
Median Position	1.50	3.08	-0.09	1.67
Differ-ence	1.58		1.76	
% 0-2	55%	40%	75%	58%
% 3-5	45%	60%	25%	42%

*
Median position.

Federals was authorized by votes in the House that identified members from middle-range districts as more willing than their colleagues from either large- or small-slaveholding areas to sanction such deliberate devastation. Both scores and scale positions fall into this pattern, and this is true for the entire House or for the Interior members apart. Yet, further inspection suggests very strongly that those willing to sacrifice were usually far from actual or immediately prospective battle zones, while the reluctant representatives spoke for the owners of property in actual danger of being destroyed in the foreseeable future. When impressment legislation was passed in the Third Session of the First Congress, such association as is found between a representative's record and slaveholding patterns in his county is most persuasively accounted for by similar elements of distance from battle theatres or other reasons for unequal incidence of impressment burdens. Before the Second Congress faced impressment issues, Federal advances had overrun almost all of the home areas of representatives from small-slaveholding societies, leaving too few observations to justify inferences about this slaveholding category. It is true that the middle-range representatives were less willing to impress than were men from large slaveholding areas, but the attitudes of the former should be judged in the light of another fact: these middle-range areas were almost all in either Governor Vance's disaffected North Carolina or Governor Brown's reluctant Georgia. Size of slaveholdings in a representative's home county, in short, tells us very little about his impressment votes that other, almost obvious considerations do not better predict. A preponderance of small slaveholdings, on the other hand, probably helps to account for keen resentment of Confederate policies in some areas of North Carolina and Georgia.

Value of Estate

There is no evidence to suggest that value of estate may have had a significant bearing on voting for property-destruction measures, and only slight evidence that it may have been an element in decisions about impressment. In Table 6-4 it is frequently the case that lower levels are assigned to the center range of wealth with both extreme categories higher, which is the same pattern exhibited by slaveownership (this includes tables not shown). The effect is also present in a scale set for the last session of Congress (Table 6-4D). The only substantial variation from this curvilinear pattern in Table 6-4 is in the scale set for the First Session of the Second Congress, among the Interior representatives only. Here (Table 6-4C) there is a more nearly linear tendency for greater wealth to produce higher scale scores. Although the small number of cases in each category of Table 6-4C makes any conclusions risky, the

TABLE 6-4

IMPRESSMENT AND WEALTH

(A)
1 Cong., 3 Sess.

Impress-ment Score	Number of Individuals Assigned Each Score				
	House				
	Absolute Estate[a]				
	0	1	2	3	4
0		4	2	2	1
1		2	4	2	1
2	1	1	4	2	1
3	2	*	3*	2	
4					
5	1	3	2	5*	1*
6	1	2	3	4	3
7	*		3	2	1
8	2			2	
9	3	2	3	3	

(B)
2 Cong., 1 Sess.

Impress-ment Score	Number of Individuals Assigned Each Score									
	Congress					Interior Members				
	Absolute Estate[a]					Absolute Estate[a]				
	0	1	2	3	4	0	1	2	3	4
0	1	1	4	3	1	1		4	2	
1	1		2	6	1	1		*	1	1
2		3	2	3			3	1	1	
3	1	2	1	4*		1*	2*	1	3*	
4	1	2		1	1		1		1	1*
5	1*	2*		2	2	1	1			
6	2	1	3*	2	1*		1	1	1	
7	2	1	2				1			
8		2	3	3	2			1		
9	1	3	2	6	3	1	1			1

* Median score.

a. Absolute Estate:
   0 = Below $10,000

1 = $10,000 - $19,000
2 = $20,000 - $49,999
3 = $50,000 - $199,999
4 = $200,000+

159

TABLE 6-4--<u>Continued</u>

(C)
2 Cong., 1 Sess.

Impress-ment Scale Position	Number of Individuals Assigned Each Position				
	Interior Representatives				
	Absolute Estate[a]				
	0	1	2	3	4
0	3*	5*	2	2	
1		1	1*_	3	
2	1		3	*	1
3					
4	1	1		2	*
5		2		3	1

(D)
2 Cong., 2 Sess.

Impress-ment Scale Position	Number of Individuals Assigned Each Position				
	House				
	Absolute Estate[a]				
	0	1	2	3	4
0	1	2	4	2	1
1	2	2	8*	3	
2	1	3*		2	
3	1*	2	2	4*	2*
4	1	2	2	2	
5	3	1	5	2	2

*
Median position.

a. Absolute Estate: 2 = $20,000 - $49,999
   0 = Below $10,000   3 = $50,000 - $199,999
   1 = $10,000 - $19,999   4 = $200,000+

TABLE 6-4--Continued

(E)
2 Cong., 1 Sess.

Impress-ment Score	Number of Individuals Assigned Each Score					
	Median-County Average Value of Land Per Acre in Congressman's District					
	House			Interior Representatives		
	Level of Land Value			Level of Land Value		
	Low	Middle	High	Low	Middle	High
0	4	1		4	1	
1	3		3	2		
2	6	2	1	4*	1	1
3	3*	4		3	3	
4	1	4*		1	2*	
5	3	1	3	2		
6	1	5	2		3	
7	2	1	3*	1		
8	1	2	5		1	
9	3	2	7	2	1	2*
Median Score	2.17	4.00	7.00	1.88	3.50	8.25
Difference	1.83	3.00		1.62	4.75	
	4.83			6.37		
% 0-4	63%	50%	17%	74%	58%	33%
% 5-9	37%	50%	83%	26%	42%	67%

*
Median score.

evident implication is that Interior members were exceedingly timid on impressment unless they were also exceedingly rich, and that congressmen of little wealth in the more positive, or sacrificing, scale positions were usually the ones from occupied territory. Some buttressing of this probability is found in Part B, where among the Interior members alone the impressment-score median level is notably below that for the entire Congress.

Just as with slaveholding, value of estate must be judged a small element in explaining responses of Confederate congressmen to roll calls on the volatile impressment issue. Although the several wealth levels behaved noticeably differently, it may be that personal estate value was related to some other individual characteristic or condition, such as geographical location or personal psychology, that had a causative relation to attitudes on impressment. Or perhaps the curvilinear pattern emerged because poorer congressmen were already wiped out by either inflation or the Federals, while the richest legislators thought they could stand the exactions of either. The man in the middle, who still had something left—but not very much—may have fought impressment the hardest. This can only be dubious conjecture. Despite the presence of the phenomenon, its explanation remains uncertain.

Land values in a representative's district are found to be associated with his impressment posture in every session that wrestled with the issue. But exclusion of the Exterior members alters the strength and nature of that association. Zones most susceptible to impressment were usually middle or low land-value areas, and reaction to the topic is probably to be understood better in terms of likelihood of impressment than of land values.

The First Session of the Second Congress offers some evidence that the greater the land value, the greater the willingness to impress (Table 6-4E). This parallels the observed association between a member's own wealth and his scale position on impressment. There may well be a clue here to first voting reactions of freshmen representatives, who were both disproportionately less wealthy themselves and spokesmen for generally poorer districts. This same pattern continues into the Second Session, but with so few men voting that North Carolinians simply dictate the pattern. Nevertheless, land values as a rough measure of affluence should not be overlooked as a possible causal consideration; perhaps the effect was achieved more through replacing the congressman than through changing his mind.

Interior or Exterior Constituency

Property destruction as an issue in the First Session of the First

Congress did not bring out any clear distinction between men representing occupied districts and those from within the region of effective Confederate control. Such destruction was most likely to affect districts neither clearly Exterior nor safely Interior. We have not employed as a separate member characteristic the experience of representing constituents currently within an active battle zone; yet, analysis in a number of instances uncovers voting behavior very probably attributable to this specific consideration. The property-destruction legislation is a good example.

The passage of the first general impressment law in the Third Session, however, involved votes that do furnish the predicted variation between Exterior and Interior members. The lower scores of Interior delegates are far more decided than the difference in medians would indicate (Table 6-5A), for in the lowest three levels there are only four (12 percent) of the Exterior but thirty-two (42 percent) of the Interior members, while the high levels contain a disproportionately large number of members from occupied territory.

By the First Session of the Second Congress the gap between these two elements in Congress had widened substantially, for both scores (Table 6-5B) and scale positions (not shown). The last session witnessed still greater difference between median scores, together with an increasing preponderance of Exterior members assigned to the highest three levels (7, 8, and 9), while the Interior lawmakers continued to appear more often in the lowest levels (Table 6-5C). The scale positions from this last session bear out the same general interpretation. Although the contrast is not quite as large for scale positions as was the case for the previous session, the Exterior (which could not be reached by the impressment officers) was heavy on the high scores and the Interior (which was repeatedly accosted by impressment agents) was abundant in the low scores. Removal of the North Carolinians from these tables only narrows differences, for, even without that group of recalcitrant Interior men, the distinction created by the status of occupied territory remains highly significant.

Summary

Destruction of property shows significant relationship only to slave-holding patterns in the member's home county. This, in turn, defines chiefly an attribute that may best be described as representing the embattled constituencies of the moment. The net effect of the association suggests simple concern for the immediate economic interests of the people back home. That none of the other characteristics or circumstances of congressmen is significantly associated with the property-destruction

TABLE 6-5

IMPRESSMENT AND FEDERAL OCCUPATION

	(A) 1 Cong., 3 Sess.		(B) 2 Cong., 1 Sess		(C) 2 Cong., 2 Sess.	
Impress-ment Score	Number of Individuals Assigned Each Score					
	Congress		Congress		Congress	
	Exterior Members	Interior Members	Exterior Members	Interior Members	Exterior Members	Interior Members
0	1	12	3	7 (4)[a]	2	8 (7)[a.]
1	1	11	7	3 (2)	4	2 (1)
2	2	9	3	6	5	3
3	7	1	1	7*(2)	4	6*(2)
4			2	3	3	
5	3	13*	5	2	8	3
6	5*	12	6*	3	7*	2
7	2	7	5	1	13	3
8	4	4	10	1	7	2
9	9	7	10	7	12	4
Median Score	5.60	4.38	5.83	2.57 (3.33)[b]	5.93	2.58 (4.83)[b]
Differ-ence	1.22		3.26 (2.50)[b]		3.35 (1.10)[b]	
% 0-4	32%	43%	31%	65%	28%	58%
% 5-9	68%	57%	69%	35%	72%	42%

*
Median score.

a. N.C. Union Whigs.

b. Without N.C. Union Whigs.

items may be because the problem arose too early for a sorting out of basic attitudes to have been accomplished. It does lead to the speculation, nonetheless, that congressmen saw government-ordered destruction and impressment as altogether distinct issues. For the taking of property in behalf of the Confederate cause, as distinguished from destroying it, produced roll-call patterns in Congress that may be recognized as somewhat similar to those associated with conscription. Except for occupied-territory status, none of the member and constituent characteristics produced more than minor associations with either pro- or anti-impressment views at the time of the original impressment law of March 1863. But the interaction between each of these variables and the issue was stronger during the Second Congress.

Slaveholding and estate values were slightly related to roll calls in this content area, but have been found to be neither a significant explanation nor even a certain influence on roll-call choices. Nevertheless, one must beware of the pitfalls of oversimplification; we cannot say that economic influences were unimportant in determining how legislators voted on impressment, because taking another man's property was obviously an economic issue. We can say, however, that simple wealth or slaveholding, either of the legislator himself or his constituents, was not the economic attribute that would best enable us to predict a congressman's stand. The most apparent determinant here was occupied-territory status. Economic influences on impressment are best displayed, therefore, not by wealth or slaveholding, but by ease of access to property which could be subjected to impressment.

Two other characteristics were also quite important, especially in the Second Congress. Former party affiliation is strongly related and secession position seems even more closely associated with impressment decisions. Whigs were clearly less sacrificing than Democrats, and Unionists were the weak ones compared to Secessionists. Nevertheless, all of the observed distinctions associated with member characteristics generally increased as prospects for Southern success grew dimmer and after the voters had been heard from in the mid-war elections. Certainly none of these factors alone, nor all combined, account fully for the impressment votes of Confederate congressmen; but party, secession stand, and occupied status of home districts do provide powerful predictive bases, especially in the Second Congress.[10]

10. Senators' voting postures on impressment are not found to have been associated significantly with either party or secession stand—or with any individual economic characteristic. Occupied status of home area was, for senators, of some significance but of less importance than on conscription matters. In the closing period of the last Congress, so few senators were voting as Interior men that little confidence may be placed in the indication that they were less sacrificing than their Exterior counterparts.

7 Habeas Corpus

THE power of a civil court to order any arresting authority to bring a prisoner in person for a court hearing was, in the English-speaking world, an almost sacred bulwark against arbitrary imprisonment by agents of the executive branch of government. Having issued such a writ of habeas corpus and having the prisoner before the bench, the courts, furthermore, had the right to decide after a preliminary hearing whether the accused could be further detained or what guarantees should be required that he would appear for trial. Some offenses justified refusal to release an accused person on any terms because, for one reason, the severity of possible punishment would probably impel the defendant to flee and avoid the jeopardy of trial at any cost in forfeited bond. The court was to decide not only whether the evidence was adequate to justify holding the accused but also whether the accused could reasonably be expected to appear for trial upon the posting of bond in an amount set by the court. Pursuant to the basic proposition that a man was innocent until proved guilty, pre-trial imprisonment was to be tolerated only after a civil court concluded that detention was absolutely necessary to guarantee appearance for trial or to protect society from a dangerous individual.

Calamitous circumstances, including war, might temporarily incapacitate civil courts and render issuance of writs of habeas corpus simply impossible. At such times, the arresting authority might be a military commander who was too busily engaged in a campaign to make an immediate and proper reply to a writ of habeas corpus requiring presentation of some civilian held in custody on suspicion of espionage or other activity endangering the operations. Such consequences of war, in simple common sense, impeded the historic and hallowed right to be free from arbitrary arrest and imprisonment. The Confederate Congress was properly aware of these facts of war and acquiesced for a time in the inevitable erosion of civil rights at certain times and places.

Legislative authorization of suspension of the writ of habeas corpus, however, was another matter entirely. If nothing else, such action was almost certainly an acknowledgment that serious internal opposition existed and that some judges would not render decisions acceptable to the executive authority. No amount of proper parliamentary language really obscured this essential point, for a judge was not compelled to order release of a person accused of a crime; if he did order release, it was a conscious and purposeful decision that the action of the detaining official was wrong and ought to be overruled. It could be interpreted as a vote of no confidence in the Confederacy. If a judge took the same view of public necessity as did the arresting authority, he could order the prisoner held for trial. Thus the real rub was simple: state judges increasingly took a very different viewpoint from that of the war-beleaguered chief executive and his military or civil agents. President Davis therefore needed, for himself and for his generals, power to seize and hold individuals whom civil courts would have released.

This was not mere caprice on Davis's part. Many of the released men were conscripts avoiding military service by finding sympathetic judges who thought conscription unconstitutional. It was a serious problem, and Davis was rightly concerned. As Senator Albert G. Brown of Mississippi remarked at the end of the crisis year of 1863, "the country should not be lost because of the opinion of every petty judge, authorized to issue a *habeas corpus.*" Pragmatically, he added that "it would be bad to have it said, after we were in our graves, that our liberty had been lost whilst we were struggling over petty constitutional questions." [1]

Martial law was a concept that complicated habeas corpus issues. The two were distinct in theory but difficult to disentangle in practice. The Confederate Congress in its first general enactment on the subject failed signally to clarify the distinction and by ambiguous language promoted a lasting confusion. Military, or martial, law applied to men in military service. Forms of procedure, agencies of decision, and types of punishment might, and usually did, differ significantly from those of civil courts. The possible jeopardy to an entire military unit from an offense by one of its members was so much greater than a civil body's probable jeopardy from one offender that the protection thrown about the accused was sharply reduced under martial law. Conviction, for example, was customarily by majority vote of a court-martial board and not by the unanimous agreement commonly required of a civil jury. The basic concept that a society must guard its general security against individual actions was not different; only the vastly more hazardous existence of a military unit was being acknowledged in this curtailment of an accused's chances of avoiding conviction. It was not primarily this aspect of martial law, however, that concerned the Confederate Congress.

In a theatre of war, civil government may be impossible to maintain, and the only law and order becomes that provided by the occupying

1. "Proceedings," L, 133.

military authority. In this case, martial law may have to be applied to the civilians of the area, and such action obviates the familiar habeas corpus procedures—producing the appearance of a suspension of the writ of habeas corpus when, in fact, the whole civil court system is no longer functioning and must therefore be supplanted by military courts. The necessity for martial law in such cases is obvious.

On the other hand, deliberate legislative approval of martial law where civil courts are functioning is of necessity an acknowledgment that these courts are inadequate, impotent, or untrustworthy. The use of military personnel as additional police or as temporary custodians of arrested persons is not martial law. Nor, for that matter, is the suspension of habeas corpus privileges an approval of martial law as long as accused persons are eventually tried in civil courts under all of the civil procedural guarantees. The Confederate Congress never intentionally authorized the supplanting of civil by martial law other than by tacitly recognizing that a commanding general had to place the security of his command above the civil rights of those unfortunate individuals found within his theatre of operations. Some congressmen even denied that the constitution of the Confederacy contemplated such a thing as the application of martial law to civilians, and went so far as to agree "that martial law . . . [was] unknown to the Constitution," and was applicable only to the armed forces, in any case.[2]

In the North, President Lincoln and his generals were plagued by parallel problems, but they were often concerned with areas in which admittedly "disloyal" people resided and "disloyal" judges were not unheard of. This was self-evidently the case in an ever-growing area of occupation and it was probably true of a large border-state zone. Disloyalty was also alleged to exist even farther north in terms of "copperheadism." In contrast, Confederate jurisdiction, with rare exceptions, was confined to an area in which all civil authorities were presumably loyal, a presumption that ought to have become increasingly justifiable as the zone of effective control shrank. Martial law over any extended area, therefore, would proclaim that entire communities remained in the Confederacy only through the persuasions of force. This is an obvious implication, and yet one which Confederates usually managed to ignore. The import of suspension of the writ of habeas corpus (as opposed to the establishment of martial law) was somewhat more easily disguised; but nonetheless, the fundamental assumption was that state courts or even Confederate civil courts were unwilling to curtail civil rights to the extent that President Davis and the Congress considered to be

2. *Journal of the Confederate Congress*, II, 325–326, 382, 394–396.

necessary for survival of the fledgling nation. It is not surprising that the question produced acrimonious and prolonged debate, or that suspension of the writ of habeas corpus was authorized for periods totaling only sixteen months of the four-year war. In a sense, this issue came as close as any confronted by the Congress to posing the ultimate question: exactly how much sacrifice should be made to support Confederate victory and independence?

Roll-Call Issues

Jefferson Davis evidently was not eager to possess the power of suspension, and he approached it gingerly, realizing both its necessity and its potential for mischief. In February 1862, he sought to achieve the desired end by working through the states. At Davis's request, Attorney General Thomas Bragg wrote to Governor John Letcher of Virginia (where suspension was thought to be most needed) to inquire whether a declaration of martial law could not be made by state authority. "It is a delicate power to be exercised by the President," wrote Bragg, with what proved to be monumental understatement. But the reply was negative,[3] and it became necessary to turn to Congress. On February 27, 1862, two days after Bragg's inquiry, Congress passed the first measure specifically authorizing President Davis to suspend habeas corpus privileges and applying it to places in danger of attack.

The Congress of the Confederate States of America do enact, That during the present invasion of the Confederate States, the President shall have power to suspend the privilege of the writ of *habeas corpus* in such cities, towns and military districts as shall, in his judgment, be in such danger of attack by the enemy as to require the declaration of martial law for their effective defence.

This, the entire text of the far-reaching legislation, placed heavy reliance upon Davis's judgment and introduced immediate confusion between suspension of the writ and martial law. The misunderstanding was increased when, on the same day, Davis proclaimed "that martial law is extended over the cities of Norfolk and Portsmouth and the surrounding country to the distance of 10 miles from said cities, and all civil jurisdiction and the privilege of the writ of *habeas corpus* are hereby declared to be suspended within the limits aforesaid." One can chart the growing threat posed by Union General McClellan's campaign on the peninsula by the similar proclamations which followed. Within a short time, martial law was declared and habeas corpus suspended in

3. Bragg to Letcher, February 24, 1862, and J. R. Tucker to Letcher, February 25, 1862, in Executive Papers, 1860–1865, Archives Branch, Virginia State Library, Richmond, Va.

Richmond, Petersburg, and a number of eastern Virginia counties. Other areas also were put under the ban. A threat in Appalachia was countered by suspension of the writ in the Department of East Tennessee and in some of the western counties of Virginia, where Unionists were dangerously numerous. Much of South Carolina was also included because of Federal operations along the coast.[4]

In April 1862, Congress reacted to such proclamations by limiting suspension to cases of arrest made by Confederate authorities for offenses against Confederate law, thereby excluding from Davis's control all civil and criminal jurisdiction of state courts. Furthermore, the suspension power was to extend only thirty days into the next session of Congress. It is clear that martial law was not at all what most congressmen had intended, and that, as in the case of conscription, its full implications were not understood until after the law was passed.

It is not surprising that the following session of Congress, meeting in August 1862, devoted much discussion, some of it rather heated, to habeas corpus and the related questions of martial law and provost marshal regulations—the last of which seemed to establish a general martial law regardless of what Congress had done about habeas corpus. Representative William P. Chilton of Alabama thought that "if it were true that the President had a right to declare martial law at his discretion, he was absolutely and essentially a dictator." Such statements made it clear that congressmen were disillusioned with the use of martial law, and many of them felt the same way about habeas corpus suspension. Oldham of Texas complained that the military commander had declared martial law in his state, "where a Yankee had not set foot since the war," and went on to object that he, a "free citizen, was not allowed to go from here [Richmond] to North Carolina without going to the Provost Marshal's office and getting a pass like a free negro." Senator John W. Lewis of Georgia echoed those very words a month later, when he outlined the various provost marshal's procedures he would have to follow simply to go home when Congress adjourned, and concluded that "it does not seem to me either just or proper that I cannot be permitted to go from this city to my home without obtaining a pass like a negro." Oldham further pointed out that the position of provost marshal was unknown to Confederate law, yet such persons had been

4. James M. Matthews, editor, *The Statutes at Large of the Confederate States of America, Commencing with the First Session of the First Congress: 1862* . . . (Richmond: R. M. Smith, 1862), p. 1; *Messages*, I, 219–227. These proclamations illustrate that initially Davis, like Congress, was either confused or at least unconcerned about the difference between martial law and the suspension of habeas corpus.

administering the martial law which he supposed was not at all authorized by the suspension of the writ of habeas corpus.[5]

As a result of such complaints, an effort was made to distinguish between martial law and suspension of the writ. The distinction was made clear in a House committee report. Martial law was military law, and "to suspend that writ is not to establish martial law with its summary proceedings and absolute power."[6] But after much discussion and disagreement between houses about how best to allow extraordinary power without permitting abuse, the Congress in October of 1862 merely reenacted the first habeas corpus suspension act, without the awkward reference to martial law, for a period ending thirty days after the start of the next congressional session.

When the First Congress reassembled for its Third Session in January 1863, it was so heedful of the rising clamor against alleged tyranny by Confederate authorities that it allowed the suspension authorization to lapse and remain almost a dead issue. Efforts in the House to re-enact the October 1862 law met swift rejection. In the election year of 1863, there was no further congressional authorization for suspension. The summer news from Gettysburg and Vicksburg, followed by the unexpected debacle at Chattanooga in November, brought the year to such a sobering conclusion for Confederates, however, that the last session of the First Congress encountered renewed habeas corpus problems as soon as it assembled in December.

Committee study of the matter brought no action until President Davis, on February 3, 1864, formally requested permission to suspend the writ again. His message, in effect, candidly admitted that vast areas were coerced to remain in the Confederacy and that, as far as Davis was concerned, part of the price of victory would be the suppression of dissent. "Public meetings have been held, in some of which a treasonable design is masked by a pretense of devotion to State sovereignty, and in others is openly avowed. Conventions are advocated with the pretended object of redressing grievances." Secret associations were being created and prominent men allegedly advocated submission to Union subjugation. People were giving information to the enemy and, when arrested, were often released. Plots were supposedly being laid to release Union prisoners in Richmond. "Spies are continually coming and going in our midst," Davis further complained, and he offered "important information of secret movement among the negroes" in the hope of adding zest to congressional reaction. The bugbear was also threatening, as Davis re-

5. "Proceedings," XLV, 226, 248–249; XLVII, 47, 86.
6. *Journal of the Confederate Congress*, V, 374–375.

ported "that [Benjamin F.] Butler is perfecting some deep-laid scheme." State judges were releasing great numbers of men properly subject to conscription, as "civil process has been brought to bear with disastrous efficiency upon the Army." If unchecked, "desertion, already a frightful evil, will become the order of the day." Habeas corpus procedure as a barrier to effective conscription was undoubtedly in the forefront of the President's mind because manpower needs were becoming desperate, and Davis felt keenly the need to remove all judicial impediments. With righteous indignation, he exclaimed, "Must these evils be endured?" He closed his melodramatic message by minimizing the perils of suspending the writ. "Loyal citizens will not feel danger, and the disloyal must be made to fear it." [7]

Within a few days, the new legislation was ready for the President's signature. Again an expiration date was set: July 31, 1864. Despite the speed of the enactment, however, elaborate provisions to avoid abuse were contained in the law, which explicitly stated that the right of suspension was "vested solely in the Congress, which is the exclusive judge of the necessity of such suspension." Furthermore, the law carefully circumscribed the suspension, limiting it to cases such as "treason or treasonable efforts or combinations to subvert the Government of the Confederate States," "attempts to incite servile insurrection," desertion, espionage, several kinds of conspiracies, and sabotage of "any bridge or railroad, or telegraphic line of communication . . . [or] the vessels or arms, or munitions of war, or arsenals, foundries, workshops or other property of the Confederate States." In addition, any arrest under this act was to be investigated so that persons improperly held could be released.[8] The elaborateness of the new legislation is a good indicator of congressional recoil from such sweeping provisions as in the initial suspension in early 1862.

Even so, indignation about this February 1864 law, passed at a "lame duck" session, was highly vocal. The newly elected Congress, meeting in its first session the following May, was therefore urged by some representatives to repeal the existing legislation immediately. Such a one was the ever-vocal Foote of Tennessee, who contended that "the disloyalty which the [habeas corpus] act was intended to fight was a phantom, a myth, a vapour; the mirage arising from a diseased eye." He was seconded by John P. Murray, also of Tennessee, who confessed himself unable to understand "that political doctrine that teaches that

---

7. *Messages*, I, 395–400.

8. James M. Matthews, editor, *The Statutes at Large of the Confederate States of America. Passed at the Fourth Session of the First Congress: 1863-4* . . . (Richmond: R. M. Smith, 1864), pp. 187–189.

in order to get liberty you must first lose it." [9] A fact hard to overlook, nevertheless, was that congressmen were sitting in a perilous locale, for General Grant's trap was slowly but surely closing its jaws. The logic of danger therefore asserted itself; repeal was staved off and the President's opinion sought by resolution of the House of Representatives on May 14. Of course Davis was strongly opposed to ending his special authority, but discretion prevented an administration bid for a new law and the suspension authority expired as scheduled at the end of July 1864. Very extensive argument and counter-argument, together with many revealing roll calls, were nonetheless produced in this First Session of the Second Congress by the habeas corpus issue.

President Davis did request a new suspension measure two days after the Second Session convened in November 1864. Richmond was almost isolated by this time, Sherman was about to march from Atlanta to the sea, and no Confederate army east of the Mississippi appeared to have any promising prospects. The day after the session opened, Lincoln was re-elected, and to many this must have been the final blow. Davis made open reference to the resulting defeatism sweeping much of Appalachian Confederate territory—referring to it in terms of "a dangerous conspiracy . . . which it is found impracticable to suppress by the ordinary course of law." [10] The House debated and amended an administration measure similar to the 1864 law, and in March finally passed it by a close vote. The Senate emasculated the bill by authorizing state courts to use the writ in all cases arising out of liability to military conscription. Since for many months the primary purpose for discontinuing habeas corpus had been to enforce draft laws against general public opinion and state judicial interference, the Senate amendment could not be acceptable to the House majority. As Lee prepared to abandon Richmond, a final plea from Davis ("the time has arrived when the suspension of the writ is not simply advisable and expedient, but almost indispensable" [11]) drove sweeping suspension through the House but not through the Senate, providing a last division of the houses on the subject of habeas corpus.

Association of Member Characteristics with Roll-Call Voting Behavior

Former Party Affiliation

One decidedly influential element in a congressman's decisions about sacrificing habeas corpus to the god of war was his former political

---

9. "Proceedings," LI, 104, 125. Foote's mention of a "diseased eye" was an oblique and slashing reference to Davis, who labored under the handicap of partial blindness.

10. *Messages*, I, 498.

11. *Ibid.*, p. 548.

TABLE 7-1

HABEAS CORPUS AND FORMER PARTY

(A)
1 Cong., 4 Sess.

Habeas Corpus Scale Position	Number of Individuals Assigned Each Position			
	Senate		Interior Senators	
	Democrat	Whig	Democrat	Whig
0	2	1	2	1
1	2	3*	1	2*
2	1		1	
3	3	1	2*	1
4	3*		1	
5	2	1		
6	2		1	
7	3	1	1	
Median Position	3.33	0.83	2.25	0.50
Difference	2.50		1.75	
% 0-3	44%	71%	67%	100%
% 4-7	56%	29%	33%	0%

*
Median position.

TABLE 7-1--<u>Continued</u>

(B)
2 Cong., 1 Sess.

Habeas Corpus Scale Position	Number of Individuals Assigned Each Position			
	House		Interior Representatives	
	Democrat	Whig	Democrat	Whig
0	1	9 (5)[a]		7*(5)[a]
1	3	2 (2)	2	2 (2)
2	2	4 (1)	1	2 (1)
3	6	5*(1)	3	1 (1)
4	14*	10	8*	1
5	9	5	2	1
Median Position	3.39	2.50 (3.20)[b]	3.25	0.00 (1.50)[b]
Difference	0.89 (0.19)[b]		3.25 (1.75)[b]	
% 0-2	17%	43%	19%	79%
% 3-5	83%	57%	81%	21%

*Median position.

a. N.C. Union Whigs.

b. Without N.C. Union Whigs.

TABLE 7-1--Continued

(C)
2 Cong., 2 Sess., Nov.-Feb.

Habeas Corpus Score	Number of Individuals Assigned Each Score			
	House		Interior Representatives[a]	
	Democrat	Whig	Democrat	Whig
0	9	17*(7)[b]	6	11*(7)[b]
1	3	2	2	
2	3	1	1	1
3	1	3 (1)	1	1 (1)
4			*	
5	2		1	
6		1		
7	2			
8		3		
9	24*	6	9	2
Median Score	8.08	-0.03 (1.50)[c]	3.50	-0.32 (-0.13)[c]
Difference	8.11 (6.58)[c]		3.82 (3.63)[c]	
% 0-4	36%	70%	50%	87%
% 5-9	64%	30%	50%	13%

*
 Median score.

a. Interior at least until the beginning of the Second Session.

b. N.C. Union Whigs.

c. Without N.C. Union Whigs.

176

TABLE 7-1--Continued

(D)
2 Cong., 2 Sess., Feb.-Mar.

Habeas Corpus Score	Number of Individuals Assigned Each Score			
	House		Interior Representatives[a]	
	Democrat	Whig	Democrat	Whig
0	3	10 (7)[b]	3	7*(7)[b]
1	3	4*(1)	2	2 (1)
2	2	2	1	
3	3	2 (1)	1	1 (1)
4			*	
5	3		1	
6	2			
7	2*	2	1	1
8	3	1		1
9	12	5	5	
Median Score	6.25	0.75 (2.50)[c]	3.50	-0.14 (6.50)[c]
Difference	5.50 (3.75)[c]		3.64 (3.00)[c]	
% 0-4	33%	69%	50%	83%
% 5-9	67%	31%	50%	17%

*Median score.

a. Interior at least until the beginning of the Second Session.

b. N.C. Union Whigs.

c. Without N.C. Union Whigs.

TABLE 7-1--<u>Continued</u>

(E)
2 Cong., 2 Sess., Feb.-Mar.

Habeas Corpus Scale Position	Number of Individuals Assigned Each Position			
	House		Interior Representatives[a]	
	Democrat	Whig	Democrat	Whig
0	8	14 (9)[b]	8	10* (9)[b]
1	1	4*		
2	3	2	1*	
3	5*	1	2	
4	5	4	2	
5	11	3	4	2
Median Position	2.90	0.00 (1.25)[c]	1.50	-0.40 (4.25)[c]
Difference	2.90 (1.65)[c]		1.90 (2.75)[c]	
% 0-2	36%	71%	53%	83%
% 3-5	64%	29%	47%	17%

* Median position.

a. Interior at least until the beginning of the Second Session.

b. N.C. Union Whigs.

c. Without N.C. Union Whigs.

affiliation. It was not, however, in the initial legislation nor its renewal that distinctions between Democrats and Whigs appeared. The original law, that of February 1862, came in response to such obvious military needs and with so little awareness of the implications that the roll-call record is slight and distinctions between groups insignificant. Even the adjustments made at the end of this First Session furnish no evidence of relation between party and issue. The more extended debate in the Second Session culminated only in simple re-enactment of the principles of the earlier law, and the several roll calls involved produced neither performance scores nor scale positions that suggest more than a slight distinction based on party. This same situation continued through the Third Session, in which few votes were taken during the notably unsuccessful efforts to revive suspension legislation.

In the Fourth Session, when Congress did renew suspension, House roll calls were inadequate for an appraisal, but Senate divisions exposed an emerging tendency for Whigs to be more doubtful about suspension than Democrats. Part A of Table 7–1 illustrates the essentially negative stance of the handful of Whig senators, and the unanimous opposition of those who were from Interior zones. By contrast, Democratic Interior senators were divided on habeas corpus, while those from the Exterior were very heavily weighted on the positive side of the suspension proposal.

The lower House of the Second Congress also revealed far greater willingness on the part of Democrats to suspend the writ. Part B of Table 7–1 refers to the First Session, in which a significant party differential appears for the entire House membership and a very sharp distinction is uncovered among the Interior representatives, within a narrow range of possible scale positions. The behavior of the First Session was continued, with increased divergence, in the Second. Supporting evidence may be found in the earlier part of the latter session, which contains so many divisions relating to habeas corpus that it provides one of the few instances of solidly based agreement scores coming from a single-subject content area. This measurement of antagonism between former Whigs and former Democrats points to a sharp disagreement along party lines. The reason for these agreement-score indications becomes obvious when habeas corpus scores and scale positions are examined.

For the entire House in the earlier portion of the last session (Table 7–1C), some men from each party background are assigned to both extremes and most score levels between, but the very large difference between medians heavily underlines the growing distinction based on previous party membership The disparity between medians approaches maximum possibility—and yet, because of extreme polarization, nine

Democrats may be found assigned to the lowest level, where more than half of the Whigs are located, while six Whigs are placed at the highest level with the majority of the Democrats. For only Interior representatives the difference between medians narrows simply because the bulk of the most determined Democrats and almost all of the like-minded Whigs have been excluded because of their Exterior status. Within this Interior group, the Democrats are seen to have been drawn almost equally to the extremes, but the Whigs continued to be drawn sharply in the direction of resistance to suspension. Excellent scale sets of roll calls on habeas corpus in both House and Senate of this session (not shown here) similarly reflect the sharp focus Confederate congressmen had achieved on this issue. It is apparent that, by November 1864, they shared a very definite concept about the questions relating to suspension and that each perceived his own position along the scale and consistently took his stand there. The members are well distributed among the scale positions, and the party-related responses of representatives (though not of senators) are apparent in differences between medians of former Democrats and Whigs for the House or just the Interior representatives. It is evident, however, that other influences besides those associated with former party affiliation were effectively at work.

The last stages of the habeas corpus issue, reflected in Table 7-1 D and E, produced no significant arresting, let alone reversal, of the trend observed in the earlier part of the session. Without the votes of their Exterior colleagues, former Whigs (almost all North Carolinians, by this late date) were virtually at the point of unanimity on the weakest scale position. It is obvious that the suspension of the writ of habeas corpus created party distinctions greater than those occasioned by the conscription or impressment issues.

Position on Secession

A congressman's position during the secession crisis of 1860–61 was even more emphatically related to his attitude toward suspension of the writ of habeas corpus than was previous party affiliation. There are exceptions to this general pattern, usually involving only senators or the Interior members at a given time, but comparing Secessionists with Unionists ordinarily yields greater differentials than contrasting Democrats and Whigs. Among the Interior representatives, position on secession was a distinctly better predictor for habeas corpus positions than was party.

In the Second Session of the First Congress, a scale set (not shown) disclosed a slightly greater willingness to sacrifice habeas corpus among Secessionists than among Unionists in the House of Representatives—a year earlier than a distinction between party groups could be discerned in the Senate. By the Fourth Session, when party differences are observable in the Senate, secession position on performance scores (not shown) is found to be similar to party pattern for the Interior senators alone, but relatively insignificant for the entire Senate. This latter finding is accurate despite a deceptively large difference between median scores for Secessionists and Unionists, since senators were assigned to levels that polarized both groups with about half at each extremity. The small numbers involved and this nearly-equal balance mean that the divergence between median levels could have been radically different if there had been change in only one senator's performance score. For the Interior senators, on the other hand, if one score had been different, the actual size of the difference between medians could still be altered somewhat without eliminating a substantial disparity based on secession position. The scale set for this Fourth Session Senate (Table 7-2A) reinforces the inferences drawn from the performance scores.

The habeas corpus issue in the First Session of the Second Congress could be observed only in the House (Table 7-2B). The Secessionist-Unionist antagonism was slightly stronger than party antagonism (as seen in Table 7-1B), although a subset of Interior members showed less antagonism than on the basis of party.

Nevertheless, the importance of secession background as a divisive force on the habeas corpus issue is illustrated by the agreement score for the Second Session of the Second Congress. Here Secessionists and Unionists were pitted against each other to such an extent that they produce an agreement level well into the minus range (−36); and, as indicated in Chapters 2 and 3, such agreement scores are extraordinary for the Confederate Congress. When scale positions (not shown) and performance scores are examined in this final session of Congress (Table 7-2C), medians again show greater differences based on secession position than they did on party, with the contrasts between antagonists being greater than usually found on other topics as they approach the maximum possible. Even though the findings are more remarkable, they are generally congruent with the patterns produced by party analysis of habeas corpus because of the close relationship of Unionism with Whiggery and Secessionism with Democracy.[12]

12. The limited differences between these two tables, and between other parallel party-secession tables, arise from the relatively few Secession Whig or Union Democrat instances (about 20 percent of those for whom both characteristics are known) together with the fact that either party or secession stand is unknown for some members. Consequently, the observably greater predictive ability of secession stand is enhanced in significance by arising from so few opportunities. Obviously, if every voting member had been either a Secessionist Democrat or a Unionist Whig, no basis for comparing the influence of party with that of secession stand could exist.

TABLE 7-2

HABEAS CORPUS AND STAND ON SECESSION

(A)

1 Cong., 4 Sess.

Habeas Corpus Scale Position	Number of Individuals Assigned Each Position			
	Senate		Interior Senators	
	Secessionist	Unionist	Secessionist	Unionist
0	2	1	2	1
1	1	4		3*
2				
3	3	1*	2*	1
4	1*	2		1
5	2	1		
6	1	1	1	
7	3	1	1	
Median Position	3.50	2.50	2.50	0.67
Difference	1.00		1.83	
% 0-3	46%	55%	67%	83%
% 4-7	54%	45%	33%	17%

*
Median position.

182

TABLE 7-2--<u>Continued</u>

(B)
2 Cong., 1 Sess.

Habeas Corpus Scale Position	Number of Individuals Assigned Each Position			
	House		Interior Representatives	
	Secessionist	Unionist	Secessionist	Unionist
0	1	9 (5)[a]	1	7 (5)[a]
1	2	2 (2)	2	2*(2)
2	2	3 (1)	2	1 (1)
3	5	4*(1)	2	1 (1)
4	14*	10	9*	3
5	8	3	2	2
Median Position	3.43	2.38 (3.20)[b]	3.22	0.50 (3.50)[b]
Difference		1.05 (0.23)[b]		2.72 (0.28)[b]
% 0-2	16%	45%	28%	63%
% 3-5	84%	55%	72%	38%

*Median position.

a. N.C. Union Whigs.

b. Without N.C. Union Whigs.

TABLE 7-2--Continued

(C)
2 Cong., 2 Sess., Nov.-Feb.

| Habeas Corpus Score | Number of Individuals Assigned Each Score | | | |
| | House | | Interior Representatives[a] | |
	Secessionist	Unionist	Secessionist	Unionist
0	6	20*(7)[b]	5	14*(7)[b]
1	1	4	1	1
2	3		2	
3	1	3 (1)	1	1 (1)
4	1		1	
5	3		2*	
6				
7	2		1	
8	1			
9	22*	6	9	1
Median Score	8.09	-0.18 (-0.04)[c]	4.50	-0.39 (-0.36)[c]
Difference	8.27 (8.13)[c]		4.89 (4.86)[c]	
% 0-4	30%	82%	45%	94%
% 5-9	70%	18%	55%	6%

*
Median score.

a. Interior at least until the beginning of the Second Session.

b. N.C. Union Whigs.

c. Without N.C. Union Whigs.

TABLE 7-2--Continued

(D)
2 Cong., 2 Sess., Feb.-Mar.

Habeas Corpus Score	Number of Individuals Assigned Each Score			
	House		Interior Representatives[a]	
	Secessionist	Unionist	Secessionist	Unionist
0	3	12* (7)[b]	3	9* (7)[b]
1	4	4 (1)	3	2 (1)
2	1	1		
3	3	2 (1)	2*	1 (1)
4				
5	1	2	1	
6	2			
7	3*		1	
8	1	1		
9	13	1	5	
Median Score	6.50	-0.04 (0.67)[c]	2.75	-0.33 (-0.25)[c]
Difference	6.54 (5.83)[c]		3.08 (3.00)[c]	
% 0-4	35%	83%	53%	100%
% 5-9	65%	17%	47%	0%

*Median score.

a. Interior at least until the beginning of the Second Session.

b. N.C. Union Whigs.

c. Without N.C. Union Whigs.

TABLE 7-2--Continued

(E)

2 Cong., 2 Sess., Feb.-Mar.

Habeas Corpus Scale Position	Number of Individuals Assigned Each Position			
	House		Interior Representatives[a]	
	Secessionist	Unionist	Secessionist	Unionist
0	6	17*(9)[b]	6	13*(9)[b]
1	3	3	2	
2	2	2	1*	
3	5	2	3	
4	4*	1	2	
5	13		4	
Median Position	3.13	-0.26 (0.00)[c]	2.00	-0.50 (-0.50)[c]
Difference	3.39 (3.13)[c]		2.50 (2.50)[c]	
% 0-2	33%	88%	50%	100%
% 3-5	67%	12%	50%	0%

*Median position.

a. Interior at least until the beginning of the Second Session.

b. N.C. Union Whigs.

c. Without N.C. Union Whigs.

186

The final votes on habeas corpus in the House again show the great significance of secession position among the entire House membership, although indicators are not as striking within Interior delegations alone. The most evident point of difference to note here is that once more secession stand was apparently more influential than party, for while there were some Whigs who could remain extremely sacrificing on habeas corpus up to the very end of the war (Table 7–1D and E) there were almost no such sacrificing Unionists (Table 7–2D and E). For example, eight Whigs are assigned performance scores of 7, 8, or 9 (compared to two Unionists), and eight are placed in the strongest half of the corresponding scale (compared with only three Unionists).

The elections of 1863 evidently aided in polarizing congressional opinions about the sacrifices being demanded of Confederate citizens. Habeas corpus was an especially easy place to take a defensive stand because of its historic sanctity. Since by 1864 the primary interest of the administration in having the writ suspended was to facilitate draft enforcement, opponents of effective conscription who were not willing to attack it directly could and evidently did find a better line of defense on the habeas corpus issue. Defeatism and common sense questions about the justification for further sacrifices also underlay much of the support for maintaining privileges under habeas corpus proceedings. And those who were most affected by defeatism were apparently the ones who had not favored an independent Confederacy in the first place. Although these Unionists had also been Whigs in the great majority of instances, it was Unionism more than former party affiliation that was associated with the most measurable extremes of antisacrificing attitudes about civil rights as opposed to the war effort.

Slaveholding

The personal economic standing of Confederate congressmen, whether measured in slaveholding or value of estate, is not a useful predictor for positions taken on habeas corpus issues. There are distinctions between slaveholding categories, to be sure, but no consistently clear relationship is observable. The curvilinear pattern noted in the Impressment chapter is again found in relation to habeas corpus: stronger scores at the lower and upper ranges of slaveholding than in the middle category. This is due simply to the fact that the middle range of slaveownership included a hard core of extremists on the habeas corpus question, most of whom were Union Whigs, whose very low scores or weak positions brought to notably lower levels the medians for this category. This same group helps to account for the frequency of the bow-shaped pattern in this and other content areas.

TABLE 7-3

HABEAS CORPUS AND SLAVEHOLDING

(A)
2 Cong., 2 Sess., Nov.-Feb.

Habeas Corpus Score	Number of Individuals Assigned Each Score				
	Congress				
	Absolute Slaveholding[a]				
	0	1	2	3	4
0	4	10	10	3	4
1		1		5	1
2		1	3*		
3		1	1	1	1
4	1	1		*	1
5	*	1	2	1	2
6		1			2
7	1	2*		1	2*
8		2			1
9	4	13	6	7	9

*
Median score.

a. Absolute Slaveholding:
   0 = No slaves
   1 = 1-9 slaves
   2 = 10-19 slaves
   3 = 20-49 slaves
   4 = 50 or more slaves

TABLE 7-3--Continued

(B)
1 Cong., 2 Sess.

Habeas Corpus Score	Number of Individuals Assigned Each Score					
	Slaveholding Pattern of Congressman's County					
	House			Interior Representatives		
	Size of Slaveholdings			Size of Slaveholdings		
	Small	Middle	Large	Small	Middle	Large
0	3	4	4	1	4	3
1		2	5		2	4
2		2	1		2	
3	2	2			2	
4		2*	*		1*	
5	1	1			1	
6	2		2	1		2*
7	4	3	3	3	3	3
8	6*	5	3	4*	4	3
9	7	2	2	5	2	2
Median Score	7.08	3.75	3.50	7.50	3.50	5.75
Difference	3.33 0.25			4.00 2.25		
	3.58			1.75		
% 0-4	20%	52%	50%	7%	52%	41%
% 5-9	80%	48%	50%	93%	48%	59%

*
Median score.

Very large slaveholders appear to have shifted their relative standing between the First and Second Congresses, displaying slightly less than average support in the First but more than average in the Second. It is possible that this reversal resulted from the large slaveholders' realization of how much they stood to lose in the impending disaster, together with a possible desire to enforce conscription in order to avoid a draft of slaves. It is more likely, however, that the difference arose from the fact that a small but significant hard core of men of relatively modest means (compared to other congressmen) were elected to the Second Congress by constituents who resented central government impositions. In contrast to the weaker stance taken by the less affluent newcomers, the large slaveowners occupied a higher range of scores. But the most impressive aspect of comparison of slaveholding with either performance scores or scale positions is not the extremely fragile thread of difference based on such trivial considerations; rather, it is the strong proof that other forces were dominant. In a notable proportion of the cross-tabulations, each of the five categories of slaveholding are represented in both high and low ranges. Frequently a cluster of legislators assigned the highest one or two scores is balanced by another cluster of congressmen at the lowest one or two scores. Table 7–3A is an excellent example of such polarization in the habeas corpus scores in the Second Session of the Second Congress. Of the ten men who owned no slaves, eight are equally divided between the most extreme levels of performance. In category 1, ten men scoring 0 are balanced by thirteen scoring at the opposite pole, and similar observations can be made for the other categories. No matter what a member's slaveowning status, therefore, he tended to take an extreme view of habeas corpus during the Second Congress. Of the 106 congressmen scored in Table 7–3A, 66 percent are scored at either the 0 or 9 levels. Such sharp polarization in all categories of a member attribute is rarely encountered, and it provides excellent evidence that this one member characteristic cannot be pointed to as a possible force in determining habeas corpus attitudes.

The slaveholding characteristics of a representative's home county appear to offer equally little, if any, clue to his habeas corpus stand. The small slaveholding category of districts is so nearly equivalent to Exterior districts by the time suspension of the writ became a serious issue that one classification almost masks the other. When Exterior districts are not included in the cross-tabulation, some association still remains, but not enough to suggest any important causal relationship. Party, secession stand, and military jeopardy seem better explanations for the roll-call behavior involved here. In the Second Session of the First Congress, for example, Interior small slaveholdings are associated more strongly with high scores on habeas corpus suspension than are middle or large slaveholdings, but the cluster of high-scoring representatives from such districts turn out to be largely Democrats or Secessionists or both (Table 7-3B). Moreover, several represented areas were so endangered that these men became Exterior delegates by the next session of Congress.

Value of Estate

For the purpose of placing him among his fellows in Congress, the value of a legislator's estate was so often comparable (at least roughly) to his slaveholding status that one would expect habeas corpus questions to bear similar relations to estate as to slaveholding. Although a wide variety of patterns could be expected when examining groups which often contain but few individuals, the arcuate model is one of those which emerges again here, as illustrated in Table 7-4A and B. In Part A, it may be observed that in the Second Session of the Second Congress, House members in the middle category (2) of absolute estate value have the lowest median score, that the two flanking categories have somewhat higher levels, and the two extreme categories have the highest levels— producing a curve running through the median positions. Inferences from this pattern are very risky, for several reasons. For one thing, the extensive polarization observed for slaveholding is repeated (except in category 4), with 70 percent of the members who could be scored being assigned 0 or 9; the median is therefore very volatile in each column and could be drawn far in either direction by the shift of only a few assignments.[13] Moreover, a better explanation than the possibility of economic influence is that, within category 2 of estate value, every one of the eight men on the 0 level were Unionist (seven also having been Whigs), while nine of the ten men in the 9 level had been Secessionists or of unknown stand on secession, leaving only one known Unionist in that highest level—a Democrat from the Exterior state of Missouri. These same ten legislators in the 9 level of category 2 were all Democrats or of unknown party affiliation except for a lone Whig from the Exterior state of Kentucky.

A scale set from the last weeks of the Confederate House (Table 7-4B) also shows the familiar arching pattern, with category 2 of absolute estate value displaying the lowest median scale position. Again, some medians

13. In the category 0 column, for example, if two men were transferred to the 0 score level, the median would move from its present 7 level all the way to 0. And in category 2, the presently established median exactly between the 2 and 3 levels would be changed all the way to 7 by placing any two of the men assigned to the lower positions at the 7 level or higher.

TABLE 7-4

HABEAS CORPUS AND WEALTH

(A)
2 Cong., 2 Sess., Nov.-Feb.

Habeas Corpus Score	Number of Individuals Assigned Each Score				
	House				
	Absolute Estate[a]				
	0	1	2	3	4
0	6	5	8	8	
1		1	2	3	
2		1	2*	1	
3		1	1	1	1
4		1*		*	
5	1			1	1
6		1			
7	1*		1	1	1
8	1	1		1	
9	6	5	10	10	4*

(B)
2 Cong., 2 Sess., Feb.-Mar.

Habeas Corpus Scale Position	Number of Individuals Assigned Each Position				
	House				
	Absolute Estate[a]				
	0	1	2	3	4
0	4	5	11*	3	1
1		1	1	5	
2		1*	1	3*	1
3	1*	1	1	2	2*
4	3	1	1	2	
5	2	4	5	4	2

*Median score or position.

a. Absolute Estate:
   0 = Below $10,000
   1 = $10,000 - $19,999
   2 = $20,000 - $49,999
   3 = $50,000 - $199,999
   4 = $200,000+

are very sensitive and could be affected by small alterations in assignment of scale positions, although this is not as volatile a configuration as in Table 7–4A. In any event, the eleven individuals in the lowest scale position of estate category 2 include eight Unionists (seven of whom had also been Whigs) and only three Secession Democrats. At the other extremity, the five men with the highest scale position in category 2 include no known Unionists or Whigs. In both tabulations 7–4A and B, estate value is even a limited predictor of attitudes toward habeas corpus only because a cluster of Union Whigs bitterly opposed to suspension fall into wealth category 2 (whether by chance or otherwise we cannot say). And once again, a tendency toward polarization seems to indicate that positions on this issue were taken without reference to wealth. Regrettably, the number of Confederate congressmen is far too small to justify any general multivariate analysis such as studying economic divisions among only Exterior Democrats or Interior Unionists.

It would appear to follow from these significant intrusions of secession and party dichotomy into a discussion of personal estate, that it was the former influences, rather than wealth, which were the meaningful ones in this pattern. Here and there a voters' revolt in the Confederate mid-war elections may well have had some economic selectivity in its impact on the membership of the new Congress, but it is difficult to believe that middle-range wealth, rather than lower-range, would have profited disproportionately from the voters' disenchantment. On balance, no meaningful relation, direct or indirect, can be inferred from the fragile evidence in these and other similar cross-tabulations of personal wealth against member responses to habeas corpus questions.

A congressional district's land-value standing, on the other hand, is very much associated with the representative's willingness to suspend the writ, but inference that any causal relationship may have existed is not justified. The wealthier districts were the ones soon captured by the Federal forces or turned into continuing battle theatres. To almost as great an extent, the middle category represented either Exterior districts or those endangered by mid-war. And the low category fell very disproportionately into the longest-protected, Interior region. What very probably motivated most members is that when suspension appeared to be applicable chiefly to battle zones, the principle opposition came from representatives of those zones, while support was strong from deep within the Confederacy. As suspension of the writ came to be more widely applicable to conscription evasion throughout the Confederacy, the Interior turned against it sharply. Such association as may be observed between land values and habeas corpus scores or scale positions is altered greatly by removing the Exterior districts. Moreover, among Interior

TABLE 7-5

HABEAS CORPUS AND FEDERAL OCCUPATION

	(A) 1 Cong., 4 Sess.		(B) 2 Cong., 1 Sess.	
	Number of Individuals Assigned Each Score			
Habeas Corpus Score	Senate		House	
	Exterior Senators	Interior Senators	Exterior Representatives	Interior Representatives
0	2	4	1	
1		5*	3	7 (6)[a]
2			3	3 (2)
3	1		2	4
4		1	1	2 (1)
5			6	3
6			7	8*
7	1		10*	11
8	5*		12	2
9	3	3	3	
Median Score	7.40	0.50	6.10	5.13 (5.69)[b]
Differ- ence	6.90		0.97 (0.41)[b]	
% 0-4	25%	77%	21%	40%
% 5-9	75%	23%	79%	60%

* Median score.

a. N.C. Union Whigs.

b. Without N.C. Union Whigs.

TABLE 7-5--<u>Continued</u>

(C)

2 Cong., 2 Sess.

Habeas Corpus Score	Number of Individuals Assigned Each Score			
	Nov.-Feb.		Feb.-Mar.	
	Congress		House	
	Exterior Members	Interior Members	Exterior Representatives	Interior Representatives
0	15	17 (8)[a]	4	11 (7)[a]
1	4	3*	5	4*(1)
2	3	1	3	1
3	2	2 (1)	3	3 (1)
4	2	1		
5	4	2	2	1
6	2	1	2	
7	4	2	4	2
8	3*	1	4*	
9	36	9	21	4
Median Score	7.50	0.83 (4.00)[b]	7.25	0.50 (2.25)[b]
Difference	6.67 (3.50)[b]		6.75 (5.00)[b]	
% 0-4	35%	62%	31%	73%
% 5-9	65%	38%	69%	27%

*Median score.

a. N.C. Union Whigs.

b. Without N.C. Union Whigs.

TABLE 7-5--<u>Continued</u>

	(D) 1 Cong., 4 Sess.		(E) 2 Cong., 1 Sess.	
Habeas Corpus Scale Position	Number of Individuals Assigned Each Position			
	Senate		House	
	Exterior Senators	Interior Senators	Exterior Representatives	Interior
0		3	4	8 (5)[a]
1	2	3		4 (2)
2		1*	3	3 (1)
3	1	3	8	5*(1)
4	2	1	21*	14
5	3*		10	5
6	1	1		
7	3	1		
Median Position	4.33	1.50	3.38	2.90 (3.29)[b]
Differ- ence	2.83		0.48 (0.09)[b]	
% 0-3	25%	77%	% 0-2 15%	38%
% 4-7	75%	23%	% 3-5 85%	62%

*
 Median position.

a. N.C. Union Whigs.

b. Without N.C. Union Whigs.

TABLE 7-5--Continued

(F)
2 Cong., 2 Sess.

Habeas Corpus Scale Position	Nov.-Feb.		Feb.-Mar.	
	Number of Individuals Assigned Each Position			
	House		House	
	Exterior Representatives	Interior	Exterior Representatives	Interior
0	9	6 (3)[a]	8	17*(9)[a]
1	10	9 (5)	4	2
2	4	5*(1)	5	1
3	3	2	4	3
4	4		7*	2
5	6*	5	19	4
6	17	5		
7	12			
Median Position	4.42	1.20 (2.25)[b]	3.36	-0.15 (1.00)[b]
Difference	3.22 (2.17)[b]		3.51 (2.36)[b]	
% 0-3	40%	69%	% 0-2 36%	69%
% 4-7	60%	31%	% 3-5 64%	31%

*Median position.

a. N.C. Union Whigs.

b. Without N.C. Union Whigs.

districts, the limited associations that remain are also clearly associated with the proximity of Federal forces. Apart from these Exterior and jeopardy considerations, variations in land value do not appear to offer any credible hypothesis about a congressman's voting reaction to the habeas corpus issue.

Interior or Exterior Constituency

A congressman would ordinarily weigh the effect upon his own constituents of limitations placed on habeas corpus privileges. For this reason, men representing Exterior constituencies could afford themselves greater freedom in applying personal value judgments to the habeas corpus issue than could the representatives of the people who were to be directly affected. It is entirely to be expected that these Exterior members would show a greater willingness than Interior members to suspend the writ. The only unexpected element is how long it took for the distinction to appear. What insight we have for the Fourth Session of the First Congress is limited to the Senate, where a clear difference between these two groups' habeas corpus scores appears for the first time. For this session, there is hardly any doubt that the status of home district with regard to Federal occupation was a major voting determinant, at least in the Senate (Table 7–5A and D). About two thirds of the Interior senators are found in the lowest two levels of the performance scores, while two thirds of the Exterior senators are at the highest two levels. In the scale analysis for this Fourth Session, the contrast is not as great, but is decisive, nonetheless.

The Exterior members of the House are found only moderately more sacrificing than the Interior members during the First Session of the Second Congress if only the disparity between median scores is considered. However, the highest two performance-score levels (Table 7–5B) are occupied almost exclusively by Exterior representatives, and the lower half of the range is the domain of the Interior men by a substantial majority. The scale set from this same session also displays limited difference between medians with similarly sharp distinctions at the highest and lowest scale positions (Table 7–5E). The moderate differences in mean were undoubtedly due to the nature of the habeas corpus debate during this session. In May and June of 1864, the question usually was not suspension of the writ, but rather repeal of an existing suspension law that was due to expire on July 31, 1864. Even legislators who detested this law could live with it for a few more weeks.

In the last session of Congress, the gap between median scores for Exterior and Interior members was considerably wider than in the previous session. There is also evidence of polarization, which is especially strong in the scores for the November-February period, when 68 percent of the congressmen scored either 0 or 9 (Table 7-5C). Despite the median score difference of 6.67, however, every score level is occupied by both Exterior and Interior congressmen, and both of these categories are polarized, which are strong indicators that other forces were at work besides occupied-territory status. Roughly similar observations may be made for the scale analyses of the same period (Table 7-5F). Although some congressmen from yet unoccupied areas stood firm for suspension and some from occupied zones still hesitated about taking such an unpopular step, the vast majority took the opposite stance, as Exterior members usually pushed suspension, and Interior delegates usually quailed. Performance scores and scale positions for the last two months confirm that this one member characteristic may have gone very far toward determining the position of most congressmen on the vital habeas corpus issue.[14]

Summary

Suspending the writ of habeas corpus, in general, served well as a clue of the extent to which each congressman was willing to sacrifice individual civil rights to the Confederate cause. It was easier in some ways for a member to take a stand on this issue than on conscription or impressment when, in fact, it was evidently these considerations he often had at heart. Consequently, it is easier to discern distinctions between groups of congressmen on habeas corpus than on other questions examined in this study. The pattern that emerges is different from the others in degree rather than in kind, for a distinguishing feature of habeas corpus is the sharpness with which lines were drawn as indicated by the −32 agreement score between Secessionists and Unionists found in the Second Session of the Second Congress.[15] The already familiar effects

14. Special comment is perhaps appropriate regarding those congressmen who score 7, 8, or 9 on this performance set from the Second Congress, Second Session, February and March, and who show up in Tables 7-1D, 7-2D, and 7-5C. Party is unknown for ten of them and secession stand is missing for sixteen. But the thirty-five congressmen who most favored suspension of the writ at this time included ten of the twelve Kentuckians and five of the seven members of the Louisiana delegation (the other two could not be scored). Only one of these fifteen men was Interior. The behavior of the Louisiana and Kentucky congressmen on the habeas corpus question helps one understand why many Interior legislators felt antagonism toward their less fortunate colleagues. See Chapter 3.

15. The unusual polarization encountered in habeas corpus performance scores and scale positions for the Second Congress probably results from the nature of the issue. Whether to suspend the habeas corpus privilege was more nearly a yes or no question, than were issues relating to conscription, impressment, or economic policy. Proponents of conscription could disagree widely about exemption policies, for example; members

of former party affiliation, stand on secession, and occupation status of home district are now exposed more starkly as significant controlling forces in the roll-call responses of Confederate congressmen. The growing weight of these factors as the war prospects of the Confederacy deteriorated is also more clearly observable than for some of the other subjects of legislation. The excellence of scalability for sets of roll calls on the habeas corpus issue may be taken as especially strong evidence that this was one question congressmen came to understand and to approach consistently. The suspension of the privilege of the writ for sixteen months was not decisive in Confederate fortunes, but congressional roll calls on the issue came close to being decisive in distinguishing dedicated from dubious Confederates. At the risk of oversimplification, one might say that the most determined congressmen (usually Exterior, Secession Democrats) desired to deny habeas corpus to the discouraged and often disaffected constituents of colleagues who were likely to be Union Whigs from the yet unoccupied core of the Confederacy.[16]

---

favoring impressment might prefer different procedures for price setting or classes of goods liable to impressment. Even suspension of habeas corpus could produce disagreement about the offenses that would justify denial of the writ or about the length of time a suspension law should remain in effect. But the degree to which congressmen took extreme positions suggests that many came to see the issue in absolute terms during much of the last year of war. Habeas corpus scale sets have a very satisfactory range of marginals, and usually a good distribution of members through the middle ranges. Yet, to a greater extent than on several other sensitive subjects, as many as half of the members assigned positions fall at one extreme or the other. The scale for the first part of the last House session, for example, includes thirty roll calls and has eight clearly defined positions; but the easiest-to-support proposition was rejected by 28 percent of those voting and the hardest-to-support accepted by 26 percent.

16. Whether senators differed greatly from representatives on habeas corpus matters, insofar as influence from member characteristics may have been concerned, is difficult to tell. Much the same pattern is found for both houses, but the small number of senators renders cross-tabulation for the Senate alone so volatile as to be untrustworthy except in the few cases already presented. Furthermore, the Exterior senators were so preponderantly Democrats that associations between voting positions and party usually are hopelessly intertwined with Exterior status. One probable distinction for the senators lies in the fact that party appears to have been a better predictor of habeas corpus stands than does secession—the reverse of the patterns for representatives.

8 Economic and Fiscal Problems

THE economy of the region which became the Confederate States of America was peculiarly vulnerable to a protracted war against a power capable of blockading Southern shores. Before 1861, these states had been engaged in a combination of subsistence agriculture and production of staple crops to exchange for manufactured goods. Cotton was, of course, the great staple export; and hardly any of this commodity was manufactured into textiles within the Confederate area. Only a fragmentary beginning had been made in iron manufacturing, and the balance of the Southern so-called industry was chiefly grist- and lumber-milling. The transportation system for the export-import economy was principally the several major river systems, each furnishing egress at a different point along the vast stretches of the coast. Railroads in 1861 were just emerging from the concept of feeder lines for water transportation, so that no effective through rail transportation facilities existed in the Confederacy. The nearest things to trunk-line transportation for the South were coastal shipping and the Mississippi-Ohio-Tennessee waterway; and when these had to be surrendered to Federal naval control, it was as though an octopus had lost its body and had been left a set of detached tentacles. The beleaguered Confederacy rapidly became a nightmare for economic planners. Severed from its antebellum sources of manufactured goods, it lacked even the capacity to move its foodstuffs and makeshift manufactures to the areas of greatest need, and this despite efforts to construct key railroad links and to control railroad operations. As the war lengthened, the consequences of such poor transportation became even more telling.

The most spectacular aspect of Confederate economic disaster, however, was the redundancy and resulting runaway inflation of the currency during the latter half of the war. This was, in one sense, only the barometer reading for stormy conditions in major components of the economy. Removing the dollar sign from the analysis of Confederate economy can advance a true understanding of the problems because preoccupation with inflation can easily distract attention from the essential nature and causes of these difficulties. Yet it cannot be denied that currency inflation grew so monstrous as to become a direct contributing cause as well as a measure of severe economic distress. So serious was

201

the problem that all segments of the population were affected by it. Congressmen often had direct, even traumatic, knowledge of inflation. Some of them were forced to double up on accommodations to cut costs, and many of them feared for their living if they were not re-elected. While soldiers grumbled about insufficient pay, townspeople clamored for bread in 1863 because they were unable to pay the high prices demanded, and legions cursed speculators and hoarders.

Perhaps the best way to demonstrate the extent of Confederate inflation is to compare gold prices between the Union and the Confederacy. In May 1861, a dollar in gold cost $1.10 in Treasury notes in Richmond; and a year later, it cost $1.50. By May 1864, the decline had gone so far that a gold dollar was worth between $18.00 and $21.00; and in early 1865, the price varied between $45.00 and $70.00. The federal greenback was also inflationary, causing some economic distress in the Union. But never did things get so out of hand as in the Confederacy. The highest premium paid on the gold dollar in New York was in the summer of 1864, when the price was $2.59 in United States Notes (greenbacks). The situation was so bad in the South, according to Representative Foote, that United States greenbacks were far more valuable on the Richmond market than Confederate Treasury notes—the humiliating premium was fourteen or fifteen to one.

No steps were taken that controlled this inflation, though many were suggested and some were enacted. One of the most obvious controls, to a twentieth-century man, would have been ceiling prices. Such a law of the maximum was actually proposed by Senator Sparrow of Louisiana on November 10, 1864. The brief bill expresses well a commonly held view of the whole frustrating problem:

Whereas, The depreciation of our currency is, in a great measure, produced by the extortion of those who sell the necessaries of life; and whereas, such depreciation is ruinous to our Confederacy, and to the means of prosecuting the war, therefore the Congress of the Confederate States of America do enact, as a necessary war measure, that the prices assessed for the army by the Commissioners of Assessment, shall be the prices established for all citizens of the Confederate States; and that any person who shall charge any price beyond such assessment shall be deemed guilty of a criminal offence, and be subject to a fine not exceeding five thousand dollars, and to imprisonment not exceeding one year.[2]

A month later, Fayette McMullin of Virginia introduced a resolution requesting the states to take such action. Bad as inflation was, however, McMullin got only fourteen votes for his resolution, and it is significant

1. Todd, *Confederate Finance,* p. 198; "Proceedings," L, 103.
2. "Proceedings," LI, 289.

that these fourteen congressmen were mostly Secessionists, almost all Democrats, and all but one were spokesmen for occupied districts.[3] It is evident, then, that there were lengths to which few of even the more determined congressmen would go. Another inflationary control was funding, and of the three compulsory funding laws—October 13, 1862, March 23, 1863, and February 17, 1864—only the last one was even temporarily effective. In the end, funding only made things worse, because it seemed to hint that outright repudiation was a future possibility.

It is evident that the complexity of the forces involved in their economy's decline were simply beyond the capacity of the Confederate leaders to manage—and often beyond their understanding, as well. Even Jefferson Davis—who, despite his faults, was certainly an able man—wrote as late as August 1862 that a proposed new issue of notes would do no harm because their convertibility to 8 percent bonds protected the currency from redundancy. But he had also just pointed out that the people preferred notes to bonds, and he apparently did not see the inconsistency between these two statements.[4]

In order to avoid further inflation and to make up for a shortage of funds, Confederate lawmakers turned to other economic expedients, such as impressment or the tax-in-kind. Substituting levies of meat and potatoes for levies of money was a controversial solution to the economic problem, however, and it impinged on constituents' interests to a sufficient degree to have exposed significant associations in roll-call responses in Congress. On the other hand, many of the proposals for economic or fiscal legislation were far too theoretical and alien to the congressmen's experience to evoke responses that can be traced to any particular influence. Although the lawmakers had reasons for what they did, these reasons may often not have been relevant to either the economic problem or its solution. Voting on many roll calls on these topics leaves an impression of almost mindless threshing about in hope that, somehow, someone's proposals would yield desirable results.

This is not to deny that Confederate administrators had a purpose and a specific objective in each major economic or fiscal move recommended to Congress; it is to deny that the individual congressman's response was necessarily very perceptive. At least partly as a result of economic naïveté among congressmen, very few of the economic issues were found to be scalable. This, in turn, so severely limits the search for influences on those responses that not even a pro-Confederate (or "strong") position could be determined for a host of the fiscal and

3. *Journal of the Confederate Congress*, VII, 320–321.
4. *Messages*, I, 235.

tax-detail divisions. Consequently, the following measurements of association of performance scores or scale positions with member characteristics apply to only a limited number of the roll calls on economic issues. On the other hand, in the levels of agreement between pairs of groups within the Congress it is possible to discern whether any signal differences existed on the entire set of economic or fiscal roll calls in each session.

Roll-Call Issues

Nothing short of a ruthless management of the economy that allocated human and material resources according to centrally determined priorities would have toughened appreciably the capacity of the Confederacy to absorb military and economic punishment. Senator Augustus H. Garland of Arkansas recognized this obvious fact and introduced a resolution which called for the creation of a "Home Department," to which should "be intrusted [sic] the development, management, and control of the internal resources of the Confederate States."[5] When Garland made his proposal, it was January 1865 and perilously late in the game. Even so, most colleagues ignored him; and though many were obviously numbed by an engulfing sense of hopelessness, others undoubtedly found such rigid control simply unthinkable under any circumstances.

Professor David Donald has explored in definitive terms in his essay, "Died of Democracy," this almost complete absence of institutional structure, individual acquiescence, or practical experience with so alien a marshaling of resources.[6] Perhaps disaster might have engendered a spirit of desperation sufficient to sustain the submersion of agrarian individualism in a leviathan state, but only if the consequences of defeat had been fully understood and totally unbearable to contemplate. By February and March 1865, many congressmen did have this spirit of desperation, and as a later chapter indicates, the result was a turn-about in voting behavior; but, by then, it was far too late. The fact was that most Confederates, at least subconsciously, placed a limit on the price they would willingly pay for independence; and for a considerable number of those who had initially gone along with secession, that price was ridiculously low. As the burdens of war and defeat came to stun the general populace, ever greater numbers were heard to complain that, in fleeing from one alleged despotism, they had fallen prey to a greater one. The efforts of the Confederate government to take unpalatable but necessary measures, such as establishing compulsory military service,

5. *Journal of the Confederate Congress,* IV, 478–479.
6. David Donald, editor, *Why the North Won the Civil War* (Baton Rouge: Louisiana State University Press, 1960).

impressing supplies, and seeking to manacle unsympathetic state judges by suspension of the writ of habeas corpus, brought widespread disaffection most clearly into view. A few of the economic and fiscal programs, including impressment, also provide an understandable index of devotion to the Confederate cause.

Congress found it necessary, from time to time, to concern itself with the railroads and telegraph system. As early as January 1862, a committee of the Provisional Congress pointed to the heavy demands war placed upon transportation and concluded "that every legitimate means should be used to increase" its capacity. The committee must have defined "legitimate means" rather broadly for the nineteenth century, since it recommended "that military control be taken of the principal railroad routes terminating at or passing through Richmond, Nashville, Memphis, Atlanta, and all routes leading to the headquarters of our several army corps," and it went on to point to the need for construction of several short but important rail links. Davis agreed and made several formal requests for railroad legislation, although, in February 1863, he thought that the telegraph system should remain under private control.[7] Regulations, special powers for military commanders, allocation of scarce materials, and even direct government appropriations for completing those vital missing rail links eventually cleared Congress, although not without much protest from some who thought such economic activity beyond the constitutional authority of the Confederate government. Despite the disastrous breakdown of transportation late in the war, Congress did not authorize complete government control of transport and communications until military collapse was only weeks away, although the topic had frequently been under discussion. Naval vessels and river-defense craft, on the other hand, were so self-evidently needed that Congress concerned itself very little with the subject beyond approving payment for whatever the Navy Department could suggest.

Trade with Europe and the North was the lifeblood of Southern economy, and its substantial interdiction by blockade and war was of great concern to Congress. Little could be done about the matter, however, except to draft largely fruitless regulations for trade more hoped for than conducted. Trade with the "enemy" was a subject of legislation on more than one occasion. An embargo on cotton export to compel foreign assistance was considered and seemed to be established on a voluntary basis in 1861. Late in the war, Confederate government rights to cargo space aboard blockade runners became a heated issue; and the "lame duck" session of the First Congress passed the most vital piece of legislation on this subject when, on February 6, 1864, it authorized

7. *Journal of the Confederate Congress*, I, 721; *Messages*, I, 307.

the president to control exports and even to forbid luxury imports for the duration of the war. Over the sometimes hysterical protests of governors, especially Vance of North Carolina, President Davis resolutely demanded half the cargo accounts of blockade runners unless they were owned outright by state governments. Even this exception demonstrates the basic weakness of the Confederacy, and yet there were those who thought the law not weak enough.

The Second Congress very early in its First Session sought to exempt from Confederate control vessels merely chartered by state governments for their own use. Davis countered with a veto, for this bill would have deprived the government of urgently needed supplies and placed the states and the central government in the self-defeating roles of competitors for the chartering of the little shipping that was available. A month before the end of the war, Congress sought to give the state governments unrestricted right to export cotton to settle obligations contracted for military goods, but President Davis pocket-vetoed this. The effective management of such foreign trade as could clear the blockade in 1864 represented one of the more extreme instances of government control of an important segment of the economy, and in turn reflected a growing awareness in the administration of the necessity for a managed economy if resistance was to be sustained.

Paying war costs was an unavoidable responsibility of the central government. As in most modern nations at war, borrowing was more popular than taxing. The Northern government, with a generally prosperous economy, found it expedient to borrow four fifths of its wartime outlay (about half of it through the issuance of United States Notes as a form of forced loan). The Confederate government ultimately found it necessary to borrow three fourths of its total of expenditures, more than two thirds of which was in the form of Treasury notes (paper money). Of the estimated two hundred millions that were raised by taxation, representing only about one fourteenth of total income, almost one third was from the tax-in-kind. Nearly one sixth of the income from all sources was from impressed property still not paid for at the end of the war. Moreover, these figures do not include the borrowing and note issues of the states or of private individuals and corporations, which added to the inflationary burden.[8] In a general way, the Confederacy may be said to have financed itself approximately 5 percent by taxes collected in money, 2 percent by tax-in-kind, 16 percent by goods impressed but never paid for, 25 percent by bonds, and more than 50 percent by Treasury notes.

Every session of Congress was concerned with one or more of the major aspects of financing the war, not to mention the innumerable

8. Todd, *Confederate Finance*, pp. 84, 120, 156, 174.

details of tax bills and Treasury note issues. As early as the First Session of the First Congress, some legislators advocated making Treasury notes legal tender for private debts as a way to strengthen their acceptability among the people, and in the North this was done with greenbacks. But the notes circulated reasonably well without a legal tender provision, and, in any case, strict constructionist views of the Confederate Constitution apparently sustained many congressmen in their natural objection to such government interference in private business arrangements. Perhaps for this reason debates on the topic seldom became very heated or interesting, and there never was much of a chance that such a provision would become law. Yet the proposal was made often enough to indicate the frustrating difficulties encountered in the acceptance of Confederate currency.

Borrowing money by floating loans abroad was included in the calculations of the Confederate Treasury Department. The most famous loan arrangement was for fifteen million dollars, and was made with the French banking house of Emil Erlanger and Company. It was approved in January 1863, during the Third Session of the First Congress. Cotton was the collateral for this bond issue, and the bond holders as well as fiscal agents stood to reap enormous profits if the Confederacy made good its independence. Congressmen could understand the long-range cost to the taxpayers of the profit opportunities involved in this bond issue, and they could also perceive the opportunities for speculation on the part of those with inside information. As a matter of fact, one congressman, Eli M. Bruce of Kentucky, saw the opportunities so clearly that the temptation was too much for him. He put some of his own money in the loan and got his hands slapped, albeit lightly, by a slightly indignant Congress.[9] The Bruce incident is important because it demonstrates that the loan was an issue the ramifications of which Congress could readily understand; member responses can therefore be expected to yield to analysis more easily than responses on most fiscal issues in the First Congress. It should be no surprise, therefore, that although the First House roll calls yielded only two economic scales, one of them concerned the Erlanger Loan. Willingness to pay dearly for quick purchasing power in Europe was a rational test of devotion to the cause of Confederate independence.

Other economic issues involved the pay of military personnel and

---

9. *Journal of the Confederate Congress*, VI, 161–164. Judith Fenner Gentry, "A Confederate Success in Europe: The Erlanger Loan," *Journal of Southern History*, XXXVI (May 1970), 157–188, offers persuasive evidence that the cost of the loan was not excessive in light of the money market. Professor Gentry describes the loan as a high-risk undertaking, justifying profits in proportion to the risk, and acknowledges that the cost "shocked" Confederate officials in Richmond (p. 179).

TABLE 8-1

CONTENT OF CUMULATIVE SCALES AND OF PERFORMANCE-SCORE SETS OF ROLL CALLS RELATING TO ECONOMIC OR FISCAL SUBJECTS

House and Session	Type of Score	No. of Roll Calls	Description of Content of Roll-Call Issues
1 House 1 Sess.	Scale	8	congressional pay and expenses, chiefly a debate between those favoring salary and those preferring per diem and mileage
1 House 1 Sess.	Performance	6	importation without duty, except from the United States; a strong trading-with-the-enemy act, and the cotton embargo question
1 Senate 3 Sess.	Scale	13	essentially the same content as in the performance set described below
1 House 3 Sess.	Scale	5	Erlanger Loan
1 House 1 Senate 3 Sess.	Performance	25 15	establishing a tax system, overriding constitutional objections that direct taxes could not be levied without a census for apportionment, and defeating various efforts to reduce anticipated revenue by special consider-
1 House 1 Senate 4 Sess.	Performance	7 14	tax bills, funding and limiting the currency, legal tender debate

TABLE--8-1--<u>Continued</u>

House and Session	Type of Score	No. of Roll Calls	Description of Content of Roll-Call Issues
2 House 2 Senate 1 Sess.	Scale	8 12	currency, taxes, general appropriations
2 House 2 Senate 1 Sess.	Performance	20 17	extensive treatment of currency problems, taxes, appropriations, and pay of civil servants occupied the House; the Senate was more concerned with taxation of banks, canals, and railroads, efforts to exempt from taxation property in areas under Federal occupation, and military compensation bills
2 House 2 Senate 2 Sess. November-February	Performance	8	new tax law and the overriding of efforts to weaken the measure by amendments, government acquisition of one half of the gold and silver held by banks or others, reduction and redemption of currency
2 House 2 Sess. February-March	Scale	14	generally the same content as in the performance set described below
2 House 2 Sess. February-March	Performance	22	tax bills, increasing the tax-in-kind, killing amendments to weaken the tax-in-kind, payment of deceased-soldier benefits in revenue bills, reduction of currency

209

civilian employees of the Confederate government. This problem repeatedly commanded the attention of Congress, as some legislators demanded better financial support for underpaid (and often unpaid) soldiers and civil servants, while others urged the necessity of holding the line against inflation. Even the remuneration of congressmen themselves produced sustained debate and many roll-call votes. Some lawmakers announced patriotically that congressmen ought to be willing to serve without pay, but were answered by those (especially from occupied territory) for whom pay and allowances provided the sole source of income.

Association of Member Characteristics with Roll-Call Voting Behavior

Every major aspect of congressional dealing with economic or fiscal matters is incorporated in the agreement-score analysis, in a broad search for evidence of distinctions between groups of congressmen identified by individual member characteristics or circumstances. The clues turned up are not numerous, and a precise cause-effect relationship between an alleged influence on the congressman and his roll-call position is impossible to establish. Only a general inference may be drawn from this agreement-level evidence that certain member characteristics had some weight in determining economic views. Scale positions or performance scores on sets of economic issues offer much more decisive evidence of influence on votes from an indicated member characteristic, and such indices have been determined for some portions of this general topic for almost every session of the House and Senate. Because the wide range of these economic and fiscal questions makes it very difficult to generalize about the subject from session to session, the content of included roll calls is provided in Table 8-1.

Former Party Affiliation

Economic issues in the Confederate Congress produced very little distinction between former Democrats and former Whigs until the First Session of the Second Congress. Even then the suggestion of party influence is considerably weakened, albeit not eliminated, by the fact that the Union Whig delegation from North Carolina accounted for a large proportion of the party differences. Toward the end of the last session of Congress, in February and March of 1865, desperation measures revealed a lessening influence from party alignment for members who still remained in Richmond, but it should be noted that the defeatist members who were departing for home during these months were disproportionately Whigs.

Agreement scores between Democrats and Whigs show no evidence of distinctions arising from the total range of economic business incorporated in the roll calls selected from the First Congress. Performance scores and scale positions yield too little evidence of influence from former party status to justify presentation of more than two tabulations from the entire First Congress. During the First Session, when remuneration for congressmen was established as per diem and mileage instead of an annual salary, a scale set composed of roll calls on that issue shows Democrats considerably more satisfied with the action taken (assigned the positive position for the scale) than were the Whigs (Table 8-2A). Polarization, however, may be noted for both groups. As will be explained later in this chapter, some other influences flowing from economic status of the individual member and from his practical ability to get home safely had a powerful influence on the stance taken here. Whigs, for instance, constituted a larger proportion of the Exterior delegations at this time than of the Interior membership, and this alone may account for the weaker median position.

The establishment of important parts of the tax structure during the Third Session revealed interesting party differences, as indicated by both performance scores and scale positions. The score levels apply to the entire Congress, but the subject yielded a scalable set of roll calls only for the Senate. Whigs proved to be somewhat higher in the range of scores than did the Democrats (Table 8-2B). The difference between median scores is not great, but distinctions in patterns of deviation from the median justify scrutiny. The Whigs are found clustered in the middle range of scores; Democrats, on the other hand, are found more evenly spread. The implication is that Democrats were severely divided, having had a wider range of opinions on taxation due to some influences that were less efficacious in drawing Whigs to either extreme. Possibly state-rights philosophy was warring with zeal for Confederate success within Democratic ranks more than among Whigs. To whatever extent the higher scores for Whigs may be adjudged significant, it can be reconciled easily with the greater awareness of central government function displayed by Whigs for some years before secession.

In a scale set (not shown) having much the same content, Whig senators are found to be weaker than their Democratic counterparts. The total absence of Whigs from the more positive part of that scale is a fair indication of their disdain for the general tax structure that won greater approval among the representatives. But the small number of individuals involved in the Senate, together with the minor distinction in medians between the two parties, provides a basis which is altogether inadequate for any generalization about influence of former party association on this scale in the Upper House.

TABLE 8-2

ECONOMIC ISSUES AND FORMER PARTY

	(A) 1 Cong., 1 Sess. Congressional Pay			(B) 1 Cong., 3 Sess. Establishing Tax Structure	
Congres- sional Pay Scale Position	Number of Individuals Assigned Each Position		Tax Structure Score	Number of Individuals Assigned Each Score	
	House			Congress	
	Democrat	Whig		Democrat	Whig
0	6	6	0	5	2
1	10	9*	1	6	1
2	5	2	2	7	1
3	3	4	3	10	3
4	3*	1	4	6	4
5	8		5	13*	5
6	11	5	6	5	8*
7	5	3	7	11	7
			8	7	2
			9	1	
Median Position	3.50	1.00	Median Score	4.12	5.06
Differ- ence	2.50		Differ- ence	0.94	
% 0-3	47%	70%	% 0-4	48%	33%
% 4-7	53%	30%	% 5-9	52%	67%

*
Median position or score.

TABLE 8-2--Continued

(C)
2 Cong., 1 Sess.
Currency, Taxes, General Appropriations

Issue Area Scale Position	Number of Individuals Assigned Each Position					
	Senate		House		Interior Representatives	
	Democrat	Whig	Democrat	Whig	Democrat	Whig
0	1			5 (4)[a]		4 (4)[a]
1		2 (1)[a]		5 (3)		4*(3)
2	2	3*(1)	4	7 (1)	1	3 (1)
3	1	1	8	3*	5	2
4	1		8*	7	3*	1
5	2*	1	7	2	1	
6	5	1	7	6	5	1
Median Position	4.50	1.67 (2.00)[b]	3.63	2.17 (3.21)[b]	3.50	0.88 (2.25)[b]
Difference	2.83 (2.50)[b]		1.46 (0.42)[b]		2.62 (1.25)[b]	
% 0-3[c]	29%	69%	24%	53%	23%	80%
% 3-6	71%	31%	76%	47%	77%	20%

* Median position.

a. N.C. Union Whigs.

b. Without N.C. Union Whigs.

c. In scale sets with an odd number of positions, the number of members assigned to the center position is divided into halves for percentage calculation.

213

TABLE 8-2--<u>Continued</u>

(D)
2 Cong., 2 Sess., Nov.-Feb.
Taxation, Gold Levy, Currency

Score on Issue Area	Number of Individuals Assigned Each Score					
	Congress		House		Interior Members[a]	
	Democrat	Whig	Democrat	Whig	Democrat	Whig
0	4	8 (6)[b]	2	6 (6)[b]	2	7 (6)[b]
1	1	6 (2)	1	5 (1)	1	5*(2)
2	4	2	4	2	1	
3	5	1	3	1	4	
4	2	2*	2	2*	2*	
5	3	3 (1)	3	3 (1)	3	1 (1)
6	3*	5	1	5	1	2
7	4	1	3*	1	2	
8	10	2	9	2	3	1
9	8	6	6	4	1	1
Median Score	6.00	3.50 (5.10)[c]	6.33	3.75 (5.10)[c]	4.00	0.30 (3.00)[c]
Difference	2.50 (0.90)[c]		2.58 (1.23)[c]		3.70 (1.00)[c]	
% 0-4	36%	53%	35%	52%	50%	71%
% 5-9	64%	47%	65%	48%	50%	29%

* Median score.

a. Interior at least until the beginning of the Second Session.

b. N.C. Union Whigs.

c. Without N.C. Union Whigs.

TABLE 8-2--<u>Continued</u>

(E)
2 Cong., 2 Sess., Feb.-Mar.
Taxation, Tax-in-Kind, Currency

Score on Issue Area	Number of Individuals Assigned Each Score			
	House		Interior Representatives[a]	
	Democrat	Whig	Democrat	Whig
0	3	6 (4)[b]	2	4 (4)[b]
1	2	3 (2)	1	2 (2)
2	3	1 (1)	3	1* (1)
3	3	5*	1	1
4	3	1	1	1
5	5*	4 (1)	3*	2 (1)
6	7	3	2	1
7	8	5	4	1
8	2			
9				
Median Score	4.80	2.80 (4.33)[c]	4.17	1.00 (5.00)[c]
Difference	2.00 (0.47)[c]		3.17 (0.83)[c]	
% 0-4	39%	57%	47%	67%
% 5-9	61%	43%	53%	33%

*
Median score.

a. Interior at least until the beginning of the Second Session.

b. N.C. Union Whigs.

c. Without N.C. Union Whigs.

The First Session of the Second Congress revealed increased distinctions, as extensive consideration of tax measures, military and civil servant pay, and currency manipulation show former Democrats notably higher than former Whigs (Table 8-2C). Both House and Senate show some party-associated difference between medians, while the general contrast among Interior representatives is distinct. There are no Democratic representatives assigned the lowest two scale positions, which are, however, occupied by a substantial cluster of Whigs. The North Carolina Union Whigs constitute such a large share of these reluctant members that for the entire House the removal of their scores would bring the medians for Whigs very close to those for Democrats. Among the Interior representatives, however, the gap is found to be so wide that even the deletion of these North Carolinians' scores would not erase distinctions along party lines, although it is true that at this late date slightly more than half of the Interior Whigs were from North Carolina. Moreover, the strongest scale position is occupied by five Democrats and only one Whig. It is evident, in any case, that new members of the Second Congress were responding differently from their predecessors. It is also probable that returning members were under increasing pressure from their constituents because of steady escalation of economic difficulties throughout the Confederacy. And both groups could understand that events called for drastic action, even though they might not be able to agree on what that action should be.

When the Second and last Session assembled in November 1864, questions relating to new taxes and extreme expedients for attacking inflation continued to reveal the influence of former party affiliation. Table 8-2D shows how much more of the support came from Democrats than came from Whigs. Elimination of the North Carolina Union Whigs would narrow this difference greatly, but would not completely remove it, while subtraction of the Exterior members would exert countering influence. Among the Interior members very few Whigs are found in the high levels. Note, for example, that in the highest level, 9, there are six Whigs, four of whom were representatives. When Interior members alone are involved, only one of these six is left—Chilton of Alabama, who ordinarily maintained a fairly high level of support for Confederate victory. It is a troublesome handicap that the North Carolina bloc constituted more than half of the Interior Whigs shown on this tabulation. Although twelve of the seventeen Interior Whigs are at the lowest two levels, eight of those twelve are the North Carolinians. It is very apparent that the melange of influences operating on this delegation intermingled old party and secession attitudes with wartime issues and Zebulon Vance's leadership in such a fashion that separate evaluation of these forces is not going to be possible.

The February and March meetings of the Congress were suffering increasing absenteeism, and more Whigs than Democrats were departing. The continuing tendency of Democrats to score higher on performance sets for this period of the session may be noted in Part E of Table 8–2 (a scale set for the same issues displayed the same result). By this time, however, most Whigs still voting in the House were from either Exterior constituencies or from North Carolina. Hardly any other Interior Whigs remained in Richmond after February of 1865—a fact significant in itself but nonetheless a serious barrier to measurement of influences on roll-call responses.

The intrinsic complications of economic issues apparently helped to delay the emergence of rivalry in Congress that might have been associated with former party considerations. Such rivalry did appear in the Second Congress and would have been more distinct had not so many of the Whigs been from the border states, which were so firmly in Federal hands by mid-war that their representatives appear to have been more affected by the occupied status of their districts than by possible influences from their earlier political affiliations.

Position on Secession

If previous findings for other subjects are any indicator, economic issues would produce differences along lines of secession position which could be expected to show only slight variation from party-based distinctions. Very few Union Democrats or Secession Whigs were in the Confederate House, although stand on secession is unknown for several members whose party affiliation has been discovered, and vice versa. The analyses of First Congress roll calls for evidences of persisting influence of secession stand has therefore brought to light nothing that differs substantially from the party analysis. Agreement scores between Secessionists and Unionists indicate no significant disagreement on over-all economic transactions. It is true that the congressional pay issue in the First Session showed Democrats scaling much more positively than Whigs (Table 8–2A) while Secessionists and Unionists display no real contrast; it was acknowledged, however, that the party differential probably was traceable to other influences.

The association of position on secession with roll-call response was stronger in the Second Congress (Table 8–3A) than in the First. This increase over time parallels findings for party. Altogether, Secessionism may be described as at least the same quality of predictor about positions of congressmen on economic issues as party proved to be, as far as most Second Congress roll calls are concerned. It was the first part of the last session, from November to February, which best brings to light the typically increased distinctions between Secessionist and Unionist

TABLE 8-3

ECONOMIC ISSUES AND STAND ON SECESSION

(A)
2 Cong., 1 Sess.
Currency, Taxes, General Appropriations

Issue Area Scale Position	Number of Individuals Assigned Each Position					
	Senate		House		Interior Representatives	
	Seces-sionist	Union-ist	Seces-sionist	Union-ist	Seces-sionist	Union-ist
0	1			4 (4)[a]		4 (4)[a]
1		2 (1)[a]		6 (3)		4 (3)*
2	2	3	2	7 (1)*	1	3 (1)
3		2*	8	2*	5	2
4			9*	7	5*	2
5	2*	1	6	4	2	
6	3	3	5	4	5	1
Median Position	4.50	2.25 (2.50)[b]	3.56	2.00 (3.29)[b]	3.60	1.00 (2.50)[b]
Difference	2.25 (2.00)[b]		1.56 (0.27)[b]		2.60 (1.10)[b]	
% 0-3[c]	38%	55%	20%	53%	19%	75%
% 3-6	63%	45%	80%	47%	81%	25%

*Median position.

a. N.C. Union Whigs.

b. Without N.C. Union Whigs.

c. In scale sets with an odd number of positions, the number of members assigned to the center position is divided into halves for percentage calculation.

TABLE 8-3--Continued

(B)
2 Cong., 2 Sess., Nov.-Feb.
Taxation, Gold Levy, Currency

Score on Issue Area	Number of Individuals Assigned Each Score					
	Congress		House		Interior Members[a]	
	Seces-sionist	Union-ist	Seces-sionist	Union-ist	Seces-sionist	Union-ist
0	2	10 (6)[b]	1	8 (6)[b]	1	8 (6)[b]
1	1	7 (2)	1	6 (1)	1	6*(2)
2	3	2*	3	2*	2	
3	4	2	3	1	3	1
4	1	2	1	2		1
5	4	3 (1)	4	3 (1)	3*	1 (1)
6	4*	2	2*	2	2	1
7	4	1	3	1	2	
8	11		10		3	
9	3	8	2	5	1	1
Median Score	5.88	1.75 (3.50)[c]	6.00	1.50 (3.50)[c]	4.67	0.25 (0.75)[c]
Difference	4.13 (2.38)[c]		4.50 (2.50)[c]		4.42 (3.92)[c]	
% 0-4	30%	62%	30%	63%	39%	84%
% 5-9	70%	38%	70%	37%	61%	16%

* Median score.

a. Interior at least until the beginning of the Second Session.

b. N.C. Union Whigs.

c. Without N.C. Union Whigs.

TABLE 8-3--Continued

(C)
2 Cong., 2 Sess., Feb.-Mar.
Taxation, Tax-in-Kind, Currency

Score on Issue Area	Number of Individuals Assigned Each Score			
	House		Interior Representatives[a]	
	Secessionist	Unionist	Secessionist	Unionist
0	1	7 (4)[b]	1	4 (4)[b]
1	3	3 (2)	1	3*(2)
2	3	1 (1)	3	1 (1)
3	6	3*	4*	
4	4*	2	1*	1
5	3*	7 (1)	2	4 (1)
6	6	1	2	
7	6	3	4	
8	2			
9				
Median Score	4.00	2.83 (4.08)[c]	3.00	0.83 (4.17)[c]
Difference	1.17 (0.08)[c]		2.17 (1.17)[c]	
% 0-4	50%	59%	56%	69%
% 5-9	50%	41%	44%	31%

*Median score.

a. Interior at least until the beginning of the Second Session.

b. N.C. Union Whigs.

c. Without N.C. Union Whigs.

median scores over those between Democrats and Whigs that we have come to expect from observation of other sensitive areas of congressional business (compare Tables 8-3B and 8-2D). The dwindling body of members still answering to roll calls in February and March of 1865, however, left a mixed record (Table 8-3C). Performance scores show less influence from secession position than from party while scale positions show the opposite.

It is evident that either former party affiliation or secession position is an excellent clue to attitudes about the critical economic issues of the Confederacy's desperation days during the Second Congress. But neither characteristic has much value for the First Congress.

Slaveholding

The individual economic status of a congressman, as reflected by his estate or slaveholdings, is simply not a major measurable determinant of his attitudes on most of the economic and fiscal questions confronting the Confederate Congress. Economic standing may have exerted some pull on a few very specific topics, however, including some of the general tax and currency issues. Of course, there are occasional single divisions in which economic standing is quite important, but these are relatively infrequent. Nevertheless, slaveholding and wealth characteristics can provide a few useful contributions to an explanation of votes on economic issues.

During the First Session of the First Congress, major policy questions failed to reveal any consequential dissimilarities in behavior among slaveholding levels, but a sharp tussle in the House concerning congressional pay produced exactly this type of distinction. The decision to pay per diem and mileage instead of an annual salary, at levels finally incorporated in a conference committee compromise bill, was pressed through by the wealthier slaveholders—over the stubborn opposition of the smaller holders. Table 8-4A displays the relatively weak scale positions of the lower slaveholding categories *versus* the higher standings for the larger slaveowners. As usual, the presence of both large and small holders in every scale position warns of other influences. And, in any case, one key probably is geography. The congressmen who most needed a regular and adequate salary were often those from the occupied regions, where slaveholdings were typically small.

A more important emergence of slaveholding influence was during the Third Session of the First Congress, when legislators wrestled with the problem of establishing a permanent tax structure—over numerous objections of a constitutional or other nature. Part B of Table 8-4 displays a marked progression in median scores, from strong for the smallest

TABLE 8-4

ECONOMIC ISSUES AND SLAVEHOLDING

(A)
1 Cong., 1 Sess.
Congressional Pay

Congres- sional Pay Scale Position	Number of Individuals Assigned Each Position						
	House						
	Absolute Slaveholding[a]					0-19 Slaves	20 or More Slaves
	0	1	2	3	4		
0	3*	7	1	1	2	11	3
1	2	7*	4		4	13	4
2		1	1	5	1	2*	6
3		3	2		2	5	2
4			2*	1	1*	2	2
5		2	1	2*	2	3	4*
6		5	7	2	5	12	7
7	1		1	4	3	2	7
Median Position						1.50	4.13
Differ- ence						2.63	
% 0-3						62%	43%
% 4-7						38%	57%

*Median position.

a. Absolute Slaveholding:
   0 = No slaves
   1 = 1-9 slaves
   2 = 10-19 slaves
   3 = 20-49 slaves
   4 = 50 or more slaves

222

TABLE 8-4--Continued

(B)
1 Cong., 3 Sess.
Establishing Tax Structure

Tax Structure Score	Number of Individuals Assigned Each Score						
	Congress					Congress	
	Absolute Slaveholding[a]					0-19 Slaves	20 or More Slaves
	0	1	2	3	4		
0		1	2	1	3	3	4
1		2	2	1	2	4	3
2		1	1	2	5	2	7
3	2	1	3	3	5*	6	8
4		2	4*	3*		6	3*
5		7*	2	3	4	9*	7
6	4*	4	1	1	3	9	4
7	2	6	8	3	1	16	4
8	1	3	1	2	3	5	5
9					1		1
Median Score						5.00	3.33
Difference						1.67	
% 0-4						35%	54%
% 5-9						65%	46%

*
Median score.

a. Absolute Slaveholding:
  0 = No slaves
  1 = 1-9 slaves
  2 = 10-19 slaves
  3 = 20-49 slaves
  4 = 50 or more slaves

slaveholders to weak for the largest, which is a great contrast to the curvilinear pattern noted so frequently in other content areas. Dividing the entire Congress and the House into two slaveholding categories only dramatizes differences and exposes the wider variations among representatives. In this case, a further analysis of Interior members exclusively reveals the same findings (not shown). This session also dealt with the Erlanger Loan, a subject that might seem likely to have elicited distinctions based on personal economic status. Contrary to that expectation, slaveholding does not appear to have been meaningfully related to the votes on this issue, though value of estate, to be discussed below, proved to be a somewhat better clue.

The Second Congress was concerned with attempts to stave off financial and economic disaster, and its members probably experienced so much difficulty in foreseeing the immediate effects of much of the legislation that self-interest as a motive was inhibited. Eventually, the conclusion that the economy was too far gone to be rescued may also have exorcised any significant association between individual member welfare and public policy. Scale analysis furnishes some evidence that the larger slaveholders in this Second Congress were more willing to make sacrifices to achieve victory than small holders—who were, perhaps, mindful that the planter's sacrifice was disaster when exacted from the small farmer. In any case, the weakest scale positions for the scale set on currency, taxes, and general appropriations from the First Session were almost pre-empted by the lowest three slaveholding categories.

The last weeks of the Congress produced roll calls on matters of the Confederate economy that ordinarily ought to have divided members along economic lines, if self-interest had been foremost. But voting patterns on economic questions, instead of becoming more obvious as in other content areas, were altered inexplicably by impending defeat. It is important, nevertheless, to remember that attendance declined so sharply during these weeks that we are very nearly dealing with a different Congress. Evidently, the handful of legislators who remained continued to be sharply divided on economic issues, but not along lines of personal economic status. In early March of 1865, for example, a funding bill passed both houses; yet, in the often perfunctory committee of conference, the bill encountered such fierce personal antagonisms that no acceptable compromise emerged, and this vitally needed measure never became law. Member differences at that date were hardly created by slaveholding status; it was too late for that. By March of 1865, slavery's future was so dismal that few, if any, congressmen could seriously weigh their slave property in the balance as they confronted the terminal roll calls of the Confederate Congress.

As with previous legislative topics, the average size of slaveholdings in a representative's home area is associated with his economic-issue votes—but only because the small slaveholders predominated in the Upper South. In early 1862, the small slaveholding spokesmen were reluctant to approve trading-with-the-enemy legislation, but thereafter the fact that almost all of them were Exterior representatives apparently dictated their sacrificing stance. Toward the end of the war, the weaker positions were taken by Interior men from small slaveholding communities, it is true, but these men were also from the Appalachian land of disaffection. It is probably the case that the economy and general character of these districts is intimately associated with the initial high level of Unionism and subsequent defeatism, if not defiance. It would be simplistic, however, to assume that slaveholding, apart from the manifold influences of the highland region, can be accepted as an effective influence on voting about economic matters. The really striking aspect of associations between slaveholding patterns and voting on economic matters is that they are so generally weak when not actually insignificant.

Value of Estate

Value of a congressman's estate, incorporating slaves and other forms of property as well, served as a differentiating characteristic in the struggle about congressional pay in much the same manner as slaveholding. The tax-structure issues of the Third Session also yield a pattern parallel to the one associated with slaveholding categories (Table 8–5A), although if median difference is the indicator used, estates proved less able than slaveholdings to account for variations in member response on these roll calls. Property value is even less helpful in examining the Erlanger Loan, although interesting differences in medians and percentage quadrants seem to indicate that wealthier members were less willing than the owners of more modest estates to consent to the terms of the loan (Table 8–5B). Apparently, they were reluctant to approve the great profits that would accrue to the European firm should the Confederacy win its independence, or perhaps they could foresee lost opportunities for profit for themselves in the action. Moreover, they were probably better acquainted with the normal costs of European financing and hence more alarmed at this excessive long-range loss to the Southern cotton producers and factors.

Interior representatives of greater relative wealth were, during the Second Congress sessions, clearly less sacrificing than Interior men of lesser estate. Two cumulative scales (not shown), one from each session, reveal this point as well as could be expected from the small remnant of members from unoccupied territory who were still present and voting.

TABLE 8-5

ECONOMIC ISSUES AND WEALTH

(A)
1 Cong., 3 Sess.
Establishing Tax Structure

Tax Structure Score	Number of Individuals Assigned Each Score						
	Congress					Congress	
	Absolute Estate[a]					$49,999 or Less	$50,000 or More
	0	1	2	3	4		
0		1	2	2	2	3	4
1	1	1	1	2	2	3	4
2		1	2	6		3	6
3	3		4	5	3*	7	8
4		1	4	4*	1	5	5*
5	1	5*	4*	4	2	10*	6
6	3*	5	1	4		9	4
7	4	2	7	6		13	6
8	1	1	5	2	1	7	3
9					1		1
Median Score						4.90	3.30
Difference						1.60	
% 0-4						35%	57%
% 5-9						65%	43%

*
Median score.

a. Absolute Estate:
   0 = Below $10,000
   1 = $10,000 - $19,999
   2 = $20,000 - $49,999
   3 = $50,000 - $199,999
   4 = $200,000+

TABLE 8-5--<u>Continued</u>

(B)
1 Cong., 3 Sess.
Erlanger Loan

Erlanger Loan Scale Position	Number of Individuals Assigned Each Position	
	House	
	$49,999 or Less	$50,000 or More
0	2	4
1	1	6
2	5	3
3	12	9*
4	25*	10
Median Position	3.10	2.33
Difference	0.77	
% 0-2[a]	12%	36%
% 2-4	88%	64%

*Median position.

a. In scale sets with an odd number of positions, the number of members assigned to the center position is divided into halves for percentage calculation.

As Congress approached the day of final adjournment, almost none of the Interior lawmakers in the highest relative wealth category were found outside the lowest positions in the scale set involving various tax measures, including a proposed increase in the tax-in-kind. Among all congressmen, but especially among the wealthy, incentive to sacrifice on economic questions apparently dissolved as the hope of victory was dashed.

Land values in a representative's district are nearly useless as predictors of his general stance on economic questions. The association that pertains is merely a reflection of the now familiar Exterior-Interior dichotomy. For Interior members only, there is little association until the last months of the war, and even then the principal distinction pits Virginia districts (high land values) against North Carolina and Georgia districts (low or middle values).

Interior or Exterior Constituency

Whether a member's district was under effective Confederate authority made a great deal of difference in attitudes toward economic matters. During the First Session of the First Congress, members from outside the perimeter of Confederate control were less willing to adopt tough regulations for trade with the United States, specifically a trading-with-the-enemy act or an apparently permanent discrimination against imports from the United States (Table 8-6A). At this early date, the few Exterior members represented states bordering the United States and, in war or peace, they would have to live with the practical effects of proximity. Understandably, they were reluctant to cut long-established commercial ties.

The congressional pay decision also was unsatisfactory to most of the men from occupied areas for the oft-mentioned reason that per diem and travel allowance were not calculated to serve the interests of those who dared not go home and had to live as refugees in Richmond for most, if not all, of the time. An Interior legislator could, if he wished, practice law between sessions, and he could obtain money from his agricultural enterprise at any time. This was not the case for most of those members from occupied territory. Regardless of their wealth in 1860, in 1862 they had to have an adequate salary, and the little extra they gained by a mileage allowance which could not be used to go home was insufficient recompense. The cumulative scale on the congressional pay matter (Table 8-6D) reveals starkly how opposed the bulk of the Exterior representatives were to the plan ultimately adopted, for two thirds of them are scaled at one of the weakest two positions and three fourths at one of the weakest three positions. On the other hand,

Interior representatives were more normally distributed, though both columns show evidence of polarization.

Exterior congressmen were evidently quite as unwilling as Interior members were to sacrifice on those issues of direct concern to themselves and their constituents; but, when the question involved had more remote consequences, they were ready to support more exacting efforts. In the Third Session of the First Congress, when vital parts of the tax structure were being established, the congressmen whose constituents were far beyond the reach of the tax gatherers tended to be more dedicated to effective taxation than Interior congressmen (Table 8–6B). Senators, by contrast, tended to occupy weak positions in the scale set on this subject without significant distinction as to whether they were from Interior or Exterior states (table not shown for senators separately). The Erlanger Loan votes in this same session, however, reveal in a scale set for the House only slightly different median scores and percentage quadrants for Exterior and Interior representatives, but again a paucity of Exterior men appear at the weakest two scale positions (not shown).

The last session of the First Congress tangled with the disaster of inflation, considering funding proposals to limit the currency and repeated attempts to make Treasury notes legal tender for private debts. Congressmen from occupied districts were understandably more willing to support the tough financial measures, partly because their constituents were probably using greenbacks (Table 8–6C). The differences between Exterior and Interior are not great, either in medians or percentage quadrants. The principal evidence of distinction is that only three occupied-territory congressmen are scored at any of the lowest three levels, as opposed to fifteen colleagues from the unoccupied areas.

The currency, tax, and general appropriations measures of the opening session of the Second Congress brought out only a faint continuation of the more sacrificing stands by occupied-district men (Table 8–6F). The difference between Interior and Exterior median scores is not large in this session and can, furthermore, be traced almost entirely to the North Carolina Union Whig votes among the Interior members. In the earlier part of the last session, with new taxes as well as old currency problems under review, the Exterior delegates increased the margin by which their scores exceeded those of Interior spokesmen (Table 8–6G). Without the North Carolina delegation a significant distinction would still have existed. Especially indicative of the impact of this member characteristic is the large cluster of Exterior members scored at one of the highest two levels (twenty-eight men contrasted with only six from Interior zones, or 42 percent of the Exterior and 20 percent of the Interior members).

TABLE 8-6

ECONOMIC ISSUES AND FEDERAL OCCUPATION

	(A) 1 Cong., 1 Sess. (Trade with U.S.A.)		(B) 1 Cong., 3 Sess. (Establishing Tax Structure)		(C) 1 Cong., 4 Sess. (Taxation, Funding, and Legal Tender)	
Score on Issue Area	Number of Individuals Assigned Each Score					
	House		Congress		Congress	
	Exterior Representatives	Interior Representatives	Exterior Members	Interior Members	Exterior Members	Interior Members
0	1	1	4	3		5
1	1	5	2	5		5
2	3	2	1	8	3	5
3	2	6	2	13	4	7
4			3	7	1	2
5	4*	6	5	13*	8	12*
6		10*	5*	9	8*	11
7		5	8	12	9	10
8	3	12	7	5	3	6
9	3	11		1	9	3
Median Score	4.38	5.90	5.30	4.15	5.81	4.75
Difference	1.52		1.15		1.06	
% 0-4	41%	24%	32%	47%	18%	36%
% 5-9	59%	76%	68%	53%	82%	64%

*
Median score.

TABLE 8-6--Continued

	(D) 1 Cong., 1 Sess. Congressional Pay		(E) 2 Cong., 2 Sess. Feb.-Mar. Taxation, Tax-in-Kind, Currency	
	Number of Individuals Assigned Each Position			
Scale Position on Issue Area	House		House	
	Exterior Representatives	Interior	Exterior Representatives	Interior
0	6	9	6	10 (6)[a]
1	8*	12	9	4*(1)
2	2	6	5	3 (1)
3		8*	12*	2 (1)
4		4	10	7
5	1	7	3	1
6	3	16	5	
7	1	8		
Median Position	0.56	3.00	2.42	0.88 (2.00)[b]
Difference	2.44		1.54 (0.42)[b]	
% 0-3	76%	50%	% 0-3[c] 52%	67%
% 4-7	24%	50%	% 3-6 48%	33%

* Median position.

a. N.C. Union Whigs.

b. Without N.C. Union Whigs.

c. In scale sets with an odd number of positions, the number of members assigned to the center position is divided into halves for percentage calculation.

During the final weeks of Congress critical economic deterioration evoked such proposals as an increase in the tax-in-kind for relieving the government of some part of its embarrassment. This attempt to circumvent the money problem only emphasized the degree of desperation to which still-loyal Confederates had been driven. Another proposal, not in itself critical to Confederate economy but attended by painfully obvious implications, was to pay government obligations to families of deceased soldiers, not in regular (though inflated) Treasury notes that could be spent, but in revenue bills. Such bills would not add to the currency in circulation but would provide these most pitiable victims of war only a promise to pay later. President Davis fully understood the currency problem by this time, and, in February 1865, he begged Congress for any new tax law that would meet the country's needs. Faced with last-ditch expedients, Congress continued to divide in part on the basis of whether Federal forces held or threatened a member's home district (Table 8–6H). Several Interior members other than the North Carolinians are found in the low score levels. More than twice as many Interior congressmen as Exterior are assigned one of the lowest three scores, while the Exterior members in turn dominate the highest three levels by twenty-six to five. The scale table (8–6E) shows comparable contrast in the high positions but not in the low ones. As well on economic questions as on others, outsiders continued to play a large roll in directing the destinies of insiders.

Summary

In their votes on economic and fiscal issues, Confederate congressmen revealed many of the same tendencies they had displayed on more explosive subjects. Some of these economic issues were decidedly associated with the member attributes under scrutiny in this study, although much of this legislative business was too involved or theoretical to measure distinctions between various classes of membership with any reasonable degree of accuracy.

Neither former party nor secession position had much influence on member responses to economic issues during the first half of the war. But, as was found to be the case in several other areas of congressional business, Democrats and Secessionists were more sacrificing than Whigs or Unionists on those late-war roll calls for which a victory-bent position could be identified.

Personal economic status of members was not a consistent influence but decidedly affected many in their approach to a general taxation system or to something as immediate as their own pay and allowances. Those to be taxed the heaviest were sometimes inclined to be less enthusi-

TABLE 8-6--<u>Continued</u>

	(F) 2 Cong., 1 Sess. (Currency, Taxes, Pay, and General Appropriations)		(G) 2 Cong., 2 Sess. Nov.-Feb. (Taxation, Gold Levy, Currency)		(H) 2 Cong., 2 Sess. Feb.-Mar. (Taxation, Tax-in-Kind, Currency)	
	Number of Individuals Assigned Each Score					
Score on Issue Area	Congress		Congress		House	
	Exterior Members	Interior Members	Exterior Members	Interior Members	Exterior Representatives	Interior Representatives
0	1	3 (3)[a]	6	7 (6)[a]	3	6 (4)[a]
1	1	5 (3)	5	4 (2)	2	4 (2)
2	5	6 (2)	5	2	1	4 (1)
3	9	7 (1)	3	3*	8	3*
4	9	5*	2	2	5	1
5	11*	7 (1)	6	2 (1)	6	6 (1)
6	11	3	7*	2	11*	2
7	5	5	4	2	12	3
8	7	2	11	4	3	
9	4	3	17	2		
Median Score	4.59	3.40 (4.17)[b]	5.86	2.67 (4.50)[b]	5.05	2.17 (3.50)[b]
Difference	1.19 (0.42)[b]		3.19 (1.36)[b]		2.88 (1.55)[b]	
% 0-4	40%	57%	32%	60%	37%	62%
% 5-9	60%	43%	68%	40%	63%	38%

*Median score.

a. N.C. Union Whigs.

b. Without N.C. Union Whigs.

astic for the arrangements being established—unless they were so wealthy as to be free from personal economic concerns. The very wealthy were sufficiently concerned for possible postwar profit opportunities to be wary of the terms of the Erlanger Loan. Neither the land values nor the slaveholding patterns back home seemed to bear any general relationship to economic issues in Congress, although some associations do appear, chiefly because these constituent characteristics were so strongly correlated with other and better indices to a congressman's votes. The signals provided by economic circumstances are therefore so mixed that one must be quite wary about any conclusion, other than to say that both indicators, slaveholding and estate value, agree in providing the apparently paradoxical finding that personal and constituent economic status had little consistent relation to member voting on economic issues. While an expectation that these analyses should produce positive results may be considered a particularly crude form of economic determinism, economic influences may have operated less in the realm of property owned than in the more tenuous and subtle sphere of member aspirations and perceptions, and are, in any case, items which we have not been able to measure.

Whether Federal troops yet occupied a member's home district, on the other hand, was a powerful influence on his votes, even on these economic and fiscal subjects. Sometimes it was as specific as the preference for an adequate annual salary instead of per diem and mileage on the part of refugee congressmen. Generally, however, it was the familiar readiness of spokesmen for those beyond the Confederacy's authority to favor ever more sacrificing steps urged upon Congress by an administration at its wit's end. As with conscription, impressment, or suspension of the writ of habeas corpus, so with taxation and monetary policy: those who did not have to pay the piper were quickest to call the more difficult tunes.

It would be nonsense to conclude that the tortuous course of each member of Congress through the economic labyrinth could have been predicted from the personal characteristics used for this investigation. It would be equally unjustified to dismiss these characteristics as insignificant or immeasurable. Men in Congress, as well as those out of it, were well attuned to the consequences of some of the legislation for their own segment of society, so that sometimes personal affluence or that of one's neighbors must have been a distinct contributing force in molding a congressman's views on a given economic issue. Men who had not supported the secession movement or been affiliated with the party credited with the success of secession were usually less committed than their rivals to sacrificial efforts in behalf of independence. And a delegate's constituents were never far from his thoughts when policies affecting them were under consideration. The behavior of those in Congress from occupied areas was a typical political reaction, even though to a very extraordinary set of conditions. Governments-in-exile were not familiar to the Civil War generation of Anglo-Americans, but the implications of release from immediate constituent reaction were plainly illustrated in the contrast on economic issues between those from occupied and those from unoccupied districts.[10]

10. However slender and limited the evidence of associations between member characteristics and various economic issues, it is even less significant for senators than for representatives. Not even the Exterior-status factor is convincingly demonstrated in cross-tabulations for the Senate alone to have had major impact except for the First Session of the Second Congress; yet the close examination of each senator's circumstances at the time of each session does sustain the conclusion that being an Exterior member, or in clear danger of becoming one, was likely to incline even a senator toward greater sacrifices in economic legislation. And for the First Session of the Second Congress, economic issues revealed party distinctions not unlike those in the House.

9 The Price of Nationhood

ON many occasions, the members of the Confederate Congress found themselves, consciously or not, making decisions that were guided by the value they placed on Southern independence. Congressional decisions on certain important subjects have been under sustained analysis in preceding chapters in search of probable determinants of each member's threshold of recoil from further sacrifice. Throughout the life of the Congress, however, many other critical issues were confronted only in such isolated instances that they provided no adequate basis for a separate examination. These issues for each session and house, wherever feasible, have been grouped together here as a broad-covering basis for estimating depth of resolve. In addition, other occasional but significant votes are included that fall within the subjects examined in previous chapters but were not numerous enough in a given session to justify the computation of a separate performance score (even though the topic may have caused numerous divisions in another session). Both of these occurrences contribute items left until now for analysis, and scores in this chapter are based in part on some subjects examined before but principally on concerns not heretofore analyzed. Cumulative scales would not normally be expected in groups of issues that pertain to such diverse subjects, which nevertheless frequently include some of the most pressing questions in the Confederacy.

Roll-Call Issues

For example, scores in this chapter include a wide variety of issues relating to administration of military affairs, beyond the basic legislation of conscription, impressment, or financing. The internal administration of the affairs of Congress provided many of the diverse roll calls, especially determination of meeting and adjournment dates, demands for secret sessions, and amendment of parliamentary rules. Efforts on the part of the sponsors of positive legislation to cut off debate and force action led to many important procedural votes. Determined congressmen frequently had to struggle feverishly to prevent adjournment during the same weeks when General Grant's encirclement of Richmond was becoming nearly complete in 1864 and 1865. Nothing, however, seemed sufficient to stop the melting away of members in attendance toward the end of a session, especially in the closing weeks of the war—a development that emasculates the search for influences on voting posture in the latter part of the last session.

Retaliation against the Federal forces for alleged violations of the practices of civilized warfare also came up from time to time, as did the inevitable dilemma produced by having to re-elect congressmen in 1863 from districts and states beyond Confederate military control. Late in the war, proposals for peace negotiations began to surface in Congress, and rising criticism of the Davis administration was reflected in legislative investigation of an executive department or in a resolution calling for removal of an executive appointee.

The Confederate Senate had the responsibility for considering nominations made by President Davis for important civil positions and for commissions in the army or navy. Perhaps because of this necessary concern with military affairs, the Senate brought to roll-call vote far more issues relating to military administration than did the House. Furthermore, taking seriously its role as "advisor" to the president, the Senate more commonly than the House voted on requests for information from executive departments or for specific action by Davis. The small size of the Senate kept disagreements about procedure from becoming as frequent as in the House. In other respects, Senate votes on diverse issues considered in this chapter were on subjects similar to those in the House.

Some of the apparently varied issues may have had an interrelation within a framework of the state-rights mode of opposing centralization, or so many congressmen seemed to think. State rights in the Confederacy has received considerable emphasis in discussions of behind-the-lines problems during the Civil War. Probably at the root of this problem was the individualism and localism that was characteristic of most of the thinly-settled areas of the United States at the time. Citizens rarely submitted tamely to centralization of authority or regimentation as long as they were unaware of any general welfare requirement for constraint and conformity. Dwellers in the burgeoning cities hardly needed to be reminded that one could exercise only very limited freedom to do as he pleased without infringing upon the rights of others. An isolated farmer could burn down an old smoke house if he wanted to clear it away for a new one; a city dweller would not consider the cleansing value of fire at all. In the constitutional development of the United States, the very special status accorded the state as a political entity created the American idiom for localism and individualism that carried constitutional and traditional sanctity. This idiom, state rights, not only was endowed with special appeal but also had an ever-present spokesman in the person of the state governor, who customarily felt a heavy responsibility for protesting any infringement of the powers "reserved to the States, respectively, or to the people thereof." [1]

The plea of state rights, used to justify persistent opposition on almost any issue, has been mentioned in previous chapters. On problems of habeas corpus, conscription, impressment, and even taxation, there were always some who saw dark dangers to state authority lurking behind pleas of military necessity or appeals to common sense. But there were also other issues that provoked those who feared for the rights of states. Efforts to have the Confederate government underwrite the cost of critically needed railroad construction evoked for some in the Provisional Congress the spectre of an all-powerful central authority, as indicated in an earlier chapter. Occasionally, this issue recurred in later sessions; Senator Oldham even claimed to have "been elected to the Senate on the principle of opposition" to such measures and asserted that state rights had precedence over military necessity.[2]

An especially sensitive subject with state-rights implications throughout the life of the Confederacy was the establishment of a supreme court. The constitution had provided for it, and Jefferson Davis called for it in his message to the First Session of the First Congress. But Congress could never agree to its creation, for the very idea was a disturbing reminder of the old government. The debates reflect this anxiety, with Louis T. Wigfall of Texas going so far as to tell the Senate that the Union had been split by its Supreme Court and by John Marshall's decisions. "Had Chief Justice Marshall been a man of bad character or inferior intellect, the old Union would still have been in existence. But his unimpeachable character, his great intellect enabled him to fasten his principles of nationality upon our institutions." Basically, the question concerned the nature of Confederate government, for if a supreme court was to be supreme, what would happen to state rights? And if it were not supreme, could it be effective? Senator Clement C. Clay preferred weakness to strength, and the major contest revolved about his proposal to deny the court the right of hearing appeals from decisions of state courts. State authorities were equally apprehensive lest restrictions on central authority be eroded by judicial decisions. In consequence of delay upon delay, a supreme court was never established.[3]

1. Permanent Constitution of the Confederate States of America, Article VI, Paragraph 6, from Lee, *The Confederate Constitutions,* p. 197.
2. "Proceedings," XLV, 159.
3. *Ibid.,* XLVII, 208, 210, 220-221.

The desire of a governor to appoint officers of high rank to command troops from his state was not infrequently at the root of state-rights protests. In Davis's judgment, efficiency in the army was too often at odds with the appointive ambitions of governors and the officer-election practices of the men. Lack of competent officers was indeed a problem, partly because men in the ranks often voted for popular rather than able men. Sparrow of Louisiana told the Senate of "an instance where a company in a tiff had elected as captain a man who was in the guard house on a charge of theft," and James Phelan stated that the weakest man was sometimes elected "just as men sometimes on the occasion of a Presidential election will vote for the greatest *** in town [sic]." The result was that many officers, in the words of Major General T. L. Rosser, "have never had the moral courage to perform their duties in a fearless and manly way." Whenever Congress encountered this dilemma, some flare-up of localism was likely.[4]

The right of a state to interpose its police powers in contravention to the claims of authority of provost marshals also led to much debate and several roll-call divisions. And toward the end of the war, the peace concerns in and out of Congress brought out conflicts between the Davis supporters and some who thought that the states should retrieve the powers granted to the central government and hold a convention to negotiate terms of peace. Although many subjects of congressional business inherently involved localism and individualism in contest with centralization of authority, in these limited state-rights sets a clearer theoretical foundation for this tug-of-war may perhaps be found.

Other important issues, which threatened the very foundation of the Confederacy, concerned the role that slaves were to play in the war effort. While some mention has been made of this previously, notably on the question of the twenty-Negro exemption, slaves have appeared remarkably seldom in this study. Whatever else they disagreed on, congressmen usually agreed fully on the role of black men in the Confederacy. For that reason, few votes were taken which involved slaves directly, and roll-call analysis has tended to obscure their significance. The manpower problem near the end of the war changed this, however; and many votes were taken during the last session of Congress on proposals to employ blacks more extensively in the war effort, even touching on the possibility of enlisting them as soldiers. Slave labor had been legislated and utilized before the eleventh hour, although not to the extent many Confederates thought sufficient. In his message of November 7, 1864, Davis asked for more of such labor, but he drew back from calling for black soldiers while ominously warning that "should

4. *Ibid.*, XLVI, 247–248; *O.R.*, ser. IV, vol. III, p. 1080.

the alternative ever be presented of subjugation or of the employment of the slave as a soldier, there seems no reason to doubt what should then be our decision." This was certainly the most momentous question the Congress faced, for, if slaves could be soldiers, they were not likely to be docile, or even slaves. As Howell Cobb, by then a major general, put it, "if slaves will make good soldiers our whole theory of slavery is wrong." [5] And Senator Robert M. T. Hunter of Virginia voiced the misgivings of a number of his colleagues by warning that "if we are right in passing this measure we were wrong in denying to the old Government the right to interfere with the institution of slavery and to emancipate slaves." [6]

It is not at all surprising that this disquieting question had been postponed longer than it should have been, and that officially Davis never did request Congress to authorize black troops. By February 1865, however, it was obvious that only inordinate measures could salvage the Confederate cause, and Davis was advocating this step in private correspondence, explaining that "we are reduced to choosing whether the negroes shall fight for or against us, and . . . all arguments as to the positive advantages or disadvantages of employing them are beside the question." Years later, Davis recalled that he had "argued the question with members of Congress who called to confer" with him, and that he had used his experience in once leading an armed group of his own slaves "against a lawless body of armed white men" as proof that slaves could be effective soldiers. He also remembered warning a senator who was reluctant to undertake the experiment that "if the Confederacy falls, there should be written on its tombstone, 'Died of a theory.' " Many congressmen, however, needed more than these slender reeds, and they continued to the end to raise much opposition to slave soldiers. J. T. Leach of North Carolina thought that arming slaves "would make a San Domingo of our land"; Josiah Turner, Jr., also from North Carolina, even opposed using slave labor in the army on the grounds that laborers could be made to drill, and added that "the country was beginning to learn that all the abolitionists were not in the North," and that Davis had "proposed abolition in a way that created suspicion as to his soundness." Obviously, the issue generated much heat, and the resulting roll calls are of great importance. [7]

Other issues included here concern establishment of a court of claims,

5. *Messages*, I, 495; *O.R.*, ser. IV, vol. III, p. 1009.

6. *The American Annual Cyclopaedia and Register of Important Events of the Year 1864* . . . (New York: D. Appleton and Co., 1867), p. 218.

7. *O.R.*, ser. IV, vol. III, p. 1110; Jefferson Davis, *The Rise and Fall of the Confederate Government* (New York: D. Appleton and Co., 1881), I, 518; "Proceedings," LII, 241–242.

TABLE 9-1

SELECTED ISSUES AND FORMER PARTY

	(A) 1 Cong., 2 Sess. Diverse Issues		(B) 1 Cong., 3 Sess. Military Issues			

	Number of Individuals Assigned Each Score					
Score on Issue Area	House		House		Interior Representatives	
	Democrat	Whig	Democrat	Whig	Democrat	Whig
0	2	1				
1	4	1	4	2	4	2
2	6	1	3	2	1	2
3	7		3	9	2	7*
4			2		1	
5	9*	6	9	3*	6	2
6	12	9*	9*	4	7*	2
7	3	4	7	3	4	2
8	1	1	5	5	4	3
9	4		4		3	
Median Score	4.56	5.28	5.22	4.33	5.29	2.86
Difference	0.72		0.89		2.43	
% 0-4	40%	13%	26%	46%	25%	55%
% 5-9	60%	87%	74%	54%	75%	45%

*Median score.

241

impressment of raw cotton, free postage for newspapers sent to soldiers, regulation of railroads, distilling of liquor, pay and mileage for congressmen, military pay and allowances, demands for resignations and confirmations of appointments, peace negotiations, war goals, and numerous other questions. A very wide array of subjects is, therefore, incorporated in the general diverse, military, state rights, and race-related sets of divisions. Such roll calls, none of which were included in earlier specific topical treatments, have been, where feasible, assigned a "strong" side for the analysis of possible influences on members. Although a large number of votes were too indefinite in content to justify such an assignment, almost every major facet of congressional business is sufficiently represented among the divisions used here as bases for performance scores or scale analysis.

Association of Member Characteristics with Roll-Call Voting Behavior

Former Party Affiliation

Analysis of the associations between former party and votes on a wide assortment of military, state rights, and generally diverse issues provides insights that tend to sustain the judgments of previous chapters. Party-secession resemblance on these issues is marked; nevertheless, the few distinctions will be given a secession-stand subsection treatment as usual.

In the First Congress, former Whigs gave evidence on a variety of items that they were as concerned as former Democrats with making the Confederacy a success. Indeed, a performance set from the Second Session, touching upon such important questions as privateering, railroad construction, organization of a general staff, and disposal of peace-negotiation resolutions introduced by the obstreperous Foote of Tennessee (Table 9–1A), shows Whigs to be more willing to sanction vigorous measures than Democrats. Only 13 percent of the former scored on the lower half of the set, as opposed to 40 percent of the latter. Interior representatives differed little from Exterior colleagues in this respect (table not shown).

During the following session Whig representatives were slightly less determined than Democrats with regard to eight votes relating to military retaliation, more professional procedures for promotion of army officers, general staff organization, blame for the fall of New Orleans, elections within occupied territory, and the establishment of a Confederate Supreme Court (Table 9–1B). Interior representatives, however, were significantly more divided along lines of former party than was the entire House.

For the Senate exclusively during the Second and Third Sessions of the First Congress, two groups of roll calls shared some of the characteristics of state-rights issues. In the Second Session (Table 9–1C), these included a number of divisions on martial law in military theatres; role and power of provost marshals, especially in relation to requiring passes of travelers; appointment of general officers, always a source of trouble with a governor jealous of his alleged power to name commanders for troops from his state; perennial railroad construction needs; and the equally perennial Confederate Supreme Court matter. While adherents of both former parties were generally willing to sustain Confederate efforts, the former Whigs were much more so than the former Democrats. A scale set (not shown), which did not include the supreme court question, indicates essentially the same relationship. A considerably greater distinction between party contingents is revealed by a Third Session set (also not shown). Ten roll calls involved a supreme court and a proposed court of claims, including jurisdiction, salaries, and other sensitive aspects of central judicial authority. Former Whig senators proved to be decidedly more nationalistic than the majority of the former Democrats, who apparently continued to follow their antebellum state-rights proclivities. Again a scale set, based on part of these roll calls but including the same topics, reiterates the findings from the tabulation of performance scores. Essentially the same pattern appears for Interior senators only.

In the Third and Fourth Sessions of the Senate, votes on diverse military matters brought out the same higher scores for Whigs, whether all or only Interior senators are observed. The eleven divisions from the Third Session (Table 9–1D) related to creation of a provisional navy; approval of various military nominations sent in by President Davis; furloughs, pay, and transportation allowances for soldiers; and whether to move the seat of government from exposed Richmond. Another dozen votes from the Fourth Session were on such military problems as exchanged soldiers, disciplining unruly cavalrymen, officer retirement, and approval of presidential nominations; but in addition there were votes on overriding a presidential veto of a bill to aid Kentucky and a disagreement with Davis about his power to name a replacement quartermaster general. At this stage, Davis still fared better among the few Whigs in the Senate than among the Democrats. A cumulative scale from these Fourth Session roll calls (not shown) places the Whigs in a more positive range of scale positions than those assigned to most of the Democrats—with a wider gap between median positions than is the case for comparable scores.

When the Second Congress convened in May 1864, however, Whig senators (all or only Interior) were no longer as likely to occupy the

TABLE 9-1--Continued

	(C) 1 Cong. 2 Sess. State Rights		(D) 1 Cong. 3 Sess. Diverse Military Issues		(E) 2 Cong. 1 Sess. Diverse Military Issies	
	Number of Individuals Assigned Each Score					
Score on Issue Area	Senate		Senate		Senate	
	Democrat	Whig	Democrat	Whig	Democrat	Whig
0	1		2		1	
1	1		2		1	2
2	1		1			2*
3	3	1	1		1	3
4	1		1		1	
5	1*		4*	1	1	1
6	1	2	2		*	
7	1	*	4		2	
8	2		1	3*	2	
9	4	3	1	1	1	
Median Score	5.00	7.00	4.63	7.50	5.50	2.00
Difference	2.00		2.87		3.50	
% 0-4	44%	17%	37%	0%	40%	88%
% 5-9	56%	83%	63%	100%	60%	13%

*
Median score.

244

TABLE 9-1--Continued

(F)
2 Cong., 1 Sess.
Diverse Issues

Diverse Issues Score	Number of Individuals Assigned Each Score			
	House		Interior Representatives	
	Democrat	Whig	Democrat	Whig
0		2 (2)[a]		2 (2)[a]
1		5 (4)		4 (4)
2		2 (1)		1 (1)
3	1	3	1	
4	2	4		3*
5	3	6*(1)	2	4 (1)
6	9	5	6*	
7	11*	5 (1)	7	1 (1)
8	6	4		1
9	2	1		
Median Score	6.18	4.42 (5.00)[b]	5.83	3.33 (4.17)[b]
Difference	1.76 (1.18)[b]		2.50 (1.66)[b]	
% 0-4	9%	43%	6%	63%
% 5-9	91%	57%	94%	38%

* Median score.

a. N.C. Union Whigs.

b. Without N.C. Union Whigs.

TABLE 9-1--Continued

(G)
2 Cong., 2 Sess., Feb.-Mar.
Diverse Issues

Diverse Issues Score	Number of Individuals Assigned Each Score			
	House		Interior Representatives[a]	
	Democrat	Whig	Democrat	Whig
0		7 (6)[b]		6*(6)[b]
1	1	3 (2)	1	2 (2)
2	1	2		
3	5	*	4	
4	2	1	1	1
5	3	2	1*	
6	3	4	1	
7	8*	3 (1)	3	1 (1)
8	7	1	3	
9	3	1		1
Median Score	6.19	2.50 (5.13)[c]	5.00	-0.08 (6.00)[c]
Difference	3.69 (1.06)[c]		5.08 (1.00)[c]	
% 0-4	27%	54%	43%	82%
% 5-9	73%	46%	57%	18%

*Median score.

a. Interior at least until the beginning of the Second Session.

b. N.C. Union Whigs.

c. Without N.C. Union Whigs.

246

position of greater dedication (Table 9-1E). In the First Session, several roll calls on appointment of generals, procedure for handling presidential nominations, and resolutions about peace negotiations and war purposes revealed a Whig element (in both scores and scale positions) that was far weaker than its antagonist. In contrast, eight divisions during the last session, relating chiefly to defense concerns, furnish little basis for exposing alignments based on former party affiliations. Some of the questions on these roll calls were general in character, but most were, one way or another, challenges to the action or judgment of President Davis in assigning army commanders and exercising his command function.

Over on the House side of Congress, a noticeably different relationship between former Democrats and former Whigs developed on Second Congress diverse-subject roll calls. During the First Session, eighteen votes that covered most of the significant subjects grouped in the miscellaneous category found Democrats clustered at high scores, while Whigs are scored all along the range of levels (Table 9-1F). The lowest three levels were occupied exclusively by Whigs, chiefly the North Carolinians, but even without them a significant difference in median scores and in occupancy of low levels distinguishes the two groups. Among Interior representatives exclusively, former party rivals overlap only slightly in scores; indeed, party divides these Interior members roughly into three levels: low level North Carolina Whigs, other Whigs in the center, and high level Democrats. The importance of these distinctions is enhanced by the serious nature of some of the subjects confronted, which included loyalty problems, war purposes, peace negotiations, officer appointment and promotion procedure, debate limitation, members' mileage allowances, and hostility to President Davis on several other matters.

A few miscellaneous roll calls taken during the winter of 1864-1865 in the last session of Congress (not shown) suggested a continuation of greater determination among Democrats which was more evident in the House than in the Senate and was most evident among Interior members. Some Democrats, perhaps resigned to defeat, are found in the lowest levels here, in contrast to the diverse-issue pattern from the First Session. Issues underlying this tabulation include House action on military control of newspapers and congressional pay and mileage allowances, and Senate consideration of the adjournment date and of court-martial proceedings for cases of conspiracy against the Confederacy. During this same period other House votes on the emotion-charged topics of secret sessions, cutting off debate, Christmas adjournment, and extending the length of the session produced increased distinctions between Democrats and Whigs. In any case, for both of these sets, scores in each party were lower among those from the Interior than among the entire membership. Whatever the significance of party, here, as elsewhere, it is modified by other considerations.

During the last weeks of Congress, the representatives were still wrestling with their own salary and mileage allowances, suspensions of the rules for various alleged emergency resolutions, and establishment of a secret service agency. Eight roll calls of this nature (Table 9–1G) illustrate the continuation to the end of Democratic efforts to carry on, with help from some Exterior Whigs, in the face of opposition from a few Interior Democrats and a large proportion of the Interior Whigs (who were by this time almost exclusively the North Carolinians).

The last session of Congress also confronted wide-ranging topics that may be considered to have had state-rights or localist implications because they generally arose from efforts to centralize and consolidate government activities, or at least to sustain the Confederate central administration. Expulsion of Foote, railroad construction, cotton impressment, consolidation of army units and concentration of command function in a general-in-chief, resolutions on war purpose and on a convention of the states for peace negotiations, the supreme court question, establishment of professional methods of officer selection, and censure of Secretary of State Benjamin provided an excellent seventeen-division set (Table 9–1H). The Democrats in the House are found chiefly in the higher levels of scores, the North Carolina Union Whigs at the bottom levels (except for Burgess Gaither, who usually voted like a Democrat-Secessionist), with the remainder of the Whigs in the middle and upper scores. Leaving the North Carolinians out of consideration, however, little party-based distinction can be observed for the House vote. The same is true for Interior representatives, but it should be observed that, without the North Carolina representatives, only seven Interior Whigs were voting on enough of these divisions to be scored. A scale constructed from a part of these roll calls (not shown) reproduced essentially the same distinction between Democrats and Whigs as that found in the performance-score tabulation. State-rights and peace questions on six roll calls during the final weeks (not shown) revealed a continuation of the Democratic-Whig distinction, except that, in the desperate extremity of defeat, some of the Exterior Whigs are found at the highest level, joined by Representative Gaither of North Carolina.

Slavery and race questions came to a head in the last session of Congress. From November 1864 to mid-February 1865, the House divided eleven times on questions concerned with military employment of slaves and free blacks, both as laborers on fortifications and as soldiers. Eight Senate divisions occurred on the same subjects, though with greater

TABLE 9-1--Continued

(H)
2 Cong., 2 Sess., Nov.-Feb.
State Rights

State Rights Score	Number of Individuals Assigned Each Score			
	House		Interior Representatives[a]	
	Democrat	Whig	Democrat	Whig
0		7 (7)[b]		7 (7)[b]
1	1	2 (1)	1	1 (1) *
2	2	2	1	1
3	2	5 *	2	1
4	4	2	2	
5	12*	4 (1)	4*	1 (1)
6	9	5	3	3
7	8	1	3	
8	3	4	2	2
9				
Median Score	4.96	3.00 (4.50)[c]	4.75	1.00 (5.50)[c]
Difference	1.96 (0.46)[c]		3.75 (0.75)[c]	
% 0-4	22%	56%	33%	63%
% 5-9	78%	44%	67%	38%

*Median score.

a. Interior at least until the beginning of the Second Session.

b. N.C. Union Whigs.

c. Without N.C. Union Whigs.

TABLE 9-1--<u>Continued</u>

(I)
2 Cong., 2 Sess., Nov.-Feb.
Slavery and Race Issues

Slavery and Race Issue Score	Number of Individuals Assigned Each Score			
	Congress		Interior Members[a]	
	Democrat	Whig	Democrat	Whig
0	3	7 (6)[b]	3	6 (6)[b]
1	3	5 (3)	3	4*(3)
2		3		2
3	8	4	5	2
4	10	2*	2*	
5	11*	7 (1)	5	2 (1)
6	2	2		
7	8	4	2	1
8	5	5	2	1
9	3		1	
Median Score	4.23	3.25 (4.42)[c]	3.25	0.75 (2.50)[c]
Difference	0.98 (0.19)[c]		2.50 (0.75)[c]	
% 0-4	45%	54%	57%	78%
% 5-9	55%	46%	43%	22%

*Median score.

a. Interior at least until the beginning of the Second Session.

b. N.C. Union Whigs.

c. Without N.C. Union Whigs.

250

TABLE 9-1--<u>Continued</u>

(J)
2 Cong., 2 Sess., Feb.-Mar.
Slavery and Race Issues

Slavery and Race Issue Score	Number of Individuals Assigned Each Score			
	House		Interior Representatives[a]	
	Democrat	Whig	Democrat	Whig
0	2	4 (4)[b]	2	4 (4)[b]
1	1	6 (3)		3*(3)
2		1		
3	1	4*(1)	1	2 (1)
4	2	1	2	
5	7	3 (1)	6*	1 (1)
6	2			
7	9*	2	2	1
8	4	2	1	
9	5	3		
Median Score	6.17	2.50 (4.25)[c]	4.33	0.50 (4.50)[c]
Difference	3.67 (1.92)[c]		3.83 (0.17)[c]	
% 0-4	18%	62%	36%	82%
% 5-9	82%	38%	64%	18%

*Median score.

a. Interior at least until the beginning of the Second Session.

b. N.C. Union Whigs.

c. Without N.C. Union Whigs.

TABLE 9-2

PROCEDURAL ISSUES AND STAND ON SECESSION

(A)
1 Cong., 2 Sess.
Adjournment and Convening

| Score on Issue Area | Number of Individuals Assigned Each Score | | | |
| | House | | Interior Representatives | |
	Secessionist	Unionist	Secessionist	Unionist
0	1	2	1	1
1	2	8	2	8
2	4	1	4	1*
3	3	1	1	
4	1		1	
5	9	5*	7	2
6	5		4	
7	3*	3	2	3
8	13	2	9*	1
9	13	5	13	3
Median Score	6.67	4.30	7.00	1.50
Difference	2.37		5.50	
% 0-4	20%	44%	20%	53%
% 5-9	80%	56%	80%	47%

*Median score.

252

emphasis on the slave-soldier issue. This momentous issue of the role to be played by black men in the last-ditch Confederate war effort served to scatter both Democrats and Whigs all along the various score levels (Table 9-1I). Lower median scores for Whigs are found, whether the entire Congress or the Interior members only are examined, but all significant party distinction would be erased if the North Carolina Union Whigs were omitted. A scale from House votes (not shown) reinforces this finding. A few roll calls from the House of Representatives in the final weeks of Congress concerned the use of slave soldiers but also touched upon compensation schemes for owners whose slaves were lost because of war-connected activity (Table 9-1J). Democrats apparently hardened their stance in these days of desperation, but Whigs continued to vote on this subject substantially as they had earlier in the session; in this instance, however, omission of the North Carolina bloc in the entire House still leaves a significant party contrast. Both Democrat and Whig performance-level medians sag about two points when Interior representatives are considered separately. A scale set utilizing some of the same roll calls repeats this general pattern.

Position on Secession

These findings for party are very closely paralleled by the ones for secession stand. In the Senate, for example, the results obtained by comparing Secessionists with Unionists are quite similar to those indicated in Table 9-1C and D for the contrast of Democrats·and Whigs. This is especially true for the First Congress. In the Second, senators were divided less by secession stand than by former party affiliation— thereby differing from their House colleagues. The number of men involved in Senate tabulations is so small, however, that little confidence can be placed in inferences drawn from such slight distinctions.

It is in the House of Representatives that the relationship between these two membership characteristics becomes most obvious. Both performance and scale sets reveal such a close resemblance between findings on party and secession that it is not necessary to examine extensive tabulations. There are, however, a few exceptions. One is a set which consists of eight roll calls dealing with dates for adjourning the Second Session of the First Congress and convening the Third. Democrats did not differ from Whigs enough to justify offering a party table, but Secessionists and Unionists pulled much farther apart, especially among Interior members only (Table 9-2A). A second dissimilarity not justifying a party tabulation also concerned adjourning and convening, and it occurred in the Second Session of the Second Congress (not shown).

Although party and secession analyses of these diversified topics reveal

TABLE 9-3

SELECTED ISSUES AND FEDERAL OCCUPATION

	(A) 1 Cong., 2 Sess. State Rights		(B) 1 Cong., 3 Sess. State Rights	
State Rights Scale Position	Number of Individuals Assigned Each Position			
	Senate		Senate	
	Exterior Senators	Interior Senators	Exterior Senators	Interior Senators
0		1	2	1
1	1	3	2	6
2	2	2		1
3	*	2*	2*	3*
4	1	3	1	4
5	2	3	2	2
Median Position	2.50	2.50	2.25	2.17
Differ- ence	0.00		0.08	
% 0-2	50%	43%	44%	47%
% 3-5	50%	57%	56%	53%

*
 Median position.

254

TABLE 9-3--Continued

	(C) 2 Cong., 1 Sess. Diverse Issues		(D) 2 Cong., 2 Sess. Feb.-Mar. Diverse Issues	
	Number of Individuals Assigned Each Score			
Diverse Issues Score	House		House	
	Exterior Representatives	Interior	Exterior Representatives	Interior
0		2 (2)[a]	1	6 (6)[a]
1	1	4 (4)	2	4 (2)
2	1	2 (1)	4	
3	3	1	3	4*
4	4	4	2	1
5	3	6 (1)	6	2
6	10	9*	7*	2
7	10*	13 (1)	9	3 (1)
8	11	1	7	3
9	4		5	2
Median Score	6.15	5.22 (5.61)[b]	5.71	2.88 (5.00)[b]
Difference	0.93 (0.54)[b]		2.83 (0.71)[b]	
% 0-4	19%	31%	26%	56%
% 5-9	81%	69%	74%	44%

* Median score.

a. N.C. Union Whigs.

b. Without N.C. Union Whigs.

few consequential dissimilarities, the ones found do parallel the conclusions of earlier chapters. For in cases where there are important variations between the two vital member characteristics, it is almost altogether a House rather than Senate phenomenon, and secession stand commonly provides greater differences than does party. The important thing, however, seems to be not so much the differences themselves, which are relatively minor, varied in character, and uncertain as to exact meaning, but rather the fact that the exceptions occurred primarily in the Second Congress. This supports the hypothesis that the 1863 elections and the subsequent immediacy of defeat changed voting behavior. And again it has become obvious that, from mid-war onward, Whigs and Unionists sooner than Democrats and Secessionists faltered and balked at the ever steeper and more perilous way that was supposed to lead toward Confederate nationhood.

Slaveholding and Value of Estate

With exceptions here and there, no evidence suggests that roll-call responses on these assorted issues were in any way traceable to personal slaveholdings or estates. This is true even for such issues as the utilization of slaves by the army. Whether the entire House or only Interior members be considered, the same patterns occur repeatedly, from session to session. Often they appear in a curvilinear shape, such as we have frequently encountered before. Sometimes, a line connecting the median in one category with that in the others is a straight one, which may occasionally slant toward rich or poor and thereby give the table some small associative meaning. Also frequent is a zigzag pattern which hints at the basic irrelevance of these two member characteristics in determining attitudes toward the issues being examined.

The Senate, with its small membership, is more difficult to judge. A few very wealthy senators were apparently strong supporters of President Davis in military affairs. This leaves the impression, in some sets of Senate scores, that the most wealthy were inclined to greater dedication, but both the inadequate size of the group and the absence of supporting evidence from other roll-call sets warn against inferring that it was the wealth level that exerted significant influence. Some of the curvilinear patterns are found in these cross-tabulations, with center range slaveholding or wealth groups tending to lower scores than either extremes. Again, for several reasons heretofore mentioned, no inference is justified that economic status per se was a major factor.

The most impressive pattern in the majority of the tabulations by slaveholding or wealth is the remarkable similarity of distribution of scores or scale positions in each member category. Often a cluster of very high and another of very low scores may be found for each slave-holding or wealth classification—which only underscores the dominance of influences other than personal economic considerations.

The general land values of a representative's district and the slavehold-ing pattern in his home county offer equally little assistance toward understanding his votes on the diverse issues discussed in this chapter. Almost needless to say, only Interior districts can be significantly scruti-nized for possible clues. The Exterior membership of Congress was so sharply aligned with high land values and small slaveholdings that the often-documented and understandable strong stance of these men as Exterior delegates overrides any associations observed in the entire House voting between any other constituency characteristics and position on any of the diverse issues.

A few associations of strength appear for Interior districts but are readily attributable to one or another of the familiar forces dominant in molding the roll-call contours of the Confederate Congress. The two most common circumstances that account for these few definite associa-tions are the impact of the North Carolina Union Whigs and the likeli-hood of the war's bringing immediate and undesirable consequences to a member's district. Prospects of race adjustments in the interest of black manpower in arms was, for instance, less disturbing to those South Alabamians and Floridians far from actual battlefields than to Virginians and Carolinians, whose slaves were readily available in the crisis theatre of the war as Grant and Sherman forged the jaws of the final trap.

Interior or Exterior Constituency

Whether a member of Congress represented an occupied or threatened area was usually not very important where these diverse, state-rights, or race-related questions are concerned. The miscellaneous nature of the issues makes for less clear-cut results than this characteristic has provided in preceding chapters. In a general way, members of the First Congress displayed little distinction on the basis of occupied status. If any tendency existed, it was for Exterior members to be slightly more belligerent; but the association is weak.

Senate standings for two sets of state-rights roll calls are shown in Table 9-3A and B. The issues in the Second Session incorporate a wide range of problems, both war-related and long-term, including railroad building and supreme court status. A scale set (Table 9-3A) yields only minor variations between columns, but the absurdly thin basis for gener-alization is made all too evident by the small size of the group under analysis. In the next session, the Third, a far stronger level for Interior senators appears on a performance set relating exclusively to a supreme

TABLE 9-3--<u>Continued</u>

Score on Issue Area	(E) 2 Cong., 2 Sess. Nov.-Feb. Procedural Issues House		(F) 2 Cong., 2 Sess. Feb.-Mar. Procedural Issues House		(G) 2 Cong., 2 Sess. Feb.-Mar. State Rights House	
	Number of Individuals Assigned Each Score					
	Exterior Representatives	Interior	Exterior Representatives	Interior	Exterior Representatives	Interior
0	2	6 (5)[a]	3	8 (6)[a]		6 (6)[a]
1	3	4 (1)	2	5*(1)	1	1 (1)
2	4	3*(2)	2	2*(1)		
3	7	4	4	2 (1)	2	3
4		1	1			
5	9*	1	8	3	4	2
6	7	2	4	2	14	4*
7	7	2	4*	2	1*	
8	7	1	6		2*	4
9	3	1	15	2	20	7 (1)
Median Score	4.94	1.83 (2.88)[b]	6.13	1.00 (4.17)[b]	7.00	5.38 (7.13)[b]
Difference	2.11 (2.06)[b]		5.13 (1.96)[b]		1.62 (0.13)[b]	
% 0-4	33%	72%	24%	65%	7%	37%
% 5-9	67%	28%	76%	35%	93%	63%

* Median score.

a. N.C. Union Whigs.

b. Without N.C. Union Whigs.

TABLE 9-3--<u>Continued</u>

(H)
2 Cong., 2 Sess.
Slavery and Race Issues

Slavery and Race Issues Score	Number of Individuals Assigned Each Score			
	Nov.-Feb.		Feb.-Mar.	
	Congress		House	
	Exterior Members	Interior Members	Exterior Representatives	Interior Representatives
0	2	9 (6)[a]		6 (4)[a]
1	1	7 (3)	4	4 (3)
2	3	1	1	1
3	9	4*	4	1 (1)
4	14		1	2*
5	16*	7 (1)	6	7 (1)
6	5	1	4	
7	12	3	13*	3
8	10	4	5	1
9	2	1	10	2
Median Score	4.50	2.38 (4.25)[b]	6.31	3.75 (4.50)[b]
Difference	2.12 (0.25)[b]		2.56 (1.81)[b]	
% 0-4	39%	57%	21%	52%
% 5-9	61%	43%	79%	48%

*
  Median score.

a. N.C. Union Whigs.

b. Without N.C. Union Whigs.

court and a possible court of claims (not shown). On this type of long-range issue, with a stormy history known to all congressmen, the dominant association was former party affiliation, with Whigs at the high level favoring a strong judiciary and Democrats clustering in the low levels in opposition. The result is an incidental difference between Exterior and Interior senators, large at first glance but extremely volatile. If only one Exterior senator's placement were different, the results could be altered radically. As if to emphasize the hazards of analysis for so small a body, the scale set on this same topic (Table 9-3B), based on a portion of the roll calls, yields median scores for the two groups that are almost identical.

The Second Congress brought out the expected increasing differences between the members from outside the area of effective Confederate control and their colleagues from unoccupied portions of the country. The First Session, with eighteen House roll calls covering an extensive array of sensitive questions, among them war goals, peace negotiations, officer selection, and procedural matters, heralded the trend (Table 9-3C). Although median scores and percentages are not far apart, the dominance of the lowest three levels by Interior representatives and the opposite balance in the highest two levels is worth noting. By the Second Session, the difference in median scores had increased. The widening gap during the last weeks is evident in the tabulation for the February-March period of the last Congress, during which more sensitive questions were voted upon than in the November-February period (Table 9-3D).

Internal congressional administration is represented for the Second Session of this last Congress by struggles between those who wanted to keep Congress in business and get on with the work and those who were trying to recess, or adjourn, or talk on until Richmond was in flames (Table 9-3E). The greater determination of Exterior representatives is, of course, evident, as is the expected pre-eminence of Interior men with very low scores and Exterior men at the highest score levels. Even if the North Carolinians were excluded from the November 1864-February 1865 performance set, the differential between those with occupied constituencies and those from the core of the Confederacy would be significant, with 59 percent of the Interior members not North Carolinians in the lower half of the performance set (compared to 33 percent for Exterior members) and a difference between medians of 2.06. Nevertheless, it must be observed that members from both sides of the line were scored in almost every level. The occupied-status factor was significant, but far from all-pervasive. And it may be noted that, during February and March 1865 (Table 9-3F), the scores for Exterior representatives and for Interior men other than the North Carolinians increased alike in the face of disaster. When the North Carolina Union Whigs are omitted from the computation, the difference between medians of the two groups is about the same as for the November to February period.

State-rights concerns in the last House session, chiefly in terms of questions about centralization of authority and administration, form the basis for only moderate difference in median scores between Exterior and Interior representatives (Table 9–3G). At the extreme levels, however, the differences are clear (and well supported by a scale set, not shown, for the November to February period). The Interior cluster at the lowest two levels was once again composed exclusively of North Carolinians, without whom the members from unoccupied territory were surprisingly and significantly more committed than the Exterior men present. Aside from the North Carolina bloc, these Interior men were apparently persuaded by necessity. One sometimes wonders why the North Carolina delegation even bothered to remain in Richmond, for, unlike many of their colleagues, their way of escape was still open. Perhaps some credence should be given to the claim afterward made by Representative J. M. Leach that he was the leader of a peace party in the Second Congress, although his personal leadership may well be questioned and his mention of thirty-five members sounds suspiciously close to the number of Unionists in the House, not all of whom were even weak in support of the Confederacy, let alone peace men.[8]

In the last session of Congress, slavery and race issues, such as the use of slave soldiers, produced the familiar pattern of generally higher scores among the Exterior members, but with significant scattering of both sides all along the range of performance scores (Table 9–3H) and scale positions. As usual, the North Carolina delegation is responsible for many of the low-scoring Interior congressmen, and it should not be forgotten that any willingness shown by Exterior members to engage in free-wheeling decision-making about slavery issues may have been due to factors other than the approach or presence of the Federals. Much of the occupied area (e.g. Tennessee, northern and western Virginia, Missouri, and Kentucky) also had fewer slaves than did the Deep South. This may have been just as important as the Union army or location of constituents in explaining attitudes toward slavery and the Confederate war effort.

The broad scope of issues incorporated in this chapter has been responsible for a more complex pattern of relations between Exterior and

8. Barnes, *History of the Congress*, II, biographical entry for Representative James M. Leach.

Interior delegates than was true for single critical questions, such as whether to expand conscription or to suspend the writ of habeas corpus. Many influences were at work in the roll-call decisions of congressmen on these varied questions, but eventually the onset of hardships and military disaster produced some evidence that Federal occupation status was a significant factor in congressional voting behavior, though perhaps not quite so important as in previously treated topics.

Summary

The continued reappearance, even though less marked, of the same general relation between a congressman's former party, secession stand, economic status, or home-area condition on the one hand, and on the other, his likelihood of appearing at any given level of war-like zeal, strengthens inferences drawn in earlier chapters about the influences of these biographical characteristics. The two subsequent chapters offer the most extensive reiteration available in support of the conclusions emerging from these investigations. This will appear first in the form of two inclusive scale sets from the Second Congress, which cut across the subject content of that Congress and on which it is possible to establish a clear position for most members of the Second House on significantly interlocking cumulative scales. A second type of summary examination will employ intercorrelations among both performance-score and scale sets and will provide various average scores and positions.

10 Determination and Defeatism

OUR scale analysis for previous chapters has been confined primarily to roll calls grouped by subject. A cluster of habeas corpus divisions or a set of votes on conscription have been analyzed to determine the extent to which the items are scalable. The result was the discovery of a variety of dimensions which served as valuable tools of measurement. Political spectra dealing with such topics as impressment, conscription, or constitution-making have provided profitable clues in our search for those background characteristics of the congressmen which helped to determine voting behavior. But cumulative scaling can be used in ways other than those thus far involved. One of these other procedures is to search for dimensions that cut across subject-content areas in an effort to discover not only the determinants of congressional behavior but also the issues that defined congressional attitudes. A habeas corpus scale tells us much; but a scale dealing with several subjects tells us more.

Although the presence of single-subject scales seems obvious enough—too obvious, for often they do not exist where one thinks they ought to—some might question whether that which we label a cross-content scale exists at all. But in twentieth-century presidential campaigns in the United States, candidates have talked about economic policy, civil rights, crime, pollution, foreign policy, and medicare, in the same breath. Problems of poverty, gun control, renewal of the cities, and national security have been lumped together and discussed as if they were part of the same basic question. While the applicability of this illustration may be questioned on the ground of failure to differentiate between rhetoric and reality, often it is the rhetoric that makes the reality. Whether a historian thinks there is or is not an intrinsic relation between two issues may be totally irrelevant. If enough congressmen thought, however fallaciously or foolishly, that a relation existed, it did exist and will probably be uncovered in roll-call responses. And scale analysis can help us to determine whether roll calls on two or more apparently different subjects evoked voting alignments that might be expected on a single subject.

In examining the British House of Commons in the 1840s, for example, William O. Aydelotte reported debates in which a speech on representational reform also covered such varied subjects as the national debt, the Irish question, landowners, and the Corn Laws.[1] More to the point in this investigation are the wide-ranging speeches in the Confederate Congress. To cite only a single example, one debate during the last session of the Senate was on the specific issue of using slaves as army laborers. But the speakers also discussed the desertion rate in the army; Confederate evacuation of Manassas in 1861; the peninsular campaign of 1862; the military situation in Georgia and South Carolina; several generals, including Joseph E. Johnston, Robert E. Lee, and P.G.T. Beauregard; tactics; arming slaves as soldiers; emancipation; the cabinet; and even Jefferson Davis himself. Although an underlying connection between these topics may readily be seen by latter-day historians, especially as they recall the impending debacle of the Confederate armies, Senator Waldo P. Johnson of Missouri "was astounded at the range this debate had taken on this amendment." He thought it necessary to remind his colleagues that "the question was not whether we shall put negroes into the army as soldiers, but whether we shall restrict to forty thousand the number of negroes to be put at the disposal of the commanders of our armies to cook, drive, throw up fortifications, &c." But Senator Johnson went off on a tangent, too, and discussed General Joseph E. Johnston. Senator John W. C. Watson of Mississippi took this all in stride and remarked in the course of debate that he would follow the example of his colleagues and "express his opinion on other subjects not pertinent to the bill under consideration." Others tried to turn Senate attention back to the subject, but with little success.[2]

But perhaps Senator Watson was mistaken; it could be that all these ideas were pertinent. If one part of a dimension, or scale, is introduced into debate, it would be logical to expect discussion, motions, and divisions on other items in the set as well. It is quite possible that the Senate debate referred to above covered a wide-ranging military dimension which was defined only in small part by the issue of using slave labor in the army.

Dimensions defined only by speeches are not very reliable. It is simply that the rambling debates strongly suggest the hypothesis that there were scale-type clusters of roll calls, not confined to a single content area, that define basic concepts held by a large number of legislators. Indeed, such scales are frequently discovered in roll-call analysis. In the British House of Commons for the 1840s, Aydelotte found a scale covering such varied issues as Chartism, Corn Laws, income tax, and livestock

1. William O. Aydelotte, "Voting Patterns in the British House of Commons in the 1840s," *Comparative Studies in Society and History,* V (January 1963), 145.
2. "Proceedings," LII, 281–306.

duties, and another concerning poor laws and labor regulations.[3] Duncan MacRae, Jr., discovered in the United States Eighty-first Congress what he called a "Fair Deal" scale, which included rent control, social security, housing, the Taft-Hartley Act, a proposed new cabinet post, the Communist Control Act, and the House Un-American Activities Committee.[4] In effect, the scales elicited in the Confederate Constitutional Convention were of this type, as were some of those uncovered in the state-rights content areas.

Usually the detection of such dimensions calls for some different, and restricting, techniques. There is a limit to the number of roll calls which can be lumped together for scale analysis. The investigator who deals with about two thousand divisions, as has been done here, is compelled to divide his data into small groups for examination. One very reasonable approach is to subdivide votes by Congress and session, but even then there are often too many to handle. A next logical step is to separate the votes into subject-content areas, as has been done for scale analysis in the foregoing chapters.

However, if one attempts to discover scales which include a variety of subjects, the subject-content method is not very helpful. In order to reduce the number of divisions that he works with, the researcher must attempt instead to study a cross section of the votes. In short, up until now, we have studied the bulk of the votes of the Confederate Congress in a topic-by-topic search for cumulative scales; for this chapter, the Congress was divided into four parts, each roughly corresponding to a single year of its existence, and a cross section of the same roll calls was selected from each portion for further examination.[5] Thus, a type of roll-call selection enters which we have not presented before, since

3. Aydelotte, "Voting Patterns in the British House of Commons in the 1840s," pp. 137, 142.

4. Duncan MacRae, Jr., *Dimensions of Congressional Voting: A Statistical Study of the House of Representatives in the Eighty-First Congress,* University of California Publications in Sociology and Social Institutions, vol. I, no. 3 (Berkeley and Los Angeles: University of California Press, 1958), pp. 225, 240–245.

5. The four periods are Provisional Congress, February 4, 1861, to Feburary 17, 1862; First Congress, First and Second sessions, February 18, 1862, to October 13, 1862; First Congress, Third and Fourth sessions, January 12, 1863, to February 17, 1864; and Second Congress, May 2, 1864, to March 18, 1865.

These are the criteria for roll-call selection:

a. Use those that concerned issues of importance, in either contemporary or later judgments.

b. Use those of unknown importance if they appear potentially significant.

c. Use enough to get a cross section of the business of each of the four periods mentioned above.

d. Reject most items on adjournment, questions of privilege, and points of order, unless

no content area examined so far was large enough to be unmanageable. This selection process is admittedly highly subjective, in spite of conscious efforts at objectivity; but since any quantitative investigation of history is likely to incorporate subjective elements, we cannot eliminate a promising avenue of approach on that account. Instead, for this part of the study, each of the almost two thousand roll calls in the Confederate Congress was examined and seven hundred were selected for further analysis.

The results of such examination, it was hoped, would be twofold: discovery of those issues which defined the ideological origin—if any existed—of Confederate congressional voting behavior, and some insight into the influences of background characteristics on a man's position on ideological spectra. One of the advantages of scale analysis is that, by comparing scales for one period with those of another, basic concepts may be displayed as they emerge and examined for extent of persistence over time. While it is often difficult to determine just what general rationale or principle of action motivated behavior on a cross-content scale, or on any scale, it is useful simply to have discovered its existence. If there was an ideological basis for the behavior of the Confederate Congress, and if—an important qualification—that basis was registered in a sufficient number of divisions, cross-content scaling should expose it.

But for much of the Confederate Congress activity, no such cross-content scales may be found that meet the very rigorous requirements inherent in this method of wide-ranging search for scalable sets.[6] In such instances, if there was an ideological conflict, it was not manifestly defined by the roll calls. In the Provisional Congress, only two small scales totaling fifteen votes were discovered out of a cross section of fifty-eight divisions. One of these scales may be loosely called a state-rights scale, as it dealt

---

they are obviously introduced as tactical maneuvers or are especially important. Few of these will scale, except with other parliamentary issues.

e. Reject votes with less than 10 percent dissent. (Such items tend to fit almost any scale, especially if the scale is not well defined.)

f. Reject duplications.

g. Reject other roll calls lacking apparent importance.

6. In preceding chapters, the scaling technique employed inspection of a matrix of four-cell tables. The proportion of tolerated "error" relationships reached as high as 10 percent. For these cross-content searches, however, a Q matrix was used similar to that utilized by Duncan MacRae, Jr., "Intraparty Divisions and Cabinet Coalitions in the Fourth French Republic," *Comparative Studies in Society and History*, V (January 1963), 164–211. This procedure requires a higher degree of scalability for roll calls that are widely different in proportion of members voting on the positive side. Using a Q of .7 as the threshold of scalability, two roll calls with 70 percent and 30 percent respectively on the positive

with supreme court review of state court decisions, selection procedures for field grade officers (whether they should be elected or appointed), railroad construction, and a Davis veto. The other scale appeared to involve taxation and constitutional issues. Several votes concerned the tax measures of August 1861, and others came from the Constitutional Convention, including problems of court jurisdiction, status of nonslave-holding states, and internal improvements.

While these may be suggestive findings, their significance is not clear. In the chapter on the Provisional Congress, it was pointed out that, for a variety of reasons, the results of analysis for 1861 are not very useful, and all of these reasons are valid here. Some issues in these scales were decided in a Congress containing as few as forty-three members, while other divisions were held in a body approaching a hundred members. In such a legislature, the longer the time span involved, the less meaningful the results of scale analysis will be, because only a handful of delegates may have voted on both roll calls in a pairwise comparison. The scale relationship is therefore determined by a treacherously small tally of votes. The best that may be said of these Provisional Congress scales is that they heralded a possible and hardly unexpected disagreement about the problem of raising a national revenue and the role of the central government in the Confederacy.

The results of cross-content scaling for the first two sessions of the First House are less promising. A sample of eighty-eight votes was used, but only fourteen of them fit into either of the two scales discovered. The implication is that, in 1862, Congress showed even less hint of ideological orientation than it had in 1861. Although the roll calls selected for examination dealt with all of the types of business the two sessions involved, both scales incorporated only votes concerned with conscription and the accompanying problem of exemption; and, with the exception of only one roll call, each scale was confined to a single session. For 1862, therefore, a broad sweep demonstrates the absence of cross-content scales.

The Third and Fourth Sessions of the First House were apparently

---

side are not acceptable, even with only 5 percent in the error cell. Very widely divergent marginals, such as 80 percent and 20 percent respectively on the positive side, will be unacceptable if as few as 2 percent of the votes fall in the error cell. These scales therefore are extremely high in quality and have very high coefficients of reproducibility. This rigorous technique has undoubtedly filtered out a number of votes which the 10 percent method would have included. On the whole, however, the advantages should outweigh the disadvantages. In this chapter, a minimum of six votes was considered necessary to establish the presence of a scale. For further discussion of cumulative scaling techniques, see MacRae, *Issues and Parties in Legislative Voting,* Chapter II.

characterized even less by a commonly held frame of reference, for, in spite of examining a large sample (140 votes), absolutely no cross-content sets could be found that met the severe scale criteria. For the period before 1864, therefore, cross-content scale analysis is of minimal help in discovering ideological differences within Congress that could be used in search of possible influences on individual voting. But the pressures of war and impending defeat wrought striking changes in the Second Congress.

Throughout this study, the investigators have noted the remarkable lack of scalability for the bulk of Confederate Congress roll calls even in specific subject-content areas, and how this changed somewhat during the Second Congress. This may well be, at least in large part, attributable to two major factors. By the time of the Second Congress, there was a more even division by party or secession stand—two characteristics that apparently were quite influential in determining how lawmakers voted; and, most important, the Second Congress confronted impending defeat. The intervening congressional elections of 1863 reflected voter awareness along these lines by increasing the proportion of Whigs and Unionists, as well as the number of members highly susceptible to defeatism. Furthermore, while a few Confederates claimed after the war that they had had forebodings as early as 1862, by the opening of the First Session of the Second Congress in May of 1864, far more than a few could see the handwriting on the wall. It is most likely that a third factor, declining attendance, also played a role. In November and early December 1864, a total roll-call vote of eighty or even ninety members was not uncommon. In January 1865, vote totals were usually in the seventies, a figure seldom reached in March, when numerous divisions brought out less than sixty legislators. It is not that all the missing congressmen went home, for on occasion over seventy votes were cast even toward the end. Perhaps it was that the apathetic left Richmond, if they could, or passively awaited their doleful fate if they could not. This left the floor to die-hard Exterior delegates advocating warlike programs and to Interior congressmen characterized perhaps by equal determination but of more pacific points of view.

The war was in one of its seasonal lulls after the adjournment *sine die* of the First Congress on February 17, 1864. But just as the new body met, heavy fighting resumed, and it did not abate until the final capitulation of the Confederate armies a year later. During the First Session, General Grant launched his bloody attacks from the Wilderness to Cold Harbor. When Congress adjourned, Grant was in the process of establishing his siege at Petersburg, while General Sherman had begun his invasion of Georgia.

Jefferson Davis gave little public evidence of his apprehension during this session. To be sure, he informed Congress that if his power to suspend the writ of habeas corpus were repealed "it would be perilous, if not calamitous," but he had been saying things like that for the previous two years.[7] Only a few instances of apprehension openly appeared among congressmen. When Richmond's alarm bell was heard during a meeting of the House, and Samuel St. George Rogers of Florida immediately moved that Congress organize a company to defend the city from a supposed attack, many of his colleagues simply refused to take him seriously. Although Foote supported Rogers, stating that "he did not believe it would ruin or hurt the Government much if someone were killed," Henry C. Chambers of Mississippi contented himself with inquiring whether Foote spoke only for himself. Rogers's proposal was tabled.[8]

Certainly the legislation of this session showed no sense of urgency. Adjournment and congressional pay were major topics of debate from the very beginning, and there was a clamorous contest over the repeal of a habeas corpus suspension act that was due to expire in the near future anyway. Congressmen took a more realistic line in private correspondence, but it was the debates and the votes which presented the face of Congress to the general public.

Things were different in the last session. Although many lawmakers had evidently given up hope and were merely marking time until the end, there were those who advocated vigorous measures because they felt that victory or at least some concession on slavery or compensation for slave property was still possible. Real desperation is implicit in the otherwise insignificant joint resolution to provide for voluntary individual contributions to the government, or in the act providing for the safety of the archives. Most of all, desperation is evident in the eventual passage of a law providing for slave soldiers; and when a premature adjournment motion was debated on March 8, 1865, several congressmen were no longer willing to conceal their forebodings. Senator Vest of Missouri thought "the contest might almost be said to be narrowed down to the possession of the Confederate capital," and Senator Waldo P. Johnson, also of Missouri, referred to "a gloom [that] had pervaded the publick [sic] mind."[9] Even Jefferson Davis was forced to allow his anxiety to become known during that last darkening winter as he begged Congress

---

7. *Messages,* I, 452.
8. "Proceedings," LI, 47–48.
9. *Ibid.,* LII, 454, 463.

to postpone adjournment until a long list of urgent pieces of legislation could be passed.

As the end came ever closer, important changes were taking place in the voting behavior of Congress. The high quality and significance of specific content scales for the Second Congress, indicated in foregoing chapters, reflected these changes in a striking but perhaps somewhat piecemeal way. Legislators who had earlier been unable to perceive any principle underlying the broad range of congressional business evidently began to comprehend the principle of national survival; some wished to throw in the towel unless a favorable issue could be achieved without certain sacrifices, while others wished to go all out for victory. For the first time, a voting pattern emerged as coherent as normally expected in a legislative body; crisis had galvanized the Second Congress into scalability. And it is only now that these parliamentary spectra include many of the truly important and decisive roll calls. Out of a cross section of 139 divisions, twenty-five votes fit into two comprehensive scales. They cover the entire period of the Congress, although most of them are from the 1865 portion of the Second Session, and only four are from the short First Session of May and June 1864. It is significant that, even within the Second Congress, cross-content scalability increased rapidly toward the end.

Issue Content of Military-Determination Scale

The first and less important of the two scales deals with a potpourri of items which varied from adjournment to tax-in-kind (Table 10-1). It included issues directly related to the military and some which provoked pained cries of state rights (though only one directly involved the rights of states), such as a tough conscription exemption bill and a conflict over Confederate use of state-chartered shipping. Perhaps military-determination is the best label for the principle involved, since the scale provides still another measure, in some degree, of the lengths to which an individual was willing to go to attain Confederate success. Those most extreme in their unwillingness to sacrifice, least determined to achieve victory at all costs, wanted to override Davis's veto of a bill which would allow the Secretary of War or the Commanding General to promote officers under certain conditions. The President had vetoed the law on the ground that the proposal would "confer a power of appointment on a commanding general not warranted by the Constitution." [10] More importantly, such legislators also wished to ignore Jefferson Davis's appeal of March 13, 1865, that with the country "environed

10. *Journal of the Confederate Congress,* VII, 745.

TABLE 10-1

CONTENT OF SECOND HOUSE CROSS-CONTENT
MILITARY-DETERMINATION SCALE

Scale Position	Voting Posture of Representatives Assigned This Position[a]
0	No support of strong (pro-Confederate) position on any item.
1	To support President Davis in his veto of a bill providing for certain types of officer promotions. March 11, 1865. 76 percent.
2	To agree to rescind the established date for final adjournment so that the session could be extended. March 13, 1865. 70 percent.
3	To table an amendment intended to guarantee that black laborers on military defenses would not be used as soldiers. January 27, 1865. 68 percent.[b]
4	To reject an attempt to postpone indefinitely (hence, by implication, to support) a defiant pro-Confederate resolution concerning the recently-held Hampton Roads peace conference. February 24, 1865. 65 percent.
5	To pass a conscription bill that included the repeal of exemptions for overseers of slaves. January 23, 1865. And to support President Davis in his veto of a bill that would have lost to the Confederate government the critical right to one half of the cargo capacity of blockade runners (the bill exempted from this half-cargo-space right any ship chartered by a state government). June 10, 1864. 61 percent on a combined item.
6	To reject an amendment that would have exempted from the tax-in-kind law any farm that did not produce enough food to supply its inhabitants and animals (permitting instead a commutation to the nearly worthless Confederate currency). March 3, 1865. 57 percent.
7	To reject another attempt to exempt from the tax-in-kind law, this time in behalf of disabled soldiers whose farms were cultivated only by family members. March 3, 1865. 28 percent.

a. Appendix VI provides _Journal_ page location of each roll call and further explanation of the scaling procedure.

b. See Appendix VI for an explanation of the use of cutting points as close together as 68 percent and 70 percent.

with perils," and the capital "in greater danger than it has heretofore been," it was necessary that "more energetic legislation" be passed. Davis pointed to needs concerning impressment, taxation, conscription exemptions, utilization of militia, and suspension of the writ of habeas corpus, and requested Congress to postpone its impending adjournment.[11] To oppose the postponement meant, in effect, to reject his position on most of these vital issues. The determined members of Congress, on the other hand, tried to keep open the door through which black laborers in the army might eventually be made into soldiers. Even on the brink of final and total disaster, they wished to flaunt their defiance of the Union in a strongly worded joint resolution deprecating the results of the Hampton Roads conference and the unwillingness of the Union to grant "no terms except such as a conqueror grants to the subjugated." Asserting that "no alternative is left to the people of the Confederate States, but a continuance of the war or submission to terms of peace alike ruinous and dishonorable," Congress declared that fighting would continue until "the independence of the Confederate States shall have been established."[12] (The actual division at issue was on a motion to postpone the resolution indefinitely; this was defeated and the resolution then passed with concurrence of all representatives except J. T. Leach of North Carolina.) Less extreme stands were measured by votes on a strict conscription exemption law, which would virtually end the exemption of overseers, and on sustaining a Davis veto of a bill which would have excluded state-chartered shipping from an existing requirement to import goods for the Confederate government. Finally, the questions at the positive (pro-Confederate) end of the scale found the hard core of extreme-measures men opposing the weakening of the tax-in-kind, either by allowing a money commutation or by exempting families of soldiers and disabled soldiers from its levy if they employed no hands, slave or free.

Cross-content scales will not score as many individuals as the others we have used, because the longer the time span covered and the more subjects employed, the more likely it is that nonscale types and infrequent voters will cloud the record. Even so, 93 of the 107 voting members could be placed, and of those who could not, only three had erratic voting patterns. More importantly, this military-determination scale provides some interesting differences in scale scores of members with opposing characteristics.

11. *Messages,* I, 544–548.
12. *Laws and Joint Resolutions of the Last Session,* pp. 134–135.

TABLE 10-2

MILITARY-DETERMINATION POSITION AND FORMER PARTY

Military Determination Scale Position	Number of Individuals Assigned Each Position			
	Second Congress			
	House		Interior Representatives	
	Democrat	Whig	Democrat	Whig
0	2	7 (6)[a]	2	6 (6)[a]
1	2	5 (2)	2	3*(2)
2	4	2	3	1
3	2	1	1	
4	6	2	2*	1
5	3*		1	
6	15	15*(1)	5	5 (1)
7	4	4	1	
Median Position	5.00	5.07 (5.32)[b]	3.25	0.67 (5.13)[b]
Difference	0.07 (0.32)[b]		2.58 (1.88)[b]	
% 0-3	26%	42%	47%	63%
% 4-7	74%	58%	53%	38%

*Median position.

a. N.C. Union Whigs.

b. Without N.C. Union Whigs.

Association of Member Characteristics
with Roll-Call Voting Behavior

Former Party Affiliation

Among the entire membership of the House of Representatives, there was a decided tendency for Whigs to occupy weaker positions on the military-determination scale than did Democrats. Because of the polarization on the extreme ends of the scale, however, this tendency is not immediately apparent, for the Whigs actually have a higher median position than their opponents. Nevertheless, as Table 10–2 illustrates, 74 percent of the Democrats occupied the determination end of the scale, as contrasted with only 58 percent of the Whigs. Still, the presence of polarization serves to remind us that regardless of group behavior, Whigs were to be found at virtually all scale levels. The analysis of Interior members, however, is less murky, since the median scale position for Whigs is almost three levels below that for Democrats, corresponding to the greater proportion of Whigs in the lower half of the scale.

For the scale tabulations in this chapter, Interior indicates Interior at least until the beginning of the Second Session of the Second Congress, except where occupied status is the characteristic under analysis. In these two instances, Tables 10–6 and 10–11, Interior indicates not occupied until the last session of Congress had adjourned. As has frequently been noted, positions for both Democrats and Whigs are usually found to be lower as one moves from the entire House to the Interior members only. Regardless of party, congressmen from the unoccupied portions of the Confederacy were distinctly less sacrificing than their unfortunate colleagues, but the spirit of sacrifice sagged much more precipitately for Interior Whigs than for Democrats.

Position on Secession

It is obvious that the ever-present correlation between party and secession views on the one hand, and voting behavior on the other, is quite strong on this scale. Unionists take weaker positions than Secessionists; they are found at all scale levels, and, like Whigs, they are polarized strongly (Table 10–3).

When Interior members are examined, the gap between medians is significantly wider, and while both Secessionists and Unionists of the Interior took weaker positions as a group, the change in median was more impressive for the latter. It is nonetheless notable that all Secessionists on the weak half of the scale were from the unoccupied, or Interior, portion of the Confederacy except one—William G. Swan of

TABLE 10-3

MILITARY-DETERMINATION POSITION AND STAND ON SECESSION

Military Deter-mination Scale Position	Number of Individuals Assigned Each Position			
	Second Congress			
	House		Interior Representatives	
	Secessionist	Unionist	Secessionist	Unionist
0	2	7 (6)[a]	2	6 (6)[a]
1	1	7 (2)	1	5*(2)
2	4	2	4	
3	2	1	1	
4	6	2*	3*	1
5	4*	2	2	2
6	11	14 (1)	4	4 (1)
7	4	1	1	
Median Position	4.50	3.50 (5.04)[b]	3.33	0.60 (4.25)[b]
Difference	1.00 (0.54)[b]		2.73 (0.92)[b]	
% 0-3	26%	47%	44%	61%
% 4-7	74%	53%	56%	39%

*Median position.

a. N.C. Union Whigs.

b. Without N.C. Union Whigs.

Tennessee. The effect of Interior status, however, was felt less by Unionists than by Whigs. The median position of Interior Whigs was 4.40 positions below that for all Whigs, but Interior Unionists were only 2.90 positions below that for all Unionists.

Slaveholding

In measures of both absolute and relative slaveownership there is a slight tendency for those with medium-sized holdings to have lower scale scores, but this does not seem to be particularly marked or significant, and what differences do exist may be due to the geographic congruence of Unionism and small holdings. The median level for each Interior category (except category 2) is one or two positions below the corresponding level for the entire House. This across-the-board similarity merely reinforces suspicions that here geography (indirectly an economic consideration) is more important than immediate personal economic interests. A glance at Table 10-4 illustrates the situation. Constituent slaveholding patterns also add little to an understanding of voting on this scale set, as the attitude which the scale defines seems to have affected about equally men from districts characterized by each of the three levels of slaveholding (large, medium, and small slaveholdings).

Value of Estate

The combined value of personal and real estate, a much more accurate measure of wealth than slaveholding, still gives the researcher rather low yields. Lawmakers owning estates valued at less than $50,000 have a higher median position than those whose estates are larger (Table 10-5), but it would be leaning too heavily on the rather ambiguous data to try to draw any sweeping conclusions from this finding. Polarization in both economic groups warns of other and more pervasive influences; positions for Interior members, for example, are significantly lower regardless of wealth. Generally speaking, whether measured by slaves or estate totals of members, or by slaveholding patterns or land values back home, wealth gives only faint leads to those who wish to determine why congressmen voted as they did on this military-determination scale.

Interior or Exterior Constituency

The other characteristics have indicated an influence on voting behav-

TABLE 10-4

MILITARY-DETERMINATION POSITION AND SLAVEHOLDING

Military Deter- mination Scale Position	Number of Individuals Assigned Each Position									
	Second Congress									
	House					Interior Representatives				
	Absolute Slaveholding[a]					Absolute Slaveholding[a]				
	0	1	2	3	4	0	1	2	3	4
0	1	2	4	1	1	1	2	3	1	1
1		3	1	3	1		2	1*	2	1
2		1	2	1	2			2	1	1
3	1			1		1				
4	1	5	2*		2	1*	3*		*	1*
5	2	2	2		1*	1	1	1		1
6	5*	9*	6	8*	4	1	3	1	4	1
7	1	5	1	2	3					1

*Median position.

a. Absolute Slaveholding:
   0 = No slaves
   1 = 1-9 slaves
   2 = 10-19 slaves
   3 = 20-49 slaves
   4 = 50 or more slaves

TABLE 10-5

MILITARY-DETERMINATION POSITION AND WEALTH

Military Determination Scale Position	Number of Individuals Assigned Each Position			
	Second Congress			
	House		Interior Representatives	
	Absolute Estate		Absolute Estate	
	$49,999 or Less	$50,000 or More	$49,999 or Less	$50,000 or More
0	7	2	6	2
1	3	5	2	4
2	2	4	2	2*
3	2	1	1	
4	5	4*	3*	1
5	3	2	3	1
6	23*	9	7	3
7	8	4		1
Median Position	5.20	3.88	3.33	1.50
Difference	1.32		1.83	
% 0-3	26%	39%	46%	57%
% 4-7	74%	61%	54%	43%

*
Median position.

TABLE 10-6

MILITARY-DETERMINATION POSITION
AND FEDERAL OCCUPATION

Military Determination Scale Position	Number of Individuals Assigned Each Position	
	Second Congress	
	Exterior Representatives	Interior Representatives
0	1	8 (6)[a]
1	5	3 (2)
2	4	2
3	3	
4	6	4*
5	3	4
6	29*	8 (1)
7	12	1
Median Position	5.33	3.50 (4.38)[b]
Difference	1.83 (0.95)[b]	
% 0-3	21%	43%
% 4-7	79%	57%

*Median position.

a. N.C. Union Whigs.

b. Without N.C. Union Whigs.

279

ior arising from the occupation status of a representative's constituency.[13] Analysis of that factor (Table 10-6) leads to the conclusion that it was extremely important. Lawmakers with the highest scale scores were more than likely to come from areas outside effective Confederate control. More remarkable is the fact that only 30 percent of the Interior representatives were at one of the strongest two scale positions, while 65 percent of the Exterior members occupied one of these extremes. In like manner, the weakest scale position is dominated eight to one by Interior representatives. As might be expected, for the entire house, the strength of association between Exterior or Interior status and scale position is greater than that between any of the other characteristics examined and position on this scale.

Summary

The conclusions to be drawn from this analysis of the Second House military-determination scale support previous findings, but by themselves they must be considered indecisive. Strength of association is not great except for occupied-status considerations. Moreover, scoring was troublesome, because several issues were in such close proximity to each other on the scale that the distinction between positions was sometimes hazy and ill-defined.

Issue Content of Defeatism-Realism Scale

The other cross-content scale of the Second House does not have these drawbacks, and it is probably the most revealing single scale of this study (Table 10-7). It dramatizes well the basic concepts underlying Confederate congressional behavior. It is obvious from these issues and their close relationship to each other that representatives finally developed an integrated concept of events. This dimension seems to be concerned with some of the same problems as the military-determination scale of this session, but because it contains twenty-one divisions and ten scale positions, and because these positions are reasonably well distributed along the scale, it defines the problems more accurately. This is labeled a defeatism-realism scale, for most of the issues posed the question of whether the Confederacy's attempt at nationhood was to be continued, and if so, whether success was to be sought by a realistic

13. In all tables of this chapter except the ones on Occupied Status, an Interior representative is one whose home area was not occupied or seriously threatened by the Union army prior to the beginning of the Second Session of the Second Congress. For Occupied-Status tables, districts overrun during the Second Session are treated as occupied.

appraisal of events, or by continued recourse to the old, outworn, and essentially meaningless shibboleths of state rights. Here we see the vigorous advocates of independence locked in desperate legislative encounter with defeatists, or, at the very least, unrealistic opponents of the measures without which even the most remote chance of Confederate victory would have been obviated.

It is not surprising that the items comprising this dimension were all vital, and that at the weak, antinationalist, antisacrificing end of the scale are two associated divisions which demonstrate reasonably well that these issues were closely related to the peace movement. The two roll calls are not technically part of the scale because they missed meeting the criteria for inclusion by very narrow margins, but they are close enough to indicate that a relationship did exist in the minds of many of the congressmen who desired peace on almost any terms. The first of these issues concerned a resolution introduced by J. T. Leach of North Carolina that accepted the principle of peace without independence by asserting that "when ever [sic] the Government of the United States shall signify its willingness to recognize the reserved rights of the States and guarantee to the citizens of the States their rights of property, as provided in the Constitution of the United States and by the laws of Congress . . . we will agree to treat for peace." [14] The other associated peace issue is a suggested amendment by John A. Gilmer to the resolution on the Hampton Roads conference which was a part of the first scale. Gilmer proposed the establishment of an "American diet," which was to be something of a halfway house between Union and separation. There were to be only two votes in this body, one each for Union and Confederacy, and its acts would have to be ratified by the respective Presidents and Congresses. It would have been the ultimate form of John C. Calhoun's theory of concurrent majorities put into practice. [15]

The most extreme of the scale issues that do meet requirements for inclusion also demonstrate the relevancy of the peace movement, for it concerns Foote's resolution to call a convention of the states (which was a transparent means to achieve peace). Eighty-three percent of the membership clashed with Foote on the propriety of such a venture. Another of Foote's resolutions attacked Davis's conscription exemption

14. "Proceedings," LI, 377–378; *Journal of the Confederate Congress,* VII, 301–303. The resolutions were defeated 76-6, but later in the day the votes of three congressmen were changed so the *Journal* shows a vote of 79-3. Pressure may have been applied to make J. M. Leach, Ramsay, and Fuller change their votes. The other minority votes were cast by J. T. Leach, Logan, and Turner. All six were North Carolina Union Whigs who sat only in the Second House.

15. *Journal of the Confederate Congress,* VII, 606–607, 646–647.

TABLE 10-7

CONTENT OF SECOND HOUSE CROSS-CONTENT
DEFEATISM-REALISM SCALE

Scale Position	Voting Posture of Representatives Assigned This Position[a]

0 No support of strong (pro-Confederate) position on any item.

To reject a proposal condemning secession and calling for peace without precondition of independence for the Confederacy. November 25, 1864. 93 percent.[b] This roll call does not meet the criteria for inclusion within the scale, although it does scale with other roll calls in this set. It is included here to help define the upper limits of the scale. No position is assigned for this roll call.

1 To table a resolution calling for a convention of the states (the object of which was transparently the making of peace). December 2, 1864.
And to refer to committee rather than pass a proposed resolution disapproving of President Davis's request for an end to blanket exemption from conscription for editors, printers, and other newspaper employees. November 9, 1864.
And to pass a bill to allow the use of state troops outside their home states. January 20, 1865.
86 percent on the combined item.

To reject a proposal for an "American diet" as a possible way to end the war without Confederate independence. February 24, 1865. 80 percent. This roll call barely misses meeting the criteria for scale inclusion and is not assigned a position. It is listed because of the information it provides about the content of this scale.[c]

2 To reject an attempt to weaken a bill providing for control of the transportation system by the Secretary of War. February 15, 1865.
And to pass the bill providing such control of the transportation system. February 15, 1865.
And to pass a bill to raise coin to purchase military supplies. March 14, 1865.
And to table a proposal to restore the writ of habeas corpus. May 12, 1864.
And to pass a bill to pay commissioners serving under the existing act suspending the writ. June 6, 1864.
And to table a resolution denouncing the suspension of the writ of habeas corpus. May 20, 1864.
80 percent on the combined item.

282

TABLE 10-7--Continued

3   To expel Henry S. Foote from the House. January 24, 1865.
    67 percent.

4   To reject a call for the question on a proposed resolution
    denouncing suspension of the writ of habeas corpus. January
    20, 1865. 62 percent.

5   To reject an attempt to postpone indefinitely a bill to sus-
    pend the writ of habeas corpus. December 8, 1864. 60 per-
    cent.[d]

6   To reject an attempt to table a bill to suspend the writ of
    habeas corpus. March 14, 1865.
    And to order to third reading a bill to suspend the writ of
    habeas corpus. March 14, 1865.
    And to reject an attempt to reconsider passage of the bill
    to suspend the writ of habeas corpus. March 15, 1865.
    And to pass the bill suspending the writ of habeas corpus.
    March 15, 1865.
    And to pass a bill to suspend the writ of habeas corpus.
    December 8, 1864.
    And to reject an attempt to forbid suspension of the writ of
    habeas corpus in cases testing liability to conscription.
    December 6, 1864.
    51 percent on the combined item.

7   To reject an attempt to table a Senate-amended bill to sus-
    pend the writ of habeas corpus. March 1, 1865. 43 percent.

8   To reject a motion ordering to third reading a bill to pro-
    vide for the payment of local market prices for impressed
    goods. March 13, 1865. 28 percent.

9   To reject an attempt to exempt from the tax-in-kind law dis-
    abled soldiers whose farms were cultivated only by family
    members. February 22, 1865. 17 percent.

a. Appendix VI provides Journal page location of each roll call
and further explanation of the scaling procedure.

b. The Journal vote (vol. VII, 302) is 79-3; but the original vote
(76-6) had been altered when Fuller, J.M. Leach, and Ramsay changed
their votes (pages 302-303).

c. Journal, VII, 646 bottom.

d. See Appendix VI for an explanation of the use of cutting
points as close together as 60 percent and 62 percent.

proposals because they would have revoked the exemptions of several occupational classes, among them newspaper editors, a pet group of Foote's; this was opposed by 81 percent of the congressmen. Almost as extreme and unpopular was the doctrinaire, unrealistic opposition to vitally needed legislation to permit the use of state troops outside their home states. Less immoderate, but still falling into a low scale position, was opposition to a bill giving the Secretary of War control over the railroads, steamships, canals, and telegraph lines of the Confederacy, control extensive enough that civilians employed in such operations would "be subject as if serving with armies in the field," i.e., they would be under martial law.[16] Further indicating the defeatism inherent in low scale positions was opposition to a bill authorizing the Secretary of the Treasury to borrow $3,000,000 in coin, which Jefferson Davis, in his desperation message of March 14, 1865, had indicated was absolutely necessary to supply the army.

Representative Foote was also involved in an issue which was more toward the middle of the defeatism-realism spectrum, but this time the problem was Foote himself. Early in January 1865, he had been arrested while attempting to cross Confederate lines on his way to Washington, where he hoped to lay the groundwork for peace. The more realistic die-hards of the House sought to expel him, but twenty-five others opposed such action.

On the other end of the scale were issues on which the defeatists had more company. One of these was the important revision of the impressment laws that was examined in Chapter 6. Although the system of impressment was designed not only to procure goods but also to save the government money, the latter goal was abandoned as Congress ordered the army to pay local market prices for goods appropriated for its use. Since the government was about out of money, passage of this bill forcing payment of inflated wartime valuations hamstrung the military supply system, although many congressmen apparently were not convinced of that fact. The most radical stance on the high-score end of this defeatism-realism scale was supported by only 17 percent of the voting congressmen. The small minority of hard-core realists, who saw that nothing but the most extreme sacrifices could possibly bring victory, opposed another attempt to weaken the tax-in-kind by the sentimental exemption of nonslaveholding soldiers' families or disabled soldiers from the operation of the law.

The other twelve roll calls composing this defeatism-realism dimension, scattered throughout the scale, illustrated the defeatists' refusal to lay

16. *Laws and Joint Resolutions of the Last Session,* p. 60.

personal freedom on the altar of necessity, by tooth and nail opposition to any suspension, however limited, of the writ of habeas corpus. Some even refused to pay commissioners who had been appointed to administer the suspension regulations that were in effect at the start of the First Session of the Second Congress. The rather large number of habeas corpus roll calls in this dimension is due to the easy scalability of the issue and the very large number of votes taken on it. The frequency of its presence does not weaken the scale's credibility.

The usefulness of this scale is enhanced not only by its scope but also by the placement of a large proportion of the members of the House in one of its scale levels. Ninety-eight of the 107 voting delegates can be assigned positions, and of the nine who cannot, only Fayette Mc-Mullin of Virginia, whose speeches were as erratic as his roll calls, had a garbled voting pattern. Some congressmen did not vote often enough to establish a scale pattern; this includes one representative who became a Union prisoner, another who died, still another who had been injured in a carriage accident, and one of the two House members who was elevated to the Senate. The other four did not express themselves on enough roll calls, and as far as is known had no particular excuse. At least two of them simply went home. Again cross-content scaling shows decided relationships between scale positions and some of the individual member characteristics.

Association of Member Characteristics
with Roll-Call Voting Behavior

Former Party Affiliation

The uninformed observer might imagine that the longer the Confederacy lasted, the smaller would be the distinction on basic issues between those who had taken opposing sides in the party battles of the 1850s. Presumably, voting in the Provisional Congress, especially in the Constitutional Convention, when basic governing principles were at stake, should display a greater party cleavage than voting at the end of the Confederacy's life. As a matter of fact, however, exactly the opposite development occurred. Differences between former Whigs and former Democrats are greater on this defeatism-realism scale than they were in the convention in 1861; it almost appears as if party antagonism had been growing during these strife-filled years, instead of declining as most legislators had hoped. Whigs took a significantly weaker stand on the items associated with the defeatism-realism dimension than their Democratic opponents, with median positions almost four levels apart (Table 10–8). But despite bunching on the 0 level for the Whigs and

TABLE 10-8

DEFEATISM-REALISM POSITION AND FORMER PARTY

Defeat-ism Realism Scale Position	Number of Individuals Assigned Each Position			
	Second Congress			
	House		Interior Representatives	
	Democrat	Whig	Democrat	Whig
0	1	12 (8)[a]		10*(8)[a]
1	4	4	3	
2	3	3*	1	1
3	3	1	3	1
4	3	2 (1)	2	2 (1)
5	3	3	2*	
6	6*	2	2	
7	11	5	3	2
8	4	3		
9	4	2	3	1
Median Position	5.67	1.83 (4.33)[b]	4.25	-0.15 (3.00)[b]
Difference	3.84 (1.34)[b]		4.40 (1.25)[b]	
% 0-4	33%	59%	47%	82%
% 5-9	67%	41%	53%	18%

* Median position.

a. N.C. Union Whigs.

b. Without N.C. Union Whigs.

TABLE 10-9

DEFEATISM-REALISM POSITION AND STAND ON SECESSION

Defeat-ism Realism Scale Position	Number of Individuals Assigned Each Position			
	Second Congress			
	House		Interior Representatives	
	Secessionist	Unionist	Secessionist	Unionist
0		12 (8)[a]		10*(8)[a]
1	2	5	2	1
2	3	4*	2	1
3	2	3	2	3
4	6	2 (1)	5*	2 (1)
5	3	3	2	
6	4*	3	2	
7	10	3	3	1
8	5			
9	4		3	
Median Position	5.88	1.13 (2.00)[b]	3.90	-0.10 (2.17)[b]
Difference	4.75 (3.88)[b]		4.00 (1.73)[b]	
% 0-4	33%	74%	52%	94%
% 5-9	67%	26%	48%	6%

*
Median position.

a. N.C. Union Whigs.

b. Without N.C. Union Whigs.

287

TABLE 10-10

DEFEATISM-REALISM POSITION AND SLAVEHOLDING

Defeat-ism Realism Scale Position	Number of Individuals Assigned Each Position			
	Second Congress			
	House		Interior Representatives	
	0-19 Slaves	20 or More Slaves	0-19 Slaves	20 or More Slaves
0	11	2	8	2
1	6	2	1	2
2	1	6		3
3	5		5*	
4	6*	2	5	2*
5	2	5*		3
6	6	3	1	1
7	9	8	3	2
8	7			
9	2	4	2	1
Median Position	3.75	4.80	2.70	3.50
Differ-ence	1.05		0.80	
% 0-4	53%	38%	76%	56%
% 5-9	47%	63%	24%	44%

*Median position.

288

on the 6 and 7 levels for the Democrats, both parties had representatives in all scale positions, indicating that to some degree the issues involved in the defeatism-realism scale actually cut across lines of former party. As one expects, differences are accentuated when the Exterior members are deleted. Both median positions and percentage quadrants indicate a marked slippage of pro-Confederate support in the Interior tabulation.

Position on Secession

As on the previous scale, in the entire House the stand that a congressman had taken on the secession issue in early 1861 was more likely to be strongly associated with his outlook on defeatism and realism than was his former party affiliation (compare percentage quadrants in Tables 10–8 and 10–9). Unionist support for the war effort, whether judged by the entire House or Interior members only, was extremely weak; and although House Unionists once again bunched at the lower positions, on this scale there was not a single Unionist in the entire House assigned to any of the highest scale positions, and there was no Secessionist at the lowest level of support. The strength of association is very great here. Among Interior members, Secessionists are found well distributed, but only one Unionist was to be found on the stronger half of the scale.

Slaveholding

The number of slaves a legislator owned is not a significant predictor of voting behavior on the defeatism-realism scale. In both absolute and relative slaveholding, the curvilinear relationship reappears, as those with medium-sized slaveholdings seem to have been less realistic than either their small-planter or nabob colleagues. Table 10–10 shows a modest difference between members holding less than twenty slaves and those with twenty or more. The decisive element in this is the large group of small slaveowners at the lowest position. That this much association existed between voting and member slaveholding is apparently because of unusual geographic coincidence. Slaveholding patterns of constituents are no more useful predictors of position on this scale, for, as mentioned before, areas of low slaveholding are, with few exceptions, outside the area of effective Confederate control.

Value of Estate

Findings here are even less useful than those for slaveholding. The form of the very weak association is similar, with members owning medium-sized estates being less realistic and more defeatist than either

TABLE 10-11

DEFEATISM-REALISM POSITION AND FEDERAL OCCUPATION

Defeatism Realism Scale Position	Number of Individuals Assigned Each Position	
	Second Congress	
	Exterior Representatives	Interior Representatives
0	4	9 (8)[a]
1	7	1
2	6	1
3	2	3
4	2	6*(1)
5	4	3
6	8*	3
7	17	4
8	11	
9	4	3
Median Position	5.94	3.42 (4.33)[b]
Difference	2.52 (1.61)[b]	
% 0-4	32%	61%
% 5-9	68%	39%

* Median position.

a. N.C. Union Whigs.

b. Without N.C. Union Whigs.

their richer or poorer colleagues. District land values add nothing of significance to the picture, merely reflecting, as they have previously, the pattern of land holdings in occupied territory.

Interior or Exterior Constituency

The repeated skewing of other characteristics by the element of enemy occupation of a legislator's district indicates that it was an important molding force in creating voting patterns. On the defeatism-realism dimension, as on others we have examined, percentage quadrants indicate that Exterior representatives were far more likely to be found at the positive end of the scale than were their fellows from the unoccupied portions of the Confederacy (Table 10-11). So marked is this tendency that only 21 percent of the Interior delegates are to be found in the highest three levels, as opposed to 49 percent of the congressmen from "imaginary constituencies," although the latter displayed an interesting polarization by having a significant part of their number, who were mostly Union Whigs, clustered in the weakest three levels. By the same token, there are a few Interior congressmen, most of them Secessionists, in the strong positions. It is obvious that the concurrence of Secessionist record and Exterior status, or Unionist record and Interior status, was a dual attribute powerfully associated with a legislator's voting behavior on the roll calls of this scale.

Summary

Party and secession characteristics are strongly associated with the voting behavior of representatives on the defeatism-realism cross-content scale of the Second House, indeed, these indicators are more definite than they were on the previous military-determination scale. Secession stand again seems to have been more significant than former party affiliation. Economic relationships are particularly uninformative. The very rich, as a group, seem to take stronger, less ideological, less defeatist, more realistic positions than those with middling wealth. Perhaps by late 1864 these men fully realized that, having more to begin with, they had more to lose, and therefore voted with a corresponding degree of realism. Even so, the economic data associations are very weak and support no further conclusion than that our analyses have not been able to find any significant economic influence on voting on these two cross-content scales. Occupied territory status, by contrast, is quite important in itself, but even more decisive when reinforced by the appropriate party and secession views.

TABLE 10-12

CROSS-TABULATION OF CROSS-CONTENT SCALES
FROM SECOND HOUSE

Military-Determination Scale

Scale Position	Number of Individuals Assigned Each Position							
	0	1	2	3	4	5	6	7
0	7	3			1		1	
1		2				1	2	1
2			2	1	1	1	2	
3	1	1		1		1		
4	1		1		1	2	3	
5		1	1		2		2	
6					1	1	5	2
7					2	1	13	1
8				1			3	6
9			1		1		2	3

Defeatism-Realism Scale

Number of Individuals Assigned Each Position

Comparison of Cross-Content Scales

The military-determination scale does not illustrate voting cleavages as well as the larger defeatism-realism scale. Median differences are greater on the latter and associations are strong, except for economic characteristics, which seem basically irrelevant to both dimensions. We might say that positions on these scales were mainly indices to the will to survival as a separate nation-state, and were significantly associated with party, secession, and occupied-status differentials.

For these reasons, as well as because of individual scoring similarities to be discussed below, these two cross-content scales seem alike in many ways. Even the content overlaps. Although the military-determination scale leans toward military and tax issues, and the defeatism-realism scale is more concerned with peace and the organization of Southern society for the war effort, it must be admitted that the contents are so similar that the labels primarily serve an operational rather than a descriptive convenience. A cross-tabulation of these two dimensions illustrates other similarities and differences (Table 10–12). The largest clusters indicate that an extremist on one scale was more than likely to be an extremist on the other, either scoring high on both or low on both. Only a few can be placed at the low extreme on one scale and high on the other—but the small cluster found there is significant. It seems that some congressmen had somewhat different views of the underlying principles motivating congressional behavior.

The composition of these clusters reveals much the sort of trends one should expect from prior discussion. In the group which occupied low positions on both dimensions, fourteen men whose reluctance to sacrifice was most notable created what some historians have called a state-rights faction and what men in 1865 often called a peace party.[17] Eight of these congressmen were the now familiar North Carolinians. Only three had been members of the First Congress, and, at a time when approximately two thirds of the membership came from counties which had been occupied or threatened by Union troops, eleven of the fourteen represented Interior constituencies (i.e., not occupied or seriously threatened before the beginning of the Second Session of the Second Congress, in November 1864). Most significant, however, is the fact that there

17. It should be remembered that the "peace party" in the Confederacy was not a party at all, and it did not, with a mere handful of exceptions, desire peace at absolutely any price. The great majority felt that peace could be achieved on the basis of some acceptable terms if only Davis would undertake the initiative. On the losing end of a war, they quite unrealistically believed that the enemy would make major concessions at the negotiating table. The problem, they thought, was that Davis was just too stubborn to consider anything short of absolute independence for the Confederacy

were twelve Union Whigs, with only two Secession Democrats. One of the latter was William W. Boyce of South Carolina, who was a bitter critic of Jefferson Davis and who went so far as to assail the President in the public arena of the daily newspapers. Boyce did not score 0 on both scales—even he did not openly support opposition to the use of state troops in other states, or back repeal of a habeas corpus law which was due to expire in a few weeks anyway. Nevertheless, Boyce was often considered the head of the peace movement. The other Secession Democrat in this group of Whig Unionists was Jehu A. Orr of Mississippi, who is classed as Secessionist because he had espoused secession at Lincoln's election rather than after his state had seceded. His unionism up to the moment of Republican victory separates him at least from the fire-eaters of the 1850s. He had served in the Provisional Congress and then entered the army where he obtained the rank of colonel. But after 1863, he began to have grave misgivings, desiring negotiations before the South was exhausted and while presumably advantageous terms could still be obtained. He entered the Second Congress and worked with Boyce with this aim in mind. Fellow congressmen confirmed that Representative Orr was a reconstructionist, which is the more believable because he was the brother of South Carolina Senator James L. Orr, who was a prominent figure in the peace faction of the Upper House.[18]

Thus, the typical members of this cabal (as it was called) were Whig, Unionist, new in Congress, of medium wealth (measured by both slaves and estate), and from unoccupied territory. It is usually recorded of them that they opposed secession until Lincoln's call for troops or until their states left the Union. One of those to whom this applied, and who serves as a good example of the type of man constantly found in the lower levels of performance scores and scale positions throughout this study, was William N. H. Smith. He differs from the others in the cabal primarily because he had more political experience than most of them (he was the only North Carolinian in this faction to sit in the Confederate Congress before 1864). He served in the state legislature in 1840, 1848, and 1858, and was state solicitor for eight years. He entered the United States Congress in 1859 and served until the end of his term. Basically a Southern Whig, he not unexpectedly spent time in the Know-Nothing party. His estate in 1860 was about $33,000, and he owned thirteen slaves. Smith preferred compromise to secession, but after Lincoln's call for troops, he abandoned the Union. Committed thereby to the Confederacy, he was nevertheless quite unwilling to make the sacri-

18. *DAB*, XIV, 60; Jehu A. Orr petition, Amnesty Papers, Mississippi; William R. Smith petition, Amnesty Papers, Alabama.

fices necessary for Confederate victory, opposing such measures as suspension of habeas corpus, impressment, and conscription. Generally speaking, he was almost as negative as any man in Congress.[19]

Although near the fringe, Smith could not be considered a part of the lunatic fringe. Such a designation would be appropriate for J. T. Leach, who had once found himself voting in a minority of one, and who was apparently the first on the floor of Congress to hint at the possibility of accepting peace without independence. An even better candidate for this dubious honor is Josiah Turner of North Carolina. Turner's estate was worth only a very modest $5,000 in 1860 (making him one of the poorest congressmen), but his political career had been promising, for he had served several terms in the state legislature. As a former Whig, he, like most of the other North Carolina congressmen, opposed secession; but he went along with it and promptly enlisted in his state's armed forces. In 1863, he was elected to Congress as a peace candidate from an Interior constituency. He was not only antiadministration, he was anti-Democrat; and, like Smith, he was opposed to the most basic war measures: conscription, impressment, adequate taxation, and suspension of habeas corpus. He was one of those who was incensed by the continued strong stands taken by the Exterior representatives. In a letter to his wife, he wrote that he "would rather plough and feed hogs than legislate . . . with Missouri and Kentucky to help me."[20] Two other members of this faction, Thomas C. Fuller and Thomas J. Foster, were discussed in Chapter 1.

At the opposite extreme from men like Turner and W.N.H. Smith are the members of a clique that wholeheartedly supported the war and occupied the very high scale positions on both of the dimensions covered in this chapter. The fifteen most extreme war hawks, however, were not so nearly homogeneous as the peace group. They were not concentrated in a single state, although, significantly enough, ten were from areas which, being claimed by the Union as states maintaining normal constitutional relationships and being represented in the federal Congress, could well be lost to the Confederacy even if it won the war (Kentucky, Missouri, and West Virginia); an eleventh came from Alexandria, the home of the "restored" Virginia government under Governor Francis H. Pierpont. More than any other members of the Confederate

19. *BDAC*, p. 1626; *DAB*, XVII, 366; Manuscript Census, North Carolina, Schedule I, vol. IX, p. 12, Schedule II, vol. II, p. 510.

20. *DAB*, XIX, 68–69; Ashe, *Biographical History of North Carolina*, III, 415–426; Josiah Turner petition, Amnesty Papers, North Carolina; Turner papers, quoted in Yearns, *Confederate Congress*, p. 225; Manuscript Census, North Carolina, Schedule I, vol. XII, p. 448.

Congress, these men had genuine reason to demand harsh measures for victory, for, unlike their colleagues, these congressmen could be undone by success as well as failure. A negotiated independence might find their constituents used as pawns, to be surrendered if necessary. Only an overwhelming victory, imposing peace upon a vanquished Union, could insure them a Confederate future. Eleven of the fifteen members of this faction were also in the First Congress; and, generally speaking, their wealth was quite low for congressmen. They included seven Democrats as against three Whigs, but party is unknown for five of them. Secession stand is unknown for nine, although all of the remainder were Secessionists. Perhaps the latter explains their voting behavior; but a much more credible explanation involves the characteristic created by the United States army, since twelve of these fifteen came from localities that were occupied by the start of the last session of Congress.

Francis S. Lyon, of Demopolis, Alabama, one of the few Interior members of this high-scoring group, was one of its more interesting adherents. A lawyer who also had plantation interests, he had been a member of the state legislature in 1833, 1834, and 1861, and he was a Whig in the Twenty-fourth and Twenty-fifth Congresses. Apparently a leader of party reorganization in Alabama after the Compromise of 1850, he considered secession a necessity, and he withdrew with other Southern delegates from the Charleston convention of the Democratic party. On the eve of the war, he was one of the wealthiest men in Congress, having an estate worth over $300,000 and including almost 200 slaves. Lyon favored conscription, tough economic measures, and the suspension of the writ of habeas corpus, and served on the important Ways and Means Committee in both the First and Second House.[21]

Willis B. Machen was more typical of this group of strong nationalists, especially those whom Turner did not like, since Machen was an anti-Union Democrat from occupied Kentucky. By the time he attended the Confederate Congress. he had been a member of the state legislature in 1854, 1856, and 1860, and of the state constitutional convention in 1849. His estate, including twenty-six slaves, was valued at almost $100,000 in 1860, a figure which was very substantial for the Upper South. He called himself a farmer, but he also had interests in iron manufacturing, trade, and the law. Holding about the same views as

---

21. Manuscript Census, Alabama, Schedule I, vol. VIII, p. 458, Schedule II, vol. III, p. 131; *DAB*, XI, 528–529; *BDAC*, p. 1246; Owen, *History of Alabama*, IV, 1079–1080; Lewy Dorman, *Party Politics in Alabama from 1850 Through 1876* (Wetumpka, Alabama: Wetumpka Printing Co., 1935), pp. 65, 77; Wiley and Milhollen, *Embattled Confederates*, p. 267.

Lyon on legislation before Congress, Machen is a good example of the lawmaker who did not have to be concerned about whether or not his constituents could carry the burdens he proposed to place on other backs. Being from Eddyville, not far from the Ohio River in western Kentucky, he did not labor under the remotest possibility of any assertion of Confederate control at home.[22]

Two other extremist categories remain to be examined. One of these, defined by a high score on the defeatism-realism scale but a low one on the military-determination scale, really does not exist, for only one congressman came close to straddling the apparently irreconcilable positions. The other high-low group is more distinctive. There were nine representatives who are placed low on defeatism-realism issues, but whose scores are high on the military-determination scale. The meaning of this is uncertain, but it is possible that here we have a group of men who desperately desired peace, but who could see no realistic alternative to fighting it out vigorously so as to obtain the best possible settlement. Such men would be distinguished from the North Carolinians and their followers, who also wanted peace desperately, but who did not desire to engage in sacrificial military action to achieve it. Some of the members of this third faction could see no inconsistency of principle in increasing the power of Confederate authority by forcing states to share chartered shipping with the central government, while refusing at the same time to sustain Confederate power by a suspension of the writ of habeas corpus. Indeed, it is true that there does not appear to be any intrinsic conflict between such positions, if one can accept the viability of persistent military activity without civilian involvement or regimentation.

The personal history of these maverick congressmen does not reveal backgrounds similar to those of men placed high on both scales. Rather, they were like those who are low on both. Party is not known for two of these nine men, but six of the others were Whigs and only one was a Democrat, and Unionists outnumbered Secessionists eight to one. The importance of this similarity is underscored by the presence in this group of two of the leading peace men in Congress, Arthur S. Colyar of Tennessee, and John B. Baldwin of Virginia, both Union Whigs, whose pressure to force Confederate negotiations prior to the Hampton Roads conference became the subject of long postwar controversy among old Confederates. Furthermore, the one Democrat in the group was from

22. Manuscript Census, Kentucky, Schedule I, vol. XVI, p. 769, Schedule II, vol. II, p. 417; *BDAC*, p. 1248; *The Biographical Encyclopedia of Kentucky of the Dead and Living Men of the Nineteenth Century* (Cincinnati: O.J.M. Armstrong and Co., 1878), p. 253.

Texas, where the Whigs had never been active enough to justify much confidence in party affiliation as a distinguishing characteristic. However, four came from territory occupied prior to November 1864.

One of the most prominent of these "third force" congressmen was Humphrey Marshall of Kentucky. A man of extensive political experience, Marshall served as commissioner to China from 1852 to 1854, and sat in Congress for four terms, 1849 to 1852 and 1855 to 1859, first as a Whig and then as an American. In 1860, he became a Democrat, supporting the presidential candidacy of Breckinridge. In the secession crisis, he sought to keep Kentucky both peaceful and neutral; but when this failed, he went to Tennessee, joined the Confederate army, and became a brigadier general. He later wrote that he left the army when "Jeff Davis treated me badly." He then moved to Richmond to practice law, entered the Second Congress, and served on the Military Affairs Committee. "My offenses are rank it is true," he wrote, in his postwar request to Johnson for pardon, "but I hope there is balm in Gilead." His general voting record is mixed. Soft on habeas corpus and the tax-in-kind, he was sometimes hard-bitten on conscription, impressment, and other economic issues.[23]

Perhaps congressmen who took any of the extreme positions were an unusual group. But because they did occupy the extreme positions, they add important support for the answers provided by the cross-content scales to the basic question in this investigation: how much might biographical characteristics have influenced a member's roll-call voting? The scales, examined both separately and in cross-tabulation, indicate that, in the House of Representatives of the Second Congress, economic influences were so minor as to be hardly worth mentioning. Party background was reasonably important, as those at opposite ends of the major scales had generally differing party backgrounds. It is possible, however, that this apparent significance of party is due to its strong correlation with secession stand, for differences in the latter characteristic were more notable than party distinctions. Moreover, the influence of Unionism appears to have been more decisive than that of Secessionism. The major indicator, however, was the military-occupation status of the home district.

An important collateral observation is the dramatic change in voting patterns in the Second House. As defeat approached, so did conceptualization, so that scalability was a product of the slipping away of

23. Humphrey Marshall petition, Amnesty Papers, Kentucky; *DAB*, XII, 310–311; *BDAC*, p. 1265; Ezra J. Warner, *Generals in Gray; Lives of the Confederate Commanders* (Baton Rouge: Louisiana State University Press, 1959), pp. 212–213.

dreams of nationhood. This observation may be supported by reference to the Confederate Senate. In this chapter, the Senate has been ignored because cross-content scaling for a small legislative body, with frequent and extended absences, produces results which are questionable at best. While scales can be discovered, their validity is marginal, and it is unproductive to analyze the positions of specific individuals under such conditions. But tentative Senate scales do show a significant increase in scalability as defeat approached. The first two sessions of the First Senate provide two scales, and the last two sessions reveal three. But for the Second Senate, scalable sets incorporate twice as large a proportion of the roll calls of the sample cross-section as for the First Senate, and in its two sessions five cross-content dimensions have been uncovered. In both houses of Congress, it is evident from scale analysis that impending defeat altered voting behavior markedly. The changed, almost dichotomized roll-call pattern is certainly the product of great transformations in the thought processes of the legislators. It may also have another significance. If this development is evidence of increasing importance of ideology in voting, it may mean that, in 1864 and 1865, Congress was beginning to behave in the traditional party manner, as segments of the membership began to coalesce under the influence of secession stand and occupied-territory status. Continued efforts to understand voting behavior by other forms of cross-content analysis are offered in the following chapter.

11 Determinants of Decision Making

THE various methods of cross-content analysis employed in this chapter and the one preceding it offer promising avenues of approach to the investigator of legislative behavior. For a congress which stubbornly resists analysis, perhaps because it does not fit the historian's stereotype of a legislative body, a variety of analytical tools is needed to fashion a credible account of the degree and meaning of association between roll-call voting and the biographical characteristics of the membership. Two helpful devices are here introduced which incorporate all roll calls used in any topical set: intercorrelations of the performance sets and of the scale sets, and an average adjusted score designed to measure each congressman's total impact upon congressional behavior.

Intercorrelation of Cumulative-Scale and Performance Sets

Comparing the scores or positions assigned to congressmen on one set with such assignments on another set of roll calls makes it possible to observe and measure the strength of association between the two sets of member levels. On each scale or performance set, members have been assigned to as many as ten levels, which constitute ordered categories from weakest (0) to strongest (9). If each member receives the same score on two different sets, a brief glance at the cross-tabulation table will indicate perfect association, all members falling into a straight diagonal line of cells. If these two sets were as simple as three levels each, every member appearing with a score on both sets would fall into either the high row and high column, the middle row and middle column, or the low row and low column. If the reverse, or negative, form of association pertained, every member would fall into either high row and low column, the center cell, or the low row and high column. Weak associations are also evident from superficial examination.

It is impractical and unnecessary to present all of the cross-tabulations of scales and performance sets. The intercorrelation strength and form (if linear) can be indicated more quickly and usually more accurately with Gamma coefficients. Gamma is a statistic for measuring the association between standings on two different ordered-category classifications, and its values range from $+1.00$ to -1.00, with 0.0 reflecting lack of measurable association. This statistic has severe limitations, especially when the number of cases is small or the distribution is very much polarized or otherwise concentrated. Inspection of the cross-tabulations, however, can mitigate these limitations, so that Gamma is a useful device for summarization. The Gamma value for the intercorrelation of the two cross-content scales in the previous chapter, for example, is $+.6$, suggesting a definite positive association but with significant amounts of deviation from exact correlation.

Scale and performance sets have been separately intercorrelated for each house. Table 11-1A provides the Gamma values for intercorrelation of House performance scores, and Table 11-1C the counterpart for the Senate. Gamma values for scale-set intercorrelation are in the B and D parts of this table.

The most pervasive implication found in the Gamma values for the House arises from the fact that almost all reflect positive association between the great majority of pairs of performance sets. The straightforward interpretation is that, if a member is scored high on one set of a pair, he is more commonly than not scored high on the other set—or, if low on one, then low on the other. In more general terms, for each of our assignments of score along a continuum from weak to strong in support of Confederate survival, a given member's level in one set is a clue to his level in the other—in the form of positive relationship. Or, to employ the hazardous term *predict*, one could have predicted a member's level on most sets somewhat better by knowing the member's level on another set than by simply assigning him the median member's level.

A pattern of Gamma values for pairwise comparisons of roll-call standings that are not substantially associated would probably cluster not far from 0.0 and range about equally into positive and negative values. The matrix we are considering is far from such a pattern. Some of the associations are so strong that one could come close to predicting a member's level in one set from knowing his level in the other. And even when association is weaker, it is still positive association for the pattern of relationships among sets on the sensitive subjects of habeas corpus suspension, impressment, conscription, race, and state rights, as well as on some of the economic issues. On the other hand, associations are weaker or are erratic when other economic, legislative housekeeping, or miscellaneous topics provide one of the pair of sets under analysis.

Such negative Gamma values as are found are chiefly in relation to the property-destruction issue and the economic roll calls in the First Session of the First House. The reason is clear; each in turn touched a sensitive spot for border-state members, who in these instances took

TABLE 11-1

INTERCORRELATION OF ROLL-CALL SETS

Matrix of Gamma Values for
Pairwise Comparison of
Score Sets as Ordered-Category
Member Attributes[a]

(A)
House Performance Scores
Issue Area Identifications

Roll-Call Set Number	2	3	4	5	6	7	8	9	10	11	12	13	14	15	16	17	18	19	20	21	22	23	24	25	26	27	28	29	30	31	32	33	34	35
1	6	6	4	5	1	4	4	3	3	3	4	2	5	3	3	7	−1	3	1	2	5	1	1	−1	3	−1	−1	1	2	4	4	1	5	2
2		5	5	7	6	4	3	1	4	4	5	5	5	5	4	6	0	2	2	3	5	1	1	0	1	−1	0	0	1	3	6	6	6	7
3			4	7	5	3	1	3	4	4	4	3	5	3	5	5	0	3	1	4	4	1	1	1	−2	1	−2	1	5	5	5	1	5	2
4				9	6	5	6	0	5	6	4	4	6	4	6	6	−2	4	3	6	6	2	−1	−1	1	0	−1	2	5	6	5	−2	2	7
5					5	4	6	0	6	6	5	6	6	6	6	6	−2	4	4	6	5	2	0	−1	−2	0	−2	1	3	6	3	−2	7	7
6						4	4	1	3	5	4	4	3	3	4	4	−1	2	2	2	2	2	−1	−1	−1	−3	1	0	2	3	4	4	4	1
7							5	0	2	4	3	4	4	4	5	5	2	3	3	4	3	2	1	−1	0	0	1	2	4	3	6	5	5	3
8								−1	3	4	4	3	6	6	6	6	1	3	3	4	4	3	−1	2	1	−1	2	2	5	4	5	4	−2	−2
9									2	2	5	3	4	0	6	4	0	5	5	0	0	2	−1	−2	−1	0	1	1	3	5	5	6	0	−2
10										5	3	3	2	4	5	4	0	2	4	4	4	4	1	0	1	1	3	2	2	3	3	5	4	0
11											6	4	3	5	5	5	2	1	4	5	2	3	0	4	0	−1	0	4	5	0	0	2	6	2
12												3	6	3	5	4	1	4	3	4	6	1	1	1	1	2	2	2	3	1	1	5	5	7
13													4	4	6	4	1	3	4	5	6	3	−1	3	2	1	1	3	3	2	4	4	5	7
14														3	6	3	−1	3	3	2	5	3	2	4	2	0	1	2	4	4	2	1	3	7
15															6	6	−2	4	4	4	5	5	4	2	3	−2	1	1	5	5	5	3	6	7
16																6	3	2	3	5	5	5	0	0	4	3	0	0	3	3	2	3	5	2
17																	6	4	4	4	5	5	−1	3	5	1	0	−1	5	4	4	4	4	2
18																		1	1	2	−2	−1	−2	−2	2	0	0	0	1	1	2	−3	−3	4
19																			2	2	2	−1	2	1	1	−1	−1	−1	2	2	1	1	−1	5
20																				5	5	3	−1	−4	0	1	2	1	2	4	3	3	3	4
21																					4	3	−4	2	−1	−1	1	1	2	5	5	6	4	1
22																						5	2	5	1	1	1	2	4	4	4	4	4	5
23																							5	3	3	1	1	1	4	5	5	5	5	3
24																								4	3	−3	0	2	2	4	3	4	2	4
25																									6	−2	1	0	0	3	5	5	4	6
26																										−4	−1	−1	2	4	4	4	2	5
27																											2	−2	0	0	3	4	3	4	−1
28																												1	1	−1	0	3	3	3	0
29																													0	−1	0	−2	0	0	3
30																														2	2	3	1	−1	0
31																															5	5	1	3	4
32																																5	4	6	5
33																																	3	4	3
34																																		5	6

Habeas Corpus
1. 1 House, 2 Sess.
2. 1 House, 3 Sess.
3. 2 House, 1 Sess.
4. 2 House, 2 Sess.
5. 2 House, 2 Sess.

Impressment
6. 1 House, 3 Sess.
7. 2 House, 1 Sess.
8. 2 House, 2 Sess.

Property Destruction
9. 1 House, 1 Sess.

Conscription
10. 1 House, 1 Sess.
11. 1 House, 2 Sess.
12. 1 House, 3 Sess.
13. 1 House, 4 Sess.
14. 2 House, 2 Sess.
15. 2 House, 2 Sess.

Racial Issues
16. 2 House, 2 Sess.
17. 2 House, 2 Sess.

Economic Issues
18. 1 House, 1 Sess.
19. 1 House, 3 Sess.
20. 1 House, 4 Sess.
21. 2 House, 1 Sess.
22. 2 House, 2 Sess.
23. 2 House, 2 Sess.

Legislative Procedural Issues
24. 1 House, 2 Sess.
25. 2 House, 2 Sess.
26. 2 House, 2 Sess.

Diverse Issues
27. 1 House, 1 Sess.
28. 1 House, 2 Sess.
29. 1 House, 3 Sess.
30. 2 House, 4 Sess.
31. 2 House, 1 Sess.
32. 2 House, 2 Sess.
33. 2 House, 2 Sess.

State Rights
34. 2 House, 2 Sess.
35. 2 House, 2 Sess.

a. Gamma values are multiplied by 10 for table entries.

TABLE 11-1--Continued

(C)

Senate Performance Scores

Issue Area Identifications

No.	Session	Issue Area
1.	1 Senate, 4 Sess.	Habeas Corpus
2.	2 Senate, 2 Sess.	
3.	1 Senate, 3 Sess.	Impressment
4.	2 Senate, 1 Sess.	
5.	2 Senate, 2 Sess.	
6.	1 Senate, 1 Sess.	Conscription
7.	1 Senate, 2 Sess.	
8.	1 Senate, 3 Sess.	
9.	1 Senate, 4 Sess.	
10.	2 Senate, 2 Sess.	
11.	2 Senate, 2 Sess.	Racial
12.	1 Senate, 2 Sess.	Military
13.	1 Senate, 3 Sess.	
14.	1 Senate, 4 Sess.	
15.	2 Senate, 1 Sess.	
16.	2 Senate, 2 Sess.	
17.	1 Senate, 3 Sess.	Economic
18.	1 Senate, 4 Sess.	
19.	2 Senate, 1 Sess.	
20.	2 Senate, 2 Sess.	
21.	1 Senate, 2 Sess.	Procedural
22.	1 Senate, 1 Sess.	Diverse Issues
23.	2 Senate, 2 Sess.	
24.	1 Senate, 2 Sess.	State Rights
25.	1 Senate, 3 Sess.	

Senate Performance Scores (triangular matrix of Set Numbers)

Column headers (Set Number): 2, 3, 4, 5, 6, 7, 8, 9, 10, 11, 12, 13, 14, 15, 16, 17, 18, 19, 20, 21, 22, 23, 24, 25

Set	2	3	4	5	6	7	8	9	10	11	12	13	14	15	16	17	18	19	20	21	22	23	24	25
1	6	0	1	6	6	6	4	9	8	5	2	-3	-3	3	-2	1	5	5	2	0	0	4	5	-2
2		-3	3	3	3	5	5	2	6	6	5	1	1	-3	2	3	4	5	2	-3	2	4	4	4
3			6	-2	3	-1	-2	5	-1	-4	1	5	2	6	3	-5	-7	1	-5	1	5	0	2	-3
4				4	3	5	5	2	3	2	2	6	3	-1	4	1	-1	0	3	3	4	-5
5					5	3	3	5	5	3	3	6	2	1	0	-1	4	1	4	6	2	2	5	4
6						6	6	2	6	5	3	1	3	-2	4	-3	4	1	3	6	0	4	3	-1
7							5	5	5	5	4	0	4	-2	0	-3	4	4	-2	4	-2	0	1	5
8								2	5	5	0	2	2	-1	0	-1	2	3	3	0	0	2	2	0
9									4	5	2	1	2	-3	0	0	2	4	4	-1	2	3	6	-2
10										6	6	0	-2	-5	-1	-2	4	1	7	5	3	5	2	2
11											6	2	-1	-3	0	1	4	3	-4	-4	1	1	1	2
12												4	5	2	6	-3	-6	0	-6	2	0	0	-1	4
13													7	-4	6	-6	3	-5	-4	5	3	0	3	4
14														0	0	-5	2	-6	-5	7	2	3	3	2
15															0	1	-1	3	1	1	5	0	3	-5
16																-4	-1	-4	-3	1	1	1	1	-1
17																	-3	6	3	-6	2	2	-1	-3
18																		2	-2	5	5	4	2	7
19																			6	-5	-2	2	1	0
20																				-2	5	3	1	4
21																					1	5	2	1
22																						5	0	1
23																							-4	1
24																								-1

Set No.	2	3	4	5	6	7	8	9	10	11	12	13	14	15	16	17	18	19	20	21	22
1	7	5	5	5	4	-2	3	3	2	4	4	6	-1	3	2	2	-1	5	4	4	3
2		6	6	4	6	-1	6	4	0	4	4	5	-1	5	2	2	1	2	4	5	6
3			8	5	6	0	4	6	4	5	4	4	0	4	2	2	0	3	5	6	8
4				4	7	1	2	5	6	5	3	3	0	5	3	2	-2	2	6	5	8
5					5	1	3	5	2	5	4	4	1	5	4	1	-1	6	4	4	4
6						2	1	6	5	5	5	6	-1	6	3	2	-2	0	6	5	8
7							-1	-2	0	-1	0	-1	0	1	1	-2	1	2	2	0	1
8								5	3	0	3	3	-3	4	0	1	1	3	4	5	4
9									5	3	3	5	-3	2	3	2	-1	4	6	4	6
10										1	3	2	-1	2	1	1	-2	3	5	3	6
11											5	6	-1	4	4	-2	1	3	6	4	5
12												4	-4	3	4	1	0	3	5	5	4
13													-1	4	3	-1	0	0	4	3	4
14														-1	0	0	1	-1	-4	-3	-1
15															2	2	-1	0	3	5	6
16																0	-3	3	4	4	3
17																	-4	1	1	5	1
18																		-1	-1	0	0
19																			7	2	3
20																				6	6
21																					6
22																					

TABLE 11-1--
Continued

(B)
House Scale Positions

Issue Area Identifications

Habeas Corpus
1. 1 House, 2 Sess.
2. 2 House, 1 Sess.
3. 2 House, 2 Sess.
4. 2 House, 2 Sess.

Impressment
5. 2 House, 1 Sess.
6. 2 House, 2 Sess.

Property Destruction
7. 1 House, 1 Sess.

Conscription
8. 1 House, 1 Sess.
9. 1 House, 2 Sess.
10. 1 House, 4 Sess.
11. 2 House, 2 Sess.

Racial Issues
12. 2 House, 2 Sess.
13. 2 House, 2 Sess.

Congressional Pay
14. 1 House, 1 Sess.

Economic
15. 2 House, 1 Sess.
16. 2 House, 2 Sess.

Procedural
17. 1 House, 2 Sess.
18. 1 House, 1 Sess.

Erlanger Loan
19. 1 House, 3 Sess.

Military-Determination
20. 2 House, both Sess.

State Rights
21. 2 House, 2 Sess.

Defeatism-Realism
22. 2 House, both Sess.

Set Number	2	3	4	5	6	7	8	9	10	11	12	13	14	15	16
1	2	0	4	8	1	3	5	7	-1	4	-1	1	8	4	-3
2		0	0	-1	6	4	-1	0	5	3	2	-3	1	8	3
3			-2	0	-1	-1	-1	-5	4	-8	0	-4	-3	4	-4
4				1	-2	2	4	8	-5	7	-1	1	8	1	0
5					4	4	8	7	3	2	-1	1	6	0	-5
6						8	1	0	3	8	4	0	6	3	3
7							2	3	6	4	4	-1	4	2	1
8								8	1	1	-5	3	6	-4	1
9									-4	7	-4	5	8	-3	-2
10										-4	5	-4	-2	0	2
11											2	4	7	6	0
12												-7	1	5	1
13													-1	-4	1
14														8	2
15															-4
16															

TABLE 11-1--
Continued

(D)
Senate Scale Positions

Issue Area Identifications

Habeas Corpus
1. 1 Senate, 4 Sess.
2. 2 Senate, 2 Sess.

Impressment
3. 1 Senate, 3 Sess.
4. 2 Senate, 2 Sess.

Conscription
5. 1 Senate, 1 Sess.
6. 1 Senate, 2 Sess.
7. 1 Senate, 3 Sess.
8. 1 Senate, 4 Sess.
9. 2 Senate, 2 Sess.

Military
10. 1 Senate, 4 Sess.
11. 2 Senate, 1 Sess.
12. 2 Senate, 2 Sess.

Economic
13. 1 Senate, 3 Sess.
14. 2 Senate, 1 Sess.

State Rights
15. 1 Senate, 2 Sess.
16. 1 Senate, 3 Sess.

weak positions in contrast with generally strong stances in their role as Exterior members. On such matters as stringent penalties for trading with the enemy and wholesale destruction of private property to keep it from falling into the hands of the Federals, representatives from districts already occupied or in immediate jeopardy were prone more to reluctance than to resolve. The level assigned to these border-state men on these two sets is generally a low one, which yields negative association when cross-tabulated with their high levels on many subsequent performance sets.

The scale set from the House that relates to congressional pay and allowances (shown in Table 11-1B) is another example of an understandable source of negative associations in pairwise comparison with other scale sets. The Exterior members, who are generally scored at the high, sacrificing levels on most sensitive issues, unable to go home between sessions, voted for an expensive plan to provide annual salaries for congressmen. Most of the Interior men, who soon fell into low levels on other scale sets, were satisfied with the customary per diem and travel allowance. When we designated the less expensive per diem system as the strong, or pro-Confederate, position, we were unintentionally placing the Exterior members in weak positions and producing the negative associations observable in the Gamma values.

The matrix of Gamma values for the performance sets taken from Senate roll calls evidently differs from the House counterpart. A large number of strong negative associations and some very erratic associations even within a single content area may readily be observed. Senators were not voting in a random manner, to be sure; but they were considerably less inclined than representatives to consistent voting in the framework of the polarity assigned for these performance sets. This matrix corroborates earlier comments about the more volatile Senate roll-call patterns, although it furnishes only limited help in identifying forces that may have influenced senators. It may also indicate that, in some pairwise comparisons, too few senators could be scored on both sets to permit confidence in the test of association.

The principal inference to be drawn from intercorrelation of House performance (and scale) sets is that representatives displayed some modest but telling consistency in taking positions in most of the subject-content areas, with a high order of predictability on key issues. Senate performance sets provide evidence of considerable consistency across at least habeas corpus suspension, two of the three impressment sets, conscription, and racial issues, but highly unpredictable responses on military, economic, miscellaneous, and even state-rights subjects. Senate scale sets are highly intercorrelated for only a limited number of pairs and generally reflect an unpredictable pattern. Some further assistance toward an understanding of these over-all postures, even in the Senate, may be obtained from the analyses of average adjusted scores and positions.

Over-All Average Performance Scores or Scale Positions

Another useful tool for cross-content analysis of legislative roll-call responses is an average of the several individual performance scores or scale positions for each member of Congress. Adjustment of the raw scores or scale positions was undertaken as a prudent defense against the possibility that exceptionally differing proportions of the membership appeared on the determined side of some but not other content areas. A member whose score primarily represents agreement with the majority on divisions which had only little dissent, and who had failed to participate on some wracking issues, would turn up with a level almost certainly far higher than he was entitled to. In any case, the scale positions are incompatible, for they are not even on a uniform ten-level basis, ranging from as few as five to the maximum of ten positions. In order to make all scores more nearly comparable, each score was adjusted so as to represent an approximation of the member's percentile ranking among his voting colleagues of the session. If, for example, only 10 percent of those voting in a content-area set are assigned the lowest score, 0, the adjusted score is one half of 10 percent, or 5.[1] If, in this same set, the score of 1 is assigned to 30 percent, those with the score of 1 are adjusted to 25 (representing approximately the center of the range from 11 to 40 that is encompassed by those scoring 1). At the high end of the scores, if 10 percent of the members with scores on that set were at the level of 9, an adjusted score of 95 would be assigned to each (midway through the 90-to-100-percent range). On the other hand, if only 4 percent were at the 9 level, each would have an adjusted score of 98. The adjustments were made for scale positions according to the same arrangement.

These adjusted scores and positions are assumed to represent a generally useful estimate of the member's rank order within the voting membership of the session. A man with a score of 0 in a set in which one half of those voting are scored at 0 is not treated in adjusted scores in the same manner as one who scores 0 when only 1 percent share his level. The former adjusted score would be 25 (one half of the 50

---

1. The precision of median value to the fractional percentile was considered useless for scoring intended to be collapsed again into ten levels, since only 1 percent difference in adjusted score could result in any case.

percent); the latter would be only 0.5. The percentage values that serve as the adjusted scores or positions have been averaged for each member and used in ten-percentile ranges, so that a member with a percentile standing of 4 or 6 would receive an average adjusted score of 0, one with 11 or 16 would receive 1, and any with percentile averages at 90 or above would be scored at 9. The adjusted average scores or positions have been used for cross-tabulation just as the original 0 through 9 assignments were.

It is of some confidence-inspiring value to note that the raw scores differ from the adjusted ones very little and that the same is true of raw and adjusted scale positions. The average performance score is the same as the average adjusted score for 198 members and differs by only one level for 55 of the remaining 57 legislators with any scores to average. The other two legislators had only three and four scores respectively to average, and their two forms of average are only two levels apart. The same is generally true for the average of adjusted scale positions. The stability of the scores and positions under these and other forms of adjustment provide assurance that any reasonable altering of the research design would not have produced markedly different results. This stability probably arises from the two considerations that Confederate congressmen recorded such a vast number of roll calls and that their divisions provide a broad-range distribution from near unanimity to tied votes. It is also because almost all of the roll calls after the earliest portion of the war have been employed. Any very limited selection of roll calls would have yielded a baffling pattern for most of the members of Congress, although the extreme postures could undoubtedly have been identified from a small sample of votes.

In spite of its presumed reliability, however, the average adjusted score cannot serve as a quick one-glance summary of an individual's voting record. Only a few members of the Confederate Congress had scores that were even approximately uniform. Considerable variation in level is often noted even for sets on the same general subject, and extreme variation from one subject to another is not uncommon. Economic issues are particularly conspicuous in this regard, frequently producing one or more levels for a member that may be far out of line with most of his other scores. This erratic pattern of subject-content measurements is compatible with the previously emphasized absence of all-pervading ideological orientation, as well as the absence of party structure in the Congress through which voting could have been channeled and disciplined. A member's average adjusted score, therefore, is likely to fall nearer the center of the range than does each of his individual content-area scores because of the neutralizing effect of inconsistent stances.

Distinctions between groups, such as between Democrats and Whigs, are smaller. But the average has the compensating advantage of being more inclusive. Despite attendant difficulties, average adjusted performance scores (or scale positions) do measure, in a broad-gauge manner, the impact of a member's voting record on the Confederacy's chances of survival.

The relations between the average of adjusted scores and positions and the several individual performance and scale sets help to define the usefulness of the averages. In addition, these relationships further illustrate how member responses vary from topic to topic. Gamma values summarize the cross-tabulations of the average adjusted scores and positions with the raw scores and positions of each individual content-area set. Table 11–2A demonstrates that the strongest associations in the performance group are between the average adjusted scores and the scores of the habeas corpus content area of the Second House, but also that the association between averages and most of the single sets are so strong that the average may be taken as a close approximation for the large majority of members of their postures on all but a few topics. Gamma values of .6 or higher dominate the issue areas of habeas corpus, impressment, conscription, race, and state rights. Property destruction has previously been cited as an instance of negative associations with many other sets, and its negative, though insignificantly weak, association with averages is not unexpected.

One of the more significant groups of relationships portrayed in Table 11–2 is that involving economic sets, for, with one exception, the Gamma values are so high (.5, .6, or .7) as to suggest that a member's general level on performance scores is a strong clue to his economic-issue posture. This fact did not appear very distinctly when member attributes were compared with individual economic-set scores because none of the attributes being measured was very strongly associated with any one of the general economic-issue areas. At this stage, it appears evident that stand on the full range of sensitive questions presented to Congress was, for most members, impressively correlated with stand on economic questions.

The Gamma values that we are discussing, generally clustering about the value .6, are not evidence that anything close to perfect association exists in the cross-tabulations. Table 10–12, displaying the cross-tabulation of the two cross-content scales from the Second Congress, can serve to illustrate the possible implications of a Gamma value of very close to +.6. This table shows a very strong positive association between the two sets of scale-position assignments for most of the members. Yet, almost a quarter of the members involved are found in the wrong

TABLE 11-2

RELATION BETWEEN AVERAGE ADJUSTED SCORES AND POSITIONS
AND INDIVIDUAL CONTENT-AREA PERFORMANCE AND SCALE SETS

(A)
House

| Issue Area | Cong. | Sess. | Gamma Values by Issue with Average Adjusted | |
			Performance Score	Scale Position
Habeas Corpus	1	2	5	6
	1	3	6	no scale
	2	1	8	7
	2	2	8	8
	2	2	8	8
Impressment	1	3	4	no scale
	2	1	6	7
	2	2	7	8
Property Destruction	1	1	-1	1
Conscription	1	1	5	7
	1	2	7	7
	1	3	6	no scale
	1	4	6	5
	2	2	7	7
	2	2	7	no scale
Racial Issues	2	2	7	6
	2	2	7	6
Economic Issues	1	1	1	-1 Pay
	1	3	5	6 Loan
	1	4	5	no scale
	2	1	6	6
	2	2	7	4
	2	2	6	no scale
Procedural Issues	1	2	2	3
	2	2	5	1[a]
	2	2	4	no scale
Diverse Issues	1	1	1	no scale
	1	2	3	no scale
	1	3	2	no scale
	1	4	5	no scale
	2	1	7	no scale
Military-Determination	2	1-2	6	7
Defeatism-Realism	2	1-2	6	8
State Rights	2	2	7	6
	2	2	7	no scale

a. This is a Procedural Scale from 1 Cong., 1 Sess.

310

TABLE 11-2--<u>Continued</u>

(B)
Senate

Issue Area	Cong.	Sess.	Gamma Values by Issue with Average Adjusted	
			Performance Score	Scale Position
Habeas Corpus	1	4	9	8
	2	2	8	4
Impressment	1	3	2	1
	2	1	5	no scale
	2	2	7	6
Conscription	1	1	7	5
	1	2	6	2
	1	3	5	6
	1	4	7	6
	2	2	8	8
Racial Issues	2	2	5	no scale
Military Issues	1	2	4	no scale
	1	3	3	no scale
	1	4	-1	0
	2	1	2	5
	2	2	1	-1
Economic Issues	1	3	-2	3
	1	4	6	no scale
	2	1	5	8
	2	2	4	no scale
Procedural Issues	1	2	3	no scale
Diverse Issues	1	1	3	no scale
	2	2	6	no scale
State Rights	1	2	7	5
	1	3	-1	2

quadrants for positive association—and one tenth are located far into a transverse corner range reflective of negative association. In other words, a measure of strength of association between member performance on two ordered-category attributes can be as high as +.6 and still allow for considerable amounts of poor association or even negative association in the case of a minority of members involved.[2] Attempting to predict a member's score on one set from his score on the other would work out in average error to much less than assignment of median-member score as the prediction. But sometimes the prediction would be far from the mark or even entirely reversed from a member's true score. This is merely another way of reiterating that what we have found in our measurements of association is a tendency, a likelihood, but not a certainty.

It follows that considerable association may exist between sets of scores from a single-issue area, such as the economic area, and a set of average adjusted scores, and that there may be further association between the averages and certain member attributes, such as stand on secession (see Table 11-4 below), without there necessarily being a strong association between economic-issue voting and stand on secession. In other words, A may be substantially related to B, and B to C, without a significant relation of A to C. This could not be true if associations were almost perfect, but Gamma values of .5 or .6 or .7 by no means preclude such a possibility.

The relations between average adjusted scale positions and the issue areas in the House (shown with scores on Table 11-2A) add little to the general contours of association more broadly illustrated in the performance scores. In both measurements of member response patterns, it turns out that averages of adjusted scores or positions on merely habeas corpus, impressment, and conscription would serve just as well as the average of all of the adjusted scores or positions to predict performance on any roll-call set. The Gamma values (not shown here) for cross-tabulation of each issue-area set with the averages over these three topics are almost identical with the Gamma values shown on Table 11-2A.

For senators, the relations between average adjusted scores or positions and each content-area set are surprisingly similar to those for the House, considering previous evidence of less predictable stance for senators than for representatives (Table 11-2B). The large area of weak associations

2. Collapsing Table 10-10 into the same quadrants and applying Yule's Q, which is a measure of one-way association and therefore applicable to a fourfold table with one nearly empty cell, produces a coefficient of association of .86.

is in military issues, although one impressment, one economic, and one state-rights set show no significant strength of association with averages. The Gamma values for average adjusted scale positions in association with issue-area sets vary somewhat from the corresponding association with performance scores. This is much more pronounced than for the House members. In part, the variation reflects one of the limitations of Gamma, for the small number of senators voting produces many distributions for which Gamma is actually indeterminate. Inspection of the cross-tabulations, nevertheless, provides evidence that the general thrust of the Gamma value is sound, even though less definite than for the much larger House.

As is the case with House members, the average adjusted scores or scale positions of senators across the combined habeas corpus, impressment, and conscription areas are approximately as useful as the over-all averages for predicting a senator's position in any particular subject-content area. Were it not for the large number of roll calls in the Senate involving military matters, which were less directly confronted in the House, Senate patterns would apparently have been less distinct from the House than is the case. All in all, even in the Senate, men tended to find roughly comparable levels of dedication from one issue to another, outside the military or a very few other roll-call sets.

Association of Member Characteristics
with Roll-Call Voting Behavior

It has frequently been noted that the Confederate Congress behaved differently from one period to another, as circumstances changed between Congresses and even between sessions. Moreover, many of the congressional seats changed hands as a result of mid-war elections. the Provisional Congress was unique for many reasons discussed in Chapter 4. Comparison of average adjusted scores with member characteristics is most useful if a group so studied contains only men who sat in Congress for approximately the same period. In addition, the environment in which voting records were established and the array of issue areas on which scores are based differ markedly between the houses of Congress, so that separate treatment of senators and representatives is called for. Cross-tabulation of member characteristics with average adjusted scores, therefore, is usually made for three separate classifications of members: those who served only in the First Congress, those who served in both, and those who served only in the Second Congress. No separate consideration of the Provisional Congress seems justified, but scores assigned to members of the Permanent Congress on the basis of Provisional Congress roll-call sets are not excluded from their averages.

TABLE 11-3

AVERAGE ADJUSTED PERFORMANCE SCORE AND FORMER PARTY

(A)

Average Adjusted Score	Number of Individuals Assigned Each Score					
	Representatives Serving in					
	First House Only		Both Houses		Second House Only	
	Democrat	Whig	Democrat	Whig	Democrat	Whig
0						4 (4)[a]
1				1 (1)[a]		5 (4)
2	1	1	1		1	3*
3	7	2	5	4	5	
4	10*	6*	5	4 *(1)	1	3
5	8	4	9*	2*	2*	3
6	7	3	8	5	4	4
7	1	1	2	2	2	
8						
9						
Median Score	3.90	3.92	4.44	4.00 (4.50)[b]	4.25	1.67 (4.00)[b]
Difference	0.02		0.44 (0.06)[b]		2.58 (0.25)[b]	
% 0-4	53%	53%	37%	50%	47%	68%
% 5-9	47%	47%	63%	50%	53%	32%

* Median score.

a. N.C. Union Whigs.

b. Without N.C. Union Whigs.

TABLE 11-3--<u>Continued</u>

(B)

Average Adjusted Score	Number of Individuals Assigned Each Score					
	Interior Representatives Serving in					
	First House Only		Both Houses		Second House Only	
	Democrat	Whig	Democrat	Whig	Democrat	Whig
0						4 (4)[a]
1				1 (1)[a]		4*(4)
2	1	1	1		1	1
3	5	2	4	3	3*	
4	10*	5*	3	3*(1)		1
5	6	2	5*	2	1	
6	4	3	4	2		3
7	1	1	2			
8						
9						
Median Score	3.75	3.80	4.30	3.50 (3.75)[b]	2.50	0.63 (5.17)[b]
Difference	0.05		0.80 (0.55)[b]		1.87 (2.67)[b]	
% 0-4	59%	57%	42%	64%	80%	77%
% 5-9	41%	43%	58%	36%	20%	23%

*Median score.

a. N.C. Union Whigs.

b. Without N.C. Union Whigs.

315

TABLE 11-4

AVERAGE ADJUSTED PERFORMANCE SCORE AND STAND ON SECESSION

(A)

Average Adjusted Score	Number of Individuals Assigned Each Score					
	Representatives Serving in					
	First House Only		Both Houses		Second House Only	
	Seces-sionist	Union-ist	Seces-sionist	Union-ist	Seces-sionist	Union-ist
0						4 (4)[a]
1				1 (1)[a]		5 (4)
2	1	1	1			4*
3	3	5	6	4	2	3
4	12*	5*	2	5*(1)	1	3
5	7	5	12*	1	1	4
6	5	4	7	3	5*	2
7	2		2		2	
8						
9						
Median Score	3.92	3.80	4.50	3.40 (3.50)[b]	5.30	1.88 (3.17)[b]
Difference	0.12		1.10 (1.00)[b]		3.42 (2.13)[b]	
% 0-4	53%	55%	30%	71%	27%	76%
% 5-9	47%	45%	70%	29%	73%	24%

* Median score.

a. N.C. Union Whigs.

b. Without N.C. Union Whigs.

TABLE 11-4--Continued

(B)

Average Adjusted Score	First House Only		Both Houses		Second House Only	
	Seces-sionist	Union-ist	Seces-sionist	Union-ist	Seces-sionist	Union-ist
			Number of Individuals Assigned Each Score			
			Interior Representatives Serving in			
0						4 (4)[a]
1				1		4* (4)
2	1	1	1			2
3	2	5	5	3	2	2
4	12*	4*	2	3* (1)[a]	1*	1
5	7	1	9*	1	1	1
6	3	4	5	1	2	1
7	2		1			
8						
9						
Median Score	3.88	3.38	4.39	3.17 (3.00)[b]	4.00	0.88 (2.75)[b]
Difference	0.50		1.22 (1.39)[b]		3.12 (1.25)[b]	
% 0-4	56%	67%	35%	78%	50%	87%
% 5-9	44%	33%	65%	22%	50%	13%

*Median score.

a. N.C. Union Whigs.

b. Without N.C. Union Whigs.

317

Former Party Affiliation

A representative's former party affiliation was barely associated with his average adjusted performance score (Table 11–3A) except for those serving in the Second House only. In this case, the familiar decisive role of the North Carolinians is evident. The same general pattern of association is present for the Interior representatives taken separately (Table 11–3B), except that so few Interior Democrats were first-term members of the Second House that comparison is crippled beyond repair. Interior Democrats and Whigs who served in both Congresses show substantial differences, which are not entirely erased by removal of the North Carolina factor. This otherwise modest distinction between medians is accentuated when one takes into account the compressing effect of averaging. Not enough senators served in only one Congress to justify a comparison by former party affiliation.

Position on Secession

Representatives who served only in the First House differ very little along lines of secession attitudes (Table 11–4A). For those who served in both, however, the familiar distinction appears. The difference between median scores is significant, but more indicative is the fact that more than two thirds of the Secessionists are scored at one of the highest three populated levels in the tabulation (5, 6, and 7), while barely more than one fourth of the Unionists are found there. Two thirds of the Unionists are located in the lower half of the levels. Representatives who served only in the Second House predictably display a much stronger association between stand on secession and levels of average adjusted scores, verifying once again the nature of the reaction against secession which was expressed in the 1863 elections. Even the removal of the North Carolinians (who, after all, were not Unionists merely through some quirk of fate) leaves a strong association, much stronger than that displayed for the party variable in Table 11–3A. Examination of Interior members apart (Table 11–4B) adds little to the image of determined Secessionists and defeatist Unionists. Clearly, secession stand is more strongly associated with average adjusted scores than is former party affiliation for House members. Among senators, this same tendency is noted, but very faintly. Perhaps the inference is justified that, from one session and one topic to another, the Unionist senator was a bit more susceptible to disintegration of resolve than a Secessionist in that body.

Slaveholding and Value of Estate

Personal economic status appears to bear no strong relationship to average adjusted scores for either senators or representatives when Exterior status is neutralized. The high-scoring low-wealth men were almost all Exterior delegates—only one fifth of them remaining Interior to the end.

Slaveholding patterns in the home county bear no clear relationship to average scores, except for Interior members serving in the Second House only. Even in this limited group, the North Carolina members from small slaveholding communities account for all of the association found. Land values in the member's district appear to be unrelated to average scores, except for the Second Congress members only. Here, the association is very strong for all members or for Interior members apart. The number of congressmen involved is not large, but the tough stand of the few representatives of the wealthier districts is unmistakable. The low-value districts are represented all along the range of levels, although concentrated in the lower half of the range.

There is some reason to conclude that this relationship is not entirely a reflection of other elements. These men were elected as new members in the 1863 contests. The tendency toward revolt among the small farmers was not universal but was evident. It may be very significant, for example, that a constituency economic distinction may be observed for those Second Congress freshmen who came from a county different from that of their respective predecessors. In a large majority of these instances, the average size of slaveholdings was smaller in the home counties of the mid-war victors than in the home counties of the "lame ducks." This pattern holds for all nine districts involved in Virginia, North Carolina, South Carolina, and Mississippi, and for two of the three such instances in Georgia. Contrary cases for the Interior South of 1863 include only one district in Alabama in addition to the one in Georgia—and two Tennessee districts that were actually in military jeopardy and doubtless had trouble with the election process. In Texas, one district sent a man from a smaller slaveholding county, while two sent representatives from larger slaveholding ones; but in the election summer of 1863, Texas had been in quite different circumstances from other Interior districts in the Lower South. When due allowance is made, the electing of new men from small-farmer-dominated home communities appears to be highly suggestive of middle and lower class agrarian unrest. And taken together with other evidence offered in earlier chapters, this clue buttresses the inference that association between district affluence and average scores of exclusively Second Congress members is indicative of a form of mild economic influence on voting patterns. Again the North Carolinians partially dictate the strength of association, but again their characteristics need not be treated lightly because they hailed from a single state, however exceptional.

TABLE 11-5

AVERAGE ADJUSTED PERFORMANCE SCORE AND FEDERAL OCCUPATION

(A)
House

Average Adjusted Performance Score	Number of Individuals Assigned Each Score		
	Always Exterior	Changed During Service From Interior to Exterior	Always Interior
0			4 (4)[a]
1	1		5 (4)
2	2	1	4 (1)
3	5	9	11 (1)
4	5	8	21*(1)
5	13*	8*	14
6	16	9	13
7	8	2	3
8			
9			
Median Score	4.92	4.06	3.64 (3.90)[b]
Difference	0.86 1.28 (1.02)[b]	0.42 (0.16)[b]	
% 0-4	26%	49%	60%
% 5-9	74%	51%	40%

* Median score.

a. N.C. Union Whigs.

b. Without N.C. Union Whigs.

TABLE 11-5--Continued

(B)
Senate

Average Adjusted Perform-ance Score	Number of Individuals Assigned Each Score		
	Always Exterior	Changed During Service From Interior to Exterior	Always Interior
0			
1			1
2			2
3		4	4
4	2	3*	3*
5	2*	3	3
6	3	1	1
7	1		
8			
9			
Median Score	5.00	3.50	3.00
Differ-ence		1.50 0.50	
		2.00	
% 0-4	25%	64%	71%
% 5-9	75%	36%	29%

*
Median score.

Interior or Exterior Constituency

Federal forces occupying a member's district, or even campaigning near it, affected his votes in Congress, a point reiterated frequently, but especially manifest in Table 11–5. For both House and Senate, through differences between median scores as well as in the occupation of the extreme positions, Exterior firmness is demonstrably greater than Interior. The coalescing produced in the process of averaging scores automatically reduces the probable extent of differences and should be considered in weighing the significance of these tables. The inference to be drawn is that the summary measure of average adjusted score reinforces the repeated emphasis on this attribute as a major influence on voting behavior.

Member Characteristics of Concurring Thrust

By this point, it is clear enough that Exterior status, Secessionist background, and perhaps former Democratic party affiliation share the same form of association with voting stance in the Confederate Congress. The same is true of the other side of the coin, Interior Union Whig patterns. Because very few members of Congress can be identified as having cross-thrust backgrounds of party and secession stand, it is not feasible to consider these two elements separately in a combined attribute analysis. Secession stand has proved again and again to have had stronger associations with voting alignments than former party affiliation. Having to exclude one of these, we eliminate party consideration with the final reminder that four fifths of those for whom both attributes are known were either Secession Democrats or Union Whigs.

To pit Exterior Secessionists against Interior Unionists summarizes much that has been provided throughout this study. Table 11–6 offers a stark contrast that not even the removal of the North Carolinians can dilute very much, although strength of association is less because of the small population in the Exterior Secessionist columns. To compensate for this weakness, to take into consideration those for whom stand on secession has not been determined, and to enlarge the universe under analysis, Table 11–7 excludes only those of known conflicting attributes—Exterior Unionists or Interior Secessionists. To incorporate one further element suggested by our findings, that members of the First Congress only were not extensively exposed to at least one of the influences that apparently affected voting behavior, this tabulation eliminates such members and examines only the two-term and Second Congress representatives. Comment seems redundant. If one were willing to collapse the eight levels actually occupied by these average adjusted scores

TABLE 11-6

AVERAGE ADJUSTED PERFORMANCE SCORE AND BOTH
STAND ON SECESSION AND FEDERAL OCCUPATION

Average Adjusted Score	Number of Individuals Assigned Each Score					
	Representatives Serving in					
	First House Only		Both Houses		Second House Only	
	Exterior Secessionist	Interior Unionist	Exterior Secessionist	Interior Unionist	Exterior Secessionist	Interior Unionist
0						(4)[a]4
1				(1)[a]1		(3) 4
2		1				2*
3	1	4	1	2		3
4		4*		(1)[a]2*		2
5		1	3*	1		1
6	2*	4	2	1	3*	1
7			1		2	
8						
9						
Median Score	5.25	3.50	4.83	3.25 (3.50)[b]	5.83	1.25 (2.67)[b]
Difference	1.75		1.58 (1.33)[b]		4.58 (3.16)[b]	
% 0-4	33%	64%	14%	71%	0%	88%
% 5-9	67%	36%	86%	29%	100%	12%

* Median score.

a. N.C. Union Whigs.

b. Without N.C. Union Whigs.

TABLE 11-7

AVERAGE ADJUSTED PERFORMANCE SCORE
AND STAND ON SECESSION, FEDERAL OCCUPATION,
OR ABSENCE OF KNOWN CONFLICT
BETWEEN THESE TWO ATTRIBUTES

Average Adjusted Performance Score	Number of Individuals Assigned Each Score	
	Representatives Serving in Both First and Second Congresses, or in Second Only	
	Exterior	Interior
	Secessionists or of Unknown Stand on Secession	Unionists or of Unknown Stand on Secession
0		4 (4)[a]
1		5 (4)
2		2
3	1	6*
4	2	6 (1)
5	7	2
6	14*	3
7	8	2
8		
9		
Median Score	5.43	2.67 (3.30)[b]
Difference	2.76 (2.13)[b]	
% 0-4	9%	77%
% 5-9	91%	23%

* Median score.

a. N.C. Union Whigs.

b. Without N.C. Union Whigs.

TABLE 11-8

COMPARISON OF ROLL-CALL VOTING BY SECESSIONISTS AND UNIONISTS
AMONG INTERIOR MEMBERS IN THE CONFEDERATE CONGRESS

Percent Instances of	First House				Second House	
	Session				Session	
	1st	2d	3d	4th	1st	2d
Concurrence	66 (74)[a]	60 (63)[a]	67 (68)[a]	49 (60)[a]	36 (58)[a]	37 (47)[a]
Dissimilarity	33 (25)	40 (36)	32 (33)	45 (38)	52 (38)	45 (42)
Antagonism	1 (1)	0 (1)	1 (0)	6 (2)	12 (4)	18 (10)
Agreement Score	64 (73)	60 (62)	66 (68)	43 (58)	24 (54)	19 (37)
Difference[b]	-9	-2	-2	-15	-30	-18

Percent Instances of	First Senate				Second Senate	
	Session				Session	
	1st	2d	3d	4th	1st	2d
Concurrence	47 (63)	52 (52)	44 (54)	54 (57)	39 (57)	45 (60)
Dissimilarity	43 (35)	42 (45)	45 (43)	34 (40)	24 (39)	33 (37)
Antagonism	10 (2)	6 (2)	11 (3)	12 (2)	37 (4)	22 (3)
Agreement Score	37 (61)	46 (50)	32 (51)	43 (55)	2 (53)	23 (57)
Difference[b]	-24	-4	-19	-12	-51	-34

a. Percentages shown in parentheses are for all members,
Exterior as well as Interior (see Table 2-2).
b. This is the difference between Agreement Scores for
Interior members and for all members.

into only two, a strong and a weak posture (using the 0-4 and the 5-7 levels), he could predict over-all voting stance on the dimension we have specified with only ten of the sixty-two men out of place—and eight of them would not be out of place if their original scores had been one or two levels different. Señators are not as readily pigeon-holed; yet, even in a group too small to be sliced into segments according to these several attributes, something of the same pattern prevails.

Agreement Scores and Cohesion Among Interior Members Only

In Chapters 2 and 3, a commentary on general voting behavior in the Confederate Congress emphasized a general conclusion that comparisons of neither former Democrats with former Whigs, Secessionists with Unionists, nor Exterior members with Interior members provided the degree of antagonism expected of rival parties in a congress. Agreement scores for these pairs were well into the positive range, rather than in the negative levels characteristic of party rivalry. It should now be noted that these comparisons incorporated elements tending to neutralize antagonism, for two Secessionists were not playing the same role when one was from an Interior and the other from an Exterior constituency. Nor were two Exterior members necessarily alike if one had been an original Secessionist and another a Unionist until the last fateful decision had to be made. The fact stands that Democrats and Whigs, Secessionists and Unionists, and the other classifiable groups discussed earlier fell short of voting behavior typical of party. Nevertheless, by excluding one member characteristic, Exterior status, more may be discovered about the relations of Secessionists with Unionists (or Democrats with Whigs). Tables 11–8 and 11–9 offer some further measurements based exclusively on Interior members at any given session.

Agreement scores between Secessionists and Unionists of the Interior in the House of Representatives did not differ much from scores for all of the two groups during the first three sessions of the First Congress. After the military disasters of the summer and fall of 1863, however, the Interior agreement score is fifteen points lower than for all Secessionists and Unionists. And for the two sessions of the Second Congress, agreement levels for Interior only are thirty and eighteen points lower. Moreover, the percentage of actual antagonism instances among roll calls rises sharply. The score of 19 as a measure of Secessionist-Unionist voting agreement is not negative-range party voting, but it is lower than any other House score for these groups, and it is low enough to suggest the evolving rivalry that might have grown into party antagonism had time remained to the Confederacy.

Senate scores measuring Secessionist-Unionist agreement levels are lower in general than are House scores, and a notably larger proportion of antagonism instances appear. Much of the difference may be attributed to the effect of very small numbers of voting members on the score calculation. Interior senators were but a portion of the whole body, which was itself probably too small for agreement-score measurement to have much stability. Nonetheless, the greatly lowered scores and the much higher proportion of antagonism instances for Interior Secessionists and Unionists alone exceed a reasonable estimate of the impact of smaller group involvement. The score of 2 for the First Session of the Second Senate, incorporating as it does 37 percent antagonism instances, is very strongly indicative of association between position on secession and over-all voting stance in this session.

The comparison of cohesion levels for Interior members with those for the entire membership brings out the trend toward greater cohesion, especially for Unionists, as the war wound down toward oblivion for the Confederacy. A major shift began in the last session of the First Congress, stunned by the military disasters of the summer of 1863 and by the elections for the Second Congress; thereafter the Interior Unionists moved sharply toward a pattern of cohesion typical of party. The small number of involved members in the Senate accounts for a part of the greater cohesion in that house, but not for all of the dramatic shift to cohesive voting by both Secessionists and Unionists in the Second Senate. Congressmen in both houses also were responding to other influences and circumstances, to be sure, but isolating Interior members clearly enhances the evidence of association between position on secession and general voting record.

To compare Exterior Secessionists with Interior Unionists is to combine in mutual reinforcement the two attributes most associated with members' roll-call responses. As should be expected by now, agreement-score measurements for these two segments of the House expose a sharp tendency toward antagonism in the Second Congress. The score for the First Session is 19, and contains 21 percent instances of antagonism; and the score for the Second Session is actually negative, −4, with 29 percent antagonism instances—involving a total of 306 roll calls.

Summary

The several efforts to obtain an overview of Confederate roll-call voting behavior yield concurring implications about the association of member

TABLE 11-9

COHESION IN ROLL-CALL VOTING IN THE CONFEDERATE CONGRESS AMONG INTERIOR MEMBERS ONLY

Percentage of Selected Roll Calls in Each Session on Which Indicated Groups Voted Together at Each Level of Cohesion

Congress	Level of Cohesion	Representatives		Senators	
		Seces-sionists	Union-ists	Seces-sionists	Union-ists
1 Cong.	90-100%	11 (8)[a]	10 (10)[a]	16 (14)[a]	29 (8)[a]
1 Sess.	80-89%	14 (16)	16 (15)	6 (6)	0 (20)
	70-79%	7 (8)	18 (11)	18 (18)	31 (31)
	60-69%	30 (26)	28 (31)	29 (31)	10 (14)
	50-59%	38 (41)	28 (32)	31 (31)	31 (27)
1 Cong.	90-100%	5 (6)	6 (5)	10 (12)	43 (18)
2 Sess.	80-89%	14 (12)	9 (6)	15 (13)	0 (15)
	70-79%	23 (23)	23 (20)	20 (16)	21 (17)
	60-69%	31 (30)	27 (31)	34 (34)	19 (28)
	50-59%	27 (30)	34 (38)	22 (24)	17 (22)
1 Cong.	90-100%	6 (5)	6 (3)	9 (8)	32 (12)
3 Sess.	80-89%	8 (7)	16 (13)	17 (19)	9 (19)
	70-79%	13 (13)	19 (19)	19 (15)	16 (14)
	60-69%	27 (35)	27 (25)	27 (21)	25 (29)
	50-59%	47 (41)	33 (39)	27 (38)	18 (26)
1 Cong.	90-100%	5 (2)	12 (4)	16 (15)	36 (12)
4 Sess.	80-89%	11 (12)	20 (12)	18 (17)	20 (13)
	70-79%	27 (24)	20 (21)	4 (13)	13 (12)
	60-69%	21 (29)	27 (33)	46 (33)	22 (23)
	50-59%	36 (33)	20 (30)	16 (22)	9 (40)
2 Cong.	90-100%	12 (11)	20 (9)	35 (8)	47 (14)
1 Sess.	80-89%	14 (17)	20 (7)	0 (12)	4 (10)
	70-79%	21 (15)	22 (21)	4 (8)	20 (20)
	60-69%	30 (24)	22 (25)	41 (41)	12 (43)
	50-59%	23 (33)	15 (38)	20 (31)	16 (12)
2 Cong.	90-100%	17 (10)	33 (11)	44 (14)	56 (17)
2 Sess.	80-89%	17 (14)	23 (16)	0 (19)	0 (8)
	70-79%	16 (19)	19 (20)	12 (24)	0 (13)
	60-69%	25 (28)	17 (26)	31 (23)	22 (33)
	50-59%	24 (30)	8 (28)	14 (21)	22 (30)

a. Percentages shown in parentheses are for all members, Exterior as well as Interior (see Table 2-3).

characteristics with voting posture. Some of the slender bases for inference obtained in working with one content area at a time have been broadened by cross-content analysis. It would appear that knowing a member's Exterior or Interior status, his secession stand, and when he served in Congress is almost all that is needed to place the great majority in at least the proper half of a spectrum from strong to weak dedication to Confederate survival. A concluding chapter will attempt to fill out the skeleton of this, the anatomy of the Confederate Congress.

12 The Anatomy of the Confederate Congress

EVERY member of the Confederate Congress faced a political vacuum created by the disappearance of the old and familiar landmarks of section and party that had furnished considerable direction for congressional roll-call behavior prior to 1860. The unsuccessful search for substitutes for these lost antebellum guidelines is a crucial part of the history of the Confederate Congress. One of the alternatives was a wide-open kind of constituent-interest voting on the part of most members—vividly displayed in the pervasive and often sectional distinction between Exterior and Interior delegates. This was not altogether surprising, for sectionalism in the United States had been largely a thinly veneered localism, which in the Confederacy easily emerged naked when not even the deterrent of party was present. As stress became increasingly greater, however, conditioning from early party association and from more recent confrontations on the secession issue also appears to have exercised influence behind a deteriorating façade of unity. For the greater proportion of responses by most members, these were probably unconscious forces—at least until 1864. The temperamental or other personal elements which had underlain party choice or secession stand, even though they may be indistinguishable, undoubtedly constituted durable components of political stance; and these old influences surfaced more readily after the Confederacy's relatively peaceful and secure days were past.

Forces of continuity thus revealed themselves in roll-call response and also in the qualities of the members themselves. The congressmen were, for the most part, continuing a political role of long standing. No jolting change of leadership or displacement of an elite took place in the selection of these men. Their personal and political characteristics speak chiefly of stability of political frame of reference. Secession, long a theoretical possibility, had finally been espoused when the First House was elected, but for most voters this was culmination rather than revolution. The stunning cost of that decision was dawning on the voters when they elected the Second House, and recoil was apparent even though no viable alternative was systematically offered. The dominant theme of 1863 to be read from member characteristics of the Second House was a turning toward the rivals of secession, but even these were usually old and familiar faces. The popular stirrings of 1863 reveal only a suggestion that the mass of voters would have reacted to prolonged disaster in their personal worlds, not only by revising the currently operational policies, but even by supplanting much of the political officer corps that had allowed the surviving options to become so few and so costly.

The disruption caused by the Confederate schism becomes more apparent from the configuration of the would-be nation's political institutions. Most obviously lacking from an otherwise familiar edifice was the framework created by a two-party system. Although partisan balance had been damaged in the North during the 1850s, it had nevertheless survived to undergird political behavior in the wartime Union. The Confederate Congress, on the other hand, showed only a bare remnant of two-party behavior and not even a relic of two-party organization. It is easy enough to discover that no party caucuses met regularly, or that no one was recognized as a party floor leader. The election of the House speaker obviously produced no party division. Nevertheless, the matter is not as simple as it might seem. Party opposition in a national congress was the rule in the lifetimes of Confederate congressmen, and a ready basis for such rivalry existed in a continuation of prior Democrat-Whig divisions or in an adoption of the more recent Secessionist-Unionist alignment. Since these two bases of potential division were nearly the same, all the more reason would appear to have existed for resuming the congressional game according to familiar rules. Moreover, party idiom and partisan recrimination abounded in private correspondence, crept into the press, and intruded on the floors of Congress. The reasonable expectation would be to find that, lacking overt party organization, the Confederate Congress members quietly divided in party-like manner. No form of analysis applied to the bulk of roll calls, however, has exposed more than a hint of two-party performance. This decisive absence of continuity calls for explanation.

One of the elements contributing to this avoidance of party structure or partisan voting was the personal risk Whigs or Unionists would have borne in creating an organization which would represent continuity of the co-operation of those who had sought to destroy the Confederacy in the womb. Another reason is that Southern Whigs in the United States Congress had come to hold the same views as Southern Democrats on many vital issues of the 1850s, and so were habituated to voting with their Southern party opponents. Furthermore, from early in the life of the Confederacy, problems confronted by Congress were usually without precedent in recent party experience; it is significant that, in the Constitutional Convention and occasionally in later sessions of Congress, conflict did emerge on issues that had important conceptual bases in either antebellum party disagreements or in disunion contests. Finally, the single six-year presidential term, obviating the necessity for re-election effort, together with the generally prevalent Democratic party control of much of the Lower South during the 1850s, militated against Democratic continuance of partisan organization that might have stimulated retaliatory Whig or Unionist cohesion. Whatever the contributing causes may have been, as far as the totality of congressional business revealed, the members acted wholly without party discipline.

Lawmaking was every man for himself, for the Congress was an amorphous body in which it seemed that almost every atom behaved according to its own rules. Often, as one pores over the tedious and roll-call-laden pages of the *Journals,* it appears as though confusion and caprice played vital roles. Clearly, many legislators did not understand what it was they were called upon to do, an accusation made by many of the congressmen themselves. Warren Akin, for example, complained to his wife that "Congress seems not to realize the magnitude of the duties devolved upon it. . . . Here is the difficulty with the people and with Congress. They do *not consider. I wish they would."* [1] While this is a fault found in any deliberative body, it seems to have been unusually prevalent in the Confederate Congress, where the bench mark of party stance was not available. This Congress therefore provides a case study of confusion in a leaderless legislature, which was aggravated because the Vice-President, Alexander H. Stephens, decided to spend most of his time sulking at home. Administration officials from Davis down could only hope for a sympathetic committee chairman or for an *ad hoc* supporter to provide some degree of floor leadership. Obviously, a smoothly functioning two-party Congress would have been a substantial asset to the Davis administration until after the 1863 elections. Such an overt two-party pattern would, on the other hand, have provided more leadership and organization for crystallizing the discontent that erupted almost unbidden in the elections for the Second House. Davis's policies might thereafter have been in straits even more dire than was actually the case, for defeatists might have had a vehicle for opting to negotiate short of unconditional surrender.[2]

1. Bell I. Wiley, editor, *Letters of Warren Akin, Confederate Congressman* (Athens: University of Georgia Press, 1959), p. 105.

2. Eric L. McKitrick, in his essay "Party Politics and the Union and Confederate War Efforts," discusses at length the various advantages Lincoln had because of the continuing two-party system in the North and comments not only on Davis's difficulties with the Confederate Congress but also on his troublesome relations with governors in terms of the tools and weapons denied him by the absence of a two-party structure. (Chapter V

Some persistent divisions along lines other than former party or seces- sion stand might have developed quietly—for example, along lines of wealth or other individual or constituent considerations. Yet neither an economic nor any other factor created even a consistent major bloc, to say nothing of a substantial minority faction. Combinations formed and shifted in unpredictable fashion, so that the historian is rarely able to predict with whom a given member would be standing as he made his day-to-day roll-call decisions. Yet, underneath these swirling surface currents, a tide was impelling men of a certain combination of charac- teristics toward decisions against further sacrifice more often than was true of the remainder of their colleagues. Eventually, defeatism spread over the land and penetrated the halls of Congress, where men who proved to have least resistance to its ravages also proved to have definite identifiable attributes.

Proof of strong association of roll-call behavior with some of these identifiable member characteristics employed for this study comes from examination of member performance on sets of divisions directly related to significant topics. Cumulative scales on specific subjects were sought assiduously in the roll calls for each house for every session. An important finding is that these divisions generally do not yield many useful scales until after mid-war. In striking contrast to the United States Congress of either the antebellum or the Civil War period, a shared sense of the relative importance of each roll-call on a coherent topic was lacking from most Confederate congressional voting. It is very doubtful that these men responded to many votes from a common conceptual orienta- tion.

This is partly because a vast number of the roll calls involved more than one dimension. A clear-cut issue like habeas corpus suspension was therefore much more scalable than were the economic questions, which often involved two or three basic principles at once. Hand in hand goes the discovery that there were more dimensions than previous researchers had suspected. Where writers like Frank L. Owsley saw the major frame of reference in the Confederate Congress to be state rights, we have discovered a variety of state-rights scales.[3] It was easy for a man to be cool on the supposed state-rights issue of railroad construction

of William Nisbet Chambers and Walter Dean Burnham, editors, *The American Party Systems: Stages of Political Development* [New York: Oxford University Press, 1967]. See also David M. Potter, "Jefferson Davis and the Political Factors in Confederate Defeat," in Donald, *Why the North Won the Civil War*, 91–114, especially pp. 113–114.)

3. See Frank L. Owsley, *State Rights in the Confederacy* (Chicago: University of Chicago Press, 1925). As Owsley expressed it (p. 1), the Confederacy "Died of State Rights."

and not on the equally state-rights issue of conscription. If all the topics that historians have heretofore called state-rights questions were actually that, then it is obvious that the concept represented not one dimension but many. Ultimately, however, impending disaster introduced most members to a common and terrifyingly simple frame of reference, with the consequence that roll-call scalability was far greater for the Second Congress than for prior years.

Partly because of limited results from cumulative scale analysis, and partly because a broader if less precise measurement can be obtained, one side of as many roll calls as seemed feasible was assigned as the position of commitment to Confederate success. Performance scores were then calculated for each member on each of numerous specific topics. By comparing both scale positions and performance scores with member characteristics, progress was made in unraveling some major threads from the tangled skein of roll-call records. In the process, there has been frequent repetition, because the techniques employed and the issues and sessions examined have produced conclusions that point in the same direction. The successive reiterations were important for establishing the similarity of responses to separate issues.

The Provisional Congress was, for many reasons, an intractable body to analyze through its divisions. One important exception is its work as a Constitutional Convention. In that brief roll-call record, there is strong evidence that former Whigs and Unionists were far more desirous of bestowing adequate powers on the government they had tried to forestall than were the Democrats and Secessionists who called it into being. By implication, at least, this relative centralism supports prior Whig claims to greater appreciation for the functions and benefits of an effective national government. It certainly ties in with the frequent wartime claim of Union Whigs that those most adroit at wrecking the old government seemed singularly inept at erecting a new one. What could not have been so readily foreseen was that these same Southern Unionists who so gracefully accepted the verdict and looked only to the Confederacy's future quailed sooner than Secessionists when the cost was more realistically assessed.

Perhaps the most significant pattern in the roll calls of the Provisional Congress, aside from its intervals as a Constitutional Convention, is the indication that, had a permanent Confederacy materialized, an Upper South *versus* Lower South antagonism would have appeared on some crucial questions. This ironic intra-Confederate sectionalism shows continuity with the problems of the Union. Regrettably however, it was not traceable for long, because much of the Upper South was soon an occupied portion of the Confederacy, whose delegates to Congress were so strongly affected by considerations associated with their Exterior status as to render unmeasurable any influences flowing exclusively from the Upper South location of their constituents.

The Permanent Congresses yielded better than the Provisional Congress to analysis of roll calls drawn from specific subjects of deep concern to Confederates. Analyses of such subjects were sometimes enlightening for sessions before the crisis of the war and usually so for those meeting after the major engagements of 1863. Most of the economic problems, especially those of the monetary mare's nest, crucial though they were, could not serve as a basis for measuring the influence of member characteristics, either because most members could not perceive them uniformly enough, or because solutions remained too elusive. Yet, even in this thicket, some movement could be discerned that proved to be parallel to that observed on questions which produced the keenest popular reactions. It was the sensitive and eventually inflamed issues of conscription, impressment, and suspension of the writ of habeas corpus in the First but especially the Second Congress that starkly exposed the rapid acceleration after mid-war of distinctions that were associated with identifiable differences among members. Several less persistent problems that were intensely critical at one or a few points only furnished reiteration of these same associations. Cross-content cumulative scales for the Second House and average performance scores and scale positions reinforced inferences about the effects of certain member circumstances or experiences.

Of the several variables tested in our analyses, the four associated with member wealth (number of slaves owned, relative slaveholding status in home county, amount of estate, and relative value of estate in home county) were least associated with voting behavior. Except for isolated issues, such as the "twenty-Negro" exemption, the pay and travel arrangements for the members of Congress, and some of the basic tax structure, no clear pattern was found to be attributable to these economic characteristics. While weak correlations sometimes exist, they are usually traceable to the presence of other factors. Members from the Upper South, for example, were not as wealthy as those from the Lower South and were more likely to have been Unionists. Hence, what sometimes appears on the surface to have been a wealth differential may really be based on opinions about secession. At the same time economic or slaveholding attributes of the congressional district tended to divide the Confederacy into regions too similar to the overriding Interior-Exterior dichotomy to permit effective measurement of associations between these constituent economic or racial considerations and roll-call patterns.

Party proved to be a more significant portent of behavior in the

Permanent Congress, despite the lack of formal alignment. To know which party had claim on a congressman's allegiance in the 1850s would certainly not enable one to predict his vote on any given roll call but would improve one's chances of guessing correctly his general attitude on the basic issues facing the Confederacy. However, the close parallel between party and secession stand (four fifths of the men for whom both positions are known were either Secession Democrats or Union Whigs) sometimes makes it difficult to tell which consideration was the more influential—if, indeed, the two can be considered as separate characteristics. To the extent that judgment can be made, former political affiliation was the weaker of the two, except on a very few issues with direct antecedents in the major party battles of the antebellum period.

Throughout this study, it has been demonstrated that secession position is generally a more important predictor of congressional voting than is party. This is very notable in the subject-content-area chapters, especially the one on habeas corpus, although it emerges in other portions of the roll calls as well. The closest approaches to typical party behavior witnessed at any time in the life of the Congress were displayed by the low agreement score between the Secessionists and the Unionists in the Constitutional Convention, together with the relatively high cohesion levels of Unionists in that convention, and the low agreement score between Exterior Secessionists and Interior Unionists in the Second Congress.

Whether a member's home district was occupied by Federals seems to have been increasingly more important than even secession stand as an influence on his roll-call responses. Time and again, Exterior members proved to be, on the average, more committed and sacrificing. They may have felt that they had less to go back to, in case of Confederate defeat, and that, once an area was occupied, it would become "Unionized" and inhospitable to those who had supported the South. In any event, these men knew more about the tragedy of war than did their Interior colleagues. Their homes were occupied, their families were either separated from them or living as refugees, and their personal incomes usually were limited to the pittance they were paid as members of Congress. It cannot be overlooked that their constituents were not likely to pay the price of any sacrificing legislation they supported. Yet, some of the members classified as Exterior because their districts were war zones, or occupied perhaps temporarily, could not count on immunity of their constituents from the impact of Confederate legislation; and it is just such members of the Exterior group who often prove to be the notable cases of deviation from the normal association of Exterior classification with high scores and positions. East Tennessee in 1863 offers one example, for her people were technically occupied by Federal forces but actually subject to impressment by campaigning Confederate forces and even to pre-emptory conscription when Confederates temporarily controlled a community. It is not surprising, therefore, that the Confederate senator from East Tennessee, Landon C. Haynes, was notably less sacrificing on impressment and conscription than would have been anticipated from his technically Exterior status at that time. Whatever the parameters directing the individual's thought process, however, the significance of this background characteristic can hardly be overemphasized.

All three of the significant predictors—former party, secession stand, and Exterior or Interior status—became more important as the Confederacy approached final defeat. As we have seen, in the 1863 elections, a Southern peace movement was partly responsible for the election of a few pro-peace men, eight of whom were North Carolina Union Whigs whose constituencies remained in the Interior to the very end.[4] These North Carolinians were responsible for much, sometimes most, of the voting differences between Democrats and Whigs, Secessionists and Unionists, and Exterior men and Interior men. Deletion of their votes usually narrows and sometimes eliminates the distinctions we have noted so frequently in previous chapters. It is obvious that these men and their followers in both Senate and House often perceived issues in a way very different from other congressmen; and although they were affected by the same influences as their colleagues, their reaction was more extreme and much more consistent. The importance of the North Carolina legislators themselves should not be overemphasized, however, for they had an important following from other states. It is no coincidence, moreover, that they were all Whigs, all Unionists, and all Interior delegates. These uncommitted congressmen created an alienated, frustrated, and obtrusive opposition to the demands of a majority of their colleagues on certain of the most sensitive topics. Whether their districts were within the Confederate defense perimeter was the most important single ascertainable influence for many congressmen; but for these doctrinaire and uncommitted North Carolina legislators, the most consequential common attribute seems to have been a vengeful memory of a Unionism relinquished with anguish.

These important characteristics of party, secession stand, and occupied status did not always work harmoniously, as they did in North Carolina

4. The home areas of James T. Leach and Thomas Fuller were penetrated by the Union army in March 1865. This was so close to the end, however, that they have been considered Interior.

in 1864 and 1865. A Secession Democrat whose constituency was occupied by Union forces was powerfully impelled toward support of drastic measures necessary for Confederate victory. A Union Whig from an Interior district would experience equally powerful tugs in the opposite direction. Much more complicated were the forces at work on Secession Whigs, or Union Democrats, or those drawn in opposite directions perhaps by Interior status and Secessionist background. Each congressman came to his own accommodation with events when faced with such ambivalent pressures, and there seems to be no way to predict what the accommodation would be, at least without much more refined and complete data than we have been able to use—perhaps more than is still extant. In instances of conflict, Unionism at times appears to have been the strongest single force; yet this cannot be applied as a rule. The erratic pattern of performance scores or scale positions for a single member from topic to topic, or even on the same topic from session to session, continues to stand as a warning of unmeasured influences at work. The member characteristics we have employed did not singly or collectively, even by inference, fully determine a member's stance. They constituted, rather, the above-mentioned tide that appears to have swept Whigs, Unionists, and Interior members along a somewhat different course from that charted by their Democratic, Secessionist, and Exterior colleagues. The exact bearing or precise location at any given instant is not the predictable element; the ultimate drift apart on crucial matters is what can be measured and found to be associated with these member characteristics.[5]

The Confederate senators left a roll-call record that differs enough from that for the House members to require comment. Length of term, responsibility more to legislators than to voters, broader scope of constituency, and perhaps greater experience in political action account in part for a senator's differing roll-call behavior. The small size of the Senate, moreover, affected the nature of committee work on bills, the character of floor discussion, and the quality of associations among senators. The intimacy of voting in as small a group as a score or so of men may well have evoked a large array of interpersonal considerations as well

---

5. One of the difficulties encountered by several students of Confederate government has arisen because of the wish to be able to classify each individual as pro-Davis or anti-Davis, pro- or anti-state rights, Southern nationalist or reconstructionist. Such monolithic implications are closer to the mark when votes are disciplined by party or some other marshaling agency; but when a member had as much freedom as was characteristic of Confederate congressmen, dichotomous classification proves not to fit reality for most of these men—tendencies and directions, not fixed positions, were the legacies of their individual characteristics or circumstances.

as a special sensitivity to one's image in the eyes of his colleagues that might have been dulled in the greater anonymity of a voting body two or three times as large as the Senate. For whatever combination of reasons, the influences on voting behavior that have been documented for the representatives apparently bore less decidedly on the senators. Individualistic behavior and personal attitudes of untraced origins account for the lion's share of senatorial decision making. And yet, even the senators can at many points be understood reasonably well in terms of other than purely personal predilections or prejudices. Particularly in matters associated with the location of Federal forces and the concomitant liability of constituents to effective Confederate law enforcement, senators behaved much like the representatives.

Limitations notwithstanding, the evidence adduced concerning some of the forces affecting a Confederate congressman's decisions ought to contribute to redressing a balance in interpretation of motivation that is still weighted too heavily on the side of survivals from the Age of Reason. Some students of American political history who would unhesitatingly acknowledge behaviorist influences in the private life of a subject take very seriously his political speeches and letters and leave a reader assuming that his announced reasons are to be accepted unless the author injects a caveat. It ought to be healthful to recognize that, whatever the rhetoric in the Confederate congressional proceedings, many a roll-call response was predictable from knowing where the member lived, which antebellum party he had espoused, and how he had reacted to the secession movement. On the other hand, the Confederate roll-call record is admittedly replete with responses that are not even approximately predictable and are wholly unrelated to the predictive characteristics we have applied—as well as to the speeches some legislators were making on the subject. Upon balancing, there may be encouragement to students of politics that appropriate tools have made possible the uncovering of considerable form and predictability in what seemed to be an almost random mass of individual decisions. Moreover, in the process, individual identity has not so much been submerged as rescued. We know something, often much, about behavior of rank-and-file Confederate Congress members who formerly were little more than names on a roster for this important segment of their lives. One purpose for furnishing detailed information on these individuals, set in a frame of reference too costly in effort to have been constructed for a single subject, is to facilitate biographical study.

Defenders of the theory of Confederate nationhood must surely have doubts when contemplating the helter-skelter operations of the Confederate Congress. The essentially constituent-oriented behavior implied by the Exterior-Interior dichotomy belies any general submerging of private and personal concerns in an overriding cause. The ready revival of former Unionism under pressure of sacrifice, discouragement, and disaster is inconsistent with the kind of commitment that could be classed as beyond the threshold of mere awareness of common concerns and into the realm of a taken-for-granted sense of perpetual nationhood. Had Confederate independence been maintained, nationalism would perhaps have emerged eventually; but in 1861, a country was created on paper before it was a reality in the hearts of a sufficient number of its would-be citizens. Despite the far-reaching efforts of Confederate leaders to create a modern nation-state, the infighting and the nature of influences profoundly affecting much of the roll-call behavior of Confederate lawmakers after 1863 cannot easily be equated to the operations of an assembly of revolutionary nationalist zealots.

The expression of strong peace sentiments in the 1863 elections was responsible for much of this change in legislative behavior, because the new Congress brought to Richmond an influx of Unionists and Whigs who had new ideas. The change was also due to a contraction of the area under reliable Confederate control. By November of 1864, the majority of Confederate congressmen came from the Exterior. Inasmuch as the most important determinants of voting were secession view and military-occupation status, it is not surprising that these changes in the character of the members of the Second Congress also produced a change in its performance. It was obvious from the early moments of the First Session of the Second Congress in June 1864 that increasing numbers of Confederate voters no longer saw their politics as that of decisions on how to make war. Rather, they began to question the basic assumption upon which the Confederacy rested, namely, that it could win its place in the family of nations by the force of arms. The issue for these voters, as for the North Carolinians and their followers in the Second Congress, was between peace, whether achieved by successful negotiations for independence or humiliating surrender, and war, with its continued sacrifices. Increasingly, Confederates and their congressmen chose the former rather than the latter, as the blight of disaffection continued to spread after 1863. Had the Confederacy retained a large enough heartland for meaningful congressional elections to have been held in 1865, the new House probably would have presented a startling complexion to a veteran observer of the American political scene. That the Interior members of such a House would have been preponderantly reconstructionist goes almost without saying; that they might also have been the spearhead of a kind of populist revolt a quarter-century in advance is altogether possible.

The workings of the Confederate Congress also help to document the extent of blunders of Southern leadership in the 1840s and 1850s, a leadership that had sought to make a mortal god of an institution and a holy terror of a race issue that together could not command adequate sacrifice from even the congressmen of the Confederacy. Foreshadowing the future, Congress also revealed that the singular prevalence of Union Whigs and Union Douglas Democrats elected under Johnsonian reconstruction in 1865 in most of the former Confederate states was a continuation of a trend line established in mid-war by Confederate voters and extended during the Second Congress by a significant segment of the men they elected.

The paucity of American experience with governments-in-exile may be slightly alleviated by the record of the Confederate Congress. Exterior members were understandably bitter at being denounced as the authors of unconstitutional and evil legislation and threatened with reduction to nonvoting territorial-delegate status. Yet there are instructive nuances in the frustrations of those Interior members who were repeatedly defeated by votes of men from phantom districts. The Confederate Exterior delegates were highly visible examples of policy-determining representation from constituencies immune to the consequences of those policies.

To paraphrase a familiar *bon mot,* nothing is more instructive about the life of the Confederacy than its manner of taking leave of it, for it offers a sight the benefits of which have rarely been enjoyed by citizens of the United States. It is a view of the devastating problem of ending a war that is manifestly lost. Professor C. Vann Woodward, in his 1952 Southern Historical Association presidential address entitled "The Irony of Southern History," [6] pointed out that the Southern people could teach the rest of their compatriots one lesson: that one does not always win a war and that the assumption of invincibility can betray a people into disaster. The Confederate Congress, by the same token, manifested the constitutional and parliamentary agonies involved in trying to liquidate a lost effort. Certainly by Christmas of 1864, with Lincoln re-elected, Richmond beseiged, Sherman in Savannah, and General John B. Hood's tattered Confederates recoiling from Nashville, the fate of the Confederacy was sealed. A large number of members of Congress had already revealed their defeatist and reconstruction state of mind in their quiet votes on roll calls. Yet it seemed beyond the grasp of any constitutional official to effect a sensible acknowledgment of the obvious. Congressman

---

6. C. Vann Woodward, "The Irony of Southern History," *Journal of Southern History,* XIX (February 1953), 3–19.

William R. Smith might thunder that the "soldier in the trenches, knee-deep in blood and mire, has the right *to look to the statesman* and require him to act his part"; but it will be recalled that, by this time, the dogs of war had long been leashed, for it was October of 1865.[7] When it might have counted, before April of 1865, he had simply left Richmond early because he feared that he might get into trouble because of his "treasonable" policies.

A basic reason for such difficulties was that, in rejecting a two-party system such as that of the Union, the congressmen rejected all hope of establishing effective alternatives to whatever executive policies they might oppose. While party politics can be carried to unreasonable extremes, the party itself can and must perform the useful function of providing a rallying point for opposition congressmen. These legislators could have insisted upon a more vigorous prosecution of the war, or on the other hand, they might have brought an earlier and therefore less painful capitulation. But the absence of continuing party channels forestalled direction and management of majority-supported programs and denied respectability, standing, and effectiveness to minority opposition. Whatever an organized resistance to the Davis administration might have done, there was none at times when it seemed to be needed. Within the American tradition in which these politicians had always operated, there was no source of alternative leadership except through a party structure. Military dictatorship was discussed but not resorted to because it was utterly foreign to the American experience. Even an attempt to rally the state governors to co-operation failed in this patrimony of state rights. This study has indicated that, by the end of the war, discontent within Congress was forcing large numbers of delegates, like William R. Smith, quoted above, to take deadly issue with President Davis. But without an opposition political party, there was no way to mobilize this opposition effectively. By contrast, Lincoln's Conservative opponents in the North, bitterly frustrated at his addition of emancipation to the original war objectives, at least had some vehicle of legitimate protest through the Democratic party's 1864 platform. While Davis felt that for him to weaken was death to a nation, what was a responsible member of the policy-making branch of the Confederate government to do? The structure was not just faulty; it was fatally deficient.[8]

7. Selma (Alabama) *Times,* October 19, 1865.

8. Frank E. Vandiver, *Their Tattered Flags: The Epic of the Confederacy* (New York: Harper's Magazine Press, 1970), p. 306, offers the following information about Davis: "He planned secretly how to end the war according to the constitution. Perhaps if he resigned the states might each conclude a treaty. It was legal and proper that he should think this way, for he was the President and could not yield."

In some ways, the Confederate Congress was just what James Madison, writing in the tenth *Federalist,* both desired and feared. Congressmen consciously and successfully avoided the divisiveness of formal parties, an action Madison would have approved, but they failed just as Madison had failed, almost three quarters of a century earlier, to evade the clash of faction. And as the Confederacy fell, it appears as though that dreaded monster, faction, was about to become institutionalized. In the Second Congress, the peace bloc of North Carolinians and their followers from other states voted as a fairly cohesive unit on important issues, and it is not unlikely that they would have created inadvertently the first political party within the new nation if the Confederacy had lived. One can see the possibilities of this in the increasing scalability of congressional roll calls during the last weeks. Had it not been cut short, Congress's quest for a substitute for the old political guidelines might have eventuated in a party that combined sectionalism with the supposedly rejected Union-Secession axis of the decade before 1861.

The best opportunity for voter response to the consequences of administration policy would have been a real party contest in 1863, but that was denied by the combination of circumstances that smothered this customary vehicle for registering dissent. The reason for the inability to build such a "loyal opposition" party is transparent: the opposition at points of greatest significance was not particularly loyal. Fidelity to a cause outside one's nation, or even in conflict with a national administration's basic policy, was not unheard of in the nineteenth century; but espousing the obliteration of one's alleged nation was not really respectable in an era of enshrined nationalism.

The Confederate Congress is therefore one of the few examples in United States history of a national legislative body attempting to operate without party discipline. A very similar shattering of pattern and coherence on roll-call responses resulted from the upheaval and realignment of parties in the United States House of Representatives between 1853 and 1855. These two periods of highly personalized decision-making suggest that actual implementation of the theory of geographic district representation in the democratic rationale of the day could very probably have led only to disaster in designing national policy. That major public policy can safely be left to the almost accidental proportion of Exterior delegates, or original Secessionists, or former Democrats who happened to be present and voting is not a very sophisticated concept of lawmaking dynamics. If the intense individualism and localism that was equated to "democracy" is properly singled out by Professor David Donald as the most appropriate cause of death to be inscribed as the Confederacy's epitaph, the anatomy of the Confederate Congress displays a central government institution that unwittingly mirrored faithfully the most fateful characteristic of its constituency.[9]

To sit in on the Confederate Congress, from the initial stroke of the gavel to the last *sine die,* as we have done, is therefore much like watching men willingly preside over their own destruction. In establishing a Constitution of such limited power (and not even implementing it fully), the Confederate Congress made itself an institution which was ill-equipped to meet emergencies which proved to be far beyond expectations. It would appear that the history of the Confederacy and its Congress demonstrates the inadequacy of ostensibly free institutions under the pressures of almost total war, unless liberty be seriously compromised. A free Congress refused to surrender to the Union; it also refused to give Jefferson Davis the instruments of war that he considered necessary (suspension of habeas corpus, effective taxation, and military details, for example), and Davis in turn refused to seize them.

Actually, however, the lesson does not involve the failure of free institutions, but rather, as David Donald points out, their extraordinary success. It is remarkable, for example, that under the pressure of a steadily worsening military situation, the Congress existed at all. Many a nation born in revolution has postponed its congresses until the coming of peace should allow such a luxury. But at the darkest moments, Davis and Congress still talked the game of constitutional liberty. Perhaps that was part of the unreality of the whole Confederate situation. But it may also have been a genuine dedication to constitutional order and the feeling that unless this could be preserved the game would not be worth the candle. The prize would be worthwhile only if unsullied. Representative John P. Murray doubted "that in order to get liberty you must first lose it." [10] There was simply a limit beyond which most Confederates would not go.

Exactly where that limit lay was a decision each had to make for himself. Though his own past may have partially dictated the outcome, every congressman probably made this decision with some anguish. If more of them had decided that independence was to be prized above all else, what then of their constituents' reactions? But congressmen rarely reached such a conclusion, for they represented truly a people who never ventured the ultimate commitment.

Tragedy abounds in the story of the Confederacy. In 1898, as he received copies of the *Official Records of the War of the Rebellion,* former

9. See David Donald, "Died of Democracy," in Donald, *Why the North Won the Civil War.*

10. "Proceedings," LI, 125.

Representative Jehu A. Orr could not even bear to look at them. "They have got the same effect on me," he revealed, "that Poe's 'Raven' would have. They are a constant reminder of disaster and defeat." [11] Frank E. Vandiver's *Their Tattered Flags* evokes well this poignant awareness of Southern travail. But an ironic twist may be felt in the fulfillment by the Congress of the age-old prophecy, reiterated by Abraham Lincoln, that a house divided against itself cannot stand. Former Senator William A. Graham's lament in 1867 that, after sectional conflict had actually begun, "the only alternative left us, was the choice of the side we should espouse, when a favorable result to either, was to be little short of ruin to us" highlights this truth.[12]

It is through the experiences of Confederate Congress members, such as Graham, that one may readily understand what William Faulkner later characterized as "the problems of the human heart in conflict with itself." [13]

11. Orr to Marcus J. Wright, September 14, 1898, Eldridge Collection. This item is quoted by permission of the Huntington Library and Art Gallery, San Marino, California.

12. Graham to Robert C. Winthrop, February 1, 1867, Robert Charles Winthrop Papers.

13. James B. Meriwether, editor, *Essays, Speeches, and Public Letters by William Faulkner* (New York: Random House, 1965), p. 119.

Appendix I

Biographical Directory
of the Confederate Congress

Sources and Criteria

The sources used in compiling this directory will be obvious to many readers. One of the most important was the *Dictionary of American Biography*. Almost as useful was the *Biographical Directory of the American Congress, 1774–1961*. These were supplemented by numerous minor national directories and a variety of regional and state directories. Equally valuable were pardon petitions filed by the congressmen during Presidential Reconstruction, which are now in the National Archives, and which often included rough biographical sketches and even physical descriptions.

The most valuable source is the manuscript 1860 census, which is also located in the National Archives, and which gives such vital data as age, state of birth, occupation, value of personal and real estate, and slaveholdings for almost all members of Congress. Census information, however, is not as reliable as one would wish, and cross-checks with other records sometimes reveal great discrepancies. For this reason, and because of frequent name confusion, the census must be used with great care. Hardy Strickland of Georgia illustrates the problem, as three entries were found under that name, and a fourth was listed under H. Strickland. All had the same occupation, two were born in Georgia and two in North Carolina, and the wife's name was the same in two cases and similar in a third. The estates varied between $2,830 and $34,000, and three had slaveholdings. In this instance, age was verified by Strickland's pardon petition in 1865 and the proper entry was tentatively picked out. The large number of inaccurate age entries in the census also gives one pause, and it must be recognized that, in this, as in many cases, the researcher's judgment may be in error. Few cases presented the problems that Strickland presented, but anyone working in census materials is advised to know the age, place of birth, spouse's name, and occupation of the individual he seeks before going to the manuscript. This information is invaluable in distinguishing between fathers and sons, cousins, and other namesakes, and in identifying those who are listed only by initial and last name. "W. D. Simpson," for example, may not be a particularly useful entry, especially if there are similar names in the same county. But if it is known that Congressman William D. Simpson was born in South Carolina in 1823, that he was a lawyer, and that he was married to Jane Young, one can be sure of proper identification.

For a variety of reasons, and those mentioned above are only a few, sources have often been unclear or conflicting. One very basic confusion is the spelling of some names; those in this appendix are, as far as we can determine, spelled in the way they were most frequently used unless we have definite information that common usage was incorrect. A good example of the problem is Thomas M. Forman of Georgia, who is listed in the *Journals* of the Congress and in the *Official Records of the War of Rebellion* as *Foreman*. The census spells it *Forman* and is corroborated by Forman's own signature on his pardon request. Thus, he will be listed as Forman, *Journals* and *Official Records* notwithstanding. Other variant spellings are frequently encountered by anyone doing research on the Confederacy. Walker Brooke is sometimes listed as Walter Brooke, Chesnut becomes Chestnut, Macfarland is frequently MacFarland. Further deviations are Mitchell for Mitchel, Rawls for Ralls, Ramsey for Ramsay, Walter Staples for Waller R. Staples, and William C. Wickham for Williams C. Wickham. Confusion is compounded because men of the era sometimes changed the spelling of their names, so that their own signatures may not match.

Name forms are equally muddled. Most men used their middle initials, but for others like Robert A. Toombs it was dropped in common usage. Sources sometimes do not agree on given names, and middle names and sometimes even first names are often unavailable. Names in the appendix are as complete as contradictory sources and limited resources would permit; but in the text and index, they are in the form by which these men are most frequently known. In case of conflicting references, the style employed is that of the *Journals,* the *DAB*, or the *Biographical Directory of the American Congress.*

The list of names does not include a few men who are sometimes thought to have been congressmen. There are a number of individuals listed in almanacs, directories, and commentaries who were not congressmen at all. Some of these were actually elected, such as Williamson R. W. Cobb, who was expelled from the Second Congress because he had voluntarily entered the Federal lines. A symptom of North Alabama Unionism, Cobb preferred not to attend Congress. Other names also crop up occasionally. For example, Gideon D. Camden was supposedly elected as a Virginia delegate to the Provisional Congress; John Hyer of Missouri was apparently elected to the First Congress; and Samuel H. Christian of North Carolina was chosen for the Second Congress but died before it met. Many other errors are found in the pages of *The Confederate States Almanac*, which was published in Vicksburg and later in Mobile. As the war progressed, the almanac deteriorated, and it ended its life in rather sad shape. But one must not underrate the difficulties of effective communication in the South during the war years, and it is not surprising that several congressmen, such as Alfred Boyd of Kentucky, Micajah Bullock of Tennessee, S. S. Scott of Kentucky, J. F. Lewis of Louisiana, and E. C. Yellowby of North Carolina, appear only in the records of the *Alamanac* and never in the *Journals* of Congress. In any case, we have considered as congressmen only those persons who actually claimed their seats.

The residences of the legislators proved not as difficult to determine as expected, but the procedure is cumbersome. First, biographical directories, state histories, and similar works were examined to determine an individual's home town or county. Frequently, sources conflicted, giving the impression that someone was living in two or three places at once. In such cases, the census records for all counties involved were searched to insure that the congressman was found and not his namesake. In a few instances, the only record available was a district represented, either in the United States Congress, a state legislature, or the Confederate Congress. Then, apportionment records had to be checked to see which counties were included in the district, and each of these counties was checked in turn. In the case of the relatively few urban dwellers, city directories and maps were consulted to determine ward of residence; time would not permit examination of the large cities unless this information was known for at least a few urban congressmen. Despite this laborious procedure, or perhaps because of it, at least partial census entries were found for all except seventeen congressmen. There were other cases, however, in which only the listing in the slave schedule or population schedule could be found.

Having determined residence in order to use the census, the census either confirms or denies that previous information. In almost all cases in this appendix, the residence listed is that in the census record (if available). Sometimes it was quite difficult to determine domicile. Alexander R. Boteler of Virginia, to take one example, is listed in the *Biographical Directory of the American Congress* as living in Shepherdstown in 1860, but the census locates him in Charleston (now Charles Town) about ten miles away—fortunately, in the same county. The opposite problem involved Charles M. Conrad of Louisiana, whom various sources place in Washington, D.C., and in New Orleans in 1860. We were unable to find him at either location in the census and therefore considered New Orleans his home. Often, the census indicates some small town which no longer seems to be on the map. Herschel V. Johnson came from Speir's Turnout, Georgia, while Albert G. Brown lived in or near Temp's Depot, Mississippi. Many of these locations were nothing more than post offices, depots, or local landmarks, so a congressman's home actually may have been several miles away. Nevertheless, the census listing is usually taken as the place of residence in 1860. Residence is unknown for only one congressman, Michael W. Cluskey of Tennessee. Congressional district is given for every representative. A map of the Confederacy by district is at the beginning of Chapter 1.

If there is occasional confusion surrounding the location of a congressman's home, there is less about what Congress he was in. But there is not as much certainty as one might reasonably expect, since not all records are correct. Even the *Official Records* omit two Missouri congressmen from the rolls of the Provisional Congress. Other errors crop up because of unexpected deaths. Thus, John Tyler of Virginia is often listed as a member of the First Congress, to which he was elected, as well as of the Provisional Congress, in which he did participate. David M. Currin of Tennessee sat in the Provisional Congress and First House and was elected to the Second, but he died before it met. A congressman's stated year of birth, on the other hand, is frequently in error, though often by only one or two years. Sources tend to be quite contradictory here.

The sources are more confusing in their designations of congressmen as Secessionists, Unionists, or Co-operationists. Here the decision was made to eliminate the Co-operationist classification, since every congressman was actually either Secessionist or Unionist. Some could be labeled Co-operationist because they wished to secede in co-operation with other states, but such individuals were obviously Secessionists. Others masqueraded in Co-operationist guise because the secession steamroller had to be slowed before it could be stopped; such men were Unionists. Congressmen were labeled either Unionist or Secessionist on the basis of their feelings about the basic issue and not their tactical positions. But so many individuals changed their minds in the year following Lincoln's election that it becomes difficult to determine what real feelings were. Accordingly, the Secession or Union label was used with reference to the date of key events. When a state seceded before the firing on Fort Sumter, the designation was Unionist, if, at the time of secession, an individual desired to remain in the Union; if he favored secession, he was, of course, Secessionist. For states that left the Union in the second wave of secession, the key is Abraham Lincoln's call for troops on April 15, 1861. With the exception of the Kentucky and Missouri delegations, which are cases unto themselves, anyone from the states which seceded after Fort Sumter is considered Unionist if he opposed secession until Lincoln's call. For Missouri, the key event is the Camp Jackson affair, when, on May 10, 1861, Federal forces disarmed the Missouri militia. Those who held out as Unionists until then are counted as Unionists, while those who turned toward secession at any time before then are Secessionists. In Kentucky, the breakdown of neutrality provides the criterion. A congressman favoring secession before September 1861 is counted as Secessionist; but to be Unionist, one still had to believe in union when neutrality was abandoned. In both Kentucky and Missouri, the basic presumption was Secessionist, although presumption alone was not enough to place the label. However, congressmen from those two states had a choice that members from other states did not have. They could be Secessionists and yet remain in the Union without acting inconsistently with their political philosophies. Obviously, care had to be exercised in making the Secession-Union decision, but more so for Kentucky and Missouri than elsewhere. At times, conflicting evidence would not permit a decision; such men were labeled unknown, and a large number of unknowns are from Missouri or Kentucky.

Although criteria for party are less complicated, several cases of indecision had to be settled by making no decision at all. This appendix lists only one party, which is the member's major affiliation in the 1850s. Members of the American and Constitutional Union parties are considered Whigs (since, in the South, the former parties were essentially the latter under different nomenclature) unless they had a Democratic party affiliation between 1848 and the time they became Know-Nothings or Constitutional Unionists. In the very few cases falling into the last category, the designation has been Democrat. If a Whig became a Democrat before the crisis of 1850–1852, as many Calhoun Whigs did, the listing is Democrat; if the switch was made afterwards, the individual remains a Whig. An asterisk indicates membership in any of a variety of other political parties, ranging from Jeffersonian Republican and Georgia Union of 1850 to American or Constitutional Union.

Vocations are as confusing as any other class of biographical information. The reader may remark at the exceptional number of congressmen engaged in two, or even three, occupations. This may tell us something of the nature of Southern society in the middle of the nineteenth century, but it may also reflect the type of biographical information available. One reason for so many dual occupations is that many congressmen who are listed as lawyers in the sources are shown by the census to own vast numbers of slaves and to live in rural areas. These legislators are considered engaged in agriculture unless there is good evidence to the contrary. Since very few large slaveholdings were used for anything but agriculture, it is probable that such educated guesses are correct. James B. Dawkins of Florida was a lawyer, but he hired an overseer and owned twenty-seven slaves. Grandison D. Royston of Arkansas is listed in the census as a lawyer, but he owned a hundred slaves, maintained five slave houses, had $60,000 worth of real estate, and lived in a rural area. Such men obviously were planters as well as lawyers.

Slaveholding statistics are more clear-cut. Occasionally, the information comes from an individual's pardon request or some other biographical source; but in the vast majority of cases, slaveholding figures are those listed in the 1860 census. Some difficulty is encountered in identifying congressmen who held slaves outside their county of residence, and it would not be practical to search an entire state or region for such holdings. Unless there was some clue as to the location of other slaves (and sometimes there was), only the legislator's home county was searched, but it was checked thoroughly. Figures include slaves owned, whether in full or part interest, and employed, on the theory that part-ownership or employment of a slave would give a man an emotional stake in slavery equal to that of the man who held full ownership. In any event, such cases seldom occurred. Slaves held in trust for others, again a rare instance, are not included. The category of relative slaveholding is based upon the size of the average holding in a congressman's county of residence, determined by dividing the number of slaves in the county by the number of slaveholders. (This information may be found on pp. 223–247 of Volume II of the 1860 census report.) The congressman's holding was then expressed as a percentage of the average, and the percentage was categorized according to this schedule: 0 = no slaves, 1 = 1 to 50 percent of the average holding in the county of residence, 2 = 51 to 200 percent, 3 = 201 to 600 percent, and 4 = 601 percent or more. This reveals some startling results. A few large slaveholders were little men at home, and some small holders were real nabobs in their own counties. The average size of slaveholdings in a member's home county has also been used, this time without further manipulation, as one of the constituency characteristics. This measurement has been omitted for senators because their constituencies consisted of entire states, but for each House member the index number is assigned as follows:

Average Holding Per County	County Type	Index Designation
0– 1.9		0
2.0– 3.9	"small"	1
4.0– 5.9		2
6.0– 7.9		3

8.0– 9.9		4
10.0–11.9	"middle"	5
12.0–13.9		6
14.0–15.9		7
16.0–17.9	"large"	8
18.0–37.9		9

A map displaying these district slaveholding levels is found in Chapter 5.

Figures on wealth, like those on slaveholding, come primarily from the census. In a few instances, no census listing could be located. Some congressmen indicated in their pardon requests that their estates were more than $20,000, and others could be found in the slave schedule of the census, but not in the listing of free inhabitants. In some of these instances, estates were projected from the pardon papers and slave schedules, valuing each slave at an average of $500. Relative estate categories were computed in a manner similar to those for slaves. The aggregate estate valuation for each congressman's home county was divided by the number of families and single men residing in that county. The congressman's estate was then categorized as a percentage of this figure, and assigned a category code in the same way as for slaveholding (the necessary information is on pp. 296–319 and 340–351 of Volume IV of the 1860 census report).

The general level of the economy among a member's constituents has been represented by the average value of land per acre in the county of the district holding median rank in this respect: less than $8 per acre classified as "low," $8 but less than $12 as "middle," and $12 or more as "high." [1] A map of land values by district is also in Chapter 5.

The last item charted for each congressman is the session in which his home area was first occupied or seriously threatened by the Federal army. In most cases, th creates no problem, since a large number of delegates had either left Congress by the time of Federal occupation, or else represented areas occupied before they came to Richmond. For such men, the designation is simply "After Term" or "Before Term." Further precision is not necessary because the effect upon voting behavior had already been created. If the legislator was in Congress when the

1. Land values by county are from Thomas J. Pressly and William H. Scofield, *Farm Real Estate Values in the United States by Counties, 1850–1959* (Seattle: University of Washington Press, 1965).

Federal threat first became real, the session in which this occurred is indicated, or, if it occurred at any time during the Provisional Congress, a notation to that effect is made. Because of their special political (and strategic) situation, all Missouri and Kentucky delegates were considered to be from occupied territory—certainly Confederate Missouri and Kentucky were always in greater danger from the Federals than were any other states of the Confederacy. On the other hand, because of the small number of engagements in their area, the Texas delegates are automatically considered unoccupied until after the end of Congress. The designations were nevertheless flexible. Once the Federal army approached northern Mississippi, it was never far away again. That area is accordingly considered occupied or threatened thereafter. By contrast, if the Federals came and went, and stayed away for extended periods of time, as in parts of western Virginia, the area is considered unoccupied. If the Federal presence was confined to minor raids, the area is also considered unoccupied. But if Northern soldiers approached and did not occupy, the question varies. When the Union presence is merely enclaves along the coast, which could not be bases for any offensive action except occasional small raids, the area is unoccupied and unthreatened, because life went on much the same. Mobile, for example, was not threatened by the small garrison at Fort Pickens. But if Federal power was large enough to permit extensive operations, an adjacent area is considered occupied or threatened because of the ever-present danger. The general rule of thumb is this: what is the likelihood that the Confederacy would be able to enforce its laws and glean its resources from these areas? Presumably, this is the question that would have been in the minds of legislators from occupied and threatened districts. A map in Chapter 5 indicates the approximate date each district was occupied or seriously threatened for the first time.

Obviously, opportunities for error in this appendix are countless; no one will be more surprised than the authors if, despite their pains, errors are not discovered. Nevertheless, while some data for any single individual may be wrong, the over-all insights this biographical information gives should be reasonably helpful. This, in fact, is the reason this appendix is added. Even though we have employed this information throughout, no pretense is made that we have exhausted its usefulness.[2]

2. This appendix has been corrected or filled in with information obtained even after it was too late to incorporate the adjustments in the computations. The few entries not directly reflected in the text would not have an appreciable effect on the results reported.

Confederate Congress Member and Representative's District	1860 Residence	Member of	Birth State	Year
Akin, Warren (10)	Cassville, Ga. (Cass Co.)	2 House	Ga.	1811
Anderson, Clifford (4)	Macon, Ga. (Bibb Co.)	2 House	Va.	1833
Anderson, James Patton	Monticello, Fla. (Jefferson Co.)	Prov.	Tenn.	1822
Arrington, Archibald Hunter (5)	Hilliardston, N.C. (Nash Co.)	1 House	N.C.	1809
Ashe, Thomas Samuel (7)	Wadesboro, N.C. (Anson Co.)	1 House	N.C.	1812
Atkins, John DeWitt Clinton (9)	Paris, Tenn. (Henry Co.)	Prov. 1 House 2 House	Tenn.	1825
Avery, William Waightstill	Morganton, N.C. (Burke Co.)	Prov.	N.C.	1816
Ayer, Lewis Malone (3)	Buford's Bridge, S.C. (Barnwell Dist.)	1 House 2 House	S.C.	1821
Baker, James McNair	Lake City, Fla. (Columbia Co.)	1 Senate 2 Senate	N.C.	1822
Baldwin, John Brown (11)	Staunton, Va. (Augusta Co.)	1 House 2 House	Va.	1820
Barksdale, Ethelbert (6)	Jackson, Miss. (Hinds Co.)	1 House 2 House	Tenn.	1824
Barnwell, Robert Woodward	Beaufort, S.C. (Beaufort Dist.)	Prov. 1 Senate 2 Senate	S.C.	1801
Barry, William Taylor Sullivan	Columbus, Miss. (Lowndes Co.)	Prov.	Miss.	1821
Bartow, Francis Stebbins	Savannah, Ga. (Chatham Co.)	Prov.	Ga.	1816
Bass, Nathan	Rome, Ga. (Floyd Co.)	Prov.	Ga.	1810

Secession Stand	Party	Vocation	Slaves Holding	Cate-gory	Estate 1860 Value	Cate-gory	Dist. Land Value Index	County Slave Holding Index	Session Occupied
Union	Whig*	Lawyer Agric. Clergy	14	2	$ 67,380	4	8	5	Before Term
Seces.	Whig	Lawyer	19	3	23,000	2	7	4	2 Cong. 2 Sess.
Seces.	Dem.	Lawyer Agric.	30	2	41,500	3			After Term
Seces.	Dem.	Lawyer Agric.	105	4	316,225	4	7	4	After Term
Union	Whig*	Lawyer	17	2	17,575	3	4	5	After Term
Union	Dem.	Agric.	27	3	35,000	4	13	3	1 Cong. 1 Sess.
Seces.	Dem.	Lawyer Agric.	20	2	37,500	4			After Term
Seces.	Dem.	Agric.	160	4	67,000	3	9.5	7	2 Cong. 2 Sess.
Union	Whig*	Lawyer Agric.	13	2	59,550	4			1 Cong. 4 Sess.
Union	Whig*	Lawyer	11	2	29,000	3	14	3	2 Cong. 1 Sess.
Seces.	Dem.	Jour.	6	1		1	9	7	1 Cong. 4 Sess.
Seces.	Dem.	Agric. Lawyer	158	3	107,000	3			Prov. Cong. 5 Sess.
Seces.	Dem.	Lawyer Agric.	18	2	115,000	3			After Term
Seces.	Whig*	Lawyer Agric.	89	4	34,000	3			After Term
Union	Dem.	Agric.	55	3	66,855	4			After Term

Confederate Congress Member and Representative's District	1860 Residence	Member of	Birth State	Year
Batson, Felix I. (1)	Clarksville, Ark. (Johnson Co.)	1 House 2 House	Tenn.	1816
Baylor, John Robert (5)	Weatherford, Tex. (Parker Co.)	2 House	Ky.	1822
Bell, Caspar W. (3)	Brunswick, Mo. (Chariton Co.)	Prov. 1 House	Va.	1818
Bell, Hiram Parks (9)	Cumming, Ga. (Forsyth Co.)	2 House	Ga.	1827
Blandford, Mark Hardin (3)	Buena Vista, Ga. (Marion Co.)	2 House	Ga.	1826
Bocock, Thomas Stanley (5)	Appomattox Court-house, Va. (Appomattox Co.)	Prov. 1 House 2 House	Va.	1815
Bonham, Milledge Luke (4)	Edgefield Court-house, S.C. (Edgefield Dist.)	1 House	S.C.	1813
Boteler, Alexander Robinson (10)	Charles Town, (W.)Va. (Jefferson Co.)	Prov. 1 House	Va.	1815
Boudinot, Elias Cornelius	Little Rock, Ark. (Pulaski Co.) (Cherokee Nation)	1 House 2 House	Ga.	1835
Boyce, William Waters (6)	Winnsboro, S.C. (Fairfield Dist.)	Prov. 1 House 2 House	S.C.	1818
Bradford, Alexander B.	Holly Springs, Miss. (Marshall Co.)	Prov.		
Bradley, Benjamin F. (11)	Stamping Ground, Ky. (Scott Co.)	2 House	Ky.	1818
Branch, Anthony Martin (3)	Huntsville, Tex. (Walker Co.)	2 House	Va.	1824
Breckinridge, Robert Jefferson Jr. (11)	Lexington, Ky. (Fayette Co.)	1 House	Md.	1835

Seces- sion Stand	Party	Vocation	Slaves		Estate		Dist. Land Value Index	County Slave Holding Index	Session Occupied
			Hold- ing	Cate- gory	1860 Value	Cate- gory			
Seces.		Lawyer	14	3	$ 40,000	4	7.5	2	1 Cong. 4 Sess.
Seces.		Lawyer	0	0	12,700	3	5	1	After Term
Union	Whig*	Lawyer	0	0	3,050	2	10	3	Before Term
Union	Whig*	Lawyer	0	0	5,360	3	4	2	2 Cong. 2 Sess.
		Lawyer Merchant			14,000	3	8	4	After Term
Seces.	Dem.	Lawyer	25	3	30,000	3	11	4	After Term
Seces.	Dem.	Lawyer Agric.	60	3	67,000	3	11.5	7	After Term
Union	Whig*	Agric. Manuf'r	15	3	41,000	4	21	3	After Term
Seces.	Dem.	Jour.	0	0	400	1			1 Cong. 4 Sess.
Seces.	Dem.	Lawyer Agric.	27	2	58,559	3	9	9	2 Cong. 2 Sess.
Union	Whig								After Term
		Agric.	0	0	1,500	1	42.5	3	Before Term
Union		Lawyer	4	1	11,310	2	3	5	After Term
	Dem.	Lawyer	0	0	14,500	2	42.5	4	Before Term

Confederate Congress Member and Representative's District	1860 Residence	Member of	Birth State	Year
Bridgers, Robert Rufus (2)	Tarboro, N.C. (Edgecomb Co.)	1 House 2 House	N.C.	1819
Brockenbrough, John White	Lexington, Va. (Rockbridge Co.)	Prov.	Va.	1806
Brooke, Walker	Vicksburg, Miss. (Warren Co.)	Prov.	Va.	1813
Brown, Albert Gallatin	Temp's Depot, Miss. (Hinds Co.)	1 Senate 2 Senate	S.C.	1813
Bruce, Eli Metcalfe (9)	Nicholas County, Ky.	1 House 2 House		
Bruce, Horatio Washington (7)	Louisville, Ky. (Jefferson Co.)	1 House 2 House	Ky.	1830
Burnett, Henry Cornelius	Cadiz, Ky. (Trigg Co.)	Prov. 1 Senate 2 Senate	Va.	1825
Burnett, Theodore L. (6)	Taylorsville, Ky. (Spencer Co.)	Prov. 1 House 2 House	Ky.	1829
Callahan, Samuel B.	Sulphur Springs, Tex. (Hopkins Co.) (Creek & Seminole Nations)	2 House		1834
Campbell, Josiah Abigal Patterson	Kosciusko, Miss. (Attala Co.)	Prov.	S.C.	1830
Caperton, Allen Taylor	Peterstown, (W.)Va. (Monroe Co.)	1 Senate 2 Senate	Va.	1810
Carroll, David Williamson (3)	Pine Bluff, Ark. (Jefferson Co.)	2 House	Md.	1816
Caruthers, Robert Looney	Lebanon, Tenn. (Wilson Co.)	Prov.	Tenn.	1800
Chambers, Henry Cousins (4)	Robson Landing, Miss. (Coahoma Co.)	1 House 2 House	Ala.	1823

Secession Stand	Party	Vocation	Slaves Holding	Slaves Category	Estate 1860 Value	Estate Category	Dist. Land Value Index	County Slave Holding Index	Session Occupied
Seces.	Dem.	Lawyer Agric. Finance	111	4	$203,000	4	9	7	After Term
Seces.	Dem.	Lawyer Agric. Educat'n	21	3	48,692	4			After Term
Union	Whig*	Lawyer	5	1	85,000	3			After Term
Seces.	Dem.	Lawyer Agric.	78	3	108,500	3			1 Cong. 4 Sess.
	Dem.	Merchant					25	2	Before Term
	Whig*	Lawyer	5	2	14,000	3	43	2	Before Term
Union	Dem.*	Lawyer	10	2	10,000	3			Before Term
	Whig	Lawyer	4	2	10,000	2	23	2	Before Term
									After Term
Seces.	Dem.	Lawyer Agric.	11	2	38,500	4			After Term
Union	Whig	Lawyer Agric. Finance	43	4	187,000	4			After Term
		Lawyer	0	0		1	10	6	Before Term
Union	Whig*	Lawyer Agric.	119	4	400,000	4			After Term
	Dem.	Agric.	127	3	330,000	4	17	9	1 Cong. 2 Sess.

Confederate Congress Member and Representative's District	1860 Residence	Member of	Birth State	Year
Chambliss, John Randolph (2)	Hicksford, Va. (Greensville Co.)	1 House	Va.	1809
Chesnut, James, Jr.	Camden, S.C. (Kershaw Dist.)	Prov.	S.C.	1815
Chilton, William Parish (6)	Montgomery, Ala. (Montgomery Co.)	Prov. 1 House 2 House	Ky.	1810
Chrisman, James Stone (5)	Monticello, Ky. (Wayne Co.)	1 House 2 House	Ky.	1818
Clapp, Jeremiah Watkins (1)	Holly Springs, Miss. (Marshall Co.)	1 House	Va.	1814
Clark, John Bullock (3)	Fayette, Mo. (Howard Co.)	Prov. 1 Senate 2 House	Ky.	1802
Clark, William W. (6)	Covington, Ga. (Newton Co.)	1 House	Ga.	1820
Clay, Clement Claiborne	Huntsville, Ala. (Madison Co.)	1 Senate	Ala.	1816
Clayton, Alexander M.	Hudsonville, Miss. (Marshall Co.)	Prov.	Va.	1801
Clopton, David (7)	Tuskegee, Ala. (Macon Co.)	1 House 2 House	Ga.	1820
Cluskey, Michael W. (11)	Tenn.	2 House		
Cobb, Howell	Athens, Ga. (Clarke Co.)	Prov.	Ga.	1815
Cobb, Thomas Reade Rootes	Athens, Ga. (Clarke Co.)	Prov.	Ga.	1823
Collier, Charles F. (4)	Petersburg, Va. (Dinwiddie Co.)	1 House	Va.	1827

Secession Stand	Party	Vocation	Slaves Hold-ing	Cate-gory	Estate 1860 Value	Cate-gory	Dist. Land Value Index	County Slave Holding Index	Session Occupied
Union	Whig*	Lawyer Agric.	48	3	$ 60,000	3	7.5	7	After Term
Seces.	Dem.	Lawyer Agric.	76	3	50,000	3			After Term
Union	Whig	Lawyer	8	1			12.5	8	After Term
	Dem.	Lawyer	6	2	12,000	3	7	2	Before Term
Seces.	Dem.*	Lawyer Agric.	16	2	175,600	4	13.5	6	1 Cong. 2 Sess.
Union	Dem.	Lawyer Agric.	27	3	42,000	3	10	3	Before Term
		Lawyer Agric.	54	3	84,000	4	6	4	After Term
Seces.	Dem.	Lawyer Agric. Jour.	89	4	45,000	3			Before Term
Seces.	Dem.*	Lawyer Agric.	142	4	350,000	4			After Term
Seces.	Dem.	Lawyer Agric.	12	2	29,500	2	7	8	After Term
Seces.	Dem.						13		Before Term
Seces.	Dem.*	Lawyer Agric.	146	4	80,000	4			After Term
Seces.	Dem.	Lawyer Agric. Educat'n	23	3	120,000	4			After Term
Union	Dem.	Lawyer Agric.	23	3	30,500	3	12.5	3	After Term

Confederate Congress Member and Representative's District	1860 Residence	Member of	Birth State	Year
Colyar, Arthur St. Clair (3)	Winchester, Tenn. (Franklin Co.)	2 House	Tenn.	1818
Conrad, Charles Magill (2)	New Orleans, La. (Orleans Par.)	Prov. 1 House 2 House	Va.	1804
Conrow, Aaron H. (4)	Richmond, Mo. (Ray Co.)	Prov. 1 House 2 House	Ohio	1824
Cooke, William Mordecai (1)	St. Louis, Mo. (St. Louis Co.)	Prov. 1 House	Va.	1823
Craige, Francis Burton	Salisbury, N.C. (Rowan Co.)	Prov.	N.C.	1811
Crawford, Martin Jenkins	Columbus, Ga. (Muscogee Co.)	Prov.	Ga.	1820
Crockett, John Wesley (2)	Henderson, Ky. (Henderson Co.)	1 House	Ky.	1818
Cruikshank, Marcus Henderson (4)	Talladega, Ala. (Talladega Co.)	2 House	Ala.	1826
Currin, David M. (11)	Memphis, Tenn. (Shelby Co.)	Prov. 1 House	Tenn.	1820
Curry, Jabez Lamar Monroe (4)	Talladega, Ala. (Talladega Co.)	Prov. 1 House	Ga.	1825
Darden, Stephen Heard (1)	Gonzales, Tex. (Gonzales Co.)	2 House	Miss.	1816
Dargan, Edmund Strother (9)	Mobile, Ala. (Mobile Co.)	1 House	N.C.	1805
Davidson, Allen Turner (10)	Murphy, N.C. (Cherokee Co.)	Prov. 1 House	N.C.	1819
Davis, George	Wilmington, N.C. (New Hanover Co.)	Prov. 1 Senate	N.C.	1820
Davis, Nicholas	Huntsville, Ala. (Madison Co.)	Prov.	Ala.	1825

Secession Stand	Party	Vocation	Slaves Hold-ing	Slaves Cate-gory	Estate 1860 Value	Estate Cate-gory	Dist. Land Value Index	County Slave Holding Index	Session Occupied
Union	Whig*	Lawyer Agric.	26	3	$ 65,000	4	10	3	Before Term
Union	Whig*	Lawyer Agric.					51	1	1 Cong. 2 Sess.
Seces.		Lawyer					13	2	Before Term
Seces.	Dem.	Lawyer	1	1	400	1	72	1	Before Term
Seces.	Dem.	Lawyer Agric.	31	3	84,705	4			After Term
Seces.	Dem.	Lawyer Agric.	100	4	160,500	4			After Term
Union	Whig	Lawyer	4	1	10,000	2	9	4	Before Term
Union	Whig*	Lawyer Agric. Jour.	11	2	35,000	3	6	5	Before Term
Seces.	Dem.	Lawyer	11	2	30,000	3	13	4	1 Cong. 2 Sess.
Seces.	Dem.	Lawyer Agric.	47	3	47,335	4	6	5	After Term
Union	Dem.	Agric.	14	2	25,000	3	3	4	After Term
Seces.	Dem.	Lawyer	13	3	80,000	4	6	3	After Term
Union	Whig*	Lawyer Finance	2	1	21,800	4	4	2	After Term
Seces.	Whig	Lawyer	10	2	23,500	3			After Term
Union	Whig*	Lawyer	13	2	50,000	3			After Term

Confederate Congress Member and Representative's District	1860 Residence	Member of	Birth State	Year
Davis, Reuben (2)	Aberdeen, Miss. (Monroe Co.)	1 House	Tenn.	1813
Dawkins, James B. (1)	Ocala, Fla. (Marion Co.)	1 House		
De Clouet, Alexander	St. Martinville, La. (St. Martin Par.)	Prov.	La.	1812
De Jarnette, Daniel Coleman (8)	Bowling Green, Va. (Caroline Co.)	1 House 2 House	Va.	1822
De Witt, William Henry	Dixon Springs, Tenn. (Smith Co.)	Prov.	Tenn.	1826
Dickinson, James Shelton (9)	Grove Hill, Ala. (Clarke Co.)	2 House	Va.	1816
Dortch, William Theophilus	Goldsboro, N.C. (Wayne Co.)	1 Senate 2 Senate	N.C.	1824
Dupré, Lucius Jacques (4)	Opelousas, La. (St. Landry Par.)	1 House 2 House	La.	1822
Echols, Joseph Hubbard (6)	Lexington, Ga. (Oglethorpe Co.)	2 House	Ga.	1817
Elliott, John Milton (12)	Prestonsburg, Ky. (Floyd Co.)	Prov. 1 House 2 House	Va.	1820
Ewing, George Washington (4)	Russellville, Ky. (Logan Co.)	Prov. 1 House 2 House	Ky.	1817
Farrow, James (5)	Spartanburg, S.C. (Spartanburg Dist.)	1 House 2 House	S.C.	1827
Fearn, Thomas	Huntsville, Ala. (Madison Co.)	Prov.	Va.	1789
Foote, Henry Stuart (5)	Nashville, Tenn. (Davidson Co.)	1 House 2 House	Va.	1804

Secession Stand	Party	Vocation	Slaves Holding	Category	Estate 1860 Value	Category	Dist. Land Value Index	County Slave Holding Index	Session Occupied
Seces.	Dem.*	Lawyer Agric.	42	3	$ 84,025	3	7	7	After Term
Seces.		Lawyer Agric.	27	2	13,500	2	7	7	After Term
Seces.	Whig*	Agric.	275	4	341,000	4			After Term
Seces.	Dem.	Agric.	67	3	56,605	3	14	7	2 Cong. 1 Sess.
Union	Whig	Lawyer	0	0	4,000	2			After Term
Seces.	Dem.	Lawyer	13	2	45,630	4	6	5	After Term
Seces.	Dem.	Lawyer Agric.	54	3	94,600	4			After Term
Seces.	Whig	Lawyer			70,000	4	23	5	2 Cong. 1 Sess.
Union		Agric. Clergy	151	4	116,256	4	6	7	2 Cong. 2 Sess.
Union	Dem.	Lawyer	0	0	8,600	4	2	1	Before Term
	Whig	Lawyer Agric.	22	3	26,525	3	9	3	Before Term
Seces.		Lawyer	0	0	8,800	2	8	4	After Term
Union		Medicine Agric. Finance	51	3	174,000	4			After Term
Union	Whig*	Lawyer	4	2	130,000	4	20	3	Before Term

Confederate Congress Member and Representative's District	1860 Residence	Member of	Birth State	Year
Ford, Samuel Howard	Louisville, Ky. (Jefferson Co.)	Prov.	England	1819
Forman, Thomas M.	Savannah, Ga. (Chatham Co.)	Prov.	Ga.	1809
Foster, Thomas Jefferson (1)	Courtland, Ala. (Lawrence Co.)	1 House 2 House	Tenn.	1809
Freeman, Thomas W. (6)	Bolivar, Mo. (Polk Co.)	Prov. 1 House	Ky.	1824
Fuller, Thomas Charles (4)	Fayetteville, N.C. (Cumberland Co.)	2 House	N.C.	1832
Funsten, David (9)	Alexandria, Va. (Alexandria Co.)	1 House 2 House	Va.	1819
Gaither, Burgess Sidney (9)	Morganton, N.C. (Burke Co.)	1 House 2 House	N.C.	1807
Gardenhire, E. I (4)	Sparta, Tenn. (White Co.)	1 House	Tenn.	1815
Garland, Augustus Hill (3)	Little Rock, Ark. (Pulaski Co.)	Prov. 1 House 2 House 2 Senate	Tenn.	1832
Garland, Rufus King (2)	Hempstead Co., Ark.	2 House	Tenn.	1830
Garnett, Muscoe Russell Hunter (1)	Lloyds, Va. (Essex Co.)	1 House	Va.	1821
Gartrell, Lucius Jeremiah (8)	Atlanta, Ga. (Fulton Co.)	1 House	Ga.	1821
Gentry, Meredith Poindexter (6)	Richmond, Tenn. (Bedford Co.)	1 House	N.C.	1809
Gholson, Thomas Saunders (4)	Petersburg, Va. (Dinwiddie Co.)	2 House	Va.	1813
Gilmer, John Adams (6)	Greensboro, N.C. (Guilford Co.)	2 House	N.C.	1805

Seces- sion Stand	Party	Vocation	Slaves Hold- ing	Cate- gory	Estate 1860 Value	Cate- gory	Dist. Land Value Index	County Slave Holding Index	Session Occupied
		Clergy	1	1	$ 9,000	2			Before Term
	Dem.	Agric.	15	2	112,000	4			After Term
Union	Whig*	Agric. Manuf'r	128	4	178,000	4	10.5	8	1 Cong. 2 Sess.
	Dem.	Lawyer	4	2	7,100	3	7	1	Before Term
Union	Whig*	Lawyer	0	0	0	0	3	3	After Term
		Lawyer	6	2	6,400	2	19	2	Before Term
Union	Whig*	Lawyer	7	2	15,200	3	5	5	After Term
	Dem.	Lawyer Agric.	10	3	16,200	4	5	2	1 Cong. 4 Sess.
Union	Whig*	Lawyer	3	1	10,500	2	10	4	1 Cong. 4 Sess.
Union	Whig	Lawyer Agric.	9	2	16,177	2	7	6	Before Term
Seces.	Dem.	Lawyer Agric.	128	4	193,700	4	16	8	After Term
Seces.	Dem.*	Lawyer	37	3	20,000		7	3	After Term
Union	Whig*	Agric.	50	4	120,150	4	25.5	3	1 Cong. 4 Sess.
	Whig	Lawyer Finance	16	3	220,000	4	12.5	3	2 Cong. 2 Sess.
Union	Whig*	Lawyer Agric.	53	4	112,000	4	9	3	After Term

Confederate Congress Member and Representative's District	1860 Residence	Member of	Birth State	Year
Goode, John Jr. (6)	Liberty, Va. (Bedford Co.)	1 House 2 House	Va.	1829
Graham, Malcolm D. (5)	Henderson, Tex. (Rusk Co.)	1 House	Ala.	1827
Graham, William Alexander	Hillsboro, N.C. (Orange Co.)	2 Senate	N.C.	1804
Gray, Henry (5)	Bienville Par., La.	2 House	S.C.	1816
Gray, Peter W. (3)	Houston, Tex. (Harris Co.)	1 House	Va.	1819
Gregg, John	Fairfield Tex., (Freestone Co.)	Prov.	Ala.	1828
Hale, Stephen Fowler	Eutaw, Ala. (Greene Co.)	Prov.	Ky.	1816
Hanly, Thomas Burton (4)	Helena, Ark. (Phillips Co.)	1 House 2 House	Ky.	1812
Harris, Thomas A. (2)	Hannibal, Mo. (Marion Co.)	Prov. 1 House	Ky.	1825
Harris, Wiley Pope	Jackson, Miss. (Hinds Co.)	Prov.	Miss.	1808
Harrison, James Thomas	Columbus, Miss. (Lowndes Co.)	Prov.	S.C.	1811
Hartridge, Julian (1)	Savannah, Ga. (Chatham Co.)	1 House 2 House	Ga.	1829
Hatcher, Robert Anthony (7)	New Madrid, Mo. (New Madrid Co.)	2 House	Va.	1819
Haynes, Landon Carter	Jonesboro, Tenn. (Washington Co.)	1 Senate 2 Senate	Tenn.	1816
Heiskell, Joseph Brown (1)	Rogersville, Tenn. (Hawkins Co.)	1 House 2 House	Tenn.	1823
Hemphill, John	Austin, Tex. (Travis Co.)	Prov.	S.C.	1803

Seces-sion Stand	Party	Vocation	Slaves Hold-ing	Slaves Cate-gory	Estate 1860 Value	Estate Cate-gory	Dist. Land Value Index	County Slave Holding Index	Session Occupied
Seces.	Dem.	Lawyer	7	2	$ 15,500	3	10	4	After Term
Seces.	Dem.	Lawyer	7	2	12,500	2	5	4	After Term
Union	Whig*	Lawyer Agric.	59	4	39,500	4			After Term
	Whig*	Lawyer					12	7	After Term
Seces.	Dem.	Lawyer	5	2	3,000	1	3	2	After Term
Seces.	Dem.	Lawyer	4	1	16,360	2			After Term
Union	Whig*	Lawyer Agric.	12	2	55,000	3			After Term
Seces.	Dem.	Lawyer Agric.	13	2	120,000	4	7	8	Before Term
Union	Dem.*	Jour.	0	0	7,400	2	13	1	Before Term
Seces.	Dem.	Lawyer	0	0	36,000	2			After Term
Union	Whig*	Lawyer Agric.	100	4	250,000	4			After Term
Seces.	Dem.	Lawyer	4	1	17,500	2	2	6	2 Cong. 2 Sess.
Seces.	Dem.	Lawyer	4	2	22,500	3	7.5	3	Before Term
Seces.	Dem.	Lawyer	0	0	11,145	3			1 Cong. 4 Sess.
Union	Whig	Lawyer	2	1	19,400	4	10	3	1 Cong. 4 Sess.
Seces.	Dem.	Lawyer							After Term

Confederate Congress Member and Representative's District	1860 Residence	Member of	Birth State	Year
Henry, Gustavus Adolphus	Clarksville, Tenn. (Montgomery Co.)	1 Senate 2 Senate	Ky.	1804
Herbert, Caleb Claiborne (2)	Eagle Lake, Tex. (Colorado Co.)	1 House 2 House	Va.	1814
Hill, Benjamin Harvey	La Grange, Ga. (Troup Co.)	Prov. 1 Senate 2 Senate	Ga.	1823
Hilton, Robert B. (2)	Tallahassee, Fla. (Leon Co.)	1 House 2 House	Va.	1821
Hodge, Benjamin Louis (5)	Shreveport, La. (Caddo Par.)	2 House	Tenn.	1824
Hodge, George Baird (8)	Newport, Ky. (Campbell Co.)	Prov. 1 House	Ky.	1828
Holcombe, James Philemon (7)	Charlottesville, Va. (Albemarle Co.)	1 House	Va.	1820
Holder, William Dunbar (2)	Pontotoc Co., Miss.	1 House 2 House	Ky.	1826
Holliday, Frederick William Mackey (10)	Winchester, Va. (Frederick Co.)	2 House	Va.	1828
Holt, Hines (3)	Columbus, Ga. (Muscogee Co.)	1 House	Ga.	1805
House, John Ford	Clarksville, Tenn. (Montgomery Co.)	Prov.	Tenn.	1827
Hunter, Robert Mercer Taliaferro	Lloyds, Va. (Essex Co.)	Prov. 1 Senate 2 Senate	Va.	1809
Ingram, Porter (3)	Columbus, Ga. (Muscogee Co.)	1 House	Vt.	1810
Jemison, Robert Jr.	Tuscaloosa, Ala. (Tuscaloosa Co.)	1 Senate 2 Senate	Ga.	1802
Jenkins, Albert Gallatin (14)	Green Bottom, (W.)Va. (Cabell Co.)	1 House	Va.	1830

Seces-sion Stand	Party	Vocation	Slaves Hold-ing	Cate-gory	Estate 1860 Value	Cate-gory	Dist. Land Value Index	County Slave Holding Index	Session Occupied
Union	Whig*	Lawyer Agric.	13	2	$170.000	4			Before Term
Seces.	Dem.	Agric.	48	3	404,082	4	5	5	After Term
Union	Whig*	Lawyer Agric.	57	3	100,000	4			After Term
Seces.	Dem.	Lawyer Jour.	1	1	50	1	5.5	8	After Term
Seces.	Whig*	Lawyer Agric.	26	2	115,000	4	12	7	After Term
Union	Whig*	Lawyer					26	1	Before Term
Seces.	Dem.	Lawyer Agric. Educat'n	12	2	33,500	3	14	5	After Term
Union	Whig	Agric.	45	3	66,500	4	7	4	2 Cong. 2 Sess.
		Lawyer					21	2	Before Term
Union	Whig*	Lawyer Agric.	119	4	137,100	4	8	4	After Term
Union	Whig*	Lawyer	4	1	11,300	2			After Term
Seces.	Dem.*	Lawyer Agric.	116	4	173,690	4			2 Cong. 1 Sess.
Union	Dem.	Lawyer Agric.	56	3	60,000	4	8	4	After Term
Union	Whig	Agric. Manuf'r	178	4	569,000	4			After Term
Union	Dem.	Agric.			100,000	4	4	1	Before Term

Confederate Congress Member and Representative's District	1860 Residence	Member of	Birth State	Year
Johnson, Herschel Vespasian	Speir's Turnout, Ga. (Jefferson Co.)	1 Senate 2 Senate	Ga.	1812
Johnson, Robert Ward	Pine Bluff, Ark. (Jefferson Co.)	Prov. 1 Senate 2 Senate	Ky.	1814
Johnson, Thomas	Mount Sterling, Ky. (Montgomery Co.)	Prov.	Ky.	1813
Johnson, Waldo Porter	Osceola, Mo. (St. Clair Co.)	1 Senate 2 Senate	Va.	1817
Johnston, Robert (15)	Clarksburg, (W.)Va. (Harrison Co.)	Prov. 1 House 2 House	Va.	1820
Jones, George Washington (7)	Fayetteville, Tenn. (Lincoln Co.)	1 House	Va.	1807
Jones, Henry Cox	Florence, Ala. (Lauderdale Co.)	Prov.	Ala.	1821
Jones, Robert M.	Red River Co. (Choctaw Nation)	1 House 2 House		
Jones, Thomas McKissick	Pulaski, Tenn. (Giles Co.)	Prov.	N.C.	1816
Keeble, Edwin A. (6)	Murfreesboro, Tenn. (Rutherford Co.)	2 House	Va.	1808
Keitt, Lawrence Massillon	Orangeburg, S.C. (Orangeburg Dist.)	Prov.	S.C.	1824
Kenan, Augustus Holmes (4)	Milledgeville, Ga. (Baldwin Co.)	Prov. 1 House	Ga.	1805
Kenan, Owen Rand (3)	Kenansville, N.C. (Duplin Co.)	1 House	N.C.	1806
Kenner, Duncan Farrar (3)	New River, La. (Ascension Par.)	Prov. 1 House 2 House	La.	1813
Lamkin, John Tillman (7)	Holmesville, Miss. (Pike Co.)	2 House	Ga.	1811

Secession Stand	Party	Vocation	Slaves Hold-ing	Cate-gory	Estate 1860 Value	Cate-gory	Dist. Land Value Index	County Slave Holding Index	Session Occupied
Union	Dem.*	Lawyer Agric.	115	4	$142,800	4			2 Cong. 2 Sess.
Seces.	Dem.	Lawyer Agric.	193	4	800,000	4			1 Cong. 4 Sess.
		Agric. Merchant							Before Term
Union	Dem.	Lawyer	3	2	140,000	4			Before Term
		Lawyer	1	1	15,000	3	7	1	Before Term
Union	Dem.	Lawyer	11	2	40,000	4	13.5	3	1 Cong. 4 Sess.
Union	Dem.*	Lawyer	7	2	7,550	2			After Term
		Agric.	227						
	Dem.	Lawyer Agric.	54	4	91,500	4			After Term
Seces.	Dem.	Lawyer Agric.	32	3	120,990	4	25.5	4	Before Term
Seces.	Dem.	Lawyer							After Term
Union	Whig*	Lawyer	3	1	9,000	2	7	5	After Term
Seces.	Dem.	Lawyer Agric.			87,000	4	6	5	After Term
Seces.	Whig*	Agric.	473	4	440,000	4	33	9	1 Cong. 2 Sess.
Union	Whig	Lawyer Agric.	14	2	106,000	4	5	4	After Term

Confederate Congress Member and Representative's District	1860 Residence	Member of	Birth State	Year
Lander, William (8)	Lincolnton, N.C. (Lincoln Co.)	1 House	Ire-land	1817
Leach, James Madison (7)	Thomasville, N.C. (Davidson Co.)	2 House	N.C.	1815
Leach, James Thomas (3)	Leachburg, N.C. (Johnston Co.)	2 House	N.C.	1805
Lester, George Nelson (8)	Marietta, Ga. (Cobb Co.)	2 House	S.C.	1824
Lewis, David Peter	Courtland, Ala. (Lawrence Co.)	Prov.	Va.	1823
Lewis, David W. (5)	Mayfield, Ga. (Hancock Co.)	1 House	Ga.	1815
Lewis, John W.	Canton, Ga. (Cherokee Co.)	1 Senate	S.C.	1801
Logan, George W. (10)	Rutherfordton, N.C. (Rutherford Co.)	2 House	N.C.	1815
Lyon, Francis Strother (5)	Demopolis, Ala. (Marengo Co.)	1 House 2 House	N.C.	1800
Lyons, James (3)	Richmond, Va. (Henrico Co.)	1 House	Va.	1801
McCallum, James (7)	Pulaski, Tenn. (Giles Co.)	2 House	N.C.	1807
McDowell, Thomas David Smith (4)	Elizabethtown, N.C. (Bladen Co.)	Prov. 1 House	N.C.	1823
Macfarland, William H.	Richmond, Va. (Henrico Co.)	Prov.	Va.	1799
McLean, James Robert (6)	Greensboro, N.C. (Guilford Co.)	1 House	N.C.	1822
McMullin, Fayette (13)	Seven Mile Ford, Va. (Smyth Co.)	2 House	Va.	1808
McQueen, John (1)	Bennettsville, S.C. (Marlboro Dist.)	1 House	N.C.	1804

Secession Stand	Party	Vocation	Slaves Holding	Category	Estate 1860 Value	Category	Dist. Land Value Index	County Slave Holding Index	Session Occupied
Seces.	Dem.	Lawyer Agric.	10	2	$ 42,500	4	8	3	After Term
Union	Whig*	Lawyer	2	1	35,000	4	4	3	After Term
Union	Whig	Agric. Medicine	47	3	53,200	4	6	5	After Term
	Dem.	Lawyer	5	2	8,500	2	7	3	Before Term
Union	Dem.	Lawyer Agric.	34	2	62,185	4			After Term
Seces.	Whig*	Lawyer Agric.	75	3	70,000	4	7	9	After Term
	Dem.	Agric. Finance	17	3	60,000	4			After Term
Union	Whig	Lawyer Agric.	11	2	23,000	4	4	3	After Term
Seces.	Dem.*	Lawyer Agric.	189	4	322,000	4	13	9	After Term
Seces.	Whig*	Lawyer	27	3	19,000	2	12.5	4	After Term
Union	Whig*	Agric. Lawyer	25	3	46,500	3	13.5	4	Before Term
Union	Dem.*	Agric.	57	3	65,000	4	3	6	After Term
Union	Whig	Lawyer Finance	12	2	180,000	4			After Term
Seces.	Dem.	Lawyer Agric.	25	3	27,700	4	9	3	After Term
Union	Dem.	Agric.	8	2	60,000	4	7.5	2	Before Term
Seces.	Dem.	Lawyer Agric.	68	3	138,881	4	9	7	After Term

Confederate Congress Member and Representative's District	1860 Residence	Member of	Birth State	Year
McRae, Colin John	Mobile, Ala. (Mobile Co.)	Prov.	N.C.	1812
McRae, John Jones (7)	Waynesboro, Miss. (Wayne Co.)	1 House	N.C.	1815
Macwillie, Malcolm H.	Mesilla, Arizona Territory (Dona Ana Co.)	1 House 2 House		
Machen, Willis Benson (1)	Eddyville, Ky. (Lyon Co.)	1 House 2 House	Ky.	1810
Marshall, Henry (5)	Mansfield, La. (DeSoto Par.)	Prov. 1 House	S.C.	1807
Marshall, Humphrey (8)	Springport, Ky. (Henry Co.)	2 House	Ky.	1812
Martin, John Mason (1)	Ocala, Fla. (Marion Co.)	1 House	S.C.	1832
Mason, James Murray	Winchester, Va. (Frederick Co.)	Prov.	Va.	1798
Maxwell, Augustus Emmett	Pensacola, Fla. (Escambia Co.)	1 Senate 2 Senate	Ga.	1820
Memminger, Christopher Gustavus	Charleston, S.C. (Charleston Dist.)	Prov.	Würt-tem-berg (Ger.)	1803
Menees, Thomas (8)	Springfield, Tenn. (Robertson Co.)	1 House 2 House	Tenn.	1823
Miles, William Porcher (2)	Charleston, S.C. (Charleston Dist.)	Prov. 1 House 2 House	S.C.	1822
Miller, Samuel A. (14)	Charleston, (W.)Va. (Kanawha Co.)	1 House 2 House	Va.	1820
Mitchel, Charles Burton	Washington, Ark. (Hempstead Co.)	1 Senate 2 Senate	Tenn.	1815

Secession Stand	Party	Vocation	Slaves Holding	Cate-gory	Estate 1860 Value	Cate-gory	Dist. Land Value Index	County Slave Holding Index	Session Occupied
Union	Whig*	Finance Merchant	2	1	$100,000	4			After Term
Seces.	Dem.	Lawyer	3	1	33,000	4	5	9	After Term
		Lawyer							1 Cong. 1 Sess.
Seces.	Dem.	Merchant Agric. Manuf'r	26	3	93,540	4	10	3	Before Term
Seces.		Agric.	201	4	206,500	4	12	7	After Term
Union	Whig*	Lawyer Agric.	15	3	40,000	4	26	2	Before Term
Seces.	Dem.	Agric.					7	7	After Term
Seces.	Dem.	Lawyer	7	2					After Term
	Dem.	Lawyer	2	1	15,000	3			2 Cong. 2 Sess.
Seces.	Dem.	Lawyer	12	2	175,000	4			After Term
Seces.	Dem.	Agric. Medicine	18	3	61,300	4	8.5	3	Before Term
Seces.	Dem.	Educat'n	0	0	1,800	1	7	6	2 Cong. 2 Sess.
		Lawyer	0	0	34,100	4	4	4	Before Term
Union	Dem.	Agric. Medicine	22	2	40,000	3			2 Cong. 1 Sess.

Confederate Congress Member and Representative's District	1860 Residence	Member of	Birth State	Year
Monroe, Thomas Bell	Frankfort, Ky. (Franklin Co.)	Prov.	Va.	1791
Montague, Robert Latané (1)	Saluda, Va. (Middlesex Co.)	2 House	Va.	1819
Moore, James William (10)	Mount Sterling, Ky. (Montgomery Co.)	1 House 2 House	Ky.	1818
Morehead, John Motley	Greensboro, N.C. (Guilford Co.)	Prov.	Va.	1796
Morgan, Simpson H. (6)	Clarksville, Tex. (Red River Co.)	2 House	Tenn.	1822
Morton, Jackson	Milton, Fla. (Santa Rosa Co.)	Prov.	Va.	1794
Munnerlyn, Charles James (2)	Bainbridge, Ga. (Decatur Co.)	1 House	S.C.	1822
Murray, John P. (4)	Gainesboro, Tenn. (Jackson Co.)	2 House	Tenn.	1831
Nisbet, Eugenius Aristides	Macon, Ga. (Bibb Co.)	Prov.	Ga.	1803
Norton, Nimrod L. (2)	Fulton, Mo. (Callaway Co.)	2 House	Ky.	1830
Ochiltree, William Beck	Marshall, Tex. (Harrison Co.)	Prov.	N.C.	1811
Oldham, Williamson Simpson	Austin, Tex. (Travis Co.)	Prov. 1 Senate 2 Senate	Tenn.	1813
Orr, James Lawrence	Anderson Courthouse, S.C. (Anderson Dist.)	Prov. 1 Senate 2 Senate	S.C.	1822
Orr, Jehu Amaziah (1)	Houston, Miss. (Chickasaw Co.)	Prov. 2 House	S.C.	1828

Seces-sion Stand	Party	Vocation	Slaves Hold-ing	Cate-gory	Estate 1860 Value	Cate-gory	Dist. Land Value Index	County Slave Holding Index	Session Occupied
		Lawyer Educat'n	1	1	$ 15,508	3			Before Term
Seces.	Dem.	Lawyer Agric.	17	2	33,536	3	16	5	Before Term
Seces.	Dem.	Lawyer	6	2	3,000	1	5.5	3	Before Term
Union	Whig*	Lawyer Agric. Finance	45	3					After Term
		Lawyer Agric.	11	2	26,150	3	5	4	After Term
Union	Whig*	Manuf'r Agric. Merchant	159	4	200,000	4			After Term
Seces.		Agric.	216	4	145,000	4	6	6	After Term
	Dem.	Lawyer	1	1	10,000	3	5	2	Before Term
Seces.	Whig*	Lawyer	16	2	60,000	4			After Term
		Agric.	0	0	6,000	2	13	2	Before Term
Seces.	Whig*	Lawyer	9	2	32,900	3			After Term
Seces.	Dem.*	Lawyer	3	1	85,000	4			After Term
Seces.	Dem.	Lawyer Agric.	19	3	66,200	4			After Term
Seces.	Dem.	Lawyer Agric. Jour.	48	3	105,010	4	13.5	6	2 Cong. 2 Sess.

Confederate Congress Member and Representative's District	1860 Residence	Member of	Birth State	Year
Oury, Granville Henderson	Tucson, Arizona Territory (Arizona County)	Prov.	Va.	1825
Owens, James B.	Ocala, Fla. (Marion Co.)	Prov.	S.C.	1816
Perkins, John Jr. (6)	New Carthage, La. (Madison Par.)	Prov. 1 House 2 House	Miss.	1819
Peyton, Robert Ludwell Yates	Harrisonville, Mo. (Cass Co.)	Prov. 1 Senate	Va.	1825
Phelan, James	Aberdeen, Miss. (Monroe Co.)	1 Senate	Ala.	1821
Preston, Walter (13)	Abingdon, Va. (Washington Co.)	Prov. 1 House	Va.	1820
Preston, William Ballard	Christiansburg, Va. (Montgomery Co.)	Prov. 1 Senate	Va.	1805
Pryor, Roger Atkinson (4)	Petersburg, Va. (Dinwiddie Co.)	Prov. 1 House	Va.	1828
Pugh, James Lawrence (8)	Eufaula, Ala. (Barbour Co.)	1 House 2 House	Ga.	1820
Puryear, Richard Clauselle	Huntsville, N.C. (Yadkin Co.)	Prov.	Va.	1801
Ralls, John Perkins (3)	Centre, Ala. (Cherokee Co.)	1 House	Ga.	1822
Ramsay, James Graham (8)	Mt. Vernon, N.C. (Rowan Co.)	2 House	N.C.	1823
Read, Henry E. (3)	Larue Co., Ky.	1 House 2 House	Ky.	
Reade, Edwin Godwin	Roxboro, N.C. (Person Co.)	1 Senate	N.C.	1812
Reagan, John Henninger	Palestine, Tex. (Anderson Co.)	Prov.	Tenn.	1818

Secession Stand	Party	Vocation	Slaves Holding	Category	Estate 1860 Value	Category	Dist. Land Value Index	County Slave Holding Index	Session Occupied
Seces.	Dem.	Lawyer Agric.			$				After Term
Seces.	Dem.	Agric. Clergy	89	3	118,000	4			After Term
Seces.	Dem.	Lawyer Agric. Finance	340	4	520,000	4	18.5	9	1 Cong. 4 Sess.
	Dem.	Lawyer	0	0	6,000	2			Before Term
Seces.	Dem.	Lawyer	8	2	48,434	3			After Term
Seces.	Whig*	Lawyer	6	2	10,000	3	7.5	3	After Term
Union	Whig	Lawyer Agric.	50	4	383,330	4			After Term
Seces.	Dem.	Agric. Jour.					12.5	3	After Term
Seces.	Dem.*	Lawyer Agric.	60	3	95,000	4	4	7	After Term
Union	Whig	Agric.	32	3	56,350	4			After Term
Seces.	Dem.	Agric. Medicine	28	3	40,825	4	8.5	3	1 Cong. 4 Sess.
Union	Whig*	Agric. Medicine	5	2	10,395	3	8	3	After Term
							9.5	2	Before Term
Union	Whig*	Lawyer Agric.	19	2	50,000	4			After Term
Seces.	Dem.	Lawyer	5	2	16,850	3			After Term

Confederate Congress Member and Representative's District	1860 Residence	Member of	Birth State	Year
Rhett, Robert Barnwell Sr.	Charleston, S.C. (Charleston Dist.)	Prov.	S.C.	1800
Rives, William Cabell (7)	Charlottesville, Va. (Albemarle Co.)	Prov. 2 House	Va.	1792
Robinson, Cornelius	Lowndes Co., Ala.	Prov.	N.C.	1805
Rogers, Samuel St. George (1)	Ocala, Fla. (Marion Co.)	2 House	Tenn.	1830
Royston, Grandison Delaney (2)	Washington, Ark. (Hempstead Co.)	1 House	Tenn.	1809
Ruffin, Thomas	Goldsboro, N.C. (Wayne Co.)	Prov.	N.C.	1824
Russell, Charles Wells (16)	Wheeling, (W.)Va. (Ohio Co.)	Prov. 1 House 2 House	Va.	1818
Rust, Albert	Little Rock, Ark. (Pulaski Co.)	Prov.	Va.	1818
Sanderson, John Philip	Jacksonville, Fla. (Duval Co.)	Prov.	Vt.	1815
Scott, Robert Eden	Warrenton, Va. (Fauquier Co.)	Prov.	Va.	1808
Seddon, James Alexander	Dover Mills, Va. (Goochland Co.)	Prov.	Va.	1815
Semmes, Thomas Jenkins	New Orleans, La. (Orleans Par.)	1 Senate 2 Senate	D.C.	1824
Sexton, Franklin Barlow (4)	San Augustine, Tex. (San Augustine Co.)	1 House 2 House	Ind.	1828
Shewmake, John T. (5)	Augusta, Ga. (Richmond Co.)	2 House	Ga.	1826
Shorter, John Gill	Eufaula, Ala. (Barbour Co.)	Prov.	Ga.	1818

Seces-sion Stand	Party	Vocation	Slaves		Estate		Dist. Land Value Index	County Slave Holding Index	Session Occupied
			Hold-ing	Cate-gory	1860 Value	Cate-gory			
Seces.	Dem.	Lawyer Agric.	76	3	$ 34,000	3			After Term
Union	Whig*	Lawyer Agric.	140	4	165,000	4	14	5	Between Terms
Seces.	Dem.	Agric. Merchant			50,000				After Term
Seces.		Lawyer Agric.	83	3	90,000	4	7	7	After Term
Union	Dem.	Lawyer Agric.	100	4	131,000	4	7	6	After Term
Seces.	Dem.	Lawyer Agric.	41	3	50,000	4			After Term
Seces.	Dem.*	Lawyer	0	0	23,000	4	27.5	1	Before Term
Union	Dem.	Lawyer Agric.							After Term
Seces.	Dem.*	Lawyer Agric.	82	4	80,000	4			After Term
Union	Whig*	Lawyer Agric.	39	3	118,760	4			After Term
Seces.	Dem.	Lawyer Agric.	75	4	392,000	4			After Term
Seces.	Dem.	Lawyer	1	1	34,000	4			1 Cong. 2 Sess.
Seces.	Dem.	Lawyer Agric.	78	4	66,535	4	3.5	5	After Term
		Lawyer	4	1	10,000	2	7	4	2 Cong. 2 Sess.
Seces.	Dem.	Lawyer Agric.	100	4	170,000	4			After Term

Confederate Congress Member and Representative's District	1860 Residence	Member of	Birth State	Year
Simms, William Elliott	Paris, Ky. (Bourbon Co.)	1 Senate 2 Senate	Ky.	1822
Simpson, William Dunlap (4)	Laurens Courthouse, S.C. (Laurens Dist.)	1 House 2 House	S.C.	1823
Singleton, Otho Robards (5)	Canton, Miss. (Madison Co.)	1 House 2 House	Ky.	1814
Smith, James Milton (7)	Thomaston, Ga. (Upson Co.)	2 House	Ga.	1823
Smith, Robert Hardy	Mobile, Ala. (Mobile Co.)	Prov.	N.C.	1814
Smith, William (9)	Warrenton, Va. (Fauquier Co.)	1 House	Va.	1797
Smith, William Ephraim (2)	Albany, Ga. (Dougherty Co.)	2 House	Ga.	1829
Smith, William Nathan Harrell (1)	Murfreesboro, N.C. (Hertford Co.)	Prov. 1 House 2 House	N.C.	1812
Smith, William Russell (2)	Tuscaloosa, Ala. (Tuscaloosa Co.)	1 House 2 House	Ky.	1815
Snead, Thomas Lowndes (1)	St. Louis, Mo. (St. Louis Co.)	2 House	Va.	1828
Sparrow, Edward	Lake Providence, La. (Carroll Par.)	Prov. 1 Senate 2 Senate	Ire- land	1810
Staples, Waller Redd (12)	Christiansburg, Va. (Montgomery Co.)	Prov. 1 House 2 House	Va.	1826
Stephens, Alexander Hamilton	Crawfordville, Ga. (Taliaferro Co.)	Prov.	Ga.	1812
Strickland, Hardy (9)	Cumming, Ga. (Forsyth Co.)	1 House	Ga.	1818
Swan, William G. (2)	Knoxville, Tenn. (Knox Co.)	1 House 2 House	Ala.	1821

Seces-sion Stand	Party	Vocation	Slaves Hold-ing	Cate-gory	Estate 1860 Value	Cate-gory	Dist. Land Value Index	County Slave Holding Index	Session Occupied
Seces.	Dem.*	Lawyer Jour.	7	2	$				Before Term
Seces.	Dem.	Lawyer Agric.	31	3	43,400	3	11.5	6	After Term
Seces.	Dem.	Lawyer Agric.	16	2	30,000	2	15.5	9	1 Cong. 4 Sess.
Union	Dem.	Lawyer	4	1	12,000	2	8	4	2 Cong. 2 Sess.
Union	Whig*	Lawyer	15	3	60,000	4			After Term
Union	Dem.	Lawyer	9	2	28,355	3	19	5	1 Cong. 3 Sess.
Union	Whig*	Lawyer	3	1	11,300	2	6	9	After Term
Union	Whig*	Lawyer Agric.	13	2	33,038	3	8	5	After Term
Union	Whig*	Lawyer Writer	5	1	11,000	2	3	5	After Term
Seces.	Dem.	Lawyer Jour.	2	2	33,000	4	72	1	Before Term
Seces.	Whig	Lawyer Agric.	460	4	1,248,050	4			1 Cong. 3 Sess.
Union	Whig*	Lawyer Agric.	42	3	65,000	4	13	3	2 Cong. 1 Sess.
Union	Whig*	Lawyer Agric.	65	4	53,000	4			After Term
Seces.	Dem.	Agric.	31	4	34,000	4	4	2	After Term
Seces.	Whig*	Lawyer			70,000	4	9	2	1 Cong. 4 Sess.

Confederate Congress Member and Representative's District	1860 Residence	Member of	Birth State	Year
Thomas, James Houston	Columbia, Tenn. (Maury Co.)	Prov.	N.C.	1808
Thomas, John J.	Christian Co., Ky.	Prov.	Va.	1813
Thomason, Hugh French	Van Buren, Ark. (Crawford Co.)	Prov.	Tenn.	1826
Tibbs, William H. (3)	Cleveland, Tenn. (Bradley Co.)	1 House	Tenn.	1826
Toombs, Robert Augustus	Washington, Ga. (Wilkes Co.)	Prov.	Ga.	1810
Triplett, George W. (2)	Daviess Co., Ky.	2 House	Ky.	1809
Trippe, Robert Pleasant (7)	Forsyth, Ga. (Monroe Co.)	1 House	Ga.	1819
Turner, Josiah Jr. (5)	Hillsboro, N.C. (Orange Co.)	2 House	N.C.	1821
Tyler, John	Charles City Court-house, Va. (Charles City Co.)	Prov.	Va.	1790
Venable, Abraham Watkins	Granville Co., N.C.	Prov.	Va.	1799
Vest, George Graham (5)	Boonville, Mo. (Cooper Co.)	Prov. 1 House 2 House 2 Senate	Ky.	1830
Villeré, Charles J. (1)	Pointe à la Hache, La. (Plaquemines Par.)	1 House 2 House	La.	1830
Walker, Richard Wilde	Florence, Ala. (Lauderdale Co.)	Prov. 2 Senate	Ala.	1823
Ward, George T.	Tallahassee, Fla. (Leon Co.)	Prov.	Ky.	1810
Watkins, W. W.	Carrollton, Ark. (Carroll Co.)	Prov.	Tenn.	1826

Seces-sion Stand	Party	Vocation	Slaves Hold-ing	Cate-gory	Estate 1860 Value	Cate-gory	Dist. Land Value Index	County Slave Holding Index	Session Occupied
Seces.	Dem.	Lawyer Agric.	46	3	$ 41,350	3			After Term
		Agric.	50	3	70,000	4			Before Term
Union	Dem.*	Lawyer	1	1	8,100	3			After Term
	Whig	Agric. Merchant	17	3	106,000	4	10	2	1 Cong. 4 Sess.
Seces.	Whig*	Lawyer Agric.		4	450,000	4			After Term
	Whig	Agric. Merchant	3	2	5,000	3	9	2	Before Term
Union	Whig*	Lawyer Agric.	16	2	30,000	3	8	6	After Term
Union	Whig	Lawyer Agric.	4	2	5,000	2	7	3	After Term
Seces.	Whig*	Agric.	43	3	73,000	4			After Term
Seces.	Dem.	Lawyer Agric.	43	3	69,000	4			After Term
Seces.	Dem.	Lawyer	6	2	9,000	2	10.5	2	Before Term
Seces.		Lawyer Agric.	89	3	105,000	4	16	9	1 Cong. 2 Sess.
Union	Whig*	Lawyer Agric.	42	3	80,000	4			Between Terms
Union	Whig*	Agric.	170	4	200,650	4			After Term
Union		Lawyer	0	0	2,290	2			After Term

Confederate Congress Member and Representative's District	1860 Residence	Member of	Birth State	Year
Watson, John William Clark	Holly Springs, Miss. (Marshall Co.)	2 Senate	Va.	1808
Waul, Thomas Neville	Gonzales, Tex. (Gonzales Co.)	Prov.	S.C.	1813
Welsh, Israel (3)	Macon, Miss. (Noxubee Co.)	1 House 2 House	Ala.	1825
White, Daniel P.	Greensburg, Ky. (Green Co.)	Prov.	Ky.	1813
Whitfield, Robert H. (2)	Smithfield, Va. (Isle of Wight Co.)	2 House	Va.	1815
Wickham, Williams Carter (3)	Ashland, Va. (Hanover Co.)	2 House	Va.	1820
Wigfall, Louis Trezevant	Marshall, Tex. (Harrison Co.)	Prov. 1 Senate 2 Senate	S.C.	1816
Wilcox, John Alexander (1)	San Antonio, Tex. (Bexar Co.)	1 House	N.C.	1819
Wilkes, Peter S. (6)	Springfield, Mo. (Greene Co.)	2 House		
Wilson, William S.	Port Gibson, Miss. (Claiborne Co.)	Prov.	Md.	1828
Withers, Thomas Jefferson	Camden, S.C. (Kershaw Dist.)	Prov.	S.C.	1804
Witherspoon, James H. (1)	Lancaster Courthouse, S.C. (Lancaster Dist.)	2 House	S.C.	1812
Wright, Augustus Romaldus (10)	Rome, Ga. (Floyd Co.)	Prov. 1 House	Ga.	1813
Wright, John Vines (10)	Purdy, Tenn. (McNairy Co.)	1 House 2 House	Tenn.	1828
Wright, William B. (6)	Paris, Tex. (Lamar Co.)	1 House	Ga.	1830
Yancey, William Lowndes	Montgomery, Ala. (Montgomery Co.)	1 Senate	Ga.	1814

Secession Party	Party	Vocation	Slaves Hold-ing	Cate-gory	Estate 1860 Value	Cate-gory	Dist. Land Value Index	County Slave Holding Index	Session Occupied
Union	Whig*	Lawyer Jour.	10	2	$ 31,000	2			Before Term
Seces.	Dem.	Lawyer Agric.	45	3	55,000	4			After Term
Seces.		Lawyer Agric.	54	3	52,000	3	10	9	After Term
	Dem.	Agric. Merchant	12	2	45,000	4			Before Term
Union		Lawyer Agric.	26	3	57,000	4	7.5	3	Before Term
Union	Whig*	Lawyer Agric.	4	1	27,700	3	12.5	5	Before Term
Seces.	Dem.	Lawyer	10	2	5,200	1			After Term
Seces.	Whig*	Lawyer	13	3	12,000	3	3	2	After Term
	Dem.						7	2	Before Term
Seces.	Dem.	Lawyer	0	0	600	1			After Term
Seces.	Dem.	Lawyer Agric.	23	2	107,000	4			After Term
	Dem.	Agric.	22	3	120,000	4	9	5	After Term
Union	Whig*	Lawyer Agric.	16	2	45,000	4	8	5	After Term
	Dem.	Lawyer	8	2	367,000	4	5	2	Before Term
Seces.	Dem.	Lawyer	6	2	17,000	3	5	3	After Term
Seces.	Dem.	Lawyer Agric.	35	3	77,000	3			After Term

Confederate Congress Member and Average Adjusted Performance Score*	Subject Content Area Congress Session	Provisional All Sessions (a b c d e f)	Conscription	Impressment	Habeas Corpus	Economic	Military	Procedural	Diverse Issues	State Rights	Race
Akin, W., Ga.	(5)*		6 5	3 2				3 6	7 5	5 8	4 5
Anderson, C., Ga.	(4)		0					3 6	9 6	6	3
Anderson, J. P., Fla.	(2)	3							4	5	
Arrington, A. H., N.C.	(4)	7	9 4 4 2	2 0	5 1	9 5 0		2 7	9 6 1 8		
Ashe, T. S., N.C.	(2)		1 3 2 5	6 9	0 6	3 0 5 6		5 2	3 0 2 3	7 9	7
Atkins, J. D. C., Tenn.	(4)	0 3	2 1 5 2 8		9 6	5 9 9 7			5 6 6 5	5 6 4	7
Avery, W. W., N.C.	(8)	7 6	1 2	7	1	9 2	6 8 5 6	5	7 6		
Ayer, L. M., S.C.	(3)	9 9	1 3 5	0 6 5	0 4 0	5 4 7 0		5 1	5 1	6 7	4
Baker, J. M., Fla.	(3)									3	
Baldwin, J. B., Va.	(3)	8 8	4 1 2 3	1 3 8	0 0 3 0 0	6 2 2 7 7		7 7 8	5 2 3 1 5	2 9 3 1	3 1
Barksdale, E., Miss.	(6)	6 2	8 9 5 7	8 6 7 2	6 9 7 5 3	7 9 8 3 3	8 4 9	9 7 4	4 8 9 8 7	7 6 5	5 7
Barnwell, R. W., S.C.	(5)	2	2 7	8 9 4	5 5	0 2 6		4 2	3 6 9	0	
Barry, W. S., Miss.	(6)	8 5 9 1 7									
Bartow, F. S., Ga.	(6)	5 0 0 6									
Bass, N., Ga.	(1)										
Batson, F. I., Ark.	(5)		3 5 7	7 2	8 5	9 9 9		2 2 1	7 3 8	7 9 4	4 7
Baylor, J. R., Tex.	(6)	6	8 4 6	5 9	3	4 3		6 7	8 3	6	8 9
Bell, C. W., Mo.	(4)	9 0	9 6 4 2 1 4	5		9 7		5	2 8 7 6 4		
Bell, H. P., Ga.	(2)		5		3 0	3 1		3 1	5 2	3 7	2 5
Blandford, M. H., Ga.	(4)	0 7	7 4 4	2 3	6 9	5 7		1 1	6 6	7 5	6 6
Bocock, T. S., Va.	(4)	6 6	2 3	8 2	9 5	2 3		8 6 9 1	6 3	6	1 0
Bonham, M. L., S.C.	(4)	9 8	0 5 5	1 2		9 7 8		5	1 7 6 8		
Boteler, A. R., Va.	(6)	8 7 5	4 5 5 6	9	9 9	6 3 3		9 0	3 7 6 8	1	8 7
Boyce, W. W., S.C.	(3)	6 0 5	1 5 2 3 5	2 5	7 0 1 0	3 5 7		5 0	2 6 8 5 0		6 2 7
Bradford, A. B., Miss.	(5)	4 8 8		7 9	8 7 9	6 8 5		7 3	6 7 7	7 8 7	9
Bradley, B. F., Ky.	(7)		7 8	7 7	7 0 0	6 6		5	6 6 9	5 6 2	8
Branch, A. M., Tex.	(5)		6 3								
Breckinridge, R. J., Jr., Ky.	(3)	5 4 7 7 8	1 5 3 4 1 2	2 4	7 6	6 5 1 3		0 8	5 3 6	5 8 0	
Bridgers, R. R., N.C.	(3)							6 5			
Brockenbrough, J. W., Va.	(8)					3	3 6 1				
Brooke, W., Miss.	(6)	5 8 6 8 8 8 5	7 8 8 9	2 5	8 4 9 9 3	3 5 7 7 9 3	4 0	8 9	8 6 7	1 7 8	9 8 7
Brow.1, A. G., Miss.	(5)	6 7 5	8 6 3	8 9					2		
Bruce, E. M., Ky.	(6)										

* Adjustment procedure is described in Chapter 11.
a. Economic. b. Military. c. Diverse Issues. d. State Rights.
e. Sequestration of Enemy Property. f. Constitutional Convention.
g. Property Destruction.

Confederate Congress Member and Average Adjusted Performance Score[*]	Subject Content Area Congress / Session	a b c d e f Provisional / All Sessions	Conscription 1 1 1 1 2 2 / 1 2 3 4 2 2	Impress-ment g 1 2 1 2 / 3 1 2 1	Habeas Corpus 1 1 1 2 2 / 2 3 4 1 2	Economic 1 1 1 2 2 / 2 3 4 1 2	Military 1 1 1 2 2 / 2 3 4 1 2	Proce-dural 1 1 2 2 / 2 1 2 2	Diverse Issues 1 1 1 2 2 / 2 3 4 1 2	State Rights 1 1 1 2 2 / 2 3 4 1 2	Race 2 2 2 / 2 2 2
Bruce, H. W., Ky.	(6)*	6	6 8 8 4 6 7	6 8 6 4	5 6 6 9 5	5 6 7 6 8 3	9 5 2 7 5	5 9 9 9	7 7 8 6 7	8 0 7 9 5	5 5
Burnett, H. C., Ky.	(6)		7 7 8 8 9 9	5 9 9 8	8 8 8	0 0 6 5 5		6 1	9 6 8	5 6 7	9
Burnett, T. L., Ky.	(7)		7 6 8 8	9 8 7 8	8 8 2	8 6 5 2		8 8			9
Campbell, J. A. P., Miss.	(3)	5 6 5 1 5	3 2 2	1 0 7	1 7	4 6 0 5	8 4	1 2	9	9 8 9	3 6
Caperton, A. T., Va.	(4)		8 5	7	7	5 2	3		2		9 5
Carroll, D. W., Ark.	(5)										
Caruthers, R. L., Tenn.	(3)	3	2 6 8 4	1 6 5 6	8 7 3	1 3 5 2		6 3	6 5 8 7	8	5 1
Chambers, H. C., Miss.	(5)	4	3 4 3 7	0	0	8 6 6	5 4	5 7 7 5 6	6 7	
Chambliss, J. R., Va.	(4)									8 8	
Chesnut, J., Jr., S.C.	(2)	1 3 5 2 5	9 5 6 6 5 5	9 2 8 8	1 2	8 7 7 8 9 7	9 2 0 0	7 1 5 3	5 6 5 6 5 7	6 5 8 7 7	6 4
Chilton, W. P., Ala.	(6)	6 7 6 1 3 9	9 8 7 6 8 8		7 9 8	8 7			9 7	7	
Chrisman, J. S., Ky.	(7)				8	9			6 6		
Clapp, J. W., Miss.	(3)	2	5 3 4	3 6 1	4 0 8	4 6 9 5	5 4	5 5 8 9	6 5 6	9 8 3 8 6 6 8	
Clark, J. B., Mo.	(5)		5 4 5 5	8 9 6 7	0 2	7 4	2 0 0	5 1	5 1 6 6		
Clark, W. W., Ga.	(4)	6 9	1 2 3 5	8 8 7		9					
Clay, C. C., Ala.	(4)	9	3 4 3 6	6	9	8 3		1 3	5 5 5 4 6 3 1	9 2	5 6 5 4
Clayton, A. M., Miss.	(8)	7	9 5 7 3 4 4	5 2 5 2	0 3	5 3 0 3 2 2		9 3 0 5		5 6 5	5 8
Clopton, D., Ala.	(3)			8							
Cluskey, M., Tenn.	(7)	7 5 5 3	8 7	8 7	9 9	9 9	9 7	3 6	9 9	5	5 8
Cobb, H., Ga.	(4)	3 7 2 3 4									
Cobb, T. R. R., Ga.	(3)										
Collier, C. F., Va.	(3)	6 7 5 8 5 6	6 1 1 8 7 5 7	0 8 1	7 0 9	2 6 1 2 9 1 5	7 0 9	1 5 9 9 8 9 9 4	5 7 6 8 5 6	3 6 5 3 2 8	3 6 5 1 8 9
Colyar, A. S., Tenn.	(4)		6 2 6	8 9 9 3	9	4 9 9					
Conrad, C. M., La.	(6)			5 7		3 7					7
Conrow, A. H., Mo.	(7)	6 9 8	9 8 9 8 8 8 9	8 9 8 9	9 9	9 2 8 6 8 3	9	7 1 5 9 6	9 6 4 9	8 9 6 7 8 8	8 9 6 7
Cooke, W. M., Mo.	(6)	5 0 1	9	5 7		8 6 9		6	9		
Craige, F. B., N.C.	(5)	7 1 8									
Crawford, M. J., Ga.	(3)	7 8 1 0 0	8 6 7 6	1 0 2 0	2 0 0	2 5 2 3 1 0		2 0	8 3 0 0	1 1 0 2	
Crockett, J. W., Ky.	(5)										
Cruikshank, M. H., Ala.	(1)										
Currin, D. M., Tenn.	(6)	5 7 6 6	9 7 9 9	6 8	8 9 6	7 7 4 4 4 1		8 8	3 6 7 6 6 3	0 7	4 3 1 5
Curry, J. L. M., Ala.	(5)	6 7 3 1 2 6	7 4 7 5	8 0	0 0	2 4		1			
Darden, S. H., Tex.	(2)		6 0	0							

[*]Adjustment procedure is described in Chapter 11.
a. Economic. b. Military. c. Diverse Issues. d. State Rights.
e. Sequestration of Enemy Property. f. Constitutional Convention.
g. Property Destruction.

Confederate Congress Member and Average Adjusted Performance Score*	Subject Content Area Congress Session	a b c d e f Provisional / All Sessions	Conscription 1 1 1 2 2 / 1 2 3 4 2	Impressment 2 2 1 / 1 2 3	Habeas Corpus 1 1 1 2 2 / 2 3 4 1 2	Economic 1 1 1 2 2 / 3 4 1 2 2	Military 1 1 1 2 / 2 3 4 1	Procedural 1 2 2 / 1 2 2	Diverse Issues 1 1 1 1 2 / 1 2 3 4 1	State Rights 1 1 1 2 2	Race 2 2 2 / 2 2 2
Dargan, E. S., Ala.	(6)*	1 5 / 3 7	9 8 5 5 / 9 4 1 2	6 / 6	8	7 5 / 5 4 0		8 0 / 0 9	9 2 / 6 3		2 2 / 2 2
Davidson, A. T., N.C.	(3)	9 3 / 5 4	8 5 5 / 9 8 5	6 5 / 1 0	0	4 5			2 3 / 3 3		2 2 / 2 2
Davis, G., N.C.	(5)	4 7 / 7					4 5		8	9 9	
Davis, N., Ala.	none										
Davis, R., Miss.	(3)		2 6 8 / 6 5	6 / 0 8	0	1 0 / 8		1 8	5 4 / 3 8		
Dawkins, J. B., Fla.	(5)										
De Clouet, A., La.	(6)	5 8 8 8 5 / 7 6 3	8 7 4 4 6 / 0 1 3 3	5 / 0	7 0 / 4 3	7 9 6 / 6 9 9	6 5 6 5 8 4	9 5 / 9	9 5 2 6 7 8 3 4 / 5 6 3 3 2 3	6	4 9
De Jarnette, D. C., Va.	(5)										8 8 / 6 8
De Witt, W. H., Tenn.	(4)			1 7 0							7 5 / 6 5
Dickinson, J. S., Ala.	(5)		7 7 6 / 8 4 5	4 / 0 9	6 9 9 / 6 9 7	9 3 5 / 8 5 3		3 0 / 6 5 1	6 3 3 / 9 6 3 5 7	8 8 / 8 6 5	9 5 3
Dortch, W. T., N.C.	(5)		6 4 7 / 5 7 7	0 6 5 8		8 5 4 6 / 8 5	6		6 / 8 5		
Dupré, L. J., La.	(5)										
Echols, J. H., Ga.	(3)	9 9	9 7 / 8 7	3 9 8 / 7 4 9	6 9 8 / 9 7	7 / 9 9	0 9 4 / 8 8 6	5 5 / 5 5 7	2 6 8 / 5 6 8	2 7 3 / 6 9 7	0 3 9 / 8 7 9
Elliott, J. M., Ky.	(6)			9 9 / 9 7	9 8 / 9 5	9 8 9 / 9 9	9 4 6 / 6 6 7	0 7 / 5 7 8	6 6 8 / 6 6 7		
Ewing, G. W., Ky.	(7)										
Farrow, J., S.C.	(3)	8	3 2 2 5 5 / 0 1 3 3	0 8 3 5 6 / 5 1 6	3 0 0 / 1 0	3 0 0 / 0 0	3 3 5 6 3 / 8 7 5 3	9 7 5 / 9	3 6 4 6 7 3 1 / 5 6 3 3 2 3	4 8 5 1	8 5 1
Fearn, T., Ala.	(9)										
Foote, H. S., Tenn.	(3)										
Ford, S. H., Ky.	(7)	6 9 / 8 0	0 4 8 4 7	5 2 / 2	0 0 / 9 9	5 1	8 3 7 4 6 5	5 3	6 8 3 6 3 7	3 5 5	3 5
Forman, T. M., Ga.	(6)	7 8 / 0 7									
Foster, T. J., Ala.	(4)										
Freeman, T. W., Mo.	(6)	3 9	7 9 / 5 8 2	9 / 0 0 / 7 7	9 9 / 7 9	1 0 0 / 7 9 9	8 6 2 1 1 / 6 6 9 6	0 0 / 5 9	5 4 9 / 6 8 9	1 0 0 / 8 5	0 1 0 0 / 5 8 8 7
Fuller, T. C., N.C.	(0)										
Funsten, D., Va.	(6)										
Gaither, B. S., N.C.	(4)	8 6 6 3 5	1 3 2 5 2 / 8 7 9 6 5	5 3 3 5 / 5 2 5 1	0 4 3 3 / 9 2 5 1 0	3 3 3 / 8 7 7 6	3 5 5 5 / 7 7 6	2 3 7 / 0 1	1 5 7 7 7 / 7 3 5	5 9 5 5	5 9 5 5
Gardenhire, E. L., Tenn.	(6)		5 5 5 9	2					7 9 8 / 7 3 5		
Garland, A. H., Ark.	(4)						6 4 0	0 1			
Garland, R. K., Ark.	(2)		1 4 3 / 7 5 6 7	6 / 1	8 5	0 0 / 0 9	2 2 / 9 5 9	4 3 / 2	3 3 0 / 7 6 4	3 2	3 2
Garnett, M. R. H., Va.	(2)								4 5 / 4	3	
Gartrell, L. J., Ga.	(6)										
Gentry, M. P., Tenn.	(4)	2 6	8 3 / 1 0	9 6 / 3 3	7 9 9 / 1 0 0	0	5 6 7 / 3 0 2	9 7 9 / 2 0	4 8 / 2 0 1	8 9 3 3 / 0 3 0 1	8 9 3 3 / 0 3 0 1
Cholson, T. S., Va.	(6)								4 6		
Gilmer, J. A., N.C.	(1)										

*Adjustment procedure is described in Chapter 11.
a. Economic. b. Military. c. Diverse Issues. d. State Rights.
e. Sequestration of Enemy Property. f. Constitutional Convention.
g. Property Destruction.

Confederate Congress Member and Average Adjusted Performance Score*	Subject Content Area (Congress Session)	Provisional (All Sessions) a b c d e f	Conscription	Impressment g	Habeas Corpus	Economic	Military	Procedural	Diverse Issues	State Rights	Race
Goode, J., Jr., Va.	(5)		4 6 2 6 8 3	3 1 6 3	5 2	8 8 5 5 8 6		9 7 9	2 5 5 7 7 9 4	6 9	6 9 5 4
Graham, M. D., Tex.	(4)		6 5 3 5 0	5 0 9	6 9 9	5 5 8 1 1	3 5	8	3 2 6 4 0		1
Graham, W. A., N.C.	(1)			0 0							
Gray, H., La.	(6)	7	7 3 3 6	9 4	6 5	2 3 1		3 6	5 9 8 5	6 5	6 5 7 7
Gray, P. W., Tex.	(4)	5 6 2 4			7	8 6		9	9 9 8 5		9
Gregg, J., Tex.	(4)			6						3 8	
Hale, S. F., Ala.	(6)	3 7 8 8 7	0 0 4 4 6 2	2 1 4 1	2 0 1 5	1 5 1 7 5 8 4		3 7 5	5 7 3 7 4 6 3 6	6 6	6 6 5
Hanly, T. B., Ark.	(3)	5 8	9 4 5	2 9	9 6	5 3		3 9	4 3 6		
Harris, T. A., Mo.	(5)										
Harris, W. P., Miss.	(6)	6 5 7 8 8 7	4 6 6 7	1 6 4 8	1 9	9 6 5 7 7		9 8 7	5 5 7 3 7 9 8	7 9 5 3	
Harrison, J. T., Miss.	(6)	7 8 8 7 4 6	5 4			8 5	3 2 0		5 5 7	9 9	
Hartridge, J., Ga.	(6)		5 6 5 3 9	9 8	9 9	6 2 9		8 7	2 5 6 7 8 6	3 8	6 9 5 7
Hatcher, R. A., Mo.	(6)	8 0 7 8	8 7 4	2 0 4 1 4		3 6 5 4		2 0			5 4
Haynes, L. C., Tenn.	(3)		6 1 0		9 6			0 5			
Heiskell, J. B., Tenn.	(5)										
Hemphill, J., Tex.	(5)	7 5	7 5 3 8 9	6 9 8		7 6 9 9	6 8 3 7 4	6 0	7 6	7 7 8 9	9 9	8 0 0
Henry, G. A., Tenn.	(6)			2 9	9 5	5 0 3 1			1 7 6	3 8	
Herbert, C. C., Tex.	(2)			1 0	0						
Hill, B. H., Ga.	(4)	7 5 5 0 6	1 4 0 2	6 9 5 4	0	1 6 4 6 8 2	7 8 8 1 8	8 5	6 5 5 7 7 9 8	6 9 6 9 8	8
Hilton, R. B., Fla.	(5)		4 7 4 4		9 9	6 7 1					
Hodge, B. J., La.	(6)				8 9 5				8		
Hodge, G. B., Ky.	(5)		7 7	2 2	3 8 5	6 6	3	3	6 5 5	6	6 2
Holcombe, J. P., Va.	(5)	3 7 7 5 6	3 6 4		6 0	6 7 0 3 6	9 1	4 4 0			
Holder, W. D., Miss.	(3)		5 7 3								
Holliday, F. W. M., Va.	(6)	3 7 7 5 6	9 7 8	8 6	7 9 9	5 9 6		8 9	6 5 5 3	6	6 9 5 5
Holt, H., Ga.	(6)	4 8 8 4	6 5 6 2 4	6	6	0 6 0 0	7 9 8 7 8 9	9	4 1 1	7 1	
House, J. F., Tenn.	(5)		6 5	7	9 9	7 2	9 3				
Hunter, R. M. T., Va.	(5)		7 8 5	1 6	0 6 0 0		5	7	3	
Ingram, P., Ga.	(6)			7 2						
Jemison, R., Jr., Ala.	(3)		1	1						
Jenkins, A. G., Va.	(5)	5 3 9 3 5	9	5 9 5	0 0	2 2 4 3	7 9 5 7	6	1	2	3
Johnson, H. V., Ga.	(3)		7 3 5	1 0	0 8	5 8 5	8 3 3		3	8 7	
Johnson, R. W., Ark.	(5)		0 1 1								

*Adjustment procedure is described in Chapter 11.
a. Economic. b. Military. c. Diverse Issues. d. State Rights.
e. Sequestration of Enemy Property. f. Constitutional Convention.
g. Property Destruction.

Confederate Congress Member and Average Adjusted Performance Score	Subject Content Area / Congress / Session	Provisional / All Sessions (a b c d e f)	Conscription	Impressment g	Habeas Corpus	Economic	Military	Procedural	Diverse Issues	State Rights	Race
Johnson, T., Ky.	(9)*	9	5 7 4 6 9 7 · 3 9	7 0 9 7 5 · 1 7	8 9 7 9 8 9 9 1	9 1 6 8 9 7 5 9 7	5 9 2	9 7 9 6 5	3 6 8 9 8	8 9	8 9 8 9
Johnson, W. P., Mo.	(6)	2 9							4 0 1 2		4
Johnston, R., Va.	(7)	9 6							7 7 9		
Jones, G. W., Tenn.	(3)	6 6 7 3 1	3 3 4 2	5	7 7	3 4 2		8			
Jones, H. C., Ala.	(4)	5 5									
Jones, T. M., Tenn.	(3)										
Keeble, E. A., Tenn.	(7)	2	6 6 · 8 9	5 · 8 9	9 9 · 8 9 9	5 8 6 · 7		1 · 6 5	5 · 8 9 8	2	5 9 7 9
Keitt, L. M., S.C.	(1)	3 7 7 2 9									
Kenan, A. H., Ga.	(6)										
Kenan, O. R., N.C.	(5)	6 7 5 8 6 4	6 4 0 5 5 7 7 · 3	5 6 8 0 · 7 7	8 7 7 9 6 6 1 0	7 5 7 3 8 7 2 1		7 9 1	5 6 1 5 8 6 8 7 7 4 0	2	1
Kenner, D. F., La.	(6)										
Lamkin, J. T., Miss.	(1)										
Lander, W., N.C.	(5)		8 7 8 7 · 0 0 · 0 1	5 · 0 0 · 1 0	8 2 0 0 1	8 5 1 0 0 0 5		5 0 0 1 1	3 3 8 1 0 0 0 0 0		0 0 0 0 0 1
Leach, J. M., N.C.	(0)										
Leach, J. T., N.C.	(1)										
Lester, G. N., Ga.	(3)	6	1 · 9 5 7	1 · 7	4 0 7	2 2 6 7			8 6 8 9	2 3	3
Lewis, D. P., Ala.	(6)										
Lewis, D. W., Ga.	(7)										
Lewis, J. W., Ga.	(3)		5 4 9 7 6 4 8 3	3 7 9 8 1 · 0	1 0 1 8 9 7	5 9 8 0 0 1 9 8 8 5	6	9 0 0 7 9 7	1 5 0 0 8 9 3 9 6 6 7	1	0 0 7 9 8 7
Logan, G. W., N.C.	(0)										
Lyon, F. S., Ala.	(6)										
Lyons, J., Va.	(4)	4	7 5 4 4 7 2 0 1 · 8	6 8 7 · 6	8 5 7 3 3	1 3 6 6 5 5 3		8 8 1	4 5 6 5 6 1 3 7 6	5 6	8
McCallum, J., Tenn.	(5)	2 2									
McDowell, T. D. S., N.C.	(3)	7 7			3						
Macfarland, W. H., Va.	(5)	2 5 7 7 7	8 3 6 4 · 3 1	1 2 3 · 5	2 5 9 5	8 3 6 2 0 0		5 5 5	5 4 7 4 5 2	5 6 4 6	5 6 4 6
McLean, J. R., N.C.	(4)										
McMullin, F., Va.	(3)										
McQueen, J., S.C.	(4)	8 5 6 8 3 4	0 3 3 5 7 7 8 7	9 · 2 9 · 2	8 9 8 9	7 3 3 8 8 9		6 6	2 1 9 6 4 7 6 9		
McRae, C. J., Ala.	(5)										
McRae, J. J., Miss.	(7)										
Machen, W. B., Ky.	(6)	7 3 9 3	8 7 6 7 7 6 3 1 5 · 7 4	8 3 6 2 5 8 8 2	7 9 8 3 0 1	3 7 9 8 6 8 8 3 3 9		3 5 8 2 6	5 9 6 8 9 9 9 6 6 5 2 6	7 9 6 8 4 6 1 5	7 9 6 8 5 5
Marshall, H., La.	(4)										
Marshall, H., Ky.	(4)										

* Adjustment procedure is described in Chapter 11.
a. Economic. b. Military. c. Diverse Issues. d. State Rights.
e. Sequestration of Enemy Property. f. Constitutional Convention.
g. Property Destruction.

Confederate Congress Member and Average Adjusted Performance Score*	Subject Content Area		Conscrip-tion	Impress-ment g	Habeas Corpus	Economic	Military	Proce-dural	Diverse Issues	State Rights	Race
	Congress Session	a b c d e f Provisional / All Sessions									

*Adjustment procedure is described in Chapter 11.
a. Economic. b. Military. c. Diverse Issues. d. State Rights.
e. Sequestration of Enemy Property. f. Constitutional Convention.
g. Property Destruction.

Members listed:

Martin, J. M., Fla. (4)*
Mason, J. M., Va. (4)
Maxwell, A. E., Fla. (4)

Memminger, C. G., S.C. (4)
Menees, T., Tenn. (5)
Miles, W. P., S.C. (5)

Miller, S. A., Va. (6)
Mitchel, C. B., Ark. (4)
Monroe, T. B., Ky. (6)

Montague, R. L., Va. (6)
Moore, J. W., Ky. (6)
Morehead, J. M., N.C. (5)

Morgan, S. H., Tex. (7)
Morton, J., Fla. (3)
Munnerlyn, C. J., Ga. (6)

Murray, J. P., Tenn. (4)
Nisbet, E. A., Ga. (6)
Norton, N. L., Mo. (5)

Ochiltree, W. B., Sr., Tex. (3)
Oldham, W. S., Tex. (3)
Orr, J. L., S.C. (2)

Orr, J. A., Miss. (3)
Owens, J. B., Fla. (3)
Perkins, J., Jr., La. (5)

Peyton, R. L. Y., Mo. (5)
Phelan, J., Miss. (6)
Preston, W., Va. (3)

Preston, W. B., Va. (4)
Pryor, R. A., Va. (5)
Pugh, J. L., Ala. (6)

Puryear, R. C., N.C. (5)
Ralls, J. P., Ala. (4)
Ramsay, J. G., N.C. (0)

Confederate Congress Member and Average Adjusted Performance Score*	Subject Content Area Congress Session	a b c d e f Provisional	a b c d e f All Sessions	Conscription 1 2 3 4	Impressment 1 2 3 1 2 1	Habeas Corpus	Economic	Military	Procedural	Diverse Issues	State Rights	Race
Read, H. E., Ky.	(7)*											
Reade, E. G., N.C.	(2)	8	6 1 6	6 6	8 9 9	2 9 9 9 0	8 8 4 7 3	1	1 8 9 3	3 9 7 9 3	6 9 8 6 9	6 9 8 6
Reagan, J. H., Tex.	(3)											
Rhett, R. B., Sr., S.C.	(2)	6 5 3 2 3 2	3 7 9 8 7		9	2 9	7 5			5 3		
Rives, W. C., Va.	(6)											
Robinson, C., Ala.	none											
Rogers, S. St. G., Fla.	(3)	1	1 9	8 4 4	3 6 5	5 7 1 7 9	1 1		0 6 1	4 6 8	6 3 2	6 3 2
Royston, G. D., Ark.	(5)											
Ruffin, T., N.C.	(4)											
Russell, C. W., Va.	(5)	1 5 5	7 8 8	2 7 5 7 7 1	3 9 7 6	7 0 7 9 9	9 0 7 3 6 8 7		9 6 7	7 1 7 8 7 7 3 5	6 6 5 6	6 6 5 6
Rust, A., Ark.	none											
Sanderson, J. P., Fla.	(6)											
Scott, R. E., Va.	(3)	1 5 1 7 7 8	7 5 8 4	7 4 5 5 3	9 8 3	3 4 7 9	0 5 2 8	5 7 5 3 6 8	5	9	2 1	3
Seddon, J. A., Va.	(5)											
Semmes, T. J., La.	(4)											
Sexton, F. B., Tex.	(5)	4 9 0 4		5 3 5 3 6 3 4	9 8 3 7 7 2	3 5 7 9 9 3	2 5 7 7 2 5 1	5 1 3	9 8 1 6	6 6 7 4 6 6 8 4 6	6 9 3 5 7 5	6 9 3 5
Shewmake, J. T., Ga.	(4)											
Shorter, J. G., Ala.	(4)											
Simms, W. E., Ky.	(7)	0 8 8 8 9 2	1 7 5 5 2	8 8 8 9 9 2 4 7 4 9 7 5	1 9 2 6 3 7	9 6 1 3 0 6 8 5	5 5 8 6 7 3 5 6 5 7 8 5 7	5 1 3	2 5 4	6 2 7 5 3 8 7 9	5 8 5 5 8	5 8 5 5
Simpson, W. D., S.C.	(4)											
Singleton, O. R., Miss.	(7)											
Smith, J. M., Ga.	(3)	4 9 8 3 7 7		4 1 9	3 1 0	7 0 1	4 1 5 3		3 3 2	6 6 6	5 5 3 7	5 3 7
Smith, R. H., Ala.	(7)											
Smith, W., Va.	(3)											
Smith, W. E., Ga.	(4)	1 6	6	5 2 1 1 0 0 3 2 3 3	2 0 0 6 5	6 1 0 0 0 0 8 6	4 1 4 3 2 0 0 5 0		1 0 0 2	2 8 1 0 0 6 3 3	7 9 5 1 0 1 3	9 3 5
Smith, W. N. H., N.C.	(1)											
Smith, W. R., Ala.	(3)											
Snead, T. L., Mo.	(6)	0 8 8 8 9 2 1 7 5 5 2		9 4 6 7 9 2 5 5 2	9 8 6 1 2 3	7 6 8 9 1	0 6 6 8 5 5 2 4	7 9 4 3 8 1	6 8 5 3	5 8 8 6 1	5 9 7 4 9 6	8 5 5
Sparrow, E., La.	(6)											
Staples, W. R., Va.	(4)											
Stephens, A. H., Ga.	(5)	3 7 4 7	5 1 3 2 5 7 9 4	6 9	5 9 0	3 9 9	9 4 7 9 7 5 4 1		1 2 3	7 2 8 6 8 6 8 7	7 3 8	7 3 8
Strickland, H., Ga.	(4)											
Swan, W. G., Tenn.	(6)											

* Adjustment procedure is described in Chapter 11.
a. Economic. b. Military. c. Diverse Issues. d. State Rights.
e. Sequestration of Enemy Property. f. Constitutional Convention.
g. Property Destruction.

Confederate Congress Member and Average Adjusted Performance Score*	Subject Content Area (Congress Session)	Provisional / All Sessions (a b c d e f)	Conscription	Impressment (g)	Habeas Corpus	Economic	Military	Procedural	Diverse Issues	State Rights	Race
Thomas, J. H., Tenn.	(6)*	5 9									
Thomas, J. J., Ky.	(9)	7 6 9 9									
Thomason, H. F., Ark.	(4)	4 2 6 7 5									
Tibbs, W. H., Tenn.	(5)	7	6 7	2	5 8 8	7 7		5	7 5		
Toombs, R. A., Ga.	(4)	1 0 8	5	4 7		3 6 6		6 9	6 3 6	6 6 8	6 8 7
Triplett, G. W., Ky.	(5)		0 3 2 3						7 6 3 9		
Trippe, R. P., Ga.	(4)		1 3	7 1 0	7 9	6 5 5		1	0 0 1	0 0 1	0 1 0
Turner, J., N.C.	(1)			8	1 0 0	1 0 0		2			
Tyler, J., Va.	(1)	1									
Venable, A. W., N.C.	(5)	1 4 8 7 7	9 6 7 6 7	3 6 8	6 6	9 5 9		2 5	6 3 7	4 7	7 5
Vest, G. G., Mo.	(5)	2	8 6 6 5	7 9 1 8	6 5	2 8 8 8 8		6 5	5 9 9 6 7 5	7 9 5	
Villeré, C. J., La.	(6)	8 5	5								6
Walker, R. W., Ala.	(3)	5 0 6		0 1	1	4	1 2				
Ward, G. T., Fla.	(3)	2 7 3 0									
Watkins, W. W., Ark.	(5)	2 7 5 7									
Watson, J. W. C., Miss.	(4)	9 6 5 7 6 4	3 4 5 5	1 2	1 6	3 9	2 5	8	5		8
Waul, T. N., Tex.	(5)		3	6 4	5	9 7 5			4 3 5 7 7		
Welsh, I., Miss.	(5)		5	2	5						
White, D. P., Ky.	(4)	5		2	7 9 0	7 9 0		5 8	8 6 2 2	3 3 1	3 1 1
Whitfield, R. H., Va.	(6)		0 0	8 3	0 0	1 2 3					
Wickham, W. C., Va.	(2)			9							
Wigfall, L. T., Tex.	(5)	9	8 6 3 6 6	7 8 9	6 6	1 7 7 6	5 6 2	1 9	6 9 5 3 7	9 2	1
Wilcox, J. A., Tex.	(5)		8 5 6 6		9	1 4 6		9 6 0	3 9	6 6 4	6 4 7
Wilkes, P. S., Mo.	(6)		9 8		9 9	9 6					
Wilson, W. S., Miss.	(9)	3 8		6 3	3 1 2	2 4 0		1 2	5 5 3	4 3 3	3 3 5
Withers, T. J., S.C.	(3)	3	4 6		0 5 0						
Witherspoon, J. H., S.C.	(3)	8 4			9 0						
Wright, A. R., Ga.	(4)	6 8	8 2 3 5	0 6 8	3 0 9 5	6 2 9	2 1	1 2 5	6 3 0 2 7 5 6	3 5	3 3 5
Wright, J. V., Tenn.	(4)	6	7 6	0 0	5	4 4			5		
Wright, W. B., Tex.	(4)		8 5 2 7	2							
Yancey, W. L., Ala.	(3)	5 1 3	5 1 3	0		8		0	8		

*Adjustment procedure is described in Chapter 11.
a. Economic. b. Military. c. Diverse Issues. d. State Rights.
e. Sequestration of Enemy Property. f. Constitutional Convention.
g. Property Destruction.

Confederate Congress Member and Average Adjusted Scale Position	Subject Content Area (Congress / Session)	a b c d — Prov. / All Sess	Conscription (1 1 1 1 1 / 1 2 3 4 2)	Impress-ment e (1 2 2 1 / 3 1 2 1 2)	Habeas Corpus (1 2 2 / 2 4 1 2 2)	Economic f (1 2 2 1 / 1 3 1 2 3)	Mili-tary (1 2 2 / 4 1 2)	g (1 1 1 2 / 2 1 2)	State Rights (1 1 1 2 / 2 3 2)	Race h i (2 2 / 2 2 both)
Akin, W., Ga.	(5)*		5 / 3	0 1	5 4 2 0	5 2 / 3 3			1 3 / 6 1	4 5 / 2 4
Anderson, C., Ga.	(3)									
Anderson, J. P., Fla.	(2)	1 / 1								
Arrington, A. H., N.C.	(3)		5 2 / 2 0	0 2	4 1 0 2	1 1 / 3 2		3 0 / 3 0	4 5 / 5 5	3 2
Ashe, T. S., N.C.	(3)		2 0 / 0 0			5 3 / 5 2				
Atkins, J. D. C., Tenn.	(4)		2 5	2 1 / 2						
Avery, W. W., N.C.	(7)	3 4	1 0 / 0	4 3 / 4 4	1 1 1 / 3	3 3 / 3 0	7 4 5	1 4 / 1 4	3 / 3 4	1
Ayer, L. M., S.C.	(3)		1 4 / 7 1							
Baker, J. M., Fla.	(5)		1 4 / 1 3							
Baldwin, J. B., Va.	(4)	5 1 1 0	3 / 4 5	5 3 1 / 4	4 0 0 1 / 4 4	1 2 5 / 5 0 2	2 6	3 / 2 5	1 1 2 / 4 3 1 / 0	1 1 / 7 1 5 6
Barksdale, E., Miss.	(5)		4 5 / 2 4			2 5 4				
Barnwell, R. W., S.C.	(4)	2	3	4 1						
Barry, W. S., Miss.	(7)	6 4								
Bartow, F. S., Ga.	(7)	3 0								
Bass, N., Ga.	(0)	4								
Batson, F. I., Ark.	(6)	2 3	5 / 4	3 1 / 5 4	7 5 6 / 2 3	4 4 2 / 4 4		4 1 / 2 3	4 2 / 4 7	6 7 / 4 4
Baylor, J. R., Tex.	(6)		0	1 3	6 0	4 4 2			4 5	4 4
Bell, C. W., Mo.	(3)	4	4					2 3		
Bell, H. P., Ga.	(2)		0	0 0 / 2 0	0 0 / 4 5	1 / 4 6		0 5	3 1 / 5 3 / 5 1	6 0 / 6 7
Blandford, M. H., Ga.	(5)	1 3	5 / 4		5 2 / 6	4 4 / 5				
Bocock, T. S., Va.	(5)		1			6				
Bonham, M. L., S.C.	(3)	0 1 / 2 3 / 3 1	1 0 / 2 3	3 4 / 1 3 / 4 1	3 0 2	1 / 4 6		3 2 / 2 4 / 2 3	0 2	2 2
Boteler, A. R., Va.	(3)	6 2 3				3 / 6 3				
Boyce, W. W., S.C.	(4)		4 2 / 4 2	5						
Bradford, A. B., Miss.	(4)	3	4 / 5	2 5 / 5 3	5 4 4 / 4 0 0	5 3 / 4 4			6 5 / 4 2 / 5	6 6 / 5 3
Bradley, B. F., Ky.	(6)									
Branch, A. M., Tex.	(5)									
Breckinridge, R. J., Jr., Ky.	(3)	3	4 2 / 1 2	2	3 3 3	3 0 1		0 4 / 3 4	1 2	2 5
Bridgers, R. R., N.C.	(3)									
Brockenbrough, J. W., Va.	(7)	4								
Brooke, W., Miss.	(5)	2 4 3 3	3 / 4	5 3 / 4 3	4 2 / 5 6 4	1 6 / 1 4	2 3	3 4	4 5 / 5 4 / 0	7
Brown, A. B., Miss.	(5)		4 9 / 4 4							
Bruce, E. M., Ky.	(6)		6							

*Adjustment procedure is described in Chapter 11.
a. Economic.   b. Const. Conv. Race and State Rights.
c. Railroad Issues.   d. Const. Conv. State Rights.
e. Property Destruction.   h. Military-Determination.
f. Erlanger Loan.   (Cross-Content Scales)
g. Procedural Issues.   i. Defeatism-Realism.

Confederate Congress Member and Average Adjusted Scale Position*	Subject Content Area Congress Session	Conscription (a b c d) Prov. / All Sess.	Impress-ment (e)	Habeas Corpus	Economic (f)	Mili-tary	State Rights (g)	Race (h i)
Bruce, H. W., Ky.	(5)*	4 5 3	3 2 1	4 4 4	1 6 0 4	4 4 3	0 4	4 4 3 7 6
Burnett, H. C., Ky.	(6)	2 3 7 9 7	3 5	4 7	0 5 2 3			4 0 4 7 5 6 7
Burnett, T. L., Ky.	(6)	4 4 4 4	4 2 3	3 5 1 0	0 4		4	
Campbell, J. A. P., Miss.	(0)	0	0 3	3	2	5 4 3		5 4 2 4 5 7
Caperton, A. T., Va.	(5)	4 2 5	4	5	0			
Carroll, D. W., Ark.	(5)						5	
Caruthers, R. L., Tenn.	(0)	0	3 3	4 4 2 0	2 0	2	3 4	6 2 7 6
Chambers, H. C., Miss.	(5)	2 3 5	1	5	7	3	3 3	
Chambliss, J. R., Va.	(4)	1 0 3						
Chesnut, J., Jr., S.C.	(3)	2 2 3 3	0 2 1	5 5	0 0 6 0	0 2	4 4	5 4 5 4 7
Chilton, W. P., Ala.	(5)	3 6 0 5 5	4 3	5 7 5	6 4 3 4	3	3 4	1 5 6 8
Chrisman, J. S., Ky.	(6)	4 3 2 5						
Clapp, J. W., Miss.	(3)	3 0 0	1 5 5	0 1 7 3	6 2 6 1	2 0	3 3 4 0	6 5 6 7
Clark, J. B., Mo.	(6)	3 2 2 4	5	3 0				
Clark, W. W., Ga.	(4)	1 0 5			4	4		
Clay, C. C., Ala.	(6)	4 2	2	7	0	4	4 5	3 3 1 0 3
Clayton, A. M., Miss.	(6)	3 5	2 1 0 0	4 2 0 6	0 6 3 2 0	0		5 3
Clopton, D., Ala.	(3)	1 0 2	4	5	2			1 3 4 7
Cluskey, M., Tenn.	(6)	4 1 3 5		7 5		2		
Cobb, H., Ga.	(5)	1 3	4					
Cobb, T. R. R., Ga.	(4)	1						
Collier, C. F., Va.	(3)	4 3 0	3	4 2 1	3 0	3	0	4 5 5 6 2
Colyar, A. S., Tenn.	(4)	5 4 4 4	4 3	3 5 4	6 4	4	1 5	4 5 5 6 6
Conrad, C. M., La.	(6)	4 3 4 4	5 1	6 5		3		
Conrow, A. H., Mo.	(7)	4 5 6	3	6 5 0	0 1 4	4 3	4 4	6 6 4 7 8
Cooke, W. M., Mo.	(5)	4 5 5	3	5 1	1 3		0 4	
Craige, F. B., N.C.	(3)	3 1						
Crawford, M. J., Ga.	(2)	2 0 4 3 0	2	0 0	1 2 0	4	2	0 0 2 0 0
Crockett, J. W., Ky.	(5)		2 1					
Cruikshank, M. H., Ala.	(1)							
Currin, D. M., Tenn.	(6)	5 3 5 4 4	2 4	1 0	2 4 0	4 0	2 4 4	4 0 3 5 1
Curry, J. L. M., Ala.	(5)	4 1 3 3	3		7 0	0		
Darden, S. H., Tex.	(4)	2 4	1		0			

*Adjustment procedure is described in Chapter 11.
a. Economic. b. Const. Conv. Race and State Rights.
c. Railroad Issues. d. Const. Conv. State Rights.
e. Property Destruction.   h. Military-Determination.
f. Erlanger Loan.   (Cross-Content Scales)
g. Procedural Issues.   i. Defeatism-Realism.

Confederate Congress Member and Average Adjusted Scale Position — Subject Content Area (Congress Session), with adjusted scale positions by subject area. Sub‑column header numbers are shown under each major heading.

Member (Avg. Adj. Scale Position)	Subject Content Area / Congress Session	a b c d (Prov. / All Sess.)	Conscription (1·1 1·2 1·3 1·4 2·2)	Impressment (1·3 2·1 2·2)	Habeas Corpus (1·1 1·2 2·4 2·1 2·2)	Economic — f (1·1 1·3 2·1 2·2 2·3)	Military (2·4 1·1 1·2 2·1 2·2)	State Rights — g (1·1 1·2 1·2 2·3 2·2)	Race — h i (2·1 2·2 2·2 2·2 2·2 both)
Dargan, E. S., Ala.	(6)*	0	5 4	1 4		5 3	3 4		
Davidson, A. T., N.C.	(4)	4	5 0 1			3 0			
Davis, G., N.C.	(6)	1 2	4 5 6 1			3 4			
Davis, N., Ala.	none								
Davis, R., Miss.	(3)		0 5	1 2		2 2	2 4	5 3	
Dawkins, J. B., Fla.	(4)		3 2			0			
De Clouet, A., La.	(5)	3 5 3 2	2 5	3 1 3	4 7 3	4 3 2 5	1 2 5	5	4 6 7
De Jarnette, D. C., Va.	(5)	2	2						
De Witt, W. H., Tenn.	(4)	3	5 3 4						
Dickinson, J. S., Ala.	(5)		2 5 4 4	1 4	4 5 5	6 1 3 2 4	3	4 3	4 3 2 2 9
Dortch, W. T., N.C.	(6)		4 3 6 4	5 3 3	7 5		7	3 6 5 0	6 5 0 8
Dupré, L. J., La.	(6)		6 4		3 1				
Echols, J. H., Ga.	(3)		5 4	3 4 2	4 1 4	4 5 5 6 6	1 3	4 7 5 6	4 7 5 6 1 6 9
Elliott, J. M., Ky.	(6)	4	5 5 6 4	4 5 3	4 3 4			4 6 5 7	4 6 5 7
Ewing, G. W., Ky.	(7)	4	6 2 5		6 6 0				
Farrow, J., S.C.	(3)	6	1 0 3 4	0 1 2	0 0 0	5 2 3 1 0	0 4 2 5	3 3 0 5	3 3 0 5 4
Fearn, T., Ala.	(9)	4	0 1	0	0 0	1 1		4	0
Foote, H. S., Tenn.	(2)		4	0	0 0	0	2 5	5	
Ford, S. H., Ky.	(8)	4	0 2			4 4 1			
Forman, T. M., Ga.	(4)	6 0							
Foster, T. J., Ala.	(4)		2 4	3	3 1 2 6	6	4 3	3 3	2 2
Freeman, T. W., Mo.	(6)	4	4	3		1 0 5 5 3	4		
Fuller, T. C., N.C.	(1)		4 3	0 0 5	0 1 0 4 6 5		0	0 0 0 0 0	0 0 0 0 0 3 7 8
Funsten, D., Va.	(7)		3 4	5				5 3 7	
Gaither, B. S., N.C.	(3)		0 4 5 5	1 2 2	3 2 0 3 0 0	2 2 4 3 3	3 0 0 1 0 0	3 3 2 6 4	3 3 2 6 4
Gardenhire, E. L., Tenn.	(5)		1 6	3 0 1	2 0	4 3			6
Garland, A. H., Ark.	(3)	3	3 7						
Garland, R. K., Ark.	(2)		1 3	3 0 2	0 1	4 0 4 4	2 1 4 1	1 1 6 1	6 1
Garnett, M. R. H., Va.	(4)		3 2	4	4 7				
Gartrell, L. J., Ga.	(6)		3						
Gentry, M. P., Tenn.	(4)	0	3 4	5 3 0	5 7 5 0 1 0	4 4 1 4 0	1 4	6 1 2 6 7 0 0 1 0 0	6 1 2 6 7 0 0 1 0 0
Gholson, T. S., Va.	(6)	3							
Gilmer, J. A., N.C.	(1)	0	4 0						

*Adjustment procedure is described in Chapter 11.
a. Economic. b. Const. Conv. Race and State Rights.
c. Railroad Issues. d. Const. Conv. State Rights.
e. Property Destruction. f. Erlanger Loan. g. Procedural Issues.
h. Military‑Determination. (Cross‑Content Scales)
i. Defeatism‑Realism.

Confederate Congress Member and Average Adjusted Scale Position*	Subject Content Area / Congress Session	Prov. (a b c d) All Sess.	Conscription 1 2 3 4 2	Impress-ment (e) 1 2 2 1 3 1 2	Habeas Corpus 2 4 1 2 1 2	Economic (f) 1 2 1 3 1 2 2 2 1 2 2	Mili-tary (g) 1 2 4 1 2 1 1 2 1 2	State Rights 2 2 2 3	Race 1 1 2 2 1 2 2	h i 2 2 2 both
Goode, J., Jr., Va.	(5)*		1 3 / 4 5	4 1 / 0	3 / 4 5	6 2 / 3 4 4	1 4 / 1 5		5 2	7
Graham, M. D., Tex.	(5)		3 2 / 2 0	3 / 3		4 5 / 0	1 / 3 4			
Graham, W. A., N.C.	(2)						1 5			
Gray, H., La.	(8)		4 3 / 5	5 / 1 4		5 / 1	1 4		6 5	6 9
Gray, P. W., Tex.	(5)	5 5	4 3	1 4						
Gregg, J., Tex.	(6)	5 5 / 1	5			4				
Hale, S. F., Ala.	(7)	5 4 3	0 0 / 5 3	0 1 0 1	3 0 1	1 1 / 3 2 1	4 1 / 0 5		3 6	5 4
Hanly, T. B., Ark.	(3)	3	2 5	5 1 / 1 5	1	1 1				
Harris, T. A., Mo.	(5)									
Harris, W. P., Miss.	(6)	4 4 4 2	2 4	0 3	1	4 1 3	4 4	1 4	4 2 2	9
Harrison, J. T., Miss.	(5)	4 4 3 2	4		4 6 5		3 4		2 5 7	6
Hartridge, J., Ga.	(5)				3					8
Hatcher, R. A., Mo.	(7)		2 4 4 4 7	5 1 / 3	1 4	7 5	3 6 / 1	3 4 / 4 0	1 4	4 2 2 / 6
Haynes, L. C., Tenn.	(5)		4 5 / 6	1 1	4		3 4			
Heiskell, J. B., Tenn.	*(6)			3 / 1 5						6
Hemphill, J., Tex.	(9)	6	3 3 4 6 7	6 0 / 4	7 7 2	2 6 0	6 2 3	4 0	5 5	0 0
Henry, G. A., Tenn.	(7)		4 0 / 0	4 0	2 0 4	0	7 1	2 5	5 5	4 6
Herbert, C. C., Tex.	(2)							3 5		
Hill, B. H., Ga.	(5)	3 6 4 4	0 2 / 0 0	4 6 / 2	5 5 / 2	2 6 / 0 2	7 1 6	2 5	3 5	4 6
Hilton, R. B., Fla.	(5)		0 2 / 3 1	1 5	5 6 4 5	5 1	4 0			
Hodge, B. J., La.	(4)		2 2		2					
Hodge, G. B., Ky.	(4)	1	4 / 6	1	1	6	0 1 5	3 1	6 2	
Holcombe, J. P., Va.	(5)	1 5	5 / 2 0	3	1 5	6	2			
Holder, W. D., Miss.	(2)							5		
Holliday, F. W. M., Va.	(6)	5 3	3 3 / 2	4 7 5	6 2 4	4 4	4 1	5 2 4	6 7	
Holt, H., Ga.	(7)			2	5		7 5 5			
House, J. F., Tenn.	(0)	0				2	7 1			
Hunter, R. M. T., Va.	(5)	2 4	2 3 6 2 3	2 / 2	3 5 / 1	0	7 2 5	4 1		
Ingram, P., Ga.	(4)		3			2	2 4			
Jemison, R., Jr., Ala.	(4)		4							
Jenkins, A. G., Va.	(6)	2 4	5 / 0 1 1	3 / 1 2	1 0 / 1 5	5 0 3 / 0 3	7 2 5 / 2 4	4 1	1 1 / 4 1	
Johnson, H. V., Ga.	(3)		4 / 1 3				2			
Johnson, R. W., Ark.	(5)	2 4								

*
* Adjustment procedure is described in Chapter 11.
a. Economic. b. Const. Conv. Race and State Rights.
c. Railroad Issues. d. Const. Conv. State Rights.
e. Property Destruction. f. Erlanger Loan. g. Procedural Issues.
h. Military-Determination. (Cross-Content Scales)
i. Defeatism-Realism.

Confederate Congress Member and Average Adjusted Scale Position*	Subject Content Area / Congress Session	Prov. All Sess. (a b c d)	Conscription (1 2 3 4)	Impressment (1 2 3 e)	Habeas Corpus (1 2 4)	Economic (1 2 3)	Military (1 2 3 4 f)	State Rights (1 2 3 g)	Race (1 2 both h i)
Johnson, T., Ky.	(8)*	4	2 5 / 4 6	6 5 5 3	4 7 5	6 / 6 4	1 5 1 / 0 5	6 6 5	6 5 7 8
Johnson, W. P., Mo.	(6)								
Johnston, R., Va.	(7)	1 4	1 0 2	1 5	4 7	6	4	4	
Jones, G. W., Tenn.	(5)								
Jones, H. C., Ala.	(4)	4	4 0 3						
Jones, T. M., Tenn.	(4)								
Keeble, E. A., Tenn.	(7)	0 2 / 0 1	5 / 3 3	5 4 / 3	5 7 5	4 3	3 1	4 6 5 / 6 7	
Keitt, L. M., S.C.	(1)								
Kenan, A. H., Ga.	(3)								
Kenan, O. R., N.C.	(5)	3 4 3 2	3 2 5 / 3 1	2 4 4 / 5 0	4 7 0 0	3 6 / 6 2	4 4 / 4 5	4 0 / 6 7 1 0	
Kenner, D. F., La.	(7)								
Lamkin, J. T., Miss.	(1)								
Lander, W., N.C.	(6)		5 5 / 5 0 0 0	2 4 0 / 0	1 0 0 0 1 0	3 0 0 / 0 3	2 2	0 0 / 0 0 2 1 0	0 0 0 0
Leach, J. M., N.C.	(0)								
Leach, J. T., N.C.	(1)								
Lester, G. N., Ga.	(2)	3	0 / 5 6	2	1 0	3 / 2	4	3 1 / 4 0	
Lewis, D. P., Ala.	(7)								
Lewis, D. W., Ga.	(7)								
Lewis, J. W., Ga.	(3)		4 0 / 5 4 0 4 4	1 5 0 / 5 4 2	0 1 0 4 6 3	0 5 / 0 1 5 6	1 3 3 / 0 4 0	1 0 1 0 / 5 3	0 0 0 0 7 9
Logan, G. W., N.C.	(1)								
Lyon, F. S., Ala.	(6)								
Lyons, J., Va.	(6)	1	4 5 / 0 3 1 2	4 5 2 1	4 3 1	2 7 / 5 0 3	0 4 4 0	4	5 6 5
McCallum, J., Tenn.	(5)								
McDowell, T. D. S., N.C.	(4)								
Macfarland, W. H., Va.	(3)	1 3	5 2 / 1	2 0	3 6	2 1 / 4	3 4	4 0 / 3 2	
McLean, J. R., N.C.	(6)								
McMullin, F., Va.	(3)								
McQueen, J., S.C.	(3)	6 6 3 2	0 0 / 5 5 5	1 5 / 1 4	5 5 5 2 0 0	0 / 4 4	0 3 1 3		
McRae, C. J., Ala.	(6)								
McRae, J. J., Miss.	(5)								
Machen, W. B., Ky.	(6)	3 0 0	5 4 / 5 4 1 0 5	2 3 1 / 4 1	5 5 5 2 0 0	5 2 6 / 5 5 4 1 2 4	2 2 / 2 2	4 4 4 / 2 5 4	4 7 7 6 1
Marshall, H., La.	(3)								
Marshall, H., Ky.	(4)								

*Adjustment procedure is described in Chapter 11.
a. Economic. b. Const. Conv. Race and State Rights.
c. Railroad Issues. d. Const. Conv. State Rights.

e. Property Destruction. h. Military-Determination.
f. Erlanger Loan.   (Cross-Content Scales)
g. Procedural Issues.   i. Defeatism-Realism.

Confederate Congress Member and Average Adjusted Scale Position*	Subject Content Area (Congress Session)	Prov. All Sess. (a b c d)	Conscription	Impress-ment e	Habeas Corpus	Economic f	Mili-tary	State Rights g	Race	h i (both)
Martin, J. M., Fla.	(2)*	3	2	3 1	2 6	0 4	5 3 5	4 4	4 5 3	2 2
Mason, J. M., Va.	(5)		1 4						4 5 4	3 4 2 / 3 3 3
Maxwell, A. E., Fla.	(4)		1 1							7 8
Memminger, C. G., S.C.	(4)	7 1 3 0	2 2 / 2 4	4 3 1	5 2 2 6	3 1 6	2 5	2 5	4 5 3	6 7 / 6 6
Menees, T., Tenn.	(5)		2 3 / 0 2	4 2 1	4 1 0 0	6 0 4 3	3 1 2	2 5	6 0 3	
Miles, W. P., S.C.	(4)	5 1								
Miller, S. A., Va.	(7)		1 3	5	4 6 5	4 6	1 5	2 4	2 4	
Mitchel, C. B., Ark.	(5)	3	3 4						2 1	
Monroe, T. B., Ky.	(4)		5 4							7 8
Montague, R. L., Va.	(7)		4 5	5 3 1	4 6 5 6 4 0	2 4 4		4	4 5 4	6 6 / 6 6
Moore, J. W., Ky.	(5)	6	3 3							
Morehead, J. M., N.C.	(8)	4			4					6
Morgan, S. H., Tex.	(6)	6 0	3	2		3		2	5	
Morton, J., Fla.	(5)	3	2							1
Munnerlyn, C. J., Ga.	(4)								4 6	6 7
Murray, J. P., Tenn.	(4)	3 1	5		0 1	2 3				
Nisbet, E. A., Ga.	(5)	4	4		6					
Norton, N. L., Mo.	(6)						7	0 4		
Ochiltree, W. B., Sr., Tex.	(3)	0 2 4 0	0 0 1 4 4	1 5 1	0 0	1 6 1 0	2 5 3	0 4	4 4	1 1
Oldham, W. S., Tex.	(4)	4 1 2	0 0 1 0 0	1 4	0 1		3 1 2	2 1	4 5	1 1
Orr, J. L., S.C.	(2)		4						3 1	9
Orr, J. A., Miss.	(2)	1 0 1 0	0 0	2 5 2 0	1 1 3 6 5 7	5 3 0	0 5	4 2 3	3 4 9	
Owens, J. B., Fla.	(1)	0 1 0 1	6 2							
Perkins, J., Jr., La.	(4)					2 0	7	0 4		
Peyton, R. L. Y., Mo.	(5)	4	2 3 2 3 3 8	4 3	6			2 1 5 2	6 5 6 6	6 6
Phelan, J., Miss.	(6)	1	3 0							
Preston, W., Va.	(4)		3 4	4				1		
Preston, W. B., Va.	(4)	2	5 3	5 1 0 5	4 6 4 1	4 4 3	3 4	6 6 5	6 6	0 0 0 0
Pryor, R. A., Va.	(6)	2	4 4							
Pugh, J. L., Ala.	(6)	0 4	3 3	1 4 1 0 0	1 0 0	5 0 0	4 4	4 4	0 0	
Puryear, R. C., N.C.	(4)		2 0							
Ralls, J. P., Ala.	(5)									
Ramsay, J. G., N.C.	(0)									

*Adjustment procedure is described in Chapter 11.
a. Economic. b. Const. Conv. Race and State Rights.
c. Railroad Issues. d. Const. Conv. State Rights.
e. Property Destruction. f. Erlanger Loan. g. Procedural Issues. h. Military Determination. (Cross-Content Scales) i. Defeatism-Realism.

Confederate Congress Member and Average Adjusted Scale Position*	Subject Content Area (Congress Session)	Conscription (a b c d) Prov. / All Sess.	Impressment (e)	Habeas Corpus	Economic (f)	Military	State Rights (g)	Race (h i both)
Read, H. E., Ky.	(5)*	/ 3 3	5 3 1	4 6 5 1 / 0	2 6 4	2	2 0 / 4 5 2 6 3	7
Reade, E. G., N.C.	(1)	4 /						
Reagan, J. H., Tex.	(5)							6 7
Rhett, R. B., Sr., S.C.	(1)	1 1 0 / 1 1 0	5	6	6		4	
Rives, W. C., Va.	(6)	1 4 /						6 7
Robinson, C., Ala.	none							
Rogers, S. St. G., Fla.	(3)	1 / 5 3	1 2 / 2 3	5 1 6	2 / 6		2 2 5	5 2
Royston, G. D., Ark.	(5)							
Ruffin, T., N.C.	(2)	1 /						
Russell, C. W., Va.	(6)	0 4 / 1 4	5 5 2 3	4 6 5 7	4 4 4 / 0	0 5	4 3 3	3 6 8
Rust, A., Ark.	(8)	4 / 6 4						
Sanderson, J. P., Fla	(2)	3 /						
Scott, R. E., Va.	(3)	1 3 /					1 1	
Seddon, J. A., Va.	(5)	1 4 /						
Semmes, T. J., La.	(4)	/ 4 2 4 5 3	6 1	3	0 2	6 2 4	1 4	
Sexton, F. B., Tex.	(5)	/ 3 2	4 2 2 / 0	5 6 5 1 / 3	6 1 3 / 3	2	4 2 3 / 6 3	3 4 7 / 4
Shewmake, J. T., Ga.	(4)	2 1 / 2 2						
Shorter, J. G., Ala.	(2)	1 / 2 2						
Simms, W. E., Ky.	(6)	/ 2 8 7	0 4 / 2 1	7 7 2 0 / 4	6 4 4 4	2 / 3	5 2 5	2 6 4
Simpson, W. D., S.C.	(4)	/ 8 7 2			4 5 3			6
Singleton, O. R., Miss.	(6)	5 / 5 1						
Smith, J. M., Ga.	(3)	3 6 0 4 / 1	0 1	4 1 0	3 3	2	2 1 5 1 3	1 3
Smith, R. H., Ala.	(6)							
Smith, W., Va.	(5)	/ 4	1	5				
Smith, W. E., Ga.	(4)	0 / 1 0 0	0 0 2 0 / 3 5	5 1 0 0 / 0 1	3 3 / 1 0	4 0 / 3 1	2 0 0 / 0 3	5 6 4 / 0 0 3
Smith, W. N. H., N.C.	(2)	2 / 0 0						
Smith, W. R., Ala.	(3)							
Snead, T. L., Mo.	(5)	0 4 / 0 3 4	3 4 4 1	5 5 7 / 4 3 1 7	6 0 5 4 / 4 3	5 4 /	4 6 5 4 / 4 2	3 4 5 / 1 5
Sparrow, E., La.	(6)	1 / 7 7						
Staples, W. R., Va.	(4)	3 / 2 4						
Stephens, A. H., Ga.	(4)	3 3 1 3 / 0 0	5 0 4	5 6 4	4 1 1	4 0 / 2 0	1 2 5 3 8	
Strickland, H., Ga.	(4)							
Swan, W. G., Tenn.	(4)	/ 3 5						

*Adjustment procedure is described in Chapter 11.
a. Economic. b. Const. Conv. Race and State Rights.
c. Railroad Issues. d. Const. Conv. State Rights.
e. Property Destruction.   h. Military-Determination.
f. Erlanger Loan.   (Cross-Content Scales)
g. Procedural Issues.   i. Defeatism-Realism.

Confederate Congress Member and Average Adjusted Scale Position*	Subject Content Area (Congress Session)	a b c d Prov. All Sess.	Conscription	Impressment e	Habeas Corpus	Economic f	Military g	State Rights	Race	h	i	both
Thomas, J. H., Tenn.	(5)*	3 3										
Thomas, J. J., Ky.	(8)	4										
Thomason, H. F., Ark.	(4)	3										
Tibbs, W. H., Tenn.	(5)	6 5 0 4	4 3	1 / 1 5	3 5 5	1 / 4	4 2	4	4 6 3 7	8		
Toombs, R. A., Ga.	(6)		3									
Triplett, G. W., Ky.	(5)											
Trippe, R. P., Ga.	(4)	1 0 0	1 0 0	0 1 / 3 4	2 1 0	6 1 0 / 2 0	4 0	0	0 1 1 1	0		
Turner, J., N.C.	(1)											
Tyler, J., Va.	none											
Venable, A. W., N.C.	(3)	1 3 3	5 4	4 5 3 / 3 4	3 6 5 / 7 6 5	0 6 4 3 / 4 4 3	0 3 3	4 6	4 7 2 7	7 9		
Vest, G. G., Mo.	(6)											
Villeré, C. J., La.	(6)	3 3	5 4 6 6 / 4 3									
Walker, R. W., Ala.	(3)	2 6	0	0	1	2	0 2					
Ward, G. T., Fla.	(8)	4 3										
Watkins, W. W., Ark.	(4)	3 2										
Watson, J. W. C., Miss.	(2)	7 4 3 1	1	1 / 4	5 4 3 1 7	1 / 4	1 2	4	4	5		
Waul, T. N., Tex.	(5)		0 4	2			0 5					
Welsh, I., Miss.	(4)											
White, D. P., Ky.	(8)	4	0	0	4 6 0 2	1 1	6 1 1	0 1 1 1				
Whitfield, R. H., Va.	(5)			5 1 4 / 5	7 2 / 7 4	1 5 / 3	2 5	1	4 2 5 6	8		
Wickham, W. C., Va.	(1)											
Wigfall, L. T., Tex.	(5)	4 5 1 6 5	3	3 5 / 5			3 4 0					
Wilcox, J. A., Tex.	(5)	5 3	5									
Wilkes, P. S., Mo.	(7)											
Wilson, W. S., Miss.	(8)	6 3 / 1 2	1	1 2	3 1 0	2 0	2 2 3 6	5				
Withers, T. J., S.C.	(3)											
Witherspoon, J. H., S.C.	(3)											
Wright, A. R., Ga.	(4)	4 1 3 1 2	2 3	4 0 / 1 5	0 2	2 6 4 / 4 1	4 0 0 / 3 3	3				
Wright, J. V., Tenn.	(4)	4 2 2 3										
Wright, W. B., Tex.	(5)											
Yancey, W. L., Ala.	(4)	2 2 2	0	6			3					

*Adjustment procedure is described in Chapter 11.

a. Economic.   b. Const. Conv. Race and State Rights.   c. Railroad Issues.   d. Const. Conv. State Rights.

e. Property Destruction.   f. Erlanger Loan.   g. Procedural Issues.   h. Military-Determination. (Cross-Content Scales)   i. Defeatism-Realism.

APPENDIX IV

SESSION DATES AND MEMBERSHIP FIGURES FOR
THE CONFEDERATE CONGRESS

Provisional Congress
    First Session   Feb. 4, 1861   Mar. 16, 1861
    Second Session   Apr. 29, 1861   May 21, 1861
    Third Session   July 20, 1861   Aug. 31, 1861
    Fourth Session   Sep. 3, 1861   (One day only)
    Fifth Session   Nov. 18, 1861   Feb. 17, 1862

First Congress
    First Session   Feb. 18, 1862   Apr. 21, 1862
    Second Session   Aug. 18, 1862   Oct. 13, 1862
    Third Session   Jan. 12, 1863   May 1, 1863
    Fourth Session   Dec. 7, 1863   Feb. 17, 1864

Second Congress
    First Session   May   2, 1864   June 14, 1864
    Second Session   Nov. 7, 1864   Mar. 18, 1865

All sessions met in Richmond, Virginia, except the first
two sessions of the Provisional Congress, which met in
Montgomery, Alabama. The second session of the Provisional
Congress met two weeks early due to a call by President
Davis. The fourth session was also called.

Membership[a]

	House	Senate	Total
Provisional Congress	117 (116)	--	117 (116)
First Congress	115 (112)	31	146 (143)
Second Congress	111 (107)	27	136 (132)

a. Two congressmen served in both House and Senate of
the Second Congress. Figures in parentheses exclude tribal
and territorial delegates.

APPENDIX V

MEASURES OF STRENGTH OF ASSOCIATION FOR CONTINGENCY TABLES

Contingency coefficients have not been placed on individual tables because the measurements of strength of association that are conveniently available do not summarize very well the relation between ordered categories and such dichotomous classifications as Secessionist or Unionist. Moreover, the small cell entries require a collapsing of categories for calculation, which thereby obscures some significant distinctions. The screening of contingency tables that was employed involved a very low threshold of acceptability so as to call our attention to any associations justifying scrutiny. This appendix offers the association-strength values of those contingency tables that we have placed with the text.

A cross-tabulation with ten performance-score levels and five wealth categories contains fifty cells. Since the Confederate House rarely had a hundred members voting at one time, each of these cells would ordinarily contain very few members and many cells would be empty. The chi-square test, from which C is calculated, requires that no marginals be zero and that no more than a small proportion of the cells have less than five observations (in our case, members falling in that cell of the cross-tabulation). The procedures that we have followed to obtain usable cells for the contingency coefficient calculations are as follows:

(a). All performance scores have been combined (0+1, 2+3, 4+5, 6+7, and 8+9) so as to produce five cells to the column.

(b). Scale positions that range over more positions than five have been combined sufficiently to collapse the number of cells in each column to five, following two guidelines-- first to eliminate empty cells or cells with only one or two observations, and then to combine in the middle range of scale positions so as to leave the more significant extreme positions intact as far as possible. No scales employed have less than five positions, and all others have been collapsed to five for C calculations.

(c). The number of cells in each row has uniformly been kept to two. In instances of former party affiliation, position on secession, and occupied status of the member's home district, only two categories exist. In the cross-tabulations employing wealth or slaveholding categories, five subdivisions of the membership or districts have been combined to make only two for C calculations. The nearest to an equal number of observations in each combined category was the objective. This was accomplished, for example, by combining the lowest three as opposed to the combined highest two categories for absolute wealth, relative wealth, and absolute slaveholding, while for relative slaveholding the highest category was balanced against the other four combined.

In a few instances, the number of members voting was so small, or the concentration of members in a few cells was so decided, that compression into a ten-cell table for calculation was not enough to eliminate empty or too-slightly-peopled cells. In these cases, the mean square contingency coefficient Phi was used.

The Contingency Coefficient is not an all encompassing summary of strength of association in our cross-tabulations, in any case, because the scores and positions are ordered categories, whereas C is applicable to nominal categories. The value of C will be the same for a differential arising from observed values in the cell next to the one in which the values would be expected, as for observed values falling at the greatest possible distance from the expected. Hence, we analyzed frequency distributions for all cross-tabulations with a value of C at .20 or higher.

CONTINGENCY COEFFICIENTS[a]

Table Number	C Value	Table Number	C Value	Table Number	C Value	Table Number	C Value
4-1A	.42	4-6F	[b]	5-3A	.25	6-1A	.29
4-1B	.24	5-1A	.15	5-3B	.16	6-1B	.27
4-1C	.27	5-1B	.18		.38		.27
4-3A	.28	5-1C	.33		.30	6-1C	.59
4-3B	.38		.51		.45		.34
4-3C	.26[b]		.17		.37		.34
		5-2A	.26		.36	6-2A	.44
4-4A	.32	5-2B	.17	5-5A	.39		.35
4-4B	.43		.26	5-5B	.13	6-2B	.36
4-5	.39		.31	5-5C	.33		.39
4-6A	.38		.38		.36		.52
4-6B	.42	5-2C	.40	5-5D	.39	6-2C	.30
4-6C	.49		.54	5-5E	.23		.52
4-6D	.56[b]	5-2D	.38	5-5F	.26		
			.39		.31		

a. Tables with more than one C value have more than one panel, and the values apply to the panels from left to right.

b. Too many empty or low entry cells for C.

CONTINGENCY COEFFICIENTS[a]

Table Number	C Value	Table Number	C Value	Table Number	C Value	Table Number	C Value
6-2D	.46	7-5D	.49	9-1A	.32	10-5	.27
	.55	7-5E	.27	9-1B	.33		.36
	.32	7-5F	.29		.39	10-6	.40
6-3A	.24		.42	9-1C	.34	10-8	.35
6-3B	.26	8-2A	.22	9-1D	.56		.44
6-3C	.36	8-2B	.25	9-1E	.57	10-9	.51
	.46	8-2C	.46	9-1F	.42		.52
6-5A	.33		.39		.62	10-10	.23
6-5B	.33		.57	9-1G	.46		.19
6-5C	.34	8-2D	.34		.58	10-11	.32
7-1A	.29		.37	9-1H	.43	11-3A	.07
	.34		.51		.49		.21
7-1B	.34	8-2E	.27	9-1I	.26		.47
	.55		.38		.33	11-3B	.12
7-1C	.34	8-3A	.34	9-1J	.45		.26
	.36		.38		.53		.63
7-1D	.38		.51	9-2A	.38	11-4A	.20
	.47	8-3B	.41		.51		.23
7-1E	.37		.43	9-2B	.39		.53[b]
	.44		.54		.53	11-4B	
7-2A	.35	8-3C	.38	9-3A	.19		.31
	.60		.55	9-3B	.29		.48
7-2B	.36	8-4A	.28	9-3C	.31	11-5A	.23
	.44	8-4B	.30	9-3D	.34		.22
7-2C	.51	8-5A	.24	9-3E	.38		.29
	.50	8-5B	.32	9-3F	.37	11-5B	.49
7-2D	.49	8-6A	.32	9-3G	.39		.20
	.49	8-6B	.25	9-3H	.43		.52
7-2E	.50	8-6C	.27		.47	11-6	.33
	.56	8-6D	.32	10-2	.26		.38
7-5A	.58	8-6E	.32		.35		.66
7-5B	.33	8-6F	.26	10-3	.32	11-7	.54
7-5C	.26	8-6G	.24		.34		
	.40	8-6H	.28				

a. Tables with more than one C value have more than one panel, and the values apply to the panels from left to right.
b. Too many empty or low entry cells for C.

APPENDIX VI

SUMMARY IDENTIFICATION OF ROLL CALLS INCORPORATED IN PERFORMANCE-SCORE AND CUMULATIVE-SCALE SETS

Each roll call used in either a performance or a scale set is listed in the following tables, one table for each set. The first column lists Journal location; the second column shows the percent voting the "strong," or "pro-Confederate," side of an issue, followed by Y or N to signify polarity-- that is, whether "Yea" or "Nay" is assigned as the "strong" position. Asterisks indicate votes used in scale sets, and broken lines denote cutting points for the assignment of the scale positions shown in the last column.

We have examined all of the roll calls of the Confederate Congress and have made the great majority machine readable for our analyses, as described in the Research Design. All data are to be deposited in the Historical Archive of the Inter-University Consortium for Political Research, Ann Arbor, Michigan. The remainder of the roll-call record is being prepared by the authors in order to round out the set for the Consortium.

PROVISIONAL CONGRESS ROLL-CALL SETS

Economic

Journal Page No.	% on Strong Side	Scale Position
Vol. I		
342	73% N	—*— 0
336	64% N	—*— 1
344-345	64% Y	
92	63% Y	
335 bottom	60% N	*
335 top	59% N	*
573	59% N	
478	55% Y	—*— 2
91	53% Y	
227	50% N	
329	42% N	
338-339	39% Y	—*— 3
242	37% N	
418-419	33% Y	—*— 4
220-221	33% Y	—*— 5
332	24% Y	—*— 6
346-347	17% Y	—*— 7

State Rights[a]

Journal Page No.	% on Strong Side	Scale Position
Vol. I		
767 top	81% Y	—*— 0
812-813	76% Y	
137 bottom	71% N	
141	68% Y	
137 top	67% N	
684 bottom	67% Y	—*— 1
821-822	66% N	
766	66% N	*
770	64% Y	—*— 2
98	62% N	
412 top	61% N	
763-764	61% Y	*
734	57% Y	*
493	54% Y	
195-196	53% N	
383	52% N	
733 bottom	44% Y	—*— 3
819	44% Y	*
222 top	39% Y	—*— 4
554-555	11% Y	

Sequestration

Journal Page No.	% on Strong Side	Scale Position
Vol. I		
786 bottom	82% N	
796-797	76% N	
806	74% Y	
747-748	67% N	
787	67% N	
393-394	65% N	
387 bottom	64% Y	
386-387	56% Y	
388-389	53% Y	
666	46% N	
790-791	46% Y	
421	43% Y	
418-419	30% Y	
397-398	29% Y	
385-386	25% Y	

Military

Journal Page No.	% on Strong Side	Scale Position
Vol. I		
391	85% N	
106	84% Y	
552-553	83% N	
555-556	81% Y	
674 bottom	77% Y	
534-535	76% Y	
655-656	73% Y	
808-809	72% Y	
668	70% Y	
673 top	70% Y	
675	64% Y	
746-747	64% Y	
669	59% Y	
645-646	57% Y	
563	56% Y	
639	50% N	
645 top	43% Y	
415	38% Y	
830-831	37% N	
820-821	33% N	
825	33% N	

a. Scale is entitled State Rights Railroad Issues.

* Roll calls used in Scale Sets as well as in Performance Sets.

PROVISIONAL CONGRESS ROLL-CALL SETS--Continued

Diverse Issues

Journal Page No.	% on Strong Side	Scale Position
Vol. I		
588-589	88% Y	
412-413	83% Y	
809 bottom	71% N	
308	66% N	
78	50% N	
254	38% Y	
445-446	9% N	

PROVISIONAL CONGRESS-AS-CONSTITUTIONAL-CONVENTION ROLL-CALL SETS

All Issues

Journal Page No.	% on Strong Side	Scale Position
Vol. I		
861	88% N	
890-891	73% N	
883	68% Y	
872-873	67% Y	
884	62% Y	
894	60% Y	
893 bottom	59% N	
893 top	58% Y	
885 middle	56% Y	
885-886	56% N	
880-881	48% N	
885 top	48% N	
881 bottom	45% Y	
880 top[a]	40% N	
868-869	39% N	
873	38% N	
871	36% Y	
892	30% N	
878	24% N	

Slavery and State Rights[a]

Journal Page No.	% on Strong Side	Scale Position
Vol. I		
861	88% N	----*---- 0
884	62% Y	---*---- 1
885 middle	56% Y	---*--- 2
885-886	56% N	---*--- 3
885 top	48% N	--*---- 4
871	36% Y	---*--- 5
878	24% N	---*--- 6

State Rights[a]

Journal Page No.	% on Strong Side	Scale Position
Vol. I		
890-891	73% N	---*--- 0
893 bottom	59% N	---*-- 1
893 top	58% Y	---*--
880-881	48% N	--*--- 2
881 bottom	45% Y	---*--- 3
878	24% N	---*--- 4

a. South Carolina members (eight) are recorded as voting Nay, but the state is listed as Yea. The latter is certainly the correct posture for the South Carolinians and is so treated here.

a. Scale Sets only.
*Roll calls used in Scale Sets.

CONSCRIPTION ROLL-CALL SETS

Senate

Journal Page No.	% on Strong Side	Scale Position
(1 Cong., 1 Sess.)		
Vol. II		
147 top	79% N	----*--- 0
154 bottom	79% Y	----*---- 1
154 top	71% N	
153	68% Y	---*---- 2
204	56% Y	
140	48% Y	---*--- 3
141	29% N	--*---
203 bottom	29% Y	---*--- 4

House

Journal Page No.	% On Strong Side	Scale Position
(1 Cong., 1 Sess.)		
Vol. V		
221	82% N	----*--- 0
259	80% N	---*--- 1
228 top	67% Y	
228 bottom	67% Y	*
250 bottom	65% Y	
292	63% Y	---*--- 2
226 top	58% N	
286	56% N	*
283	55% N	
226 bottom	54% Y	
91	53% Y	---*--- 3
224	48% N	
280 bottom	44% N	---*-- 4
225	41% Y	--- 5

*Roll calls used in Scale Sets as well as in Performance Sets.

CONSCRIPTION ROLL-CALL SETS--Continued

Senate (1 Cong., 2 Sess.) Vol. II

Journal Page No.	% on Strong Side	Scale Position
321 bottom	88% Y	* 0
321 top	79% Y	* 1
242	77% N	*
287 top	68% N	
261	64% N	
241 top	61% N	
285 top	61% N	
285 bottom	61% Y	* 2
295 bottom	57% N	*
310	57% N	
296 bottom	55% N	
310 top	53% N	
255	43% Y	* 3
311	42% N	
290	40% N	
296 middle	40% Y	
295 top	36% Y	
241 bottom	23% N	
287 bottom	23% Y	* 4
292	19% Y	* 5
286	15% N	

House (1 Cong., 2 Sess.) Vol. V

Journal Page No.	% on Strong Side	Scale Position
525 bottom	82% Y	* 0
501	77% Y	*
396 top	76% N	*
474	74% N	*
366 top	71% N	* 1
475	65% N	*
397	64% N	*
438 top	64% Y	*
443 top	62% N	* 2
354	62% Y	*
326 bottom	60% N	*
476 bottom	60% Y	*
389	59% Y	* 3
445 top	58% Y	*
452 top	57% Y	*
490	57% Y	*
400	56% Y	*
387	53% N	*
461 bottom	52% N	* 4
396 middle	51% Y	*
382 top	50% Y	*
461 top	48% Y	*
452 bottom	47% Y	*
436	42% Y	
438 bottom	42% N	*
327	41% N	*
451	41% N	*
326 top	38% N	*
399	37% Y	*
399 bottom	34% Y	*
476 top	34% Y	*
460	33% Y	*
443 bottom	31% Y	* 5
441	29% N	*
395	26% Y	

CONSCRIPTION ROLL-CALL SETS--Continued

Senate (1 Cong., 3 Sess.) Vol. III

Journal Page No.	% on Strong Side	Scale Position
100	83% Y	* 0
307	82% N	
75 top	78% N	* 1
305	72% Y	*
93	71% N	
98 top	61% N	* 2
304	61% Y	
98 middle	57% Y	* 3
301 top	50% Y	
75 middle	48% Y	*
88 bottom	45% N	* 4
75 bottom	43% Y	
299	43% Y	
300	43% Y	*
92	39% N	
97	39% Y	* 5a
340	35% Y	* 6
73	27% Y	
87 top	23% Y	* 7
87 bottom	23% N	*
88 top	14% Y	* 8

House (1 Cong., 3 Sess.) Vol. VI

Journal Page No.	% on Strong Side	Scale Position
94 bottom	82% N	
136 bottom	66% N	
93	65% Y	
273	58% Y	
98	56% Y	
373 bottom	55% Y	
284	54% Y	
43	53% N	
92 bottom	53% Y	
253	53% N	
438	53% Y	
94 top	49% N	
41	47% N	
285 bottom	45% Y	
79	40% N	
145 top	38% N	
443 top	38% N	

a. The roll call on page 340 was removed from the scale set, but scale position 5 was overlooked. No senator is at the 5 level in this scale, therefore.

*Roll calls used in Scale Sets as well as in Performance Sets.

*Roll calls used in Scale Sets as well as in Performance Sets.

CONSCRIPTION ROLL-CALL SETS--Continued

House (1 Cong., 4 Sess.)

Journal Page No.	% on Strong Side	Scale Position
Vol. VI		
561	80% Y	---*--- 0
705 top	76% Y	*
861 top	75% Y	---*--- 1
560 bottom	71% Y	*
707 bottom	71% Y	
684	62% N	*
686	60% N	---*--- 2
796 top	59% N	*
756	57% Y	
846	56% Y	---*--- 3
714 top	51% N	
585	50% Y	
742	48% N	
713	45% Y	
533	43% Y	---*--- 4
746	41% N	
717 top	41% N	*
734 top	38% Y	
687	34% Y	
560 top	30% Y	---*--- 5
770 top	26% Y	*
697	24% Y	*
770 bottom	22% N	---*--- 6

Senate (1 Cong., 4 Sess.)

Journal Page No.	% on Strong Side	Scale Position
Vol. III		
499	89% Y	---*--- 0
558	82% Y	*
518 top	79% Y	---*--- 1
498 bottom	75% N	*
582 bottom	75% Y	
573 middle	70% N	---*--- 2
568 middle	68% Y	*
568 bottom	68% N	*
556	67% Y	
572	65% Y	
768 top	57% Y	---*--- 3
498 top	57% N	
555	50% N	
719	50% Y	
547 top	45% Y	---*--- 4
554 top	45% N	*
554 bottom	45% N	*
559 top	44% Y	
568 top	42% N	---*--- 5
679	36% N	*
546	35% N	
581	32% N	
582 top	32% N	---*--- 6
573 top	29% Y	*
559 bottom	27% Y	
573 bottom	21% N	---*--- 7
518 bottom	20% Y	---*--- 8
547 bottom	15% Y	---*--- 9

CONSCRIPTION ROLL-CALL SETS--Continued

House

Journal Page No.	% on Strong Side	Scale Position
(2 Cong., 2 Sess., Nov. - Feb.)		
Vol. VII		
475	80% Y	---*--- 0
474 bottom	78% N	*
473	73% N	
485	70% N	---*--- 1
478 top	69% Y	
474 top	65% N	*
487 bottom	64% Y	---*--- 2
448	62% N	
366 bottom	58% Y	
486 bottom	57% N	---*--- 3
366 top	56% N	
452	53% Y	
479	53% N	*
478 bottom	51% Y	---*--- 4
480	48% N	*
486 top	41% Y	
448 top	39% Y	---*--- 5
(2 Cong., 2 Sess., Feb. - Mar.)		
Vol. VII		
787	61% Y	
788 top	60% N	
776	52% N	
788 bottom	47% N	
759	38% Y	
665	27% N	
761	19% N	

Senate (2 Cong., 2 Sess.)

Journal Page No.	% on Strong Side	Scale Position
Vol. IV		
562 middle	81% N	---*--- 0
557	74% Y	---*--- 1
556	68% N	---*--- 2
563 top	62% N	---*--- 3
562 bottom	60% Y	*
561 top	59% N	*
562 top	59% N	---*--- 4
563 bottom	55% N	---*--- 5
720 top	53% N	
720 bottom	50% Y	---*--- 6
544	40% N	
591	38% Y	---*--- 7

PROPERTY DESTRUCTION ROLL-CALL SETS

House (1 Cong., 1 Sess.)

Journal Page No.	% on Strong Side	Scale Position
Vol. V		
63 top	87% Y	---*--- 0
69	87% N	*
62	84% Y	---*--- 1
63 bottom	56% N	*
60	54% Y	*
59 bottom	41% N	---*--- 2
64	24% N	*
59 top	23% Y	---*--- 3
70	15% N	---*--- 4

*Roll calls used in Scale Sets as well as in Performance Sets.

*Roll calls used in Scale Sets as well as in Performance Sets.

IMPRESSMENT ROLL-CALL SETS

House

Journal Page No.	% On Strong Side	Scale Position
(1 Cong., 3 Sess.)		
Vol. VI		
107	88% Y	0
314 bottom	64% N	
419 bottom	52% N	
312	46% Y	
170 bottom	45% N	1
179 top	45% N	
314 middle	42% Y	2
(2 Cong., 1 Sess.)		
Vol. VII		
182	72% N	0
234	69% Y	1
232 top	63% Y	
231 bottom	62% Y	2
236 top	54% Y	
216	52% N	
224 bottom	49% N	3
236 bottom	48% N	
224 top	46% Y	
167 top	43% N	4
235	39% N	5
(2 Cong., 2 Sess.)		
Vol. VII		
766	80% Y	0
767 bottom	76% Y	1
765	67% N	
794 top	67% Y	
794 bottom	67% Y	
795	67% Y	
707	62% Y	
708	61% Y	
794 middle	58% Y	2
767 top	47% N	
728	44% Y	3
747 bottom	39% N	4
747 top	28% N	5

Senate

Journal Page No.	% On Strong Side	Scale Position
(1 Cong., 3 Sess.)		
Vol. III		
131	88% Y	0
327	86% Y	
355	65% Y	
133 bottom	61% N	
132 bottom	58% Y	1
128	55% Y	
143 bottom	54% Y	
132 top	50% N	
144	50% Y	2
133 middle	43% N	
143 top	40% Y	3
133 top	39% N	4
232 top	23% N	
194 top	19% N	5
148 bottom	10% N	6
(2 Cong., 1 Sess.)		
Vol. IV		
219	75% N	0
133 bottom	47% Y	1
132	43% Y	
133 top	41% N	
150	33% N	2
(2 Cong., 2 Sess.)		
Vol. IV		
444	84% Y	0
610 bottom	82% Y	
602 bottom	65% Y	
696	65% Y	1
509	63% Y	
669	53% Y	2
688 top	50% N	
602 top	44% Y	
286	39% N	3
610 top	39% Y	
597	33% N	4
447	21% N	5
		6

*Roll calls used in Scale Sets as well as in Performance Sets.

HABEAS CORPUS ROLL-CALL SETS

House

Journal Page No.	% on Strong Side	Scale Position
(1 Cong., 2 Sess.)		
Vol. V		
516 bottom	76% N	0
505	70% N	1
518	57% Y	2
517 bottom	55% N	
559 bottom	49% Y	3
517 top	45% N	4
559 middle	30% N	5
(1 Cong., 3 Sess.)		
Vol. VI		
339	65% Y	0
155 top	59% Y	1
352	37% N	2
319 top	32% Y	
(2 Cong., 1 Sess.)		
Vol. VII		
171	81% N	0
172	71% Y	1
80	69% Y	2
170 bottom	67% N	3
65	53% N	4
59	44% N	5
192	42% N	
54	26% N	

Senate

Journal Page No.	% on Strong Side	Scale Position
(1 Cong., 4 Sess.)		
Vol. III		
703	85% N	0
693 top	64% N	1
711 top	60% N	2
710 bottom	58% N	
712 bottom	58% Y	3
709 third	52% Y	
709 bottom	52% N	
710 top	52% N	
711 bottom	52% N	
702 top	50% N	
702 bottom	50% N	
709 top	48% N	
709 second	48% N	4
692	38% Y	5
693 bottom	33% N	6
712 top	28% Y	
674	26% Y	7
(2 Cong., 2 Sess.)		
Vol. IV		
386	84% N	0
384 top	75% N	1
381	74% Y	
307	71% N	2
382 middle	71% N	
387 bottom	70% Y	
384 bottom	60% N	3
723 top	53% Y	4
387 top	45% Y	5
382 bottom	44% N	
723 middle	44% Y	
721	40% Y	
723 bottom	38% Y	6
382 top	35% N	
323	21% N	7

*Roll calls used in Scale Sets as well as in Performance Sets.

HABEAS CORPUS ROLL-CALL SETS--Continued

House

(2 Cong., 2 Sess., Nov. - Feb.)

Journal Page No.	% on Strong Side	Scale Position
Vol. VII		
335 bottom	72% N	---*--- 0
323 bottom	67% N	---*--- 1
375	66% Y	*
337 top	54% Y	*
337 bottom	64% Y	*
329	62% Y	*
468	62% N	---*--- 2
348 top	60% Y	*
336 top	58% N	*
348 bottom	58% N	*
339	57% Y	*
379 bottom	57% N	*
323 top	56% N	*
342 top	56% N	*
347 bottom	55% N	*
349	55% N	---*--- 3
342 bottom	53% Y	*
347 top	53% Y	*
350	53% Y	*
580	53% N	*
331	52% N	*
332	52% Y	*
343 top	52% N	---*--- 4
343 bottom	51% N	*
335 top	51% Y	*
333	47% N	*
344 bottom	46% Y	---*--- 5
330	46% Y	*
334	40% Y	*
334	38% N	
336 bottom	35% N	---*--- 6
379 top	26% Y	---*--- 7

*Roll calls used in Scale Sets as well as in Performance Sets.

House

(2 Cong., 2 Sess., Feb. - Mar.)

Journal Page No.	% on Strong Side	Scale Position
Vol. VII		
647 bottom	70% N	---*--- 0
770	63% Y	---*--- 1
763 top	62% Y	*
672 top	56% Y	*
762 top	56% N	---*--- 2
673 bottom	55% Y	*
763 middle	55% Y	*
771 bottom	54% N	*
771 top	53% N	---*--- 3
771 middle	52% Y	*
672 middle	51% N	*
762 middle	51% N	*
763 bottom	51% N	*
764 top	50% N	---*--- 4
673 top	43% N	---*--- 5

*Roll calls used in Scale Sets as well as in Performance Sets.

ECONOMIC ROLL-CALL SETS

House

(1 Cong., 1 Sess.)

Journal Page No.	% on Strong Side	Scale Position
Vol. V		
171	81% Y	
237 bottom	79% Y	
237 top	67% Y	
257	66% Y	
167 top	53% Y	
258	49% N	

(1 Cong., 3 Sess.)

Journal Page No.	% on Strong Side	Scale Position
Vol. VI		
418	92% Y	
197	77% N	
467	76% N	
411	71% Y	
194 top	70% N	
199 bottom	64% N	
473 bottom	64% N	
234	63% Y	
180 top	62% Y	
241	59% Y	
242 bottom	57% Y	
255 bottom	55% N	
192 top	54% Y	
194 bottom	53% N	
242 top	53% N	
174 bottom	51% Y	
180 bottom	50% Y	
409 bottom	50% Y	
409 top	48% N	
138 top	45% N	
192 bottom	38% Y	
195 bottom	38% N	
213	33% N	
87	29% Y	
240	27% N	

House

(1 Cong., 1 Sess., Cong. Pay)[a]

Journal Page No.	% on Strong Side	Scale Position
Vol. V		
151	77% N	---*--- 0
121	61% N	---*--- 1
101 top	52% Y	---*--- 2
102	51% Y	*
110	46% Y	---*--- 3
99 bottom	40% Y	---*--- 4
128 bottom	32% N	---*--- 5
138	26% Y	---*--- 6
		7

(1 Cong., 3 Sess., Erlanger Loan)[a]

Journal Page No.	% on Strong Side	Scale Position
Vol. VI		
35	88% Y	---*--- 0
55	76% Y	---*--- 1
34 bottom	67% N	---*--- 2
54 bottom	64% N	*
136 top	61% N	---*--- 3
		4

Senate

(1 Cong., 3 Sess.)

Journal Page No.	% on Strong Side	Scale Position
Vol. III		
261 top	54% Y	---*--- 0
318	53% N	*
261 bottom	52% Y	*
253 top	50% Y	*
253 bottom	50% Y	*
266 bottom	42% Y	---*--- 1
339	41% Y	*
266 top	38% Y	*
265 top	36% Y	---*--- 2
29	33% Y	*
254	33% Y	*
265 bottom	32% Y	*
322	30% Y	*
260	25% Y	---*--- 3
270 bottom	19% Y	---*--- 4
269	13% Y	---*--- 5
28	6% Y	---*--- 6

a. Scale Sets only.

*Roll calls used in Scale Sets as well as in Performance Sets.

ECONOMIC ROLL-CALL SETS--Continued

House

(1 Cong., 4 Sess.)

Journal Page No.	% on Strong Side	Scale Position
Vol. VI		
844	77% N	
581	65% Y	
674	65% Y	
843	65% Y	
644 bottom	54% Y	
636 top	45% Y	
632	44% Y	

(2 Cong., 1 Sess.)

Journal Page No.	% on Strong Side	Scale Position
Vol VII		
22 bottom	89% Y	* 0
152	76% N	* 1
217	65% Y	* 2
142	62% N	
189 bottom	60% N	
147	55% Y	
186	54% N	* 3
160	51% Y	*
201 bottom	51% Y	
205 bottom	51% Y	*
168 top	49% N	
167 bottom	47% Y	
202 top	47% N	* 4
190 top	46% N	*
168 bottom	45% Y	
220 top	45% N	
169 top	41% Y	
201 top	39% N	* 5
219	33% N	* 6

Senate

(1 Cong., 4 Sess.)

Journal Page No.	% on Strong Side	Scale Position
Vol. III		
651	84% N	
586	79% N	
764	79% Y	
762	67% Y	
636	65% Y	
653	56% Y	
723	55% Y	
656 bottom	48% Y	
765	41% Y	
650	40% N	
735 bottom	33% N	
683	24% N	
738 top	24% Y	
738 bottom	16% Y	

(2 Cong., 1 Sess.)

Journal Page No.	% on Strong Side	Scale Position
Vol. IV		
195 top	81% N	* 0
229	73% Y	
195 middle	70% Y	* 1
195 bottom	70% Y	*
75	59% Y	
188	57% Y	* 2
152	52% Y	* 3
158	52% N	
191	52% Y	*
187 bottom	50% Y	* 4
192 top	48% N	*
47	47% N	
187 top	44% N	*
190	43% Y	*
192 middle	43% Y	*
192 bottom	41% N	* 5
139	32% N	6

*Roll calls used in Scale Sets as well as in Performance Sets.

ECONOMIC ROLL-CALL SETS--Continued

House

(2 Cong., 2 Sess., Nov. - Feb.)

Journal Page No.	% on Strong Side	Scale Position
Vol. VII		
382 bottom	79% Y	
461 top	62% N	
461 bottom	58% N	
492 bottom	55% N	
404	52% N	
578	52% N	
574 bottom	42% N	
608	42% Y	

(2 Cong., 2 Sess., Feb. - Mar.)

Journal Page No.	% on Strong Side	Scale Position
Vol. VII		
624 bottom	70% N	* 0
629 bottom	68% N	*
629 top	67% N	*
620 top	65% N	*
642	59% Y	*
620 bottom	58% N	* 1
686	57% N	
617 top	56% Y	
623 top	54% Y	*
622 bottom	50% Y	* 2
623 bottom	48% N	*
641	46% N	
617 bottom	43% N	
755	43% N	* 3
645	42% N	
696	42% Y	
622 top	38% N	*
687	28% N	* 4
626	27% N	
695 top	23% Y	*
695 bottom	20% Y	* 5
631	17% N	* 6

Senate

(2 Cong., 2 Sess.)

Journal Page No.	% on Strong Side	Scale Position
Vol. IV		
647 bottom	64% Y	
640	56% Y	
646	56% N	
647 top	47% N	
638	36% N	
663	20% N	

*Roll calls used in Scale Sets as well as in Performance Sets.

MILITARY ROLL-CALL SETS

Senate

Journal Page No.	% on Strong Side	Scale Position
(1 Cong., 2 Sess.)		
Vol. II		
375	81% Y	0
488	74% Y	* 1
298	72% Y	
470	72% Y	* 2
444 bottom	71% N	
429 bottom	70% N	* 3
450	68% Y	
371	59% N	* 4
429 top	53% N	
370 bottom	45% N	
483	44% N	* 5
448	39% N	
280	38% N	*
415	35% Y	
471 top	28% Y	
437	25% N	
(1 Cong., 3 Sess.)		
Vol. III		
379	78% Y	0
301 bottom	75% N	* 1
360	75% N	
238	64% N	* 2
165 bottom	57% Y	
311	57% N	* 3
337	57% N	
314	50% Y	
380	47% N	* 4
51	44% N	* 5
373 top	28% Y	
(2 Cong., 1 Sess.)		
Vol. IV		
64	78% Y	0
212 top	74% N	* 1
94	53% Y	* 2
181	48% N	
212 bottom	44% Y	* 3
220	41% Y	
101 top	39% N	* 4
211 top	37% N	* 5
78 bottom	24% N	

* Roll calls used in Scale Sets as well as in Performance Sets.

Senate (continued)

Journal Page No.	% on Strong Side	Scale Position
(1 Cong., 4 Sess.)		
Vol. III		
699	89% Y	0
750	73% N	* 1
707	65% N	
716	65% Y	* 2
779	65% Y	
674 bottom	57% Y	* 3
808	57% Y	
674 middle	52% Y	* 4
701	50% Y	
749 top	50% N	
781	47% Y	* 5
544	44% Y	
549	44% N	
621 top	41% Y	* 6
621 middle	41% N	
621 bottom	29% N	
622	29% N	*
749 bottom	25% N	* 7
667 top	24% Y	
(2 Cong., 2 Sess.)		
Vol. IV		
482	81% Y	0
457 top	73% Y	* 1
552	71% N	
512	63% N	* 2
636 bottom	53% Y	
553	50% N	* 3
710 bottom	47% N	
456	45% Y	
641	44% N	*
652	44% N	* 4
458 top	41% N	
330	37% N	
687	31% N	
458 bottom	24% N	* 5
502	24% N	
407	23% Y	* 6

* Roll calls used in Scale Sets
as well as in Performance Sets.

PROCEDURAL ROLL-CALL SETS

House

Journal Page No.	% on Strong Side	Scale Position
(1 Cong., 1 Sess.)[a]		
Vol. V		
218 bottom	75% Y	0
218 top	68% Y	* 1
230 bottom	53% Y	* 2
230 top	51% Y	
115	49% Y	*
230 middle	49% N	* 3
264	37% N	* 4
(1 Cong., 2 Sess.)		
Vol. V		
447	82% Y	0
323 bottom	79% Y	
492 bottom	79% Y	* 1
558	75% Y	*
559 top	72% Y	
492 top	66% N	* 2
408 top	51% Y	
435	49% N	* 3
387 top	47% N	* 4
411 top	27% N	* 5
(2 Cong., 2 Sess., Nov. - Feb.)		
Vol. VII		
613 top	74% N	
613 bottom	69% N	
372	57% N	
561 top	53% Y	
498	46% N	
553 bottom	44% N	
390	43% N	
560	39% N	
561 bottom	38% N	
555	35% N	

a. Scale Set only.

Senate

Journal Page No.	% on Strong Side	Scale Position
(1 Cong., 2 Sess.)		
Vol. II		
472 bottom	62% N	
418	57% N	
269 top	48% N	
458	44% Y	
269 bottom	43% N	

House

Journal Page No.	% on Strong Side	Scale Position
(2 Cong., 2 Sess., Feb. - Mar.)		
Vol. VII		
756 bottom	70% Y	
756 middle	69% N	
726 bottom	58% N	
726 top	53% Y	
683	46% N	
723 bottom	44% N	
723 top	40% Y	

*Roll calls used in Scale Sets as well as in Performance Sets.

DIVERSE ISSUES ROLL-CALL SETS

House

Journal Page No.	% on Strong Side
(1 Cong., 1 Sess.)	
Vol. V	
265	83% Y
20	79% Y
260 top	59% N
254	54% Y
230 bottom	53% Y
260 bottom	53% Y
230 top	51% Y
230 middle	49% Y
49	24% N
(1 Cong., 2 Sess.)	
Vol. V	
494	71% Y
386	69% Y
480 bottom	59% Y
534 bottom	51% N
480 top	30% N
408 bottom	25% N
(1 Cong., 3 Sess.)	
Vol. VI	
378	78% Y
172	65% N
431	63% Y
488 bottom	61% Y
63	56% N
308 top	53% N
320 top	43% N
367 top	36% N

Senate

Journal Page No.	% on Strong Side
(1 Cong., 1 Sess.)	
Vol. II	
74	68% Y
73	62% N
198	57% Y
182	48% N
203 top	42% Y
197	37% Y
148 bottom	27% Y
(2 Cong., 2 Sess.)	
Vol. IV	
361 top	69% Y
361 bottom	63% Y
601	56% N
541	50% N

House

Journal Page No.	% on Strong Side
(1 Cong., 4 Sess.)	
Vol. VI	
679	86% Y
703 bottom	85% Y
588	81% Y
764	76% Y
766	76% Y
806 top	76% Y
854 top	66% N
702	64% N
610	62% Y
785 top	59% Y
793	54% Y
802 top	39% N
548 top	23% N
516	13% N

DIVERSE ISSUES ROLL-CALL SETS

House

Journal Page No.	% on Strong Side
(2 Cong., 1 Sess.)	
Vol. VII	
12	92% Y
211 top	87% N
84	74% Y
208	73% Y
214	69% Y
124	66% N
155	65% N
206 top	62% N
131	59% Y
222	59% Y
73	57% Y
223	56% N
127 top	55% Y
119	54% Y
206 bottom	51% N
110	47% Y
120	44% N
191	42% N

DIVERSE ISSUES ROLL-CALL SETS--Continued

House

Journal Page No.	% on Strong Side
(2 Cong., 2 Sess., Nov. - Feb.)	
Vol. VII	
266	81% Y
355	52% Y
365	48% N
546	45% N
328	42% N
(2 Cong., 2 Sess., Feb. - Mar.)	
Vol. VII	
756 top	76% Y
702	59% N
652	57% Y
722 bottom	52% Y
722 top	51% N
753 top	48% N
746	45% N
633	40% N

STATE RIGHTS ROLL-CALL SETS

House

(2 Cong., 2 Sess., Nov. - Feb.) Vol. VII

Journal Page No.	% on Strong Side	Scale Position
302	96% Y	0
317	83% Y	*
586 bottom	79% N	1 *
587	74% Y	*
491 top	67% Y	2
582	66% N	
586 top	62% Y	3
464	58% Y	
310	57% Y	*
438 bottom	55% Y	
436 middle	51% Y	4
458 top	49% Y	
463 bottom	33% N	*
428	32% Y	5
462 bottom	32% Y	6
427	20% Y	*
523	17% N	

(2 Cong., 2 Sess., Feb. - Mar.) Vol. VII

Journal Page No.	% on Strong Side	Scale Position
684	89% Y	
646 bottom	80% N	
745	76% N	
646 top	65% N	
658 bottom	55% Y	
658 top	50% N	

Senate

(1 Cong., 2 Sess.) Vol. II

Journal Page No.	% on Strong Side	Scale Position
395 middle	86% Y	0
316	83% N	*
399	78% Y	1
395 bottom	77% Y	*
315	74% N	*
336	56% Y	2
396 bottom	52% Y	3
443	44% N	*
395 top	43% Y	4
444 top	29% N	5

(1 Cong., 3 Sess.) Vol. III

Journal Page No.	% on Strong Side	Scale Position
32	86% N	0
153	58% Y	*
192	55% N	1
195 middle	55% N	*
181	53% N	
195 bottom	50% N	2
36	48% N	3
194 bottom	45% N	*
196 bottom	45% N	4
176 bottom	27% N	5

RACE ROLL-CALL SETS

House

(2 Cong., 2 Sess., Nov. - Feb.) Vol. VII

Journal Page No.	% on Strong Side	Scale Position
508 top	70% N	0
562	70% N	*
508 bottom	68% Y	1
505 top	63% Y	*
509	63% Y	*
612 top	61% Y	
507 bottom	60% Y	
512 bottom	55% N	
542	55% Y	
611 bottom	53% Y	
514	52% N	
543	52% Y	2
612 middle	52% Y	*
612 bottom	51% Y	*
554	51% Y	
595	49% Y	
505 bottom	49% Y	3
610 bottom	48% Y	
553 top	48% Y	*
507 top	47% Y	
611 top	47% Y	4
610 middle	40% Y	*
552 bottom	38% N	*
510	34% N	5
610 top	34% Y	*
511	32% N	
521	29% N	6
506	16% N	*
512 top	12% Y	7 *

House

(2 Cong., 2 Sess., Feb. - Mar.) Vol. VII

Journal Page No.	% on Strong Side	Scale Position
667 bottom	83% Y	0
772 top	69% N	1 *
729	61% Y	
721	57% Y	
614	56% Y	
717	51% Y	2
773 top	47% N	3
716 top	41% Y	4
716 bottom	40% Y	5

Senate

(2 Cong., 2 Sess.) Vol. IV

Journal Page No.	% on Strong Side	Scale Position
503	65% Y	
524	60% Y	
569	59% Y	
528 top	53% Y	
670	53% Y	
585	48% N	
519	47% Y	
528 bottom	19% Y	

*Roll calls used in Scale Sets as well as in Performance Sets.

*Roll calls used in Scale Sets as well as in Performance Sets.

*Roll calls used in Scale Sets as well as in Performance Sets.

CROSS-CONTENT ROLL-CALL SETS FROM HOUSE OF SECOND CONGRESS

Journal Page No.	% on Strong Side	Scale Position		Journal Page No.	% on Strong Side	Scale Position
Military-Determination				**Defeatism-Realism**		
Vol. VII				Vol. VII		
745	76% N	------*--- 0		317	Y	------*--- 0
756 bottom	70% Y	-----*--- 1		266	Y	*
508 bottom	68% Y	-----*--- 2a		475	Y	*
646 top	65% N	-----*--- 3a		combined		
487 bottom	Y	* 4		three above (86%)	Y	-----*--- 1
206 top	N	*		586 bottom	N	*
combined				587	Y	*
two above	61% Y	* 5		contrived		
686	57% N	-----*--- 6		from two above	Y	*
687	28% N	--------- 7		767 bottom	Y	*
				54	Y	*
				172	Y	*
				80	Y	*
				combined		
				five above (80%)	Y	-----*--- 2
				491 top	67% Y	-----*--- 3
				468	62% N	-----*--- 4a
				348 top	60% N	-----*--- 5a
				762 top	N	*
				763 middle	Y	*
				771 bottom	N	*
				771 middle	Y	*
				contrived		
				from four above	Y	*
				350	Y	*
				335 top	N	*
				combined		
				three above (51%)	Y	-----*--- 6
				673 top	43% N	-----*--- 7
				747 top	28% N	-----*--- 8
				631	17% N	--------- 9

The issues incorporated in the Military-Determination scale set are described in detail in Table 10-1.

The issues incorporated in the Defeatism-Realism scale set, and two closely related roll calls that do not quite reach the desired level of scalability but aid in defining the characteristics of the set, are described in detail in Table 10-7.

*All of these roll calls relate to the scale sets described here without reference to whether any of them are also to be found included in other sets.

a. Cutting points are not always distributed as evenly as desirable. Combining two roll calls with a similar percent positive sometimes creates a new item having a percent positive which duplicates that of yet a third item. Deletion of any roll calls to avoid this mechanical inconvenience robs the scale of part of its subject content, giving an incomplete impression of the attitude it attempts to define. Furthermore, several congressmen had such poor attendance records that some could not have been assigned any scale position if either of such a troublesome pair of roll calls had been omitted. Other methods of evading such a difficulty through defining items by a group of roll calls would not have made a significant difference.

Bibliographical Comment

Because of the specialized nature of this study, an extended biblio-
graphical essay would be an exercise in pedantry, especially since the
recent appearance of J. G. Randall and David Donald, *The Civil War
and Reconstruction,* second edition, revised (Lexington, Massachusetts:
D. C. Heath, 1969), with its up-to-date bibliography, and the completion
just shortly before this manuscript went to the publisher of Allan Nevins,
James I. Robertson, Jr., and Bell I. Wiley, editors, *Civil War Books:
A Critical Bibliography,* 2 vols. (Baton Rouge: Louisiana State University
Press, 1967–1969). Any extensive attempt to outline background sources
would be a pale shadow of the bibliographic riches to be found in either
of these publications.

Rather than follow usual procedures of historical research, examining
a wide range of monographs, personal papers, diaries, newspapers, and
government documents, the authors have of necessity concentrated upon
the roll-call record found in the *Journal of the Congress of the Confederate
States of America, 1861–1865,* 7 vols. (Washington: Government Printing
Office, 1904–1905). Other materials have been used to lend meaning
to the insights gained from roll-call analysis or to provide background
needed to place issues, men, and events in the proper context, but we
have not engaged in a library-to-library search for personal papers and
manuscripts; citations to such materials evidence research previously
undertaken for purposes other than this book. Even so, the contributions
of several manuscript collections, such as those in the Library of Congress
and in the Southern Historical Collection at the University of North
Carolina are obvious to every reader who has examined our footnotes.

Several publications other than the *Journals* have proven to be indispensable. The "Proceedings of the . . . Confederate Congress" [title varies],
Southern Historical Society Papers, XLIV–LII (1923–1959) are not only
important in themselves, but are vital to a full understanding of the
Journals. Necessary to comprehension of both of the foregoing are James
M. Matthews, editor, *The Statutes at Large of the Provisional Government
of the Confederate States of America . . .*(Richmond: R. M. Smith, 1864);
the similarly titled compilations which Matthews published after all
except the last session of Congress; and Charles W. Ramsdell, editor,
Laws and Joint Resolutions of the Last Session of the Confederate Congress

(November 7, 1864–March 18, 1865) Together with the Secret Acts of Previous Congresses (Durham: Duke University Press, 1941).

Biographical information used here has come from a large number of sources. Most vital was the manuscript of Schedules I (Free Population) and II (Slaves) of the Eighth Census (1860), located in the National Archives, Record Group 29, which provided almost all of the data on individual economic status and much other personal information as well. Another comprehensive source for personal background was the collection of amnesty petitions filed by those congressmen who survived the war, which is to be found in the National Archives, Record Group 94. Also helpful were Allen Johnson, et al., editors, *Dictionary of American Biography,* 22 vols. (New York: Charles Scribner's Sons, 1928–1958); *The National Cyclopedia of American Biography* . . . , 51 vols. (New York: James T. White and Company, 1898–); James Grant Wilson and John Fiske, editors, *Appleton's Cyclopedia of American Biography,* 7 vols. (New York: D. Appleton and Company, 1894–1900); *Biographical Directory of the American Congress, 1774–1961* (Washington: Government Printing Office, 1961); and the other numerous though less comprehensive national biographical directories. On the state and local level, a large number of similar references of varying degrees of utility were used in conjunction with state histories, specialized monographs, memoirs (including several of the bench and bar variety), and geneological sources. Indeed, the most appropriate general citation for this mass of material would be simply the state and local history shelves for each of the states involved. A number of such works are listed in our footnotes, especially in Chapter 1.

Some economic characteristics were important on the county rather than on the individual level. Most such material came from the report of the *Eighth Census of the United States, 1860* . . . , 4 vols. (Washington: Government Printing Office, 1864); and Thomas J. Pressly and William H. Scofield, *Farm Real Estate Values in the United States by Counties, 1850–1959* (Seattle: University of Washington Press, 1965).

The items used in constructing the background of the Confederate Congress and the context in which it functioned are too numerous to be included, and if listed would fail to reflect those works, long since read, which leave their inevitable impressions upon the researcher's mind without enabling him to remember their titles. Some monographs have, however, been of special importance in understanding the problems we have discussed. The foremost mention must go to Wilfred Buck Yearns, *The Confederate Congress* (Athens, Georgia: University of Georgia Press, 1960), which illustrates by its well-thumbed pages that it has been an invaluable guide and an ever-present companion. We do not agree with a number of Yearns's conclusions, yet it would have been more difficult to understand the significance of much of Congress's activities had not Yearns's ground-breaking study pointed the way. Confederate congressional district information is precisely and clearly presented in John Brawner Robbins, "Confederate Nationalism: Politics and Government in the Confederate South, 1861-1865" (Ph.D. dissertation, Rice University, 1964). Less important, but nevertheless useful in their place were Albert B. Moore, *Conscription and Conflict in the Confederacy* (New York: Macmillan, 1924); Richard C. Todd, *Confederate Finance* (Athens, Georgia: University of Georgia Press, 1954); David Donald, editor, *Why the North Won the Civil War* (Baton Rouge: Louisiana State University Press, 1960); and Frank L. Owsley, *State Rights in the Confederacy* (Chicago: University of Chicago Press, 1925). This highly selective listing should not be concluded without reference to the invaluable documentary collections in James D. Richardson, editor, *The Messages and Papers of Jefferson Davis and the Confederacy, Including Diplomatic Correspondence, 1861-1865,* 2 vols. (New York: Chelsea House—Robert Hector, 1966) [variant title of the original 1905 publication] and U.S. War Department, *The War of the Rebellion: A Compilation of the Official Records of the Union and Confederate Armies,* 70 vols. in 128 (Washington: Government Printing Office, 1880-1901).

Other sources should be mentioned for the methodological contribution they have made. Any investigator using quantitative techniques for roll-call analysis must begin by acknowledging his debt to Duncan MacRae, Jr., and William O. Aydelotte. MacRae's *Dimensions of Congressional Voting: A Statistical Study of the House of Representatives in the Eighty-First Congress* (Berkeley and Los Angeles: University of California Press, 1958) was the first book-length use of Guttman scaling for this purpose. Aydelotte's "Voting Patterns in the British House of Commons in the 1840s," in *Comparative Studies in Society and History,* V (January 1963), launched nineteenth-century scaling studies. These provided the starting points not only for the present authors but for other investigators as well. See also MacRae's *Parliament, Parties, and Society in France 1946-1958* (New York: St. Martin's Press, 1967), and his recent *Issues and Parties in Legislative Voting: Methods of Statistical Analysis* (New York: Harper and Row, 1970), which discusses a number of quantitative procedures helpful for those engaged in roll-call study. We regret that this highly sophisticated analysis was not available when we began our project, although the nature of our roll-call data renders much of it unsuited to the most powerful analytical tools. A guidebook for those unfamiliar with the techniques used here is Lee F. Anderson, Meredith W. Watts, Jr., and Allen R. Wilcox, *Legislative Roll-Call Analy-*

sis (Evanston, Illinois: Northwestern University Press, 1966). In addition, a number of the variations on older procedures which we have employed were originally used in Richard E. Beringer, "Political Factionalism in the Confederate Congress" (Ph.D. dissertation, Northwestern University, 1966) and Thomas B. Alexander, *Sectional Stress and Party Strength: A Study of Roll-Call Voting Patterns in the United States House of Representatives, 1836–1860* (Nashville: Vanderbilt University Press, 1967).

Index